International Migration into the 21st Century

Reginald Appleyard

International Migration into the 21st Century

Essays in Honour of Reginald Appleyard

Edited by

M.A.B. Siddique

Director
Centre for Migration and Development Studies
The University of Western Australia

Edward Elgar
Cheltenham, UK • Northampton, MA, USA

Published by
Edward Elgar Publishing Limited
Glensanda House
Montpellier Parade
Cheltenham
Glos GL50 1UA
UK

Edward Elgar Publishing, Inc.
136 West Street
Suite 202
Northampton
Massachusetts 01060
USA

A catalogue record for this book
is available from the British Library

Library of Congress Cataloguing in Publication Data

International migration into the 21st century : essays in honour of Reginald Appleyard / edited by M.A.B. Siddique.
    p. cm.
  Includes index.
    1. Emigration and immigration. I. Title: International migration into the twenty-first century. II. Siddique, Muhammed Abu B. III. Appleyard, Reginald T. (Reginald Thomas), 1927–

    JV6032 .I574 2001
    304.8'2'09049—dc21

                       00–050290

ISBN 1 84064 531 8

Printed and bound in Great Britain by MPG Books Ltd, Bodmin, Cornwall

Contents

Figures

Tables

Contributors

Aderanti Adepoju
Professor
Chief Executive
Human Resources Development Centre
Lagos, Nigeria

Reginald Appleyard
Emeritus Professor
Graduate School of Management
The University of Western Australia
Nedlands, WA, Australia

Stephen Castles
Professor and Director
Centre for Asia Pacific Social Transformation Studies (CAPSTRANS)
University of Wollongong
Wollongong, NSW, Australia

Barry R. Chiswick
Research Professor and Head
Department of Economics
University of Illinois at Chicago

Allan M. Findlay
Professor
Geography Department
University of Dundee
Dundee

Sally E. Findley
Professor of Clinical Public Health
Center for Population and Family Health
Joseph L. Mailman School of Public Health
Columbia University, New York

Tomas Hammar
Professor
Centre for Research in International Migration and Ethnic Relations (Ceifo)
Stockholm University, Sweden

Charles B. Keely
Herzberg Professor of International Migration
Department of Demography and
Walsh School of Foreign Services
Georgetown University, Washington DC

Rebecca Kippen
Demography Program
Research School of Social Sciences
Australian National University
Canberra, ACT, Australia

Peter McDonald
Professor and Head
Demography Program
Research School of Social Sciences
Australian National University
Canberra, ACT, Australia

Anthony P. Maingot
Professor of Sociology
Florida International University
Miami, Florida

Philip Martin
Professor
Department of Agriculture and Resource Economics
University of California
Davis, CA

John Salt
Professor
Department of Geography
University College London
26 Bedford Way
London

M.A.B. Siddique
Director
Centre for Migration and Development Studies
Department of Economics
The University of Western Australia
Nedlands, WA, Australia

Ronald Skeldon
Professor and Independent Consultant (based in Bangkok),
  and Honorary Professor, University of Hong Kong
ESCAP Editorial UN Building
Bangkok, Thailand

Hania Zlotnik
Chief
Mortality and Migration Section
Department of Economic and Social Affairs
United Nations, New York

Preface

This book contains the papers prepared for a conference on 'International Migration into the 21st Century' held at the University of Western Australia during November/December 1999. The conference was organised to honour the contribution of Professor Reginald Appleyard to the field of migration in Australia and internationally. The papers were prepared by Professor Appleyard's friends and colleagues who attended the conference to celebrate his contribution to the field. They are distinguished scholars of international migration whose main research was undertaken during the last quarter of the 20th century. Each had prepared a paper that attempted to evaluate the nature and significance of change in migration from his/her own research interest and perspective, and to foreshadow emerging trends (from that perspective) into the early twenty-first century. The conference focused on the following five major issues:

1. The role and impact of changing economic trends on the volume, direction and composition of international migration. Particular attention was given to ageing trends and implications.
2. The causes of, and trends in, illegal migration and trafficking.
3. The politics of selection and restriction, including the social and economic opportunities of diversity.
4. Changing determinants of return migration.
5. Refugee migration.

The conference agenda was less formal than usual, particularly because participants had been drawn from a range of social sciences. It was structured to address the above issues and each participant had opportunity to contribute to discussion on each issue from his/her own research perspective and experience. There was no formal presentation of papers by participants.

During the concluding session of the conference, participants agreed that while the format of the conference—to discuss the five issues but not specifically the contributed papers—was appropriate, there was need for the papers to be assessed prior to publication. Accordingly, each author was asked to assess two papers. Their reports were then sent to the authors who made changes on the basis of those comments as well on their own 'second thoughts'.

As editor, I wish like to express my sincere gratitude to all the contributors whose prompt response to my frequent requests made it possible to publish this important volume on international migration within a tight schedule. I am also indebted to a number of colleagues and friends who have directly and indirectly helped me organise the Conference and edit the book. I owe a special debt of gratitude to Professor Paul Miller, Head, Department of Economics, the University of Western Australia, for his constant encouragement and inspiration. He also played a significant role in raising funds for the conference from both internal and external sources. Organisation of the Conference and publication of this volume would not have been possible without his direct help. I also wish to thank my senior colleague, Dr R.N. Ghosh, for taking the initial step to celebrate Professor Appleyard's contribution to the field of migration by his friends and colleagues. Mr Ratan Kumar Ghosh, Ms Helen Reidy and Ms Victoria Karagiannis provided excellent assistance with the organisation of the Conference.

Mrs Glenys Walter undertook the painstaking task of preparing the manuscript and I wish to thank her for completing it with her usual efficiency and cooperation.

I would like to acknowledge the understanding and support received from my wife, Naznin and daughters Farzana and Farhana.

Finally, neither the conference nor this book would have been possible without the generous financial assistance received by the Centre for Migration and Development Studies from: Department of Immigration and Multicultural Affairs (Canberra), the Vice-Chancellor's office (UWA), the Executive Dean's Office (ECEL, UWA), Graduate School of Management (UWA), Department of Economics (UWA), Department of Commerce and Trade (WA), Reserve Bank of Australia, AusAID (Canberra), Economic Society of Australia (WA Branch), Ministry for Planning (WA), and Mr Michael Wright of Voyager Enterprises, Pty Ltd (Cottesloe, WA).

M.A.B. Siddique
Department of Economics
The University of Western Australia
June 2000

In Honour of Reginald Appleyard

Reginald Thomas Appleyard occupies an eminent position in the field of migration and development studies in Australia and internationally. The present volume of essays in his honour brings together contributions by a group of scholars who have known him for many years and hold him in high esteem. Each contributor has written an essay on the theme of international migration into the twenty-first century. The fact that they belong to many disciplines is an indication of the position which Reginald Appleyard enjoys not only in the field of migration and development but also in the social sciences as a whole.

The editor of this volume does not pretend to present a comprehensive story of Appleyard's thought and action extending over half a century. Rather, it is a modest attempt to sketch a broad account of the activities of this eminent scholar who has contributed significantly in the fields of international migration theory and policy, Australian immigration and economic issues, and economic history.

Reginald Appleyard was born at Claremont, Western Australia on 16 September 1927. In 1950, he entered The University of Western Australia (UWA) where he obtained a Bachelor of Arts (1st Class Honours) degree in Economics. He was awarded a Population Council Fellowship for further study at Duke University where he obtained the MA and PhD degrees. While studying at UWA, Appleyard developed a close academic relationship with Dr Merab Tauman (née Harris), Senior Lecturer in Economic History; and at Duke University with Professor Joseph Spengler. Both had a significant influence on his scholarly works in economic history and migration.

Appleyard's formal academic career began in 1958 when he was appointed Research Fellow in Demography at the Australian National University (ANU). He was highly regarded by the Department and during the 10 years at ANU (1958–1967), his position was elevated to Fellow in Demography in 1962 and to Senior Fellow in 1965. During this decade, he became actively involved in applying migration theories into practice in the context of Australia. This is reflected in his empirical works on *British Emigration to Australia* (1964), 'Determinants of Return Migration - A Socio-Economic Study of United Kingdom Migrants Who Returned from Australia' (1962), 'The Return Movement of United Kingdom Migrants from Australia' (1962) and 'The Great Migration—Australia' (1966).

Appleyard returned to his natural home—Western Australia—in 1967, having been enticed by UWA to the Foundation Chair of Economic History.

He retained this position for 25 years until his formal retirement in 1992. While at UWA, he firmly established himself as a dynamic academic leader and international scholar in the area of migration and development. He was the Head of the Department of Economics for 17 out of his 25 years at UWA. In 1987, he founded the Centre for Migration and Development Studies. As foundation Director, he formed a research team from amongst interested colleagues to conduct research on theoretical aspects of the migration-development process, the impact of permanent migration on Australia's socio-economic development, and the impact of migration in general on processes of socio-economic change in developing countries. Academic and research staff associated with CMDS have published extensively in refereed journals and authored numerous books dealing with immigration and development issues. He also attracted funds from national and international sources for the Centre to conduct its research activities and to organise numerous international seminars and conferences on contemporary problems in immigration and development.

The year 1967 was the turning point in Appleyard's career. The dimension of his research was now extended beyond Australia. His years at ANU had equipped him with the skills and self-confidence necessary to firmly set his research agenda in international migration and development. In the next 35 years, his scholarly activities placed him so permanently in this field that it is almost impossible to write a paper on any aspect of Australian and international migration without citing Appleyard's work. Since 1967 he has authored, co-authored, edited and co-edited 19 scholarly books and over 60 journal articles and chapters in books dealing mostly with theories and policies of Australian and international migration. His books include *The Beginning: European Discovery and Early Settlement of Western Australia* (1980), *International Migration Today: Trends and Prospects* (1988), *The Impact of Migration on Developing Countries* (1989), and *International Migration: Challenge for the Nineties* (1991). His scholarly papers include 'International Migration in the Third World' (1981), 'International Migration in the ESCAP Region' (1982), 'International Migration in a Changing World' (1984), 'Migration and Development: Myths and Reality' (1989), and 'Immigration and Demographic Change in Australia' (1991).

In 1992, Appleyard was appointed Coordinator of a project funded by UNFPA and IOM to research emigration dynamics in developing countries. He recommended the appointment of research teams in four regions of the developing world and helped develop an appropriate research model for studies that extended over five years, culminating in the publication in 1998 and 1999 of four volumes, which he edited, titled *Emigration Dynamics in Developing Countries*.

An important contribution by Appleyard in the field of migration was his coining the term *professional transient*—a new class of migrant who emigrates to host countries through transnational corporations (TNCs) for a short period. Since the end of World War II, TNCs have played an increasingly vital role promoting economic development in many developing countries through direct foreign investment. Due to a very low level of human resources development, many of these countries did not have necessary skills to use the technologies transferred by TNCs for engaging in various production processes. This 'skill gap' was filled temporarily by the technical staff supplied by the TNCs whom Appleyard had identified as professional transients.

He has also made significant contributions as a demographer and economic historian. His chapter titled, 'Economic Demography of the Twentieth Century' (1980) is considered a classic. His papers on 'Western Australia: Economic and Demographic Growth' (1981), and 'Population' (1991) deal with the historical patterns of population growth in Western Australia. Spengler's influence is clearly evident from his writings in this area. As an economic historian, Appleyard's interests centre mainly around his home state (WA). His writings deal with such important issues as the State's resources boom and problems associated with it, the financing of goldmining, WA's economic relationship with Japan and so on.

Appleyard's contributions to the Australian and international communities cannot be judged only through his scholarly works in the three areas outlined above. His services to the Australian and international communities are reflected through his involvement in numerous boards and committees established by the United Nations, International Organisation for Migration (IOM), and the government of Australia in various capacities. In 1992, he was appointed Editor of *International Migration*, a position he still holds, having been responsible, with an Editorial Board, for raising the journal's standard to a very high level. In 1999, he was appointed member of the Order of Australia (AM) for his 'service to education through the research and teaching of economic history, migration and population studies, and economics'.

The volume, direction and composition of international migration changed significantly during the second half of the twentieth century. In 1988, the Centre for Migration and Development Studies, which he founded, and UNESCO (Paris), jointly published a volume titled, *International Migration Today: Trends and Prospects*. In his general introduction, R.T. Appleyard, the Editor, referred to a symposium that had been sponsored by UNESCO in 1955 on *The Positive Contribution of Immigrants*. He noted that all the papers presented at the 1955 symposium had been written by European scholars on the settlement of European migrants in predominantly European receiving countries, and concluded that it was perhaps the last occasion on which discussions on international migration would be confined to impacts on 'traditional' sending and receiving countries.

Appleyard wrote:

> For the seeds of change had already been sown which during the ensuring thirty years [to 1988], would create a phenomenon so different in type, composition and direction as to be unrecognisable from the phenomenon studied by [Oscar] Handlin [convenor of the 1955 symposium] and his colleagues.

The chapters in the CMDS/UNESCO volume confirmed that migration had indeed become a complex and pervasive phenomenon. No region of the world had remained untouched by what one contributor, Demetrios Papademetriou, called 'the widening and deepening of the reach of the migration process'.

Since the publication of the CMDS/UNESCO volume in 1988, international migration has continued to play an important role in socio-economic change and development. The year 1999 was therefore an appropriate time to assemble scholars of the experience and calibre of those who had contributed to the 1955 and 1988 volumes to evaluate the nature and significance of migration during the 1990s, and also to try and project likely changes during the early twenty-first century.

Appleyard's mission to disseminate wisdom and knowledge amongst the younger generation and to serve mankind is an on-going process. At 72, he is maintaining his energy and vigour to pursue this mission. As one of his great admirers I take this opportunity to honour him and his outstanding contribution to the field of international migration and development.

REFERENCES

Appleyard, Reginald (1962), 'Determinants of Return Migration – A Socio-Economic Study of United Kingdom Migrants Who Returned from Australia', *Economic Record*, **38** (83).

Appleyard, Reginald (1962), 'The Return Movement of United Kingdom Migrants from Australia', *Population Studies*, **15** (3), pp. 214–25.

Appleyard, Reginald (1964), *British Emigration to Australia*, Australian National UniversityPress, Canberra; Weidenfeld and Nicolson, London; University of Toronto Press.

Appleyard, Reginald (1966), 'The Great Migration – Australia', *The Round Table*, No. 222.

Appleyard, Reginald and Toby Manford (1980), *The Beginning: European Discovery and Early Settlement of Western Australia*, Nedlands: University of Western Australia Press.

Appleyard, Reginald (1980), 'Economic Demography of the Twentieth Century', in N. Stanley and R. Joske (eds), *Changing Disease Patterns and Human Behaviour*, London: Academic Press, pp. 389–402.

Appleyard, Reginald (1981), *International Migration in the Third World*, Paris: CICRED, pp. 1–59.

Appleyard, Reginald (1981), 'Western Australia: Economic and Demographic Growth, 1850–1914', in C.T. Stannage (ed.), *New History of Western Australia*, Nedlands: University of Western Australia Press, pp. 211–36.

Appleyard, Reginald (1984), 'International Migration in the ESCAP Region', *Selected papers, Third Asian and Pacific Population Conference*, New York: United Nations, pp. 212–23.

Appleyard, Reginald (1984), 'Internatinal Migration in a Changing World', *International Migration*, **22** (3), pp. 169–77.

Appleyard, Reginald (ed.) (1988), *International Migration Today: Trends and Prospects*, Paris: UNESCO.

Appleyard, Reginald (ed.) (1989), *The Impact of Migration on Developing Countries*, English and French editions, Paris: OECD.

Appleyard, Reginald (1989), 'Migration and Development: Myths and Reality', *International Migration Review*, **23**, Fall, pp. 486–99.

Appleyard, Reginald (1991), *International Migration: Challenge for the Nineties*, Geneva: IOM.

Appleyard, Reginald (1991), 'Immigration and Demographic Change in Australia', in *Migration: The Demographic Aspects*, Paris, OECD, pp. 73–7.

Appleyard, Reginald (1991), 'Population' in R.T. Appleyard (ed.) *Western Australia into the Twenty-First Century: Economic Perspectives*, Nedlands: University of Western Australia Press, pp. 77–104.

Appleyard, Reginald (ed.) (1998), *Emigration Dynamics in Developing Countries: Vol. I – Sub-Saharan Africa*, Aldershot, UK: Edward Elgar.

Appleyard, Reginald (ed.) (1998), *Emigration Dynamics in Developing Countries: Vol. II – South Asia*, Aldershot, UK: Edward Elgar.

Appleyard, Reginald (ed.) (1998), *Emigration Dynamics in Developing Countries: Vol. III – Mexico, Central America and the Caribbean*, Aldershot, UK: Edward Elgar.

Appleyard, Reginald (ed.) (1998), *Emigration Dynamics in Developing Countries: Vol. IV – The Arab Region*, Aldershot, UK: Edward Elgar.

1. International Migration into the 21st Century: Selected Issues

M.A.B. Siddique and Reginald Appleyard

As noted in the Preface, the Perth conference brought together a small group of eminent scholars of international migration whose major achievements had been made during the last twenty-five years. Each invitee had been asked to prepare a paper on a topic of his/her choice which addressed likely significant changes in international migration into the twenty-first century. However, the conference programme did not provide opportunity for authors to formally present their papers. Instead, it was structured to address five issues which the organisers had carefully selected as likely to be relevant and important in the first decade of the twenty-first century. The logic of this decision was that while the participants would not be specialists in every issue, their collective wisdom and experience would provide insights into, and understanding of, each issue's relevance and importance.

Following five formal sessions held at the University of Western Australia, participants travelled together for three days to Albany on the south coast of the state. The journey provided opportunity for further discussion, in an informal setting, of the five issues. A final session was held at Albany where each issue was revisited. This chapter contains summaries of discussion by participants on each issue; extracts from presented papers; discussion at the Perth meeting; and 'second thoughts' from the Albany meeting.

IMPACT OF CHANGING ECONOMIC TRENDS ON VOLUME, DIRECTION AND COMPOSITION OF INTERNATIONAL MIGRATION (INCLUDING AGEING)

This impact of significant changes in political and economic systems on the direction and composition of international migration, especially during the 1990s, is acknowledged by all the authors of chapters in this volume. Not only are they clearly aware of the complexities of their subject, and the need to look for 'new expressions' of international migration but, as Salt argues, for new ways of conceptualising and understanding them. Existing migration theories, it is argued, have proven to have low predictive power because of the inherent complexities of the phenomena that they seek to explain. Skeldon argues that it was inability to cope with the dynamism in new contemporary movements that actually led to the shift away from narrowly focused models to more qualitative, even introspective, interpretations, and Findley observes that migration transformations over time need to be understood in relation to global linkages.

Policy response has, of course, varied according to parameters set by each country's economic and political circumstances. Indeed, Martin shows that the number and types of migrants has increased faster than the capacity of national governments, regional bodies and international organisations and agreements to deal with them. In relation to the US/Caribbean region, Maingot shows that re-evaluation of national immigration policies has occurred in response to global economic migration, new communications and transportation networks, and the availability of rights and benefits of migrants. In Sub-Saharan Africa, on the other hand, the unstable political landscape, escalating ethnic conflict and persistent economic decline have combined to determine the volume and direction of migration between countries on that continent. And while the development of Western multicultural societies were brought about by the application of principles of the rule of law and human rights, the incorporation of immigrants into welfare systems, and the effect of social networks in maintaining the migration process, Castles asks whether similar factors exist, or are likely to arise, in Asia's migrating countries, many of which have increased rapidly their GDP per capita.

The impact of demographic change in most Western, and several non-Western countries, as a result of declining fertility and consequent ageing, has led to proposals for increased immigration. But McDonald and Kippen, in their chapter on Australia's demographic experience and prospects, conclude that persons who argue for a higher level of immigration must base their arguments on the benefits of a larger population, not upon the illusory 'younging power' of high immigration.

As would be expected, discussion at the Perth meeting on the impact of changing economic trends on international migration was both lively and catholic in its diversity. This was partly because the issue itself embraces a catalogue of sub-issues, and partly because participants were drawn from a range of social sciences.

Among the many significant points made at the session was that migration policies in the past had failed, in terms of the outcomes not being what were originally intended; for example, guest worker migration in Europe turned into permanent settlement. However, theoretical developments during the last ten to fifteen years have helped explain these failures and, hopefully, will reduce its incidence in the future. For example, the new theory of labour migration does not see migrants simply as economic atoms, but emphasises micro dimensions, supply strategies and family reunion. There has also been an integration of economics with social capital theory, migration being seen as a social process in order to understand why political and economic objectives are not always realised. Migration scholars have therefore been encouraged to integrate the micro and macro dimensions in order to unravel the totality of the migration process.

It was also argued that in the last thirty years scholars have not paid sufficient attention to the context in which states have attempted to control/regulate migration, nor to states' perceptions regarding the meaning and value of migration. Part of the reason why many scholars cannot get their minds around changes in migration is that they cannot get their minds around what is happening to the concepts of state, sovereignty and citizenship. The view, commonly held in Western countries, that regulation is supported on the general presumption that local workers will 'not give their jobs away', has also influenced thinking about the impacts of free trade and the movement of capital. While many states retain strong regulatory frameworks, they are at the same time allowing decision-making to be made beyond their borders. Indeed, discussion about the movement of labour, at least at the high end, has been increasingly introduced into discussions on trade, thus encouraging an international regime not for migration in general, but for 'pieces of it'—one for high skills; one for refugees. There is clear need to analyse the fundamental assumptions that go into states trying to set up regulatory systems in this new era.

In efforts to respond to the implications of such developments, it was suggested that the proliferation of new terms appearing in migration literature—'transient migration', 'incomplete migration', 'migration trafficking', 'petty trading' and 'labour tourism'—should be researched as part of a continuum ranging from permanent to daily patterns of movement. This could be seen as a mobility stream in which processes of metamorphosis occur: people moving from one state to another, with some on different points of the continuum at different times. The challenge, it was argued, is to come to grips with this notion of mobility, perhaps letting the notion of migration slip a little further into the background.

The issue raised in the chapter by McDonald and Kippen regarding the use of immigration to stem the ageing process in Australia was raised at a global level in terms of future labour supply for countries experiencing sub-replacement fertility. One participant argued that during the next 20-30 years, labour supply deficit would dominate the study of international migration, especially in Europe, Japan, the 'tiger' economies of Asia, and probably the US. On the other hand, expected 'massive surpluses' in Sub-Saharan Africa, the Asian sub-continent and probably China, simply will not be kept at bay, or ignored, by the ageing economies. In India alone during the next 30–40 years, the population aged 20–64 years will number 400 million, whereas in Japan the population of similar ages will decline from 80 to 60 million, no matter what happens to fertility. Global demographic dimensions will therefore inexorably underlie the migration issue, including those raised in Castles' chapter regarding some countries which are lacking experience in migration, are relatively culturally homogeneous, and do not readily provide citizenship and other rights to migrants.

These, and many other points, were raised during the discussion on issue I and inevitably revisited during discussion on other issues. At the final session of the conference held at Albany, collective wisdom had been distilled into the following suggestions:

- While migration trends in the twentieth century illustrate that economic processes are socially, culturally and politically embedded, technology on the one hand, and economic aspects of globalisation on the other, have facilitated a new intensity of interconnections around the globe. The interpretation of trends in population movement requires new approaches by migration scholars that are informed by theories which must be pertinent to the new context.

- New forms of migration need to be linked to global economic processes. Many migration flows are associated with different types of global controls. For example, skilled migrants arise from the global reach that many large cities require, and the state is only too happy to facilitate the movement without incorporating it within what it advertises as 'migration policy'. This type of flow is becoming more significant and new business legislation has been introduced to facilitate and encourage it. Indeed, states have to do this if they want to remain competitive, otherwise they stand to lose some of their global reach.

- What is interesting and new in the contemporary context is that the effects of globalisation are now more indirect in the way that they link to migration. Trade theory has proven to be a weak medium for studying recent flows of capital and people. Migration transformations over time, and into the twenty-first century, should be interpreted relative to the relationship between production and reproduction structured within specific labour markets.

- Economic and demographic pressures have been responsible for turning some international frontiers into major economic and demographic divides, setting the potential for vast migration pressures in poor, populous states. A cultural economy approach is needed to understand why low-wage labour migrants are drawn in large numbers from some countries but not others.

- Qualitative methods, and social theory, are clearly needed to examine how and why migration is seen as a threat to local and national identity. This is seen as necessary for scholars concerned with the economic dimensions of migrations, as well as those concerned with cultural issues.

- Calls for high levels of immigration to offset changes in population structures in some developed countries are both problematic and also unlikely to produce the desired effects. Prudent policies which help sustain fertility at replacement levels, combined with strategies that promote positive views of older people, offer a more effective approach.

ILLEGAL MIGRATION AND TRAFFICKING

While the chapters by Salt and Chiswick focus directly on this issue, it is referred to in at least five other chapters. Salt sets the orders of magnitude by declaring that the illegal trafficking of migrants is widely recognised to be a major international problem, bringing in an estimated annual income of about five to eleven billion dollars and perhaps as profitable as drug smuggling. According to one estimate, approximately 15–30 per cent of those managing to reach their destinations in Europe in 1993 used the services of traffickers during some part of their journey. The trafficking business is expanding, and while it is well organised, there is less evidence that organised crime is heavily involved. The main operators, suggests Salt, are more likely to be the conventional criminal groups than the internationally organised crime syndicates. Martin argues that a legacy of the series of Braccro programmes and toleration of Mexico-US migration has seen increased illegal migration alongside increasing economic migration. In Malaysia, there are an estimated two million 'irregular workers', mainly from Indonesia, who Castles shows work in industrial and plantation jobs that are not attractive to local workers. In Sub-Saharan Africa, expulsions and deportations are common policy measures directed at 'so-called illegal migrants' before, and remarkably after, the formation of sub-regional economic unions, thus negating what Adepoju calls the *raison d'être* for establishing those communities. African migrants are now adopting more daring methods to enter countries of the North, involving risky passages via more diverse transport points.

Explanation of why trafficking had increased, how it operates in relation to illegal migration, and the policies needed to control it (as well as the information necessary to devise appropriate policies), were the main questions under discussion at session II of the conference.

Chiswick argues that the supply of illegal migrants can be thought of as a rising function of the wages differential, and that illegals tend to be lower skilled than legal permanent immigrants and the average worker in the destination labour market. This explanation was not disputed, although there was general consensus that any assumption that illegals have 'choice', the power to choose where they go, removes theorisation a long way from the practical application of policy making. Such an approach, argued one discussant, ignores the intermediaries that come between those who wish to sell their labour to an employer (state) illegally, and those who do the employing.

Discussion on this complex issue, at least on its magnitude, was to some extent modulated by Salt's declaration that 'one of the things that immediately comes out when you disturb the surface is lack of any sound empirical studies'. About one-half of the literature is about trafficking of women and children in prostitution. 'Hard data are really soft data that became hard because everybody quotes them'. There is no hard evidence to indicate that trafficking is increasing in Europe, and while organised crime is certainly involved, there is also a large amount of localised involvement, for example, people who operate cross-border buses or routes through forests. Governments are normally at a disadvantage *vis-à-vis* traffickers and their operations, especially in the use of up-to-date electronic equipment to detect operations.

Taking their cue from Castles' point that illegal workers in Malaysia are tolerated because they are needed, participants spent some time discussing the manner in which illegal migration and trafficking have become 'problems', including why illegal migration has been an issue of importance in the US since the mid-1970s, and in Europe with the cutback in labour migration about the same time. Because no society has imposed hard penalties against employers of illegal migrants, researchers should be investigating the social and political functions of the phenomenon. One participant suggested that in situations such as Malaysia, the term 'illegal' is inappropriate. The workers are 'marginal', and they stay that way. It was also noted that strong welfare states seem to be less tolerant of illegal migrants because of their access to welfare.

Trafficking, on the other hand, has been openly discussed at inter-governmental meetings partly because of its security implications. No government supported it and so from an international perspective it is 'easier' to deal with than illegal migration, which governments may forbid but in many instances tolerate and even encourage. Salt's point that there are different types of trafficking led to discussion on the results of a study of about thirty asylum seekers who had obtained refugee status in the UK. The study had shown that without the service of traffickers to assist with documentation and travel, they would not have reached the UK. The activities of traffickers in such situations bordered on the illegitimate, but for some persons it is the only way that they can move from difficult situations. Perhaps some trafficking satisfies human rights needs; the problem is how to make the distinction, and to prevent the erosion of the asylum system. When liberal governments set out to protect their countries from the entry of large numbers of illegal migrants arriving and claiming their rights, they increase the pressure on persons to use illegal means of entry. It is therefore difficult for governments to support a convention that makes certain types of traffickers acceptable, but others not. The suggestion that an amnesty-type system under which individuals have rights to be legalised after a specified period received some support, especially in situations where their entry occurred 'because of the illegal behaviour of the state'.

The lack of sound empirical studies on trafficking and illegal migration identified by Salt clearly conditioned the depth and progress of discussion at the Perth meeting. Even at Albany discussion was still characterised by question posing and identifying the main topics requiring attention by researchers. For example, under the general heading *Market Development*, it was asked: What is the nature of the market developed and served by traffickers and illegal migrants? What new spatial markets are being opened up? How are these related to new route networks? How do markets work? How are trafficking and illegal workers actually linked? Under the general heading, *Trafficking, Business Organisation and Development*, it was asked: How is the trafficking industry evolving? What new niche businesses can be expected to develop? How far is organised crime involved? Are these distinctive networks based on ethnic origins? Under *Democratisation and State Dynamics*, it was asked: When does toleration of migrants change and how far is public opinion affected by the pressures of illegals? How does trafficking and illegal migration interact with broader migration policy, and in what direction? Is the balance of power between ethnic groups compromised by trafficking? Under *Inter-State Relations*, it was asked how these relations are affected by trafficking and illegal migration. To what extent do forms of co-operation exist, and how does this compare in efficiency with co-operation within and between trafficking organisations? Under *Individual Human Rights*, it was asked: What are the outcomes for the individual and how does the cycle end for the illegal migrant both in and out of debt bondage? What is the relationship between the individual and the criminal system at destination? Do illegal and trafficked migrants constitute a permanent or long-term marginal element in society?

The long list of questions elicited little response, and certainly no answers, perhaps only emphasising Salt's view concerning lack of sound empirical studies. Participants agreed that research should not be deterred by the fact that trafficking is generally seen as a 'police issue' and therefore not easily or readily available for analysis by social scientists. It should be opened up for analysis, although how effective that analysis can be is another question. Nor should we conclude on the basis of such fragmentary data available that illegal migration occurs only when trafficking is involved. There is a clear difference between smuggling (using the services of someone to get out) and trafficking (when they are victims). Great care needs to be exercised in the use of terminology. There is a range of areas in which exploitation, illegality etc. can emerge. In trying to determine whether or not trafficking is a topic that will 'run for some time', or just something that we are confronted with in a 'moment of institutional crisis', we need to focus carefully on clarifying the problems with appropriate techniques and terminology.

THE POLITICS OF SELECTION AND RESTRICTION

International migration and migration control, declared Hammar, are complex issues. The public is seldom well informed, and it is most difficult even for the attentive opinion to judge which statements are factual and serious evaluations and which are mainly threat scenarios. In Europe, until late in the twentieth century, there had been no fundamental changes in national systems of migration policy, and most of the proposals for adjustments in legislation or practice came from civil servants, not politicians. The US, on the other hand, had become a complex social and cultural plural society by the mid twentieth century, and even the most restrictive policies could not control immigration. Maingot shows that between 1953 and 1965, a period of strict quotas and emphasis on control, only thirty-five per cent of all immigrants admitted to the US were quota immigrants. In the Republic of South Africa in recent years, calls have been made for the arrest and deportation of so-called illegal immigrants—fellow Africans, including those from countries that hitherto sheltered South African freedom fighters, including members of the current ruling ANC party.

Discussion on this issue at the Perth meeting centred around the extent to which states have retained their control over selection and restriction and are likely to do so, and in what ways, in the future. While selection and restriction are the objectives of the state, decision-making has increasingly been diversified in what one participant described as a conflict-ridden area that contains more independent and institutional actors than ever. For example, ethnic networks with migration knowledge have become influential in the politics of selection, having developed over the last decade as a 'global system of netted migration'.

Since the end of World War II, receiving countries have come to realise what one participant described as the 'myth of the controllability of difference'. One approach has been for governments to admit workers to the labour market but keep them out of the cultural sub-system. This has failed. Another approach has been assimilation/integration but this had frequently led to community formation. Even the models of pluralism in Canada, Australia and Sweden led, in due course, to a tightening of immigration control. Migration networks retain and prolong migration processes whatever policy makers want to do. Indeed, once a country recognises that migration is closely connected with personal freedoms and human rights, it is difficult to impose rigid border controls and rigid assimilation policies. And while there is likely to be an increase in mobility, and a trend towards greater ethnic and cultural diversity, it should also be noted that during the last decade there has been a shift away from multicultural policies and a growth in anti-immigration movements.

Decision-making in some European countries has been transferred from the national to the regional level, and the traditional basis that restriction is designed to protect the domestic labour force is being challenged. Firms involved in global business think on a multi-states level, their executives arguing that immigration policy should facilitate the movement of personnel. The increased movement of high level personnel, usually on non-immigrant visas, has been due largely to an increase in the number of global firms and the higher content of intellectual property in the production of goods and of services. A hierarchy appears to have evolved: state policy deals with the less-skilled element of labour; increasing global integration being serviced by regional markets and regional policy. The state remains powerful in deciding about the domestic market, but the reality about regional and global exchanges of highly skilled workers has become a realm in which global business is perhaps more powerful. Even so, the power of business in this regard should not be over-emphasised. States remain strong in trade negotiations and in working out regional agreements where their interests extend beyond migration *per se*.

At the Albany meeting, participants reaffirmed that the politics of selection and restriction will remain a major issue, if only because many countries have dual labour markets and tolerate illegal migration. Because theory of the politics of selection and restriction is based largely on 'formal' migration, there is now a need to develop theories based on the diversity of migration movements around the world. The notion that governments will increasingly administer two-tier systems (formal and 'other') was seen as too simplistic a scenario. Every receiving country has multiple systems for different categories according to cultural, social, economic and humanitarian criteria. We are not looking at the evolution of a single system, but of a very complex network of arrangements.

CHANGING DETERMINANTS AND IMPACTS OF RETURN MIGRATION

Early literature on migration tended to equate return with failure: persons who emigrated with the intention of settling later changing their minds and returning 'home', or resettling in another country. Governments of 'traditional receiver' countries such as Australia, which provided financial assistance for the travel and adaptation of selected migrants, took a dim view of subsequent departures. Indeed, 'rates of return' became an index of a programme's success: the lower the rate the greater the success. However, a proportion of intending settlers, whether assisted or not, has always returned to their country of origin. Many never leave it again; others re-emigrate, and some even re-return. Skeldon's chapter cites a study which shows that during the latter part of the nineteenth and early twentieth centuries, the peak period of migration across the Atlantic, about twenty per cent of the Scandinavians and just under 40 per cent of the English and Welsh returned home.

'Return' as articulated in contemporary migration literature is essentially a generic term that incorporates a number of sub-types necessary to explain current mobility. While attempts to dichotomise return as either voluntary or involuntary have helped identify one important difference in 'type', scholars have struggled to come to terms with qualitative aspects of these categories. In the modern migration era there are many variations of return which, in both conceptual and practical terms, are difficult to handle. Nor is it easy to adequately classify the act of return. Thousands of Palestinians living in Kuwait at the time of the Gulf War were 'returned' to Jordan when most of them had never lived there. And how do ethnic Germans returning to the Federal Republic prove that they are Germans? For most, their movement represents a new migration rather than a return to something that they never knew, and are required to adapt in the manner of regular immigrants. Or Italian ethnics in Argentina who 'return' to Italy and then decide to live in Spain which, under EC regulations, they are able to do. Indeed, one problem of assessing return of these types is that it implies people going back to where they 'belong', and that the receiving state has the responsibility of taking care of them.

The changing and increasingly important role of the diaspora has also added a new dimension to the concept of return. More states are retaining contact with their nationals abroad and some are allowing double nationality to maintain the links. This type of movement, one participant argued, will increasingly be the way that states maintain the linkages. A Turkish girl in Sweden who leaves there before she reaches age twelve 'else she will not be seen as a good woman in Turkey', emphasises the importance of understanding lifetime strategy in order to understand the processes of return.

Return is also a field where the policies of both sending and receiving countries, and international organisations, can play important roles, especially in relation to economic development. For example, Taiwan retains close links with its nationals abroad, and incorporates return migration into the establishment and development of science and technology parks. This policy has facilitated achievement in high-tech industries. A substantial literature is now available on the importance of skills transfer by returning migrants and emphasises that such transfers are likely to be most successful if achieved within a context conducive to development in the society of origin. The successful returners are usually those who while away kept in contact with social and economic networks at home.

Salt argues that most 'permanent' settlement today may be associated with return migration to their home countries by former labour migrants and by certain ethnic and national groups such as German *Ausseidler,* Ingrian Finns, Bulgarian Turks, Pontion Greeks and Romanian Magyars. Adepoju argues that the xenophobic reactions to African migrants in especially France and Germany has reinforced the feeling that they are unwanted and must be returned to their countries. These and other statements presented at the Perth meeting led participants to reconsider the relevance of the two broad categories of return (voluntary and involuntary) at the Albany meeting. The former category includes not only persons who had intended to stay but did not achieve their objectives to settle, but also those who, on achieving their objectives (higher income, sufficient savings to build a house at 'home' and good education for their children) returned to their country of origin. Involuntary return, on the other hand, generally relates to causes in the host country such as war and economic crisis or, as in the situation described by Adepoju, xenophobic attitudes.

Return, for whatever reason, and stages of the mobility cycle, has been greatly facilitated by efficiency of travel and communication which will influence how we research migration in the future. Past research on 'return' migration has tended to focus on the last stage, not the coming and going. Obtaining more and better information on mobility, and identifying the variables that influence returners, are fields of research that require a great deal more attention. There is certainly a need for greater clarity of conception of the phenomenon. It needs to be seen as part of a cycle, not a discrete entity.

REFUGEE MIGRATION

Unlike other issues discussed at the conference, refugee migration was different in that it involved an international regime, i.e. collective action by states. The system is clearly under challenge partly because what had been originally designed and how it operated, and what was assumed to be the issue to be addressed, have now changed. The discussant at this session of the conference traced the history of the system since World War II, from UNRRA, IRO and UNHCR, showing that until the early 1960s focus had been on the resettlement of displaced persons in Europe.

Since 1960, two refugee regimes have developed: those relating to developed countries, and those relating to Third World countries. The first regime was based on several assumptions: most refugees would come from communist countries, numbers would be small and there would be no possibility of sending them back. The international community therefore did not build up a record of experience as to how countries may wish to bring about political situations that would allow for return. The system had been designed for one geopolitical system. But in 1983/84, large numbers of persons began arriving from places other than Eastern Europe, and while most countries were initially generous with their assistance, as the numbers increased, budgeting issues arose and some governments began to say that 'this is not what we bargained for'. Today, many arguments within countries for and against making asylum procedures more difficult, are based on concern whether or not it is acceptable to change the rules when the problem moves from one set of geopolitical structures to another.

The second regime, relating to the Third World, has involved the impacts of so-called proxy wars between East and West (e.g. Vietnam, Afghanistan, Angola, Nicaragua, El Salvador). Capacity to develop mechanisms to achieve political situations were not well developed, with the result that large, long-standing displaced populations were created outside their countries. Many conflicts in the Third World were prolonged not so much by external economic and political support, but because it did not take much to destabilise the governments. The international community was therefore faced with many complex situations. In places such as Rwanda, behaviour was so horrendous that it was difficult for international organisations to be neutral. What do you do when the refugees are under the control of military authorities? Give the country assistance that will only aid the military? But if you do not provide assistance the refugees are likely to die. 'The assumptions of the past', argued the discussant, 'are under challenge and there are no easy answers'. While many people in the West do not want to change the humanitarian tradition of the past seventy years, others are afraid of being overwhelmed by the problem.

Several participants argued that a major reappraisal needs to be made of the application of the Geneva Convention towards new refugee areas, that the Convention had been written in a way that allowed signatory states to protect their interests, that it asks for very little and leaves many responsibilities not well defined. The United Nations High Commissioner for Refugees (UNHCR) is inevitably becoming involved in situations such as to protect internally displaced persons in Iraq, simply because it is the only organisation in the UN system that has the expertise necessary to handle the problems. It was suggested that while UNHCR would like to keep the displaced person and refugee situations separate, the UN system is struggling to handle the former because it is not at all clear that displaced persons are necessarily a UNHCR mandate.

While states are likely to continue to operate through UNHCR, non-governmental organisations (NGOs) are set to play an increasingly important role in the resolution of refugee-type problems. The media has been especially effective in depicting the misery of many refugee and displaced person situations around the globe, creating an awareness not only of the numbers not moving, but awareness of the potential for relocation. As in so many facets of international migration, refugee migration is in transition in terms of policy and for scholars who attempt to find answers for its resolution. It was suggested that the issue of displacement should be placed within the context of inequality; of economic and political systems that perpetuate inequality, and the need to go back to 'root causes'. While not disagreeing with this approach, another participant argued that the main problem at the moment is to fight for retaining an adequate protection system and adapt that system to the new refugee situation.

This polemic topic was discussed frequently between the Perth and Albany meetings. At Albany, it was agreed that while refugees had been neglected by scholars as part of international migration theory, a major breakthrough had been Zolberg's research on the political theory of refugee creation in Third World countries. This had led to closer examination of the causes of conflict in multi-national states, the ideology of those states and the role of international players in the creation of refugees. From these had evolved other studies on why states reacted in the way they did to lack of stability. One finding was that states had a stake in collective action because there was a collective threat to stability. Within this framework, a number of studies were undertaken on examples of collective action, the operations and success of agencies, the inappropriateness of certain types of collective action, and the special circumstances of women. The chapter by Sally Findley shows that refugee flows in Sub-Saharan Africa are dominated by women and children who have seen their husbands and fathers killed or have left them fighting. There have also been a number of legal and historical studies on the refugee issue.

Participants agreed with the view that recent changes in the nature and direction of international migration, noted in the first section of this chapter, are also challenging the operation of states, international agencies, and the intellectual apparatus that scholars once used to study refugee migration. The political approach may have been a little too simple, taking for granted the national state system which is now very much under challenge. A contextual approach by researchers is needed to address such questions as: What are the processes that lead to the categorisation of who is a refugee? Why do some states categorise some persons as refugees but other states do not? Why do we hate the terms 'economic refugee' and 'environmental refugee'? What are the limits to the states' ability to say that they will, or will not, undertake certain obligations.

In respect to the last question, the final session at the Perth meeting had been addressed by Australia's Minister for Immigration and Multicultural Affairs, the Hon. Philip Ruddock, MP, on the basis and magnitude of his Government's refugee programme. Pointing out that of the 60,000 displaced persons and refugees identified by UNHCR as being in urgent need of resettlement, Australia takes 12,000, he vigorously defended the policy of detaining 'boat people' who, by 'illegally arriving on our shores' claiming refugee status, deprive others in more dire predicaments. His Government had therefore introduced new regulations which, instead of providing permanent residence to those judged to be a refugee, would now provide temporary refugee status to those who, having arrived illegally, are assessed as refugees. The Minister emphasised that while he did not want to suggest that 'temporary refugee' will be a magic solution that instantly eradicated the problem of unlawful arrivals, it was clearly an important component of the Government's overall strategy to address what he called 'forum shopping'.

Researchers will need to define refugee theory and link it with other issues relating to global political structure in different ways. This will certainly require greater attention to collection and analysis of appropriate data, but there is every chance that the field will attract new scholars because of new concerns and ways of looking at the issue. Among likely new topics of research are the implications for those persons excluded as refugees, and what happens to those who are repatriated whether under conflict or otherwise.

2. Politics of Immigration Control and Politicisation of International Migration

Tomas Hammar

INTRODUCTION

The study of international migration has spread into almost all disciplines in the social sciences and the humanities. Some disciplines started early; others, among them political science, are latecomers. It is my hope that the growth of academic work on international migration at the end of the twentieth century will lead to rapid future development of this important research field. Close co-operation between many disciplines and new institutional arrangements for research and studies will be necessary, and old financial and disciplinary structures at universities around the world must not be allowed to hinder the development.

Migration policy remained an apolitical issue until the middle of the twentieth century. Regulation of immigration, first practised during World War I and formalised during the 1920s and 1930s, was relaxed again after World War II, as demonstrated by the European guest worker system. In 1972–74, when recruitment virtually ceased in Western Europe, international migration was regulated anew and in partly new form. Immigration had been politicised in Britain after 1958 and in Switzerland around 1970 when a national *überfremdung* referendum was held. But these were the main exceptions. In general, the apolitical period continued.

European politicisation began in the mid-1980s for several reasons. Some were international: the growing refugee flows caused by ethnic conflicts and civil wars in non-European countries, and also intensified economic co-operation within the (then) EC. Others were domestic: structural unemployment in European immigration countries remained for years at an unexpectedly high level and, simultaneously, large immigrant groups settled for good. In many states, multicultural policies were discussed and integration policies developed. At the same time, anti-immigration groups openly criticised immigration and refugee policies as too liberal and voiced hostility to immigrants. Asylum seekers became victims of racial attacks.

Populist political parties gained votes in national elections; some even held influential positions in the parliaments. In sum, international migration was increasingly politicised in most European immigration countries.

In this chapter, Sweden will be my main example. Special attention will be paid to domestic politics dealing with real, perceived or just imagined threats that potential migration flows are about to increase and perhaps break through the 'walls'. Migration will be discussed as a more or less politicised issue which politicians under some conditions use or misuse for campaign purposes. The aim is to discuss the extent to which politics will matter in international migration. Will international migration again become an apolitical issue, or at the beginning of the new millennium will it remain politicised and even appear to be one of the top political issues? Is politicisation of migration basically positive or negative?[1] We would be better prepared to answer such questions if we knew under what conditions international migration is being politicised or instead depoliticised. Unfortunately, we know too little about this, although migration politics has recently become a matter of academic debate.

FROM AN APOLITICAL TO A HIGHLY POLITICISED MIGRATION POLICY

In 1964 my doctoral dissertation in political science was published under the title, *Sweden to the Swedes. Immigration Policy, Aliens Control, and Asylum in Sweden 1900–1932*.[2] It dealt with the emergence of a system of aliens legislation and immigration control and its implementation during the first third of the century, including unemployment years during the 1920s and 1930s and before Hitler's *Machtübernahme*. I used the protectionist slogan 'Sweden to the Swedes' to show that the immigration debate before World War I was tied to the defeat of trade liberalism as well as to the newly awakened interest in nationalism and defence. The book was not a typical political science thesis, but rather showed how this policy issue developed, and how an administration was established in reaction to immigration. It was a thesis which today I would call apolitical, and the theme itself was about a period when immigration in Sweden—and probably in most European countries—was an apolitical issue. In this chapter I will refer frequently to the Swedish case.[3]

POLITICISATION

My discussion is confined to open societies with democratic and representative governments where opinions can be expressed freely and political parties compete in general elections. Interest organisations enjoy the freedom of association and, as pressure groups, can influence the political agenda which is also influenced by political parties, their leaders and the media.

An issue is more politicised when it is a matter of political debate, confrontation and decision-making, a question about the goals to be attained, reforms to be made, and the methods to be used. An issue is less politicised when it has been settled, when everyone agrees, and when it is dealt with as a matter of routine administration. Therefore, migration policy is highly politicised when there is open confrontation between the political parties in parliament and in government, when parties incorporate migration in their platforms and in election campaigns, when there is much media attention and public debate, and when opinion is divided. In contrast, it is low when migration policy is by and large taken for granted, a matter of routine administration and continuous implementation, handled either by public authorities or by private interests on an open economic market with little or no state interference.

Most policy issues can be placed on a continuum from low to high politicisation. When an issue is moved in one direction or the other, we may call this 'politicisation' or 'depoliticisation'. During periods of rapid change we expect politicisation to be high; in status-quo periods the political system is probably less politicised and more characterised by administration than by political conflicts. This difference may have consequences for policy making and for public opinion. Without a certain level of political debate, little information about migration and migration policy may be available and the public can easily misunderstand or even be unaware of what is going on. High politicisation may bring about debates in which standpoints are formulated and alternatives discussed. In the transition from low to high politicisation and debate, when the public is not well informed, there might be a risk that simplified and emotional demagogic arguments will win over the balanced and knowledgeable.

A low degree of politicisation turns policymaking into policy administration, and the job of articulating and implementing policies is handed over to lawyers, civil servants and policy experts (such as many well-known social science experts, sometimes called 'the immigration Mafia'). The more migration policy is considered to be an apolitical issue, the greater is the influence of these 'intermediaries' on immigration policy.

In this chapter, politicisation will be assessed by a few rather crude indicators. An issue may be considered politicised the higher it is placed on the political agenda, the more political parties and interest organisations and media are activated, and the more public opinion is developed, formulated and outspoken. In contrast, an issue is less politicised (and more apolitical) when a state adopts a laissez-faire policy, not interfering in what is then often meant to belong to the market. Moreover, a less politicised issue is handled as a matter of routine, of administration and law, and also as a practical and technical problem which can best be solved by consulting the specialists.

The politicisation of migration has varied from country to country and over time. It has been low in many countries during long periods (e.g. 1945–

73), and has changed suddenly to high (1980–). As scholars, we have used various measurements and have not always agreed about whether migration policy is an apolitical or a political issue. The ideas expressed here partly deviate, for example, from those of several American authors.[4]

THE APOLITICAL TRADITION IN EUROPEAN IMMIGRATION POLICY

European migration policy was depoliticised or apolitical for long periods during the twentieth century when ideas of classical liberalism prevailed, even if temporal deviations were made. The ideal goal was a world where people could move freely and states did not interfere with international migratory movements. The hope was to return to the situation before 1914, when both transatlantic and intra-European movements were freely allowed. However, demands for protectionist systems aimed at controlling both trade and migration initiated the first politicisation in this century and resulted in the first national Aliens Acts. World War I stopped almost all voluntary migration, and depression and alarming unemployment and inflation during the 1920s and the 1930s led to prolongation, stabilisation and institutionalisation of the states' system of immigration control. Even so, the Utopia of free mobility has survived in several countries. Each time the control system was amended and prolonged, governments made wishful declarations that free movement would be restored as soon as the world situation had returned to 'normal'. In Sweden, this hope was lost only in 1954 when the provisional Aliens Act was given permanent status for the first time. The situation had become 'normal', but still the need for control was indispensable.

Migration control began as temporary crisis administration, and administrative decisions soon replaced political decisions. For half a century and more there were few political debates about migration. Immigration and aliens control was handled mainly by state administrations such as labour market bureaux, social welfare agencies and not least the aliens police. Courts were involved in adjudicating appeals against administrative decisions. In some countries, the partners in the labour market, the employers and the trade unions, were actively involved, but seldom the political parties, and not even the inflamed refugee debates in the 1930s followed traditional party lines.

Administrative agencies and courts in each country have gradually developed national systems of migration policy by 'trial and error'. No fundamental changes were made in this European migration control system, and most proposals for adjustments in legislation or practice came from civil servants, not politicians. Even during the intensive labour recruitment period in the 1960s and 1970s, migration remained largely an apolitical issue.[5]

In Sweden, Germany and France, decisions to stop recruitment of foreign labour in the early 1970s were made without public debate and parliamentary discussions. In Germany, the decision was made in 1973 by the Minister of Labour without consulting the Bundestag. Differences of opinion were expressed only after the decision. In France, a newly appointed Minister of Immigration suspended all new labour immigration in 1974. Behind this decision stood President Giscard d'Estaing who had just taken office; the National Assembly was not heard. In Sweden in 1972, neither the Government nor the Riksdag made the formal decision, but instead the central organisation of the national trade unions, the Landorganisationen, (LO). This corporativism could easily be practised, for trade unions held a 'veto'. They were always asked to advise the labour market authorities whether or not foreigners should be granted work permits. In February 1972, when the LO's advice changed from yes to no, the implication was immediate cessation of the import of foreign labour.[6]

MIGRATION AS A NATIONAL AND SYMBOLIC POLICY ISSUE

The term 'symbolic' may be given several meanings and deserves clarification. Symbols are representations: a flag represents the nation state, a crucifix the Christian church. In politics symbols are often used as representations of parties and their ideologies, for example, a rose for the Social Democratic parties. In a similar way, 'immigrant' and 'immigration' have been used as negative symbols for socio economic 'problems', blaming immigrants for being the underlying cause of unemployment, housing shortage and crime. A minority language may be seen as a symbolic threat to the national culture, so also many churches and mosques, head-scarves, and groups of immigrants.

Migration policy is often given symbolic meaning or used symbolically. It is evaluated, debated and decided not just on facts, but as a symbolic representation of something great and important: conceptions or myths about country, nation, history and origin, people, citizenship and welfare. In this sense, migration policy is not only a rational and logic issue, but rather a playground of emotions open to many different interpretations and interests. We can think of migration policy as a screen on which other policy issues are easily projected.

First, migration policy is an expression of a country's national interest: we and our country in contrast to all the others. Second, early warning and threat scenarios of large potential migration flows are uncertain and often impossible to prove or disprove: forecasts about future migration flows are seldom reliable and testable. It is hard to measure the efficiency of control and therefore to plan how much control will be needed. Moreover, a mistake could imply heavy costs, and no country could politically afford 'to lose control'. Migration policy is therefore a vague and very sensitive issue. Third, political leaders do not assess the efficiency of migration policies only by the outcome of policy decisions. More important is that they know these policies are able to reassure and please public opinion. Fourth, the electoral significance of both control and integration policies is considerable: while some politicians may fear to enter debates on this issue, others find that they can use it to promote their own interests.

Migration policy is partly a domestic issue, and its role in domestic politics must not be neglected, but it is also an issue akin to foreign policy, development and security policy. It involves citizens (and former citizens) of other countries as well as relations between these countries. International migration and migration policy may not always be of direct concern to the voters' private purse, their personal income or expenditures, nor is it a regular class issue, dividing domestic opinion. Immigration control is a 'we contra-them'-oriented issue: 'Shall *they* be allowed to stay and work among *us*?' Like many foreign policy issues, international migration can therefore credibly be presented as an external threat to the country. National interest is a key symbol which can unite 'us' against 'the others'.

In the 1990s fundamental changes in international politics have spread a feeling of insecurity. Among contributing factors are post-Cold War political and ethnic conflicts, wars and civil wars, the strengthening of the EU at the cost of the national member states, and many unsolved global international problems (poverty, pollution, population etc.). Fear of an unknown future may not always be clearly expressed but it is shared by many. Politicians can offer little but symbolic gestures, hoping to reassure their voters that international migration and other perceived threats will be kept under control.[7]

In periods of social insecurity, blame may be placed primarily on immigrants, foreign workers, refugees and other unwanted competitors who are said to cause unemployment and to live on social benefits which 'we' have to pay for. Some politicians have promised to stop migration (even when this has already been done) and to see that the country will not 'lose control of immigration' (even when the risks are low or negligible).

International migration and migration control are complex issues. Public opinion is seldom well-informed and it is most difficult even for an attentive opinion to judge which statements are factual and serious evaluations and which are mainly threat scenarios. Future migration flows are hard to predict. Many forecasts have been made, but most are more or less guesswork of little reliability. New flows often start suddenly because of an unexpected crisis. Furthermore, it is very hard to account *post factum* for the long-term economic effects of migration, and it may be even harder to make an advance assessment of a country's capability to receive new large flows and to integrate them efficiently into the national economy, especially if they arrive within a short time span. The long-term effects of large scale international migration have seldom been foreseen.

In this situation, politicians consider that the effects a policy might have on the public opinion is more significant than the actual policy outcome. In other words, they evaluate policy efficiency primarily on political and electoral grounds. In the best world, policy decisions should be resolute, effective and wise, but this is far from realistic in migration policy, and it has evidently been unrealistic in Europe in the 1990s because of complex social problems, high structural unemployment, budgetary crises, etc. Political decisions cannot be expected to change things quickly for the better, and politicians can do little but promise a better future to an audience which is increasingly sceptical and suspicious.

As long as immigration policy remains apolitical, policy alternatives are not formulated and presented, and the public is not well-informed. This may cause problems if immigration policy is suddenly politicised. In this situation—found in many European countries—some politicians are tempted to simplify facts, to place the blame on some categories of people, to exaggerate the risks and use symbols and emotions in irresponsible agitation. Politically it may be too dangerous to argue against this demagogy in front of a rather uninformed audience. It will—in such situations—take time until a re-politicised immigration policy debate brings about a more elevated and mature level of information. Too little politicisation tends to result in an uninformed public. A sudden politicisation may be fertile ground for xenophobic political parties. Perhaps a long-lasting policy debate might be the cure.

Such questions come to mind when we study change in European migration policy from a traditional apolitical to a newly-politicised status. It would be a fascinating task to unravel the interrelationships in the 1980s between migration flows, new and restrictive control policies, xenophobic movements, media attention and policies, and more general changes in public opinion. These five factors are interdependent, and it remains uncertain as to what extent control policies are the result of changes in migration flows and in attitudes and opinions, or whether more restrictive control has legitimatised a growing xenophobia. Has public opinion been too little informed, what role has the media played and how has the political leadership met the new challenges? Has fear of potential migration flows been excessive, and has migration policy been given too much attention?

PUBLIC OPINION AND POLITICAL PARTIES IN SWEDEN

Sweden's apolitical tradition lasted until around 1985 when about one million persons were first or second generation immigrants. In 1972, labour immigration ceased with the exception for Nordic citizens. In 1975, the Riksdag unanimously adopted a positive integration programme, including major reforms aimed at a vaguely envisioned future multicultural society. But migration was not a politicised issue, and there was little debate. Specialists were asked for technical solutions. The political parties expressed goodwill but made no strong commitments and there were no party differences. Some critics wrote about an existing taboo, a tacit agreement not to bring this sensitive issue into party politics.

This changed radically in the mid-1980s. In 1987–88 an open and rather vivid public debate started about the scope and methods of migration control, including demands for both more restrictions and a more liberal and humane practice. Political parties which had been unanimous in their defence of one political line, soon stood divided, as demonstrated in several Riksdag debates. For the first time, some members of Parliament demanded cessation of all immigration and a sharp reduction in public costs for refugees. With this kind of platform, a new party of discontent, the New Democracy, emerged before the general elections of 1991. It gained 8 per cent of the votes, or 28 of 349 seats in the Riksdag. How did this politicisation come about?

We find two parallel trends: increased immigration from outside Europe and a break of the 'taboo' on critical comments. After 1985 the annual number of immigrants increased. The majority were asylum seekers from wars or warlike situations in the Middle East and Africa. The Swedish administration of asylum applications, the reception centres and rising costs caused permanent reorganisations and exceeded budgets. But there was no national debate until the local government of one municipality, Sjöbo, in Southern Sweden, refused to take its share of refugees (in all 15 persons). Its decision gained support from the majority of voters in a local referendum in 1988 and initiated a national debate on migration control. Once opened, the door could not be closed. Out of this referendum emerged a strong, previously unrecognised negative opinion, which no political party had exploited. One year later, the Government launched a more restrictive refugee policy, although still verbally maintaining that the traditional generous policy continued, only that Sweden for the time being had already admitted too many refugees in a short period, and therefore was unable to receive many more.[8]

Which came first? The chicken or the egg? The negative opinion or the restrictive policy? While the answer is not easy to provide, it is clear that the local referendum in Sjöbo, which claimed national attention, had broken the ice and started the debate. It showed that many Swedes favoured a more restrictive immigration and refugee policy, an opinion supported by all the five traditional political parties, most numerous in the centre party, the conservative party (Moderaterna), and in the Social-Democratic party and least in the liberal party (Folkpartiet).

New Democracy, the first party to criticise Sweden's refugee policy in an electoral campaign (1991), completely changed the climate in the following year's parliamentary debate. To regain what had been lost, other political parties moved towards more restrictions, and continued to do so in the following years, although New Democracy disappeared in the following elections (1994) because of internal conflicts. Meanwhile, the crises in Bosnia and Kosovo had given rise to new refugee problems and new solutions. The restrictive policy was continued, but with specific qualifications for each of the refugee groups from the former Yugoslavia. The debate went on, and maybe as a result, public opinion was gradually more informed and less negative up to 1987, thereafter again turning more negative and less tolerant.

The interrelationship between public opinion and political decision-making may be interpreted in two different ways. First, many Swedes had long thought that immigration and refugee policy was too liberal, but had not openly voiced their criticism. When this changed (as it did in the Sjöbo referendum and afterwards), policymakers adjusted and made control more restrictive. The second interpretation starts in 1989 when the government decided to reduce immigration and make the control system more rigid and effective. This new policy may have induced negative attitudes towards refugees and immigrants and it may have made it legitimate to openly express such ideas. Implied in the restrictive policy decisions was that Sweden had already admitted too many refugees, that the right of asylum was often claimed with little ground, and that budgetary public costs were running too high. But the negative attitudes could easily spill over from asylum seekers and new refugees (from Bosnia and Kosovo) to foreigners (from the former Yugoslavia) already long settled in Sweden. In simplified arguments the question could be asked: If most foreigners and most new immigrants from 1989 onwards are 'unwanted', what about those foreigners who immigrated some years earlier, should not they be told to leave the country?

A WELL-EDUCATED PUBLIC OPINION

In relation to the formation of public opinion in Sweden, especially concerning immigration and immigration policy, an unusually good source of information is national opinion surveys from 1969 to the 1990s. It is therefore misleading to say that there was no information and knowledge about migration before the end of the 1980s when politicisation began. But, as already noted, there had been little political debate, and migration policy had been made by specialists on administrative and technical decisions, rather than by the parties on political decisions. Information for the public, or perhaps the 'education' of the public about immigration and migration policy, had not been the task of political parties but of the immigration authorities, notably the National Immigration Authority, SIV.

In 1964, Sweden's first daily newspaper, *Dagens Nyheter*, initiated a debate on the integration of immigrants. Should they become assimilated new Swedes (as everyone at that time naively supposed they would), or should minorities be allowed to develop and preserve their own language, culture and religion? Five years later, the Parliament established SIV as the new national immigration authority. Among other roles, it was assigned the task of promoting good mutual relations between immigrant groups and the majority population. SIV was organised in two parallel sections, one 'good' section for integration and one 'nasty' section for immigration control (permits and deportations etc.). Under Kjell Öberg, a journalist and former ambassador to China who was the first head of SIV, great efforts were made to teach Swedes about the new minorities, the immigrant organisations, their culture and religion, their needs and demands. SIV published a periodical magazine and many books, organised courses on all levels, and persuaded local governments to initiate their own information service. SIV actively fought against prejudice and discrimination, and from 1978 Kjell Öberg was director of the state's anti-discrimination programme.

This massive campaign for increased tolerance had been underway for about fifteen years before the referendum in Sjöbo. The message had been that immigration was to the advantage of everyone, Swedes and immigrants; that those who had been immigrants should enjoy the same conditions as everyone else, including full rights to participate in the society. In 1976, voting rights in local and regional elections were granted to immigrant non-citizens. Only national elections were still the privilege of citizens. While it is not possible to establish accurately the impact of these efforts on public opinion, we have some clues which have been much discussed in Sweden.

As noted above, the first survey of public opinion was made in 1969, just at the beginning of the State-administered information campaign. This was followed by other surveys in 1981, 1987, 1993 and 1995[9] which contained the same questions. From 1969 to 1981 tolerance increased, even if there were still many expressions of intolerance and hostility against immigrants. Young persons were more tolerant than older persons, urban persons more than rural, highly educated more than less educated. A critical comment often heard was that this might imply only that the Swedish people had learnt how to answer interview questions or perhaps that they now knew how they ought to behave, how tolerant they should be, and answered in compliance with such expectations. Even this would show, however, that some significant learning had taken place. The well-known sociologist Erik Allardt wrote an extremely positive review of Charles Westin's book (1984) which showed that in 1981 Swedish opinion was indeed remarkably tolerant. But would this tolerance disappear in a less prosperous period?[10]

The 1987 survey did not show dramatic changes. The level of tolerance was the same or, if anything, even somewhat better than 1981. It was shown, however, that the attitudes of the youngest cohort in this study (16–18 years olds) were more negative to immigrants. This led to an extra survey exclusively of young persons in four selected neighbourhoods which showed that the negative trend among the young had continued, being stronger among boys than among girls. Unemployment was not the cause, although four of five young persons blamed immigration for a severe housing shortage.

The surveys in 1993 and 1995 showed a general decline in tolerance, not only among young respondents. The Sjöbo referendum in 1988 and the Government decision in December 1989 which launched the more restrictive refugee policy, occurred before the 1993 survey. The appearance and success of the populist party in 1991 and the arrival of new and numerous refugee groups from Bosnia and Kosovo occurred before and during the two latest surveys. Much less tolerant attitudes were thus expected and even if the proportion of positive response was still high, the trend in these surveys was negative. As a result of several new items being included in the latest surveys, a new and important distinction can be made between attitudes to immigrants and to immigration policy. Again this corresponded to how the political debate had developed.

New Democracy had demanded a reduction in immigration and a more strict control and regulation of asylum seekers, refugees and their families. While the party's spokesmen were not always very clear in their statements, they nonetheless tried to maintain that they were not negative to immigrants already in Sweden. It was the policy that they criticised: it was far too liberal and generous. The surveys of 1993 and 1995 showed that this distinction between immigrants and migration policy was made also by the public in general. Tolerance of alien residents was combined with dislike of the policy.

THE REFUGEE MOVEMENT

Even attentive public opinion may find it difficult to understand migration and not least to recognise how migration policy may be relevant in private life situations also for members of the majority population. For those who meet immigrants, refugees, asylum seekers and illegals face to face, the situation is different. As asylum seekers often wait long periods for the final decision about their stay, they may learn to know neighbours, teachers, parents to their children's friends, etc. If a decision to deport arrives, it can provoke strong reactions from local people who have learnt to know them. Sometimes the media give publicity to what many consider unfair and outrageous treatment. The Minister of Immigration often had problems defending her decision to deport a family after several years, and explain to protesting neighbours that she had to take such a tough decision otherwise Sweden would not be able to stop unwanted immigration in the future. For many neighbours, emotional ties to the family weighed much heavier than abstract theory of migration control.

Although Ministers of Immigration had always faced such situations, after 1989 when the number of asylum seekers had increased and control had become more strict, the cases were more numerous and there was less room for individual exceptions. In order to free the Minister of Immigration from this political dilemma, which was also very time-consuming, the appeal system was depoliticised. A new administrative court, called the Aliens Board, took over appeals against negative decisions made by the Immigration Authority, SIV. In practice, this meant that evaluation of refugee status was dressed in the form of a legal interpretation, although the law itself is a vague document which gives wide room for interpretation of the grounds for asylum application as well as of Sweden's national interests as expressed in statements by the Riksdag and the Government. As a result, the rate of rejected appeals rose from ten to fifteen per cent in the 1980s to about eighty per cent at the end of the 1990s.

The Minister has in this way been freed from direct political responsibility in individual cases. The protests have continued, however, both from international and Swedish organisations, and from a pro-refugee movement that developed in protest against a too restrictive policy. The Liberal party Folkpartiet, the 'green' party Miljöpartiet, and the leftist party Vänsterpartiet, have voiced this opinion in the Riksdag (representing together some 30 per cent of the votes). The political debate about migration and migration policy has never been so vivid in the Riksdag as during the last five years of this millennium. According to surveys, public opinion has gone from a more tolerant and positive attitude towards a more restrictive, and now favours a strict control policy. So does the political majority in the Riksdag made up of the Moderates and the Social Democrats (about sixty per cent together).

CONCLUSION

International migration has been politicised in Europe both for real and symbolic reasons and in order to protect internal and external security. This occurred from 1985 to 1990, when many unwanted refugee immigrants arrived from war torn regions in Asia and Africa. Xenophobic, populist parties to the right and to the left have exploited this situation; other parties have tried to avoid debate and prolong a more or less apolitical situation.

Summing up the Swedish experience, major immigration reforms had been made without party divisions or conflicts before the politicisation in 1987–89. The general public was relatively well-informed about immigration and immigration policy, but news and views were communicated not by the political parties in public debates, but in an official information campaign which lasted several years and, according to ongoing studies, resulted in a high level of tolerance. No open opposition was heard, although in private conversations people often criticised the country's refugee policy, claiming it to be too liberal. In 1988, the referendum in Sjöbo opened the door for this silent negative opinion (negative mainly towards migration policy not towards immigrants), and demonstrated the spread and significance of negative opinion throughout the country.

At the time when this politicisation occurred, there was not much demand for foreign labour and only a few immigrants found jobs with reasonable income in Sweden. The state budget therefore had to cover great expenditure for asylum seekers and refugees. While the traditional parties at first did not want to make refugee migration an election issue, the populist party New Democracy forced them to do so, and made them understand that they had better accept demands for less generosity and more strict immigration control.

Two preliminary conclusions may be ventured: first, politicisation may, as it seems in this case, be a positive answer to a democratic deficit. If a policy issue (e.g. migration policy) remains apolitical for long period, this will have consequences for public opinion. Voters will not meet pro and contra arguments as these are never publicly articulated. Relevant opinions will not be developed and represented by the parties. When the same issue is later politicised, put on the parties' platforms and debated in elections, a simplified rhetoric and populist argumentation may win. Hopefully, in the long run, a more mature debate will emerge and in due course a depoliticisation trend will begin.

In Sweden, the five old parties paid little notice to migration policy before the Sjöbo referendum, and were even rather passive in the following national elections in 1991, in which New Democracy successfully made migration policy one of its key issues. SIV's tolerance campaign had been a public drive, education coming from above. People had been told to be tolerant, and in surveys a majority appeared to be relatively tolerant, but all the time there was also an unheard negative minority. Perhaps, as a consequence, the revolt in Sjöbo was directed against the central national authorities in Stockholm which had told people that they should receive immigrants in their local communities, although they had been recognised as refugees by these national authorities.

Second, politicisation of migration policy depends on both real, material facts and on symbolic representations. The relative weight may vary, but symbolic representations play a greater role in migration policy than in many other policy areas, because the symbolic nature is enhanced in this complex and sensitive issue about which it is difficult to make well founded, rational policy decisions. Moreover, these decisions must often be made without reliable migration forecasts, and they must be made early in prevention and defence against future potential migration. In this context coloured by uncertainty, anxiety and even excessive fear, policymakers tend to exaggerate the risk of large-scale flows from nearby and faraway countries and continents. In this sense, migration policy is a transnational issue, often apolitical but now and then politicised, that involves both real and symbolic national interests in need of full protection.

NOTES AND REFERENCES

1. I have learned a lot from colleagues in two projects, and I owe thanks to all of them. Two books emerged from these projects: Hammar, T., Brochmann, G., Faist, T., and Tamas, K. (eds) (1997) *International Migration, Immobility and Development*. Oxford: Berg; Brochmann, G. and Hammar, T. (eds) (1999), *The Mechanisms of Immigration Control. A Comparative Analysis of European Regulation* Policies, Berg: Oxford.
2. Hammar, T. (1964), *Sverige åt svenskarna. Invandringpolitik, utlänningskontroll och asylrätt i Sverige 1900-1932*, Dissertation, Stockholm University, Summary in English. Stockholm, Published by the author.
3. I have previously written on similar topics in Hammar, T. (1997), 'Flyktingpolitiken i hetluften', in *Brobyggare, en Vänbok till Nils Andrén*, Stockholm: N&S (1999), 'Closing the doors to the Swedish welfare Sstate', in Brochmann, G. and Hammar, T. (eds), *Mechanisms of Immigration Control. A Comparative Analysis of European Regulation Policies*, Berg: Oxford.
4. Freeman, G. (1995), 'Modes of immigration politics in liberal democratic states' in *International Migration Review*, 1995: 881-902; and Hollifield, J. (1992), *Immigrants, Markets and States*, Cambridge, MA: Harvard University Press.
5. Hammar, T. (1985), 'Comparative analysis' in Hammar, T. (ed.), *European Immigration Policy, a Comparative Study*. Cambridge: Cambridge University Press. pp. 279 ff.
6. Hammar, T. (1988), 'Invandringspolitikens ideologi och historia', in *Arbetarhistoria*, **12** (2), Stockholm: Arbetarrörelsens arkiv.
7. Edelman, M. (1988), *Constructing the Political Spectacle*, Chicago: University of Chicago Press.
8. Fryklund, B. and Peterson, T, (1989), *'Vi mot dom' Det dubbla främlingsskapet i Sjöbo*, Cesic Studies in International Conflict, Lund: Lund University Press.
9. In all these surveys professors Anders Lange and Charles Westin have participated, and most of the studies were developed and analysed by one of them or by the two together. During the 1980s and 1990s this work was done at the Stockholm University Centre for Research in International Migration and Ethnic Relations (Ceifo). See Lange, A. (1993), *Den mångtydiga toleransen, förhållningssätt till invandring och invandrare* 1993, Stockholm: Ceifo; Lange, A. (1996), *Den svårfångade toleransen, förhållningssätt till invandring och invandrare* 1996, Stockholm: Ceifo; Lange, A. and Westin, C. (1991), *Ungdomen om invandringen*. Stockholm: Ceifo; Westin, C. (1984), *Majoritet om minoritet, en studie i etnisk tolerans i 80-talets Sverige*, rapport från diskrimineringsutredningen, Stockholm: Liber; Westin, C. (1998), 'Xenophobic Activation, Public Opinion and Integration Policies in Europe', in Westin, C. (ed.), *Racism, Ideology and Political Organisation*, Stockholm: Ceifo.
10. Allardt, E. (1984), 'Toleransen ökar-hur länge?' in *Dagens Nyheter* (daily newspaper, Stockholm)

3. Economic Integration and Migration: the Mexico–US Experience

Philip Martin

INTRODUCTION

This chapter explores the evolution of the world's largest volume migration regime—the demand-pull, supply-push, and network linkages forged over the past century that have resulted in the movement of over seven per cent of the 106 million persons born in Mexico to the US. Migration flows are larger than these numbers suggest, since another one to two per cent of Mexico-born persons work seasonally in the US. In 1999, some four to five million Mexico-born workers were employed in the US labour market, equivalent to about one-third of the twelve million Mexicans employed in formal sector jobs in Mexico (enrolled in the pension system IMSS).

For most of the twentieth century, the major relationship between Mexico and the US has been a low-skill migration relationship, and migration was more often a source of conflict than of cooperation. Mexico complained frequently about the poor treatment of its citizens in the US, but there were few mechanisms to enable the Mexican and US governments to work cooperatively to improve conditions for legal or unauthorised Mexican migrants. On the US side of the border, fewer than 10,000 south western farm employers set the terms for most Mexico–US migration for most of the twentieth century. The US government alone, or the US and Mexican governments jointly, permitted US farmers to recruit Mexican workers for temporary US employment for about twenty-five years of the twentieth century. However, many US farmers and Mexican workers preferred to operate outside the legal guest-worker system even while it was operating; periodic crackdowns on unauthorised migrants by the US government led to mutual recriminations between the US and Mexico.

The legacy of the series of Bracero programmes and toleration of unauthorised Mexico–US migration meant that illegal migration increased together with closer economic integration. Closer economic integration was widely expected to quickly and seamlessly reduce unauthorised migration, exemplified by Mexican President Salinas's comment that 'We would rather export Mexican tomatoes than Mexican tomato pickers'. Experts cautioned that approval of the North America Free Trade Agreement would act as a substitute for migration in the long term, but that migration might increase in the short term as the Mexican economy restructured. The failure of policy makers to anticipate this migration hump, which occurred in the mid-1990s, led to a backlash that produced both Proposition 187 in 1994 in California and federal legislation in 1996 restricting the access of all poor Americans, but especially immigrants, to welfare assistance.

SETTING THE STAGE: BRACEROS AND MIGRATION

There is a long history of northward migration of unskilled labour. Between 1769 and 1833, for example, the 21 Spanish missions established along the El Camino Real in California (today's Highway 101) employed local Indians to work on surrounding farmland as a means of exercising control over them. The Spanish priests soon complained of labour shortages and, at the behest of Franciscan Father Junipero Serra in 1773, the Spanish viceroy in Mexico City agreed to permit the California missions to 'recruit' workers in what is today the Mexican state of Baja California. The rights of these 'first Braceros' were laid out in a 1773 Reglamento (Steven Street, 1996/97: 316).

There has been significant Mexico–US migration in every decade of the twentieth century, but during only two periods, 1917–21 and 1942–64, did formal bilateral agreements regulate the entry and wages and working conditions of most Mexican workers who were temporarily employed in the US. During both of these so-called Bracero (strong arm) programmes, Mexican workers were recruited to work in US agriculture because of wartime emergencies. However, both programmes expanded after the war ended, and labour and civil rights arguments were used to justify ending them over the objections of farmers and the Mexican government.

For example, US farmers, with 'Food to Win the War' as a motto, got the first Bracero programme approved by persuading the US Department of Labor (DOL) in May 1917 to suspend the head tax and the literacy test in order to admit temporary Mexican farm workers, and Mexicans arrived legally to work on US farms for the next four years, until 1921. The US Border Patrol was established in 1924, but did little to impede the movement of Mexicans migrating north to be seasonal farm workers. Mexico–US migration was stopped in the late 1920s by repatriations that were launched to open jobs for Americans during the Great Depression: between 1929 and 1933, some 400,000 Mexicans (including their US-born and US-citizen children) were returned to Mexico.

Contemporary Mexico–US migration has its roots in a series of agreements under which 4.6 million Mexican workers were admitted to the US as seasonal farm workers between 1942 and 1964. In some cases, the same workers were admitted year after year, but over the course of 22 years, one to two million Mexicans obtained work experience in the US as legal guest workers. It is important to remember that the Bracero programme was very controversial in the US from the start, and that it admitted the maximum number of Mexican workers in the mid-1950s when western water projects opened new farmland, not during World War II.

1942–64

The 'farm labor supply agreement' between the US and Mexico of 23 July 1942 was bitterly opposed by US farm labour reformers. Throughout the 1930s, 'realist' farm labour reformers argued that large farms in the western US were really 'factories in the fields' that should be covered by the same labour laws as non-farm factories. Another group of reformers, 'idealists', wanted large farms broken up into family-size parcels so that there would be no need for hundreds of thousands of seasonal farm workers; they opposed applying farm labour laws to farm factories, and instead favoured land reform.

The reformers appeared to be on the verge of forcing some major change in western agriculture in 1939–40, when a series of academic and government reports demonstrated convincingly that low farm wages were capitalised into higher land prices, and large landowners invested in the political process to ensure that they had a flexible work force willing to accommodate to seasonality and thereby preserved the land wealth acquired in part from previous immigration (Martin, 1996, Chapter 2). John Steinbeck's 1940 book, *The Grapes of Wrath*, which was soon made into a movie, provided the emotional impetus for farm labour reforms.

However, before any farm labour reforms could be enacted or implemented, World War II broke out, and young American men who may have formed the core of a farm worker union or protest movement exited the seasonal farm workforce for the armed forces or factory jobs. Many were replaced by Braceros, although they comprised less than two per cent of US hired farm workers during World War II. The availability of Braceros, plus prisoners of war, interned Japanese, and US prisoners, sent an unmistakable signal to US farm workers—economic mobility would require geographic mobility, or getting ahead in the US labour market would require getting out of the hired farm workforce.

The Mexican government, remembering the humiliation of early 1930s repatriations, insisted that the US government guarantee the contracts that farmers were required to provide to Mexican Braceros, including round-trip transportation and the payment of wages equal to those of similar American workers (Craig, 1971: 41). The US–Mexican Bracero agreement contained many safeguards for workers, but it also led to many Mexican workers paying bribes to get on the list to be hired by US farmers. US farmers who hired legal Braceros were required to pay the workers' transportation and housing costs. Thus, little encouragement was needed for Mexican workers and US farmers to operate outside the programme, and the number of so-called 'wetbacks' increased significantly in the late 1940s and early 1950s.[1]

The Bracero programme in the early 1950s became an ongoing quasi-amnesty programme for seasonal workers from Mexico, many of whom arrived illegally. Newspaper headlines that read 'Wetbacks swarm in' led to the perception that Mexico–US migration was out of control. A retired Army general was appointed to head the INS, and in 1954 he launched Operation Wetback, a massive border control and interior enforcement operation that removed from the US over one million Mexicans in the mid-1950s. Simultaneously, the US government relaxed rules for employing Mexicans as legal Bracero workers, with the result that the number of Braceros admitted peaked at 550,000 in 1955–56. One result of the expansion of the Bracero programme was that US workers, especially Mexican–Americans who faced competition from Braceros in the fields, responded by moving to cities such as Los Angeles and San Jose.[2]

The Bracero programme was ended unilaterally by the US in 1964, amid predictions that tomatoes and other commodities would have to be imported into the US from Mexico because of the lack of farm workers. These predictions—made by farmers and agricultural officials presumably closest to the farm labour market—proved to be false. Farm wages rose sharply in the mid-1960s, when the combination of the full-employment Vietnam-war economy and a smaller excess supply of farm workers permitted Cesar Chavez and the United Farm Workers to win a 40 per cent wage increase for grape pickers, increasing their minimum wages from $1.25 to $1.75 an hour in the UFW's first contract in 1966. During the late 1960s, farm wages rose faster than most other US wages, especially in California, and farm work was expected to emerge as construction-style work that paid high wages when seasonal work was available, and offered maximum unemployment insurance benefits during the off season.

1965–82

The golden era for US farm workers—the time when there were relatively few newly-arrived foreigners in the farm workforce—lasted from the mid-1960s to the early 1980s. Legal and illegal immigration brought this golden era to a close by 1982.

The legal immigration of Mexicans began as a trickle in the late 1960s, when many ex-Braceros became US immigrants. During the 1960s, US employers were permitted to sponsor unskilled Mexicans to be immigrants by sending a letter to the US government that asserted that the Mexican named in the letter was the best-qualified person to fill a vacant job. Most Mexican immigrants to the US in the 1960s were sponsored by US farmers: an estimated 80 per cent of the 222,000 immigrants from Mexico between 1957 and 1962 had been Braceros who were sponsored for immigrant status by farm employers.

There was illegal immigration as well. The UFW, the major farm worker union, complained about farmers using unauthorised workers to break strikes called in support of higher wages. The UFW was a major force behind the approval in the US House of Representatives of employer sanctions in the 1970s—the Senate refused to agree, and the US did not adopt employer sanctions until 1986. Illegal immigration rose slowly: 110,000 deportable aliens were located in FY65, 212,000 in FY68, 420,000 in FY71, and 788,000 in FY74. The number rose to just over one million in the late 1970s, but then fell back under one million a year in the early 1980s. In 1982, Mexico devalued the peso, and apprehensions began to rise again, peaking at 1.8 million in FY86.

There was a clear link between Braceros, legal immigration, and illegal immigration. Most Braceros were men aged between 18 and 40. Those sponsored by US employers in the 1960s were in their thirties when they became legal immigrants. As they reached 40 and aged out of seasonal harvest work in the 1970s, some US farm employers made them foremen, and asked them to recruit younger Mexicans to be seasonal harvest workers. The foremen, who typically visited Mexico during the winter months, recruited workers who arrived illegally the next summer. This process of network recruitment soon linked particular Mexican villages and particular farms and areas in the US.

The UFW's fortunes rose when there was little illegal immigration, and fell when immigration surged. The high water mark for the UFW came in 1978–79, when it represented about 70,000 farm workers in California, ten per cent of all those who worked for wages sometime during the year on the state's farms. As contracts expired in 1978–79, the UFW demanded 50 to 60 per cent wage increases at a time when President Carter asked US employers not to grant wage increases in excess of seven per cent.

The UFW called a strike against major lettuce growers in support of its wage demands that boomeranged. Growers, aware of the availability of newly-arrived Mexican migrants who could serve as strike breakers, harvested enough lettuce at prices that were triple normal levels to double their revenues. The UFW eventually won a 42 per cent wage increase with a few of the largest growers vulnerable to consumer boycotts, raising entry level wages on farms with contracts from $3.75 to $5.25 per hour, but most of the companies that signed agreements increasing wages to these levels went out of business in the early 1980s or adapted in some other way so that they employed no farm workers.[3]

IMMIGRATION REFORM AND CONTROL ACT (IRCA)

Farm worker wages and benefits were eroding in the early-1980s when what became the Immigration Reform and Control Act began moving through Congress. Farm labour proved to be a major stumbling block to the enactment of IRCA, with western farmers insisting there be an alternative guest-worker programme available to them that did not require growers to obtain certification from the US Department of Labor before employing foreign workers, or provide free housing to temporary farm workers employed on their farms. However, a bipartisan coalition of control-minded Republicans and worker-advocate Democrats prevented the approval of such a guest-worker programme, and the compromise was one of strangest amnesty programmes ever: the Special Agricultural Worker programme.

The SAW programme permitted unauthorised foreigners who did at least 90 days of farm work in 1985–86 to apply for US immigrant status. Because it was widely asserted that many US farm employers paid their workers in cash, the regulations implementing the SAW programme were written in a manner that put the burden of disproving an application on the government, that is, once a foreigner applied for legalisation, usually by attaching to the application a short letter from a farm employer asserting that the worker was employed at least 90 days, the burden of disproving the alien's claim rested on the US government. The government had no mechanism to cope with the flood of applications, over 1.2 million rather than the expected 400,000, and no means of disproving what were in many cases false worker applications and employer letters—for example, the application and letter might assert that the worker picked tomatoes for 92 days, but the harvesting season in that area was only 60 days. In the end, over 1.1 million foreigners were legalised under the SAW programme, including one million Mexicans, the equivalent of one in six adult men in rural Mexico.[4]

The theory of SAW legalisation was that it would reverse the early 1980s slide in farm worker wages and working conditions by enabling now legal workers to join unions and press for wage increases. With the border closed to unauthorised migrants, farmers would have no choice but to grant wage and benefit increases to retain SAWs or to win permission to obtain legal non-immigrants under one of two alternatives: (1) the H-2A guest worker programme, which required farm employers to offer workers housing and contracts spelling out wages and working conditions; and (2) the Replenishment Agricultural Worker programme, a never-implemented programme that would have given unauthorised workers a probationary immigrant status that could be converted to regular immigrant status after several years of US farm work.

This theory that Mexican men would continue to commute seasonally to US jobs without their families proved to be false. As Mexico opened its economy, many now-legal SAWs brought their families to the US. At the same time, the SAW programme taught poor Mexicans that they could buy forged documents and win legal immigrant status, encouraging more Mexicans to migrate to the US. The hired farm work force was estimated to be twenty to twenty-five per cent unauthorised in the early 1980s, about ten per cent unauthorised in the late 1980s, but then the percentage of unauthorised workers began to climb in the 1990s. By 1998–99 over half the US farm workers were believed to be unauthorised, with the highest percentage of unauthorised workers in low-profit commodities—the percentage of unauthorised is higher in raisin grapes than table grapes—and in areas of the US that have only recently begun to have significant numbers of Mexican farm workers, such as the midwest and southeast.

In sum, the Mexico–US Bracero programmes of the twentieth century turned out to be anything but a managed flow of temporary foreign farm workers:

- Bracero programmes were largest after the wartime emergencies that justified them had passed, and they created networks that linked unskilled Mexican workers with unskilled US jobs.
- Braceros in the US farm labour market encouraged US workers with other employment options to get out of the farm labour force, reinforcing exit rather than voice responses to dissatisfaction that isolated the farm labour market from other US labour markets.
- Mexico neglected West Central Mexico, the area from which many migrants came, so that emigration and remittances became the economic pillars of families and local and regional economies
- The unequal exchange involved in the various Bracero programmes and their illegal migration aftermath made it hard for the US and Mexican governments to treat each other as equals on migration matters. The normal mode was for the US to act unilaterally, and for Mexico to complain.

FROM BRACEROS TO NAFTA: MAQUILADORAS

When the Bracero programme ended in 1964, there was an unemployment crisis in Mexican border cities. US employers were required to pay transportation costs from the worker's home to the US workplace, and many Mexicans moved with their families to the border area to reduce US employers' transportation costs and thus increase the probability of being selected. This meant that in the mid-1960s thousands of families were living along the Mexico–US border who were dependent on the US labour market.

Mexico and the US co-operated on a plan to create jobs for ex-Braceros in the border region in 1965. Under the Border Industrialization Program of 1965, trade and investment laws were modified in both Mexico and the US so that foreign (US) investors could create jobs in factories in Mexico border areas, so-called maquiladoras. Mexico allowed foreign ownership of maquiladoras, and permitted the duty-free importation of components and any machinery needed to produce and assemble maquiladora goods. Finished maquiladora goods had to be exported from Mexico and, as they entered the US, the US tariff schedule was modified to limit the duty on maquiladora products to the value that was added by Mexican assembly operations. Wages and Mexican inputs usually account for 10 to 20 per cent to the value of maquiladora products entering the US.[5]

The maquiladora programme expanded slowly and has become a major Mexican success story. There were 12 maquiladoras employing 3,000 workers in 1965, 600 maquiladoras employing nearly 120,000 workers in 1980, 2,000 maquiladoras employing 472,000 workers in 1990, and 4,000 maquiladoras employing 1.1 million workers in February 1999.[6] Foreign direct investment in Mexico averaged $11 billion a year between 1994 and 1997, and much of it went into maquiladoras. By 1999, maquiladoras provided almost 10 per cent of the formal sector jobs in Mexico, about thirty per cent of the manufacturing jobs, and generated 44 per cent of all Mexican exports. In 1998, maquiladora exports surpassed oil as Mexico's leading source of foreign exchange.[7]

Maquiladoras did not create jobs for ex-Braceros. The Braceros were young men; the workers employed in maquiladoras were and still are mostly young women. Instead of hiring men who had moved to the Mexico–US border to be closer to US farm jobs, maquiladora managers hired young women, and when they ran out of local women, they recruited more from the interior of Mexico: women were believed more willing to work for low wages, to have more dexterity, and to be less likely to complain about repetitive assembly line work.[8]

Maquiladoras in Mexican border cities acted as a single firm when it came to setting wages and benefits. Most pay workers the same wages—about $1.80 per hour—and offer the same benefits, typically subsidised transportation, meals at work, and coupons that provide discounts at local stores. Instead of competing with each other on wages, maquiladoras try to maximise the number of workers seeking jobs and establish assembly operations that can tolerate high turnover—in many plants, turnover exceeds 100 per cent a year, as workers quit because of a bad supervisor or to work with relatives and friends.

The young women who dominate the maquiladora workforce tend not to migrate on to the US, but this is not the case for their husbands and the men who often accompany them to the border area. Maquiladoras thus serve as indirect stepping stones for Mexico–US migration, as men follow women in search of jobs and then continue across the border. Although many aspects of maquiladoras are debated in the US and Mexico, it is clear that:

- Maquiladoras did not achieve their original goal of providing jobs for ex-Bra.ero men who had become dependent on the US labour market.
- Maqui.adoras stimulated population and economic growth along the US–Mexican border. About eight million persons live within 50 miles of the US–Mexican border, one of the richest parts of Mexico and one of the poorest parts of the US.
- Maquiladoras create jobs that pay more than the Mexican minimum wage, although critics note that maquiladora labour and environmental practices are sometimes poor.

In addition to factory maquiladoras employing mostly women, another maquiladora-like industry has emerged in northern Mexico in which foreign investment in the border area is clearly associated with more Mexico-US migration. Mexico's export-oriented vegetable industry, financed by US growers, packers, and retail stores and symbolised by fresh tomatoes, is centred in Sinaloa, about 600 miles south of the US border. The value of Mexican fresh tomato exports, which are picked during the winter months of January through April, almost doubled between 1989–1993 and 1994–98, from $256 million a year to $477 million a year.

Both Mexican winter tomatoes and competing tomatoes in Florida are harvested by Mexican migrants. In Mexico, large farms in Sinaloa and Baja California employ about 170,000 Mexican workers, mostly indigenous and often non-Spanish speaking migrants from southern Mexico. In 1996, typical wages for tomato picking in Sinaloa were reported to be about three to five dollars per day, and children often joined their parents in the fields.[9] Seasonal work ends in Mexico just as US growers begin to hire farm workers. Most of the family migrants return to small farms in southern Mexico in April, but especially landless workers tend to migrate onward to the US if they have network connections that can help them find US jobs. One survey of Mixtecs in the US reported that two-thirds had worked in northern Mexican export-oriented agriculture before coming to the US, and they reported being encouraged to join US based friends and relatives (Zabin et al., 1993)

TRADE AND MIGRATION: NAFTA

In 1990, Mexico's President Salinas proposed a free trade agreement with the US. Canada, which had entered into a free trade agreement with the US in 1989, joined the negotiations for what became the North American Free Trade Agreement (NAFTA) which went into effect on January 1, 1994,[10] with the goal of lowering barriers to trade and investment and thus stimulating job and wage growth in the three member countries. Passage of NAFTA was not a sure thing in the US. Reform Party presidential candidate Ross Perot used opposition to NAFTA as a cornerstone of his 1992 presidential campaign, and his prediction that there would be a 'giant sucking sound' as US jobs left for Mexico was an oft-repeated phrase of NAFTA opponents.

The other and ultimately winning end of the what-will-happen-with-NAFTA spectrum was anchored by Presidents Bush and Clinton. They, along with free trade theorists, argued that NAFTA was the best means of accelerating Mexican trade and economic development, creating jobs and thereby reducing unwanted Mexico-US migration. Although general agreements on migration were explicitly not part of the NAFTA, the hope that NAFTA-led economic development would reduce the volume of illegal migration was a major reason why some wavering Congressional representatives in the end voted for NAFTA.

The NAFTA debate highlighted the larger question of whether trade liberalisation is an effective means for reducing 'unwanted' South–North migration.[11] The answer of most economists is 'Yes'. Standard comparative statics analysis highlights the fact that the migration of labour tends to be self-stopping because of the adjustment processes that economically motivated migration set in motion, speeding the growth of wages in the sending area and slowing the growth of wages in the receiving area. Thus, the standard comparative statics trade model concludes that migration and trade are substitutes in both the short and long run (Ohlin, 1933; Stopler and Samuelson, [1941] 1949; Heckscher, 1949; Mundell, 1957).

The major policy-relevant question was not what would happen in the long run, after the North American economies reach a new equilibrium, but what would happen during the adjustment period, and how long this adjustment period might last. The US Commission for the Study of International Migration and Cooperative Economic Development concluded that 'expanded trade between the sending countries and the United States is the single most important remedy' for unwanted migration. However, the Commission also noted that 'the economic development process itself tends in the short to medium term to stimulate migration' (1990, p. xv). In other words, the Commission warned that the same policies that reduce migration in the long run could increase migration in the short run, creating 'a very real short-term versus long-term dilemma' for a country such as the US considering a free trade agreement as a means to curb unauthorised immigration from Mexico (1990, p. xvi).

THE MIGRATION HUMP

The Commission embraced the hypothesis that trade and migration can be complements in the short run and substitutes in the long run, that is, closer economic integration can produce a 'migration hump'. A migration hump means that when migration flows are charted over time, migration first increases with closer economic integration and then decreases (Martin, 1993; Martin and Taylor, 1996).

Closer economic integration does not always have to be associated with a migration hump. A migration hump is most likely to occur when any or all of three conditions are met: (1) there are continued job opportunities abroad to act as a demand-pull for migrants; (2) supply-push emigration pressures rise as the sending country economy adjusts to freer trade; and (3) social networks that provide information, funds and social capital bridge the border. Mexican–US migration satisfied these three conditions, as did the experience of countries as diverse as Italy and South Korea. However, as the cases of Italy and South Korea illustrate, the migration hump can be relatively short-lived: emigration nations can turn into immigration nations, or persist for decades as with the great Atlantic migration of the nineteenth century.[12]

TRADE THEORY AND MIGRATION

The standard trade model rests on five major assumptions: identical production technologies; factor homogeneity; constant returns to scale; instantaneous adjustment; and perfect competition, full employment, and complete markets. When any or all of these assumptions do not hold, trade and migration can be complements, that is, increased trade can be associated with more migration, producing a migration hump when migration flows are plotted against time.

The standard trade model assumes that countries integrating economically share the same technologies or production functions. For example, if US farmers use herbicides to control weeds and Mexican farmers use hoes, the reason is higher wages and cheaper herbicides in the US, not the lack of herbicides in Mexico.[13] With or without Mexico–US migration, US agriculture would be expected to have a higher capital-labour ratio than Mexican agriculture because of higher US wages. Without free trade, we should observe more hand workers in Mexican cornfields and more herbicides in US cornfields.

If herbicides and other capital inputs give the US a comparative advantage in corn production, then freer trade should permit the US to produce and export more corn. This has in fact happened under NAFTA: the US produces about ten times more corn than Mexico,[14] and the US can export corn to Mexico for less than Mexican farmers can produce corn with labour-intensive technologies. About half the man-days worked in Mexican agriculture in the mid-1990s were used to produce corn. Freeing up trade in corn, as called for by NAFTA, is expected to eliminate millions of man-days of work for the three million Mexican farmers and workers employed in corn production. If these workers have no local job alternatives, and if networks link them to US labour markets, they may migrate to the US.

The second assumption is that the same worker is equally productive regardless of the country in which s/he works. Comparative advantage-based trade rests on differences in factor productivity, which are usually due to a country's endowments of land, labour and capital. However, productivity differences due to infrastructure differences—differences in transportation, communications and the legal systems—can be so significant that a labour-intensive emigration country such as Mexico may not have a comparative advantage in the production of some labour-intensive goods.

For example, if Mexican workers are more productive in the US than in Mexico because the US infrastructure is better, then the migration of Mexican workers to the US may decrease production in Mexico and increase the production of goods made with Mexican workers in the US. This is what seemed to occur in one part of the shoe industry in the 1980s. The Mexican shoe industry in Leon shrank in part due to lack of experienced workers, while the shoe industry that employed Mexican workers from Leon in Los Angeles expanded. Shoes produced by Mexican workers in the US with more capital were then exported, including to Mexico. Migration, by converting Mexican workers into US workers, in this case discouraged the production of some labour-intensive goods in Mexico, and encouraged more migration to and production in the US.

The third critical assumption of standard trade theory is that there are constant returns to scale in both countries, which means that increasing all inputs by 10 per cent increases output by 10 per cent. If there are scale economies—if per unit costs fall as production increases—then freer trade may increase the output of labour intensive industries in the US and encourage more migration from Mexico to staff expanding US production lines. When the basis for trade is scale economies, migration and trade can be complements.

The fourth assumption of the standard trade model is that adjustments to changing prices and wages are instantaneous, and the process of adjustment does not affect the comparative-static outcome. In reality, prices may drop and workers may be displaced when freer trade is implemented, but finding a new job may take time. For example, Mexican farmers can be displaced or have their incomes lowered with free trade in corn, but it may take several years for foreign and domestic investment to create additional jobs in manufacturing. This adjustment process may be more difficult and costly for older men displaced from agriculture if expanding maquiladoras prefer to hire young women.

The fifth assumption of standard trade theory is perfect markets, including full information, no risk, and no transactions costs. This assumption is rarely fulfilled, giving rise to insights that have been collected under the rubric of the new economics of labour migration. For example, suppose that the benefits of migration are significant, but there are no legal means to cross borders to take advantage of wage differences, so that the migrant must utilise the services of a smuggler who demands an up-front fee. In such situations, freer trade that speeds job and economic growth may also increase migration, as rising incomes in the sending country permit more migrants to afford smugglers' fees (Schiff, 1996).

Families in the rural areas of sending countries dependent on agriculture may treat family members as a portfolio of income earners, and deploy sons and daughters in a manner that maximises earnings and minimises risks. This means that Mexican families may send daughters to border area maquiladoras and sons to the US. If both succeed in getting jobs, the family can be much better off. However, even if the son is apprehended, the daughter's near one hundred per cent probability of getting a maquiladora job acts as insurance for the son's attempted illegal entry.

NAFTA AND MIGRATION: 1994–2000

Most economic models simulating the effect of NAFTA on Mexico and the US concluded that, as a result of NAFTA, Mexico would experience the greatest adjustments to free trade as well as the greatest benefits in the form of job creation. No one knew how quickly Mexico–US migration flows might be affected by these adjustments. However, the statements of political leaders often implied that reductions in migration would be immediate, or noticeable, after a short period of adjustment.

Many of the simulations were based on computable general equilibrium (CGE) models. The US International Trade Commission summarised the results of 10 models, and reported that estimates of how much faster Mexico's real GDP was projected to rise because of NAFTA ranged from 0.1 to 11.4 per cent, that Mexican employment was expected to be at least 7 per cent higher and that real Mexican wages would be 0.7 to 16.2 per cent higher because of NAFTA. The primary mechanism by which these results were to be achieved was through foreign investment—capital would flow to Mexico, the argument ran, bringing new technology and new management and creating jobs and hope. As a Latin American 'tiger economy', this argument ran, Mexico could have a persisting trade deficit as foreign investment built up Mexico's productive capacity and infrastructure, much as South Korea did during a similar phase of development in the 1960s and 1970s.[15]

Foreign capital had flowed into Mexico as predicted in anticipation of NAFTA in the early 1990s. However, Mexico permitted the peso to become overvalued in 1993–94, making imports of both capital and consumer goods relatively cheap. Instead of using foreign investment to create factories and jobs, much of these foreign savings were used to buy US and other foreign goods, or invest in what proved to be white elephants, such as an extensive system of little-used toll roads. In 1994, a series of events dampened foreign investor enthusiasm for Mexico, including the Zapatista rebellion in the state of Chiapas on 1 January 1994; the assassination of the leading presidential candidate in March 1994; and a sharp increase in the Mexican money supply in summer 1994 to support the ruling party's candidates in the July 1994 elections. Economic advisors recommended devaluing the peso, but President Salinas resisted. In December 1994, just after Salinas left office, Mexican and foreign investors began converting massive amounts of pesos into dollars at the fixed 3.45 pesos to $1 rate, Mexico ran out of reserves to support the peso, and the peso was devalued sharply in December 1994.

Although most migration experts had predicted that the closer economic integration symbolised by NAFTA would at least temporarily increase migration, none predicted the sharp 1994–95 devaluation and severe Mexican recession. Mexico, a country with about ten million formal sector private jobs for a paid labour force of thirty million, experienced almost one million layoffs from formal sector jobs in 1995. In the villages from which many migrants come, economic models projected a migration elasticity with respect to peso devaluations of 0.7 per cent—that is, a seven per cent increase in emigration for every ten per cent devaluation of the Mexican peso. The peso fell almost sixty per cent between November 1994 and November 1995, signalling a massive increase in emigration pressure.

In 1997, economic growth returned to Mexico. The economy expanded by three to six per cent a year in the late 1990s and long-term foreign investment returned, with the auto, electronics, and computer industries rapidly adding workers.[16] However, Mexico–US migration continues at high levels. The US apprehended 1.1 million foreigners, over 95 per cent Mexicans, in FY94; 1.4 million in FY95; 1.6 million in FY96; 1.5 million in FY97; 1.7 million in FY98; and 1.5 million in FY99.

What has changed is attitudes in both Mexico and the US toward what may be the peak of the Mexico–US migration hump. With US legislation in 1996 that implemented some of the provisions of Proposition 187, especially restricting the access of immigrants to welfare assistance, as well as an economic boom that has brought US unemployment rates to a 30-year low, migration is no longer front-page news in California and the US. Attitudes in Mexico have also changed. Many Mexicans once viewed migrants as 'traitors'. However, in 1998, Mexico took an important step to preserve ties with migrants abroad when it allowed Mexicans who naturalise in the US or elsewhere to retain Mexican nationality, and permitted Mexicans who had already naturalised abroad to re-acquire rights as Mexican nationals. Mexican nationals have several economic benefits over foreigners, including the right to buy property within 100 km of the Mexican frontier and within 50 km of the Mexican coast.

One reason for this Mexican change of attitude is recognition of the importance of the Mexican community abroad. There are about eight million Mexico-born persons in the US, and another twelve million with Mexican roots. Their per-capita income is lower than the 1998 US average of $30,000 a year, but 20 million Mexicans in the US averaging $20,000 a year have the same GDP as 100 million Mexicans with average $4000 a year incomes—each has about $400 billion.

The new attitude toward Mexicans in the US is reflected in Mexican government attitudes toward remittances. Mexicans in the US remit about six billion dollars a year to Mexico, usually in transactions that average $300.[17] Several Mexican states have established programmes to match remittances that are invested to create jobs in the migrants' areas of origin, and the Mexican government has trumpeted these programmes as a way to leverage contributions from Mexicans abroad.

For example, in Timbinal, a village of about 1,000 in the southern part of the state of Guanajuato, remittances from migrants employed in California's Napa Valley were used to create the village's first full-time jobs in a 32–machine sewing factory that pays local women the area's minimum wage—30 pesos or $3 a day. About 150 persons from Timbinal live in Napa, and they pooled their remittances under the state government's 'Mi Comunidad' programme, under which the state provides training for managers and workers in workplaces established with remittances. Remittances, as well as a grant from Sutter Homes Wineries, the US employer where some of the village's migrants work, gave Timbinal running water. Timbinal is an exception—few purely farming and ranching communities in Mexico have made the switch to industry on their own, in part because going to the US is such an easy alternative.

NAFTA and remittances can speed up economic and job growth and slow emigration, but the more important factor in the long run may be demographic and economic changes. The Binational Study on Migration in 1997 emphasised that demographic and economic factors were producing high levels of Mexico–US migration in the late 1990s, but these same factors may lead to significantly less migration by 2010. For example, the Mexican population growth rate peaked at 3.3 per cent in 1970, when 45 per cent of Mexican residents were under 15 years of age. In 1974, the Mexican government launched a programme to persuade families to have fewer children, and birth rates fell sharply. Mexico in 1997 had 1.3 million young people turn 15, and 970,000 labour-force entrants, but the number of labour-force entrants is expected to fall to between 500,000 and 550,000 per year by 2010. These lower birth rates, which are also expected to persist, are also expected to stabilise Mexico's population at about 141 million in 2025, when the US population is projected to be 335 million.[18]

The second reason to expect less emigration is economic and job growth. Between 1988 and 1995, each 1.35 per cent increment to economic growth in Mexico was associated with one per cent job growth. If this 1.35 to 1 ratio persists, five per cent economic growth can generate 3.7 per cent job growth, or 1.1 million new jobs each year, enough to employ all new job seekers and begin to reduce un- and underemployment (Mexico's economy expanded by 4.8 per cent in 1998, and is expected to grow by three per cent in 1999).

CONCLUSION

International migration has the potential for disrupting orderly relations between nations, despite the fact that the number of migrants is relatively small (Appleyard, 1991). In a world of six billion, the number of international migrants—persons living outside their country of birth or citizenship for 12 months or more—approached 150 million in 2000, meaning that 2.5 per cent of the world's residents—one in 40—were legal or unauthorised immigrants, non-immigrant guest workers, students, business persons, or refugees or asylum seekers.[19]

The number and type of migrants has increased faster than the capacity of national governments, regional bodies, or international organisations and agreements to deal with international migration.[20] However, several responses are apparent in the countries receiving unwanted migrants:

increased expenditures on immigration control and new regional forums to discuss migration issues.

More expenditures on controls are very noticeable in the US: the Immigration and Naturalization Service is one of the fastest-growing agencies in the US government, with a 1999 budget of four billion dollars and 31,000 employees. This represents a doubling of the INS's budget and manpower since NAFTA went into effect in 1994. Ironically, the INS changed its strategy to prevent illegal migration in 1994, switching from rewarding agents for apprehending as many unauthorised migrants as possible to aiming to deter entries by stationing large numbers of agents visibly along the border and using lights, fences, and other obstructions to funnel persons attempting unauthorised entry to places where they were likely to be caught. This INS strategy is often referred to as Operation Gatekeeper, the INS name for the programme along the California–Mexico border.

It is not clear if this new INS strategy is working, that is, it is hard to determine whether migration is decreasing or whether the new strategy has simply prevented high levels of Mexico–US migration from becoming larger. The General Accounting Office is required to evaluate the strategy, and in May 1999 it concluded that 'available data do not yet answer the fundamental question of how effective the strategy has been in preventing and deterring illegal entry', although it is clear that: (1) apprehensions decreased in sectors such as San Diego and El Paso, where the new strategy has been in place the longest time; (2) more foreigners were caught trying to enter with false documents, suggesting that more difficult unauthorised border entry encouraged migrants to try other means of entry; and (3) smuggling fees seem to have risen, which would suggest more difficulty entering illegally. However, there were no reliable data to indicate whether aliens apprehended were deterred from attempting re-entry or whether the new border control strategy had reduced border-area crime. Many migration experts have yet to see any evidence of fewer migrants. Surveys of migrants suggest as many as ever are trying and succeeding in getting into the US (Massey, 1998), and there is a remarkable lack of upward wage pressures in US labour markets that hire recently arrived Mexicans (Martin and Taylor, 2000).

The new border control strategy symbolised by Gatekeeper is costly in money, tensions, and lives—several hundred migrants have died trying to enter the US illegally via deserts and mountains. Some critics argue that instead of further tightening border controls, a guest worker programme should be implemented to permit Mexicans to work at least seasonally in the US. In theory, a guest worker programme could reduce or stop illegal immigration. If enough guest worker visas were available, migrants would presumably have no need to pay smugglers. US farmers have been the most aggressive advocates of a new guest worker programme. They want an alternative to the current guest worker programme for unskilled farm workers, the H–2A programme, which requires US farm employers to have their need for a foreign workers certified by the US Department of Labor, and DOL does not normally provide certification until the farmer actively recruits US workers at a DOL-determined wage and offers workers free housing and other benefits.

Farmers could avoid certification and still hire Mexican migrants legally in several ways, including legalising current farm workers who are unauthorised, or using an attestation procedure to obtain foreign workers. Under attestation, the farmer asserts that he tried and failed to find US workers, and this assertion opens the border gate—enforcement comes after the workers are in the US. US farmers in October 1999 proposed a combination of 'quasi-legalisation' for unauthorised farm workers that would permit currently illegal farm workers to become probationary guest workers, that is, migrants' work visas that would remain valid only if they did at least 180 days of farm work a year and left the US for at least 65 days each year. Migrants who satisfied these conditions each year for five of the next seven years could apply to become US immigrants.

The farmers' proposal is what the Mexican government wants. Mexico wants to play an active role in the enforcement of programme rules and regulations under any new guest worker programme, but the October 1999 proposal has no formal role for Mexico. It may never become law: President Clinton announced his strong opposition to a new guest worker programme in 1995, saying 'I oppose efforts in Congress to institute a new guest worker or 'Bracero' programme that seeks to bring thousands of foreign workers into the United States to provide temporary farm labor'.

Since 'international migration is neither a sufficient nor viable medium for alleviating the employment and development problems of developing countries', the world must find ways to create jobs and opportunity where potential migrants live (Appleyard, 1999: 2). Freer trade and investment is the closest thing to a free lunch in economics: more trade and investment can accelerate economic growth in both emigration and immigration countries, and thus they are desirable for their own sake. However, the transition to freer trade in previously closed emigration economies is disruptive, altering relative prices and thus wages, incomes, and job opportunities. If migration networks link those adversely affected by restructuring to the international labour market, and if the labour markets in which migrants seek jobs abroad do not shrink, then trade and migration are likely to be short-run complements—that is, increased trade is likely to be accompanied by increased migration.

Over time, freer trade and investment should increase the rate of income and job growth in the emigration country, thus diminishing migration pressures. However, when viewed over a decade or two, the result of closer economic integration can be a migration hump, which can be relatively small and short because, when wage differences decrease to 4 or 5 to 1 and economic and wage growth seems assured in the emigration country, economically-motivated migration often drops dramatically. Small and short migration humps are powerful arguments for freer trade and investment.

Migration humps lead to three major policy implications. First, freer trade and investment should be advocated as the best long-run policies to promote what has been called 'stay-at-home' development, not as short-term cures for unwanted migration. Second, a better understanding of migration-linked adjustment is needed, such as how to deal with the three million Mexican farmers growing corn who are affected by NAFTA's call for free trade in corn. Third, emigration countries that benefit from freer trade and investment should be expected to help immigration countries to manage migration, especially during the migration hump. Given the resistance to free trade in many ageing industrial democracies worried about unwanted immigration, it seems naive to suggest that migration can continue to be excluded from trade negotiations.

NOTES

1. The usual practice was for a Mexican worker to enter the US illegally, find a US farm job, and go to work, usually under prevailing wages, but without, for example, government-inspected free housing or other protections specified in the contracts that each Bracero worker received. If apprehended inside the US, the Mexican worker was usually taken to the Mexican border, issued work documents, and returned to his US employer, a process termed, even in official government reports, as 'drying out wetbacks'. The fact that there was no enforcement penalty on workers or employers for being outside the programme encouraged illegal immigration, leading one researcher to conclude that 'the Bracero program, instead of diverting the flow of wetbacks into legal channels ... actually stimulated unlawful emigration' (Scruggs, 1961: 151).

2. California vegetable production rose 50 per cent, as California replaced New Jersey as the 'Garden State'. According to the US Department of Agriculture, farm worker wages rose 41 per cent, from $0.85 in 1950 to $1.20 in 1960, while factory worker wages rose 63 per cent during the 1950s.

3. Growers with contracts could avoid dealing with the UFW by having lettuce and other vegetables raised under contract for them. Contract farming makes each of the 20 to 40 farmers an employer of farm workers, and the packer-marketer with a brand name to protect, only an employer of non-farm workers. Dole Food Company, the world's largest marketer of fresh fruits and vegetables, uses this strategy extensively.

4. In the mid-1980s about 30 million Mexicans were living in rural and agricultural areas-average household size was five, including two parents and three children. In most cases, fathers left wives and children in Mexico while doing farm work in the US.

5. The value-added in Mexican maquiladoras remains low. In the first six months of 1997 maquiladoras exported goods worth $20 billion, but imported goods worth $16 billion, so Mexico's value-added was only about $4 billion.

6. About 30 per cent of maquiladora jobs are in Juarez, across the border from El Paso, and 20 per cent are in Tijuana, south of San Diego.
7. About 81 per cent of Mexican manufactured products exported to the US in 1998 were products assembled in maquiladoras.
8. Young women have remarkably high labour force participation rates in Mexican border cities-60 to 80 per cent of the 20 to 24-year-old women are in the work force.
9. The schools in the camps teach from 5 to 8p.m., so that children can help their parents in the fields.
10. In 2001, the maquiladora will be incorporated into the Mexican economy and, under NAFTA, restrictions on Mexican sales and temporary imports from the US and Canada will be no more. New Mexican laws passed during the last decade also stand to stimulate joint ventures and manufacturing employment.
11. We use 'unwanted' rather than illegal to describe the migration that industrial countries are trying to reduce because much of the migration most amenable to being reduced with trade and other economic development measures involves legal but not necessarily wanted foreigners, such as 'economic refugees' in Western Europe, and Salvadorans with a 'Temporary Protected Status' in the US. In both cases, the host countries would like to reduce the number of such aliens, but their presence is not unlawful.
12. Migration humps are not new. The 48 million Europeans who emigrated from Europe between 1850 and 1925 represented about one-eighth of Europe's population in 1900, suggesting that 'large scale emigration was quite common during Europe's period of industrialization' (Massey, 1991. 17).
13. This is the same thing as saying that differences in the labour and capital intensities of production between the two countries are due solely to differences in their factor endowments.
14. The US state of Iowa alone produces about twice as much corn as Mexico.
15. However, aggregate models predicted that, meantime, agricultural liberalisation policies in Mexico, including the removal of price supports for corn, would stimulate migration from rural areas, with many migrants heading to the US.
16. Between 1994 and 1998, foreigners invested $57 billion for long-term projects, making Mexico second only to China in the receipt of foreign investment dollars.
17. In 1999, Western Union and Orlandi Valuta, subsidiaries of First Data Corp., and MoneyGram Payment Systems Inc. settled class-action lawsuits filed against them in Illinois, Texas and California that accused the companies of overcharging migrants who remitted money to Mexico by using unfavourable exchange rates. The companies agreed to provide discount coupons to those who had wired money to Mexico since 1 January 1987, and pledged more than two million dollars (First Data) and $300,000 (MoneyGram) to Latino community organisations in the US.
18. Fertility has dropped from seven children per woman in 1965 to 2.5 in 1998, so that there are fewer children to be supported. There is now a surge of 1.3 million young people turning 15 each year. Mexico includes those 15 and older in its potential labour force data, but the number of young people turning 15 is expected to drop to 650,000 a year in 2010.
19. These UN data do not distinguish foreign-born persons by their reason for migration, date of arrival or duration of stay. The UN data also do not distinguish

between people moving across borders as, for example, immigration into the US and Canada, and borders moving over people, as occurred in India and Pakistan, or with the break-up of Yugoslavia and the USSR. The UN defines developed countries to include Europe, the ex-USSR, the US, Canada, Japan, Australia and New Zealand.

20. Most of the world's residents will never be migrants. Most people will live and die within the borders of one of the world's 190-odd countries without ever spending an extended period of time abroad.

REFERENCES

Appleyard, Reginald (1991), *International Migration Today. Challenge for the Nineties*, Geneva: International Organization for Migration.

Appleyard, Reginald (ed.) (1999), *Emigration Dynamics in Developing Countries*, Aldershot: Ashgate.

Craig, Richard B. (1971), *The Bracero Program: Interest Groups and Foreign Policy*, Austin: University of Texas Press.

Heckscher, E.F. (1949), 'The effects of foreign trade on the distribution of income', in H.S. Ellis and L.A. Metzler (eds), *Readings in the Theory of International Trade*, Philadelphia: Blakiston.

Martin, P.L. (1993), *Trade and Migration: NAFTA and Agriculture*, Washington, DC: Institute for International Economics.

Martin, P.L. and J.E. Taylor (1996), 'The anatomy of a migration hump', in J.E. Taylor (ed.), *Development Strategy, Employment and Migration: Insights from Models*, Paris: Organization for Economic Cooperation and Development.

Martin, Philip (1996), *Promises to Keep: Collective Bargaining in California Agriculture*, Ames: Iowa State University Press.

Martin, Philip L. and Taylor, Edward J. (2000), 'California farm workers', *California Agriculture*, **54** (1), 19–25.

Massey, Douglas S. (1998), 'March of folly: U.S. immigration policy after NAFTA', *The American Prospect*, **37**, March-April, 22–23.

Massey, D.S. (1991), 'Economic development and international migration in comparative perspective', in Sergio Diaz-Briquets and Sidney Weintraub (eds), *Determinants of Emigration from Mexico, Central America and the Caribbean*, Boulder, CO: Westview Press.

Massey, D.S., J. Arango, G. Hugo, A. Kouaouci, A. Pellegrino and J.E. Taylor (1998), *Worlds in Motion: Understanding International Migration at the End of the Millennium*, Oxford: Oxford University Press.

Massey, D.S., R. Alarcon, J. Durand and H. Gonzalez (1987), *Return to Aztlan: The Social Process of International Migration from Western Mexico*, Berkeley and Los Angeles: University of California Press.

Mundell, R.A. (1957), 'International trade and factor mobility', *American Economic Review*, **47**, 321–35.

Ohlin, B. (1933), *Interregional and International Trade*, Cambridge, MA: Harvard University Press.

Schiff, M. (1996), 'Trade policy and international migration: substitutes or complements?' in J.E. Taylor (ed.), *Development Strategy, Employment and Migration: Insights from Models*, Paris: OECD Development Centre.

Scruggs, Otey (1960), 'Evolution of the Mexican Farm Labor Agreement of 1942', *Agricultural History*, **34**, 140–49.

Stolper, W.F. and P.A. Samuelson [1941] (1949), 'Protection and real wages', *Review of Economic Studies*, **IX**, November.

Steven Street, Richard (1996/97), 'First farmworkers, first Braceros: Baja California field hands and the origins of farm labor importation in California agriculture, 1769–1790', *California History*, **75** (4), 306–21.

US Commission for the Study of International Migration and Cooperative Development (1990), 'Unauthorized migration: an economic development response', Washington, DC.

Zabin, Carol, Michael Kearney, David Runsten, and Ana Garcia (1993), 'A New Cycle of Rural Poverty: Mixtec Migrants in California Agriculture', Davis: California Institute for Rural Studies.

4 Regional Integration, Continuity and Changing Patterns of Intra-Regional Migration in Sub-Saharan Africa

Aderanti Adepoju

INTRODUCTION

This chapter addresses intra-regional migration in Sub-Saharan Africa (SSA) within the context of regional economic groupings in a continent where intensive migration has been prompted by demographic, economic, ecological, political and related factors. The component sub-regions are characterised by distinctive forms of international migration: labour emigration from western and middle Africa to countries of the North and to the Gulf states; persistent refugee flows within eastern Africa as a result of adverse political, economic and environmental conditions; labour migration from southern African countries to the Republic of South Africa (RSA); and clandestine migration in western and eastern Africa.

These migrations, voluntary and compelled, take place within diverse political, economic, social and ethnic contexts. Changes in current migratory patterns, especially the intensification of irregular migration and trafficking, can be attributed to poverty and human deprivation, worsening social conditions and widespread unemployment. These conditions have also contributed to the sustained exodus of both skilled and unskilled persons, males and females, in regular and irregular situations on a scale not experienced before, to countries within and outside SSA.

A series of interrelated events, including the demarcation of national boundaries, the emergence of independent nation-states and especially the establishment of regulations governing immigration, have introduced a subtle distinction between internal and international migration, both of which once involved free movement across wide areas of the region. The concept of legality was also invoked, and a distinction was henceforth made between legal and illegal immigrants.

Historical, economic, ethnic and political links have fostered and reinforced intra-regional, inter-regional and international migration in SSA. Demographic momentum, unstable political landscape, escalating ethnic conflicts, persistent economic decline, severe poverty and worsening ecological conditions, have influenced trends and patterns of international migration in the region. By far the largest migration stream in Africa is intra-regional workers, undocumented migrants, nomads, frontier workers, refugees and, increasingly, highly-skilled professionals.

In the various sub-regions, migration among neighbouring countries underscores their economic interdependence. The free movement of persons, ushered in by the implementation of a protocol on free movement of persons in a few of the sub-regions, triggered and accelerated labour migration that would have occurred anyway. However, free movement of persons does not necessarily guarantee movers the right of extended residence and employment in economic ventures in the host country. In some ways, this situation reflects the weaknesses of these sub-regional economic unions, as well as faltering political support.

This chapter reviews the emergence, and the multiplicity, composition and orientation of sub-regional economic unions, as well as their economic and political constraints and weaknesses. Of importance is the impact of economic downturn in traditional countries of immigration in the region, especially core countries in the sub-regional economic groupings, and comprehensive responses to so-called illegal immigrants, including expulsions. This is followed by a discussion on traditional and changing patterns of international migration, the role of the economic unions in fostering, containing or redirecting orderly migration, and the effects of restrictions on organised migration in generating new patterns of migration within and outside sub-regional communities. The chapter concludes with a note on prospects for an African Economic Union—the ultimate integration of the economy of the region—and in particular its prospects for facilitating the unrestricted flow of persons.

THE CONTEXT OF INTERNATIONAL MIGRATION DYNAMICS IN SUB-SAHARAN AFRICA

African economies are fragile, fragmented, rely mainly on mono-products, and are highly vulnerable to fluctuating prices of commodities in international markets. Steady decline in real GDP per capita in recent years underscores their weaknesses. Difficulties have been compounded by a heavy debt burden and the adverse effects of structural adjustment programmes on living conditions.

The region's rapidly growing population has accelerated migration through linkages with labour force growth and unemployment. Unemployment has increased in part because of the link between rapid growth in the labour force and contractionary fiscal and monetary policies. The limited capacity of the labour market to absorb annual cohorts of job seekers turns them into potential emigrants. The current unemployment rate among secondary and university graduates is one-third or more (Adepoju, 1998b). In Senegal, Mali, Burkina Faso, Togo, Zaire, Cameroon, Lesotho, Congo and Ethiopia, the push of abject poverty is as compelling as the pull of enhanced living conditions in countries of the North. Spectacular disparities in development between several countries in the region have increased pressure in migration to cities, and from there to other countries within and outside the region.

Part of the problem is the scale and nature of the region's population. SSA contains many small states with small populations and weak markets and ineffective or non-existent cross-border economic linkages. Unstable political situations are closely associated with poor economic performances. Political instability resulting from conflicts is a strong determinant of migration in the region. The political landscape is unstable, unpredictable and volatile. Loss of state capacities, breakdown of states rooted in the precarious democratisation process, vacillating effects of structural adjustment programmes and human insecurity, have prompted a variety of migratory movements, including refugees (Adekanye, 1998).

Conflicts, including 'high intensity' civil wars in Angola, Liberia and Mozambique (Schmeidl, 1996) have generated millions of refugees, internally displaced persons and migrants. In Sudan, Somalia, Sierra Leone, Rwanda and Burundi, ethnic tensions have played visibly important roles in such conflicts. Sustained refugee flows are rooted in these ethnic-based conflicts (Nnoli, 1998), especially between ethnic groups with respect to access to political power and resources. In Rwanda, for example, conflict is rooted in the sharing of power and land, a particularly scarce resource, but behind it is intense demographic pressure on increasingly unproductive land: the country's population density ranks among the highest in the world.

In several ecologically fragile parts of the region, the Sahel and parts of southern Africa, especially Lesotho, unproductive landholdings, as well as unstable and lowly remunerated jobs, have compelled farmers to seek wage labour or engage in non-farm activities in the towns, and sometimes from there to more prosperous countries within the sub-regions. Migration both within and outside the region is taking place within the context of profound social and economic transformations and change. Political and economic crises are triggering migrant labour, commercial migration and refugee flows, as well as the emigration of skilled and unskilled persons to more prosperous countries. As countries of the North have tightened their borders against immigrants from developing countries, including SSA, the need for regional co-operation to promote intra-regional migration has become ever more pressing.

THE FORMATION OF SUB-REGIONAL ECONOMIC UNIONS

Historical, demographic, economic, political, ecological and ethnic factors have acted in combination to produce a variety of migration configurations in the various sub-regions of Africa: labour migrants, nomads, clandestine migrants, brain drain, refugees and internally displaced persons. Clandestine movement by ethnic groups and pastoral peoples across long, porous frontiers and undocumented migration have been facilitated by common colonial background, language, complementary economies, political systems and cultural affinities (Adepoju, 1983). In eastern Africa, for example, undocumented migration between Kenya, Uganda and Tanzania has taken advantage of common colonial background, a common language, currency and cultural affinity. Its volume and direction have depended, however, on the relationship between these countries, which changes from time to time.

National borders almost always traverse ethnic lines, thus introducing the concept of legality, residence and nationality into the migration scene. Regulations governing immigration have introduced a subtle distinction between internal and international migration, both of which once involved free movement across wide areas of the region. Changes in immigration laws prescribed specific procedures for entry and of subsequent employment of non-indigenous workers and also introduced the distinction between legal and illegal immigrants—the requirement that immigrants must possess valid travel documents and entry documentation. So-called migrants were not only illegal immigrants in the host country, but most of them left their home countries illegally, without appropriate travel documentation (Adepoju, 1996a).

National governments, anxious to identify their territories as sovereign independent states and to preserve available employment opportunities for nationals, adopted various measures to reduce the inflow of migrants, and to limit entry to authorised immigrants with special skills. Immigration and employment laws were enacted in Gabon (1962), Nigeria (1963), Botswana (1968), Tanzania (1972) and Zambia (1972) to regulate the admission and stay of foreign nationals and the inflow of unskilled persons seeking employment. Most of these laws remain on the countries' statute books in spite of the creation of sub-regional economic unions aimed at facilitating the free flow of human resources, including freedom to reside and work in member states.

By the end of the 1970s, African leaders recognised that accelerated development could not be achieved without pooling natural and human resources and removing barriers that hindered intra-African migration. The re-grouping of fragmented nations was viewed as a viable means to enlarge market sizes and facilitate movement of goods, services, labour and capital (Afolayan, 1998; Asante, 1990). Towards this end, a few sub-regional unions were set up (or revitalised) in the 1980s and 1990s to complement existing ones.

The formation of sub-regional economic unions to some extent simulated the kind of homogeneous societies that once existed in sub-regions. Understandably, in the case of the Economic Community of West African States (ECOWAS), the protocol on Free Movement of Persons was the first to be ratified and implemented, again ushering in an era of free movement of citizens within member countries. Table 4.1 summarises the features of these unions that are elaborated below.

Table 4.1 Regional organisation and groupings in Sub-Saharan Africa

Organisations and member states	Main purpose
Communauté Economique de l'Afrique de l'Ouest Benin, Burkina Faso, Côte d'Ivoire, Mali, Mauritania, Senegal	Economic co-operation
Economic Community of West African States Benin, Burkina Faso, Côte d'Ivoire, Gambia, Ghana, Guinea, Liberia, Mali, Mauritania, Niger, Nigeria, Togo	Economic co-operation
Mano River Union Guinea, Liberia, Sierra Leone	Customs union
Communauté Economique des Pays des Grands Lacs Burundi, Rwanda, Zaire	Economic co-operation
Common Market of Eastern and Southern Africa Angola, Burundi, Comoros, Congo, Eritrea, Ethiopia, Kenya, Lesotho, Madagascar, Namibia, Rwanda, Sudan, Swaziland, Tanzania, Uganda, Zambia, Zimbabwe	Common market
Southern Africa Development Community Angola, Botswana, Lesotho, Malawi, Mauritius, Mozambique, Namibia, South Africa, Swaziland, Tanzania, Zambia, Zimbabwe	Common market
Union Douaniere et Economique de L'Áfrique Centrale Cameroon, Central African Republic, Chad, Congo, Equatorial Guinea, Gabon	Customs union

Source: Browne, 1998–93

The Lagos Plan of Action and the Final Act of Lagos endorsed the approach to create sub-regional economic groups in three zones—West Africa, Central Africa, and East and Southern Africa—on the basis of a conceptual framework for phased regional economic integration. It envisaged that regional trade areas would serve as building blocks for the proposed Economic Community for Africa, initially scheduled to be established by 2000. The treaty aimed at establishing an African Economic Community by 2025 and was signed in Abuja in 1993 with the aim (amongst others) to facilitate intra-regional labour mobility. It was hoped that the sub-regional groupings would ultimately facilitate economic integration in the various sub-regions and labour mobility within member states. The more sensitive issues of right of residence, establishment of migrants, as well as the rights and obligations of the host countries, were muted in the treaties of sub-regional economic unions.

In Central Africa, the *Union Douaniere et Economique de Afrique Centrale* (Customs and Economic Union of Central Africa-UDEAC), founded in 1964, included a joint convention on free movement of people, goods, merchandise, services and capital and the right of establishment. The contiguity and common colonial experience of the member states enhanced labour mobility from poorer areas of Chad, Cameroon and Central African Republic to administrative and commercial centres in Cameroon, Gabon and Congo, and the copper mining and forestry centres of Gabon and (then) Zaire. Recently, Gabon, the richest member of the Union, and the main country of immigration, has become the strongest advocate for co-operation and integration in the sub-region, a move that culminated in the elimination of internal trade tariffs between the six member states which already share a common currency and are now building common institutions (*The Economist,* 16 May 1998). In 1983, the Economic Community of Central Africa (CEEAC) was created.

In 1974, six Francophone West African countries established the *Communauté Economique de l'Afrique de l'Ouest* (Economic Community of West Africa-CEAO). The agreement on free movement of persons signed in 1978 recognised the individual's right to travel, reside and settle within member countries. The convention on dual nationality mooted in 1966 and again in 1978 was fiercely opposed by Côte d'Ivoire which feared an unrestrained influx of migrants from poorer members of the Community with whom she shared common colonial heritage and currency. Even in the absence of the proposed convention, Côte d'Ivoire has been, and remains, the main destination for immigrants from Community countries and beyond. In 1994, CEAO was dissolved and replaced by the West African Economic and Monetary Union (UEMOA).

The Economic Community of West African States (ECOWAS) was founded in 1975 to enhance free trade and facilitate free movement of factors of production in the sixteen Member States. Its Protocol on Free Movement of Persons and the Right of Residence and Establishment of 1979 is explicit on free mobility of labour. The rights of entry, residence and establishment were to be progressively established within fifteen years from the definitive date of entry into force of the protocol.

The implementation of the first phase over the first five years abolished requirements for visa and entry permits. Community citizens in possession of valid travel documents and an international health certificate could enter Member States without visa for up to ninety days. The removal of national barriers to economic activity within the community and the Protocol on Free Movement of Persons, Residence and Establishment ensured free movement and rights of residence and establishment of nationals of member states, regarded as community citizens, within the community. These rights do not however displace the laws that govern the admittance of aliens into a foreign state. Member states can thus refuse admission into their territory of so-called 'inadmissible immigrants'. In the case of expulsion, normally at the expense of the immigrant, states undertake to guarantee the security of the citizen concerned, his family and his property.

The delayed second phase—Right of Residence—of the Protocol came into force in July 1986, but the Right of Establishment of the Protocol is yet to be implemented. All along, Côte d'Ivoire, and later Nigeria, became major receiving countries of migrants from Ghana, Mali, Togo and Burkina Faso. Senegal was both a country of immigration and emigration. In mid-1999, the ECOWAS travellers' cheque was inaugurated to facilitate commercial transactions and travel within Community States. Nationals of ECOWAS countries have taken advantage of these developments to migrate in larger numbers within the Community, especially to Côte d'Ivoire and Nigeria.

The Economic Community of the Great Lakes (CEPGL) was founded in 1976 with explicit and phased implementation of the protocol on free mobility of labour after eight years of legal residence in a member state. The preparatory, transitional and final phases of the agreement provided for unrestricted freedom of movement, with provision for regularisation of the status of illegal immigrants, expulsion of individuals, equal rights of migrants and nationals with respect to social security entitlements and freedom of association. Obstacles inhibiting free movement of labour, monetary transactions and transfer of goods were to be removed (Afolayan, 1998). Over the years, thousands of ethnic Tutsis from Rwanda have settled in the Democratic Republic of Congo (DRC), the richest of the Community countries. These provisions have however been stalled by the turbulent political situation in these countries which has led to virtual collapse of regimes in Rwanda, and later the DRC, and turned the zone into a stage of theatrical, devastating warfare. Thousands of refugees and displaced persons roamed neighbouring countries for shelter and security.

The East African Community (EAC), set up in 1967 by Kenya, Uganda and Tanzania, took over and decentralised the common services established under the colonial administration. While the Community lasted (until 1977), it facilitated intra-regional labour mobility of mostly undocumented migrants. The contiguity of the three countries, crosscutting communities, and Kenya's buoyant economy, made that country the major recipient of clandestine labour migrants. In 1996, the three countries once again instituted the East African Co-operation (EAC) to promote integration and free movement of their nationals. Early in 1999, membership of the Co-operation was expanded to include Burundi and Rwanda, traditionally the major sources of migrants and refugees to Tanzania and Uganda (Adepoju, 1998a).

The treaty that created the Preferential Trade Area (PTA) for Eastern and Southern Africa in 1981 as a Free Trade Area following the collapse of the East African Community, made no reference to free movement of persons, residence and establishment. Such a protocol was incorporated in the Treaty for the Common Market for Eastern Africa (COMESA)-which superseded the PTA. Founded in 1994 with the ultimate objective of creating a common market along the recommendation of the Lagos Plan of Action, Egypt was accepted into membership early 1999. Tanzania withdrew its membership in July on the pretext that it already belonged to EAC and SADC.

The Southern African Development Co-ordination Conference (SADCC) was established in 1980 by nine countries to reduce their economic dependence on South Africa, create a genuine and equitable regional integration, and mobilise resources to promote the implementation of national, inter-state and regional policies taking advantage of the historical circumstances and geo-politics of the sub-region. Most of the member states were at the same time members of the (then) 'Front Line States' which opposed apartheid rule in South Africa. In 1980, SADCC created the Southern African Labour Commission (SALC) to reduce the vulnerability of the labour-exporting countries—especially Lesotho, Malawi, Botswana, Mozambique and Namibia—on (and later eliminate the supply of) migrant labour to South Africa.

Subsequent political developments in South Africa led to the realisation that reduction of economic dependence on South Africa—the overriding objective of SADCC—was no longer a valid long-term aim. In 1993, the South African Development Community replaced SADCC and welcomed South Africa into its fold. The treaty was followed by special protocols on aspects of regional co-operation and movement of people across borders. By July 1994, member states agreed to abolish visa requirements for travel by nationals in SADC countries. However, Zimbabwe and South Africa decided to maintain visas for visitors between their countries in order to control illegal immigration. In August 1995, the leaders of SADC met to discuss the modalities for establishing, among others, a southern African economic community with free trade, free movement of people and a single currency by the year 2000 (*The Economist*, September 1995). The Democratic Republic of Congo (former Zaire) became a member of SADC in 1998. The protocol on Free Trade Area of SADC is expected to come into force by 1 January 2000 in the expectation that it will help attract more foreign capital and create new jobs. So far, only half the members have ratified it. Already harbouring an estimated 3 million illegal immigrants, RSA is aware that if the Community protocol facilitated free movement of persons, the dominant flow would be to the Republic (Adepoju, 1998a).

Table 4.2 Member states of major sub-regional organisations in Sub-Saharan Africa

Country	ECOWAS	UEMOA	CEEAC	CEMAC	CEPGL	COMESA	SADC	IOC
Angola						*	*	
Benin	*	*						
Botswana							*	
Burkina Faso	*	*						
Burundi			*		*	*		
Cameroon			*	*				
Cape Verde	*							
Central African Republic			*	*				
Chad			*	*				
Comoros						*		*
Congo			*	*				
Côte d'Ivoire	*	*						
Djibouti						*		
Eritrea						*		
Ethiopia						*		
Gabon			*	*				
Gambia	*							
Ghana	*							
Guinea	*							
Guinea-Bissau	*							
Equatorial Guinea			*	*				
Kenya						*		
Lesotho						*	*	
Liberia	*							
Madagascar						*		*
Malawi						*	*	
Mali	*	*						
Mauritania	*							
Mauritius						*	*	*
Mozambique						*	*	
Namibia						*	*	
Niger	*	*						
Nigeria	*							
Dem. Rep. of Congo			*		*	*	*	
Rwanda			*		*	*		
São Tomé			*					
Senegal	*	*						
Seychelles					*	*	*	
Sierra Leone	*							
Somalia						*		
South Africa							*	

Country	ECOWAS	UEMOA	CEEAC	CEMAC	CEPGL	COMESA	SADC	IOC
Swaziland						*	*	
Tanzania						*	*	
Togo	*	*						
Uganda						*		
Zambia						*	*	
Zimbabwe						*	*	

Source: Kennes, (1999): 40
Note to abbreviations

ECOWAS   Economic Community of West African States
UEMOA   West African Economic and Monetary Union
CEEAC   Economic Community of Central African States
CEGPL   Economic Community of the Great Lakes States
COMESA   Common Market for Eastern and Southern Africa
SADC   Southern African Development Community
IOC   Indian Ocean Commission

The Small Island States in Africa (otherwise called Indian Ocean Commission) met in mid-1999 to foster closer co-operation. Apart from the Island States—Cape Verde, Comoros, Madagascar, Mauritius, São Tomé and Principe and Seychelles—two other small coastal western Africa countries—Equatorial Guinea and Guinea-Bissau—also participated to facilitate economic and technical co-operation on the management of human resources and to overcome isolation in the global world economy.

Some contemporary migration within countries comprising sub-regional economic unions would have occurred anyway; in some cases, the protocols on free movement accelerated an on-going process.

CONTRADICTIONS IN SUB-REGIONAL ECONOMIC INTEGRATION AND CHALLENGES FOR INTRA-REGIONAL MIGRATION

A major area of concern is the multiplicity of and the extent to which these regional economic unions have promoted free movement of labour amongst the nationals of the member states as well as migrants' settlement rights. Economics and politics of intra-regional migration in SSA are intricately interwoven. For so long, the balkanisation of SSA countries along colonial lines—francophone, anglophone and losophone—has hindered rather than promoted regional integration and free mobility of labour in the region. Most unions take the form of concentric circles and countries often belong to more than one union with different, sometimes contradictory ideologies, aims and objectives (Adepoju, 1998a). Nationals from different groups migrate in stages across countries associated with the different communities. The countries also exhibit different levels and patterns of development, political systems and ideologies.

Although the protocols of some sub-regional organisations include free movement of persons, residence and establishment, these are rarely implemented. Only ECOWAS has, to a large extent, implemented the protocol on free movement of persons, but remains lukewarm about the right of residence and establishment. A major threat to integration efforts stems from the failure of countries to implement the numerous protocols and decisions of the economic unions. National political and economic imperatives tend to override Community treaties and their provisions. The economic problems emanating from the adoption and commitments undertaken under the aegis of structural adjustment programmes by several countries of the region are country-specific and often at variance with regional integration commitments. In the case of ECOWAS, for example, although the protocol on free movement of persons, right of residence and establishment was adopted in 1979, it merely abolished visa requirements for citizens intending to stay for a maximum of ninety days in another member state. Events that followed stalled the adoption of right of residence and establishment, and the expulsion of community citizens from Nigeria in 1983 and 1985 created a crisis of confidence. As the economic situation worsened in virtually every country in the sub-region, many industries were closed, while capacity utilisation for those operating fell to 25–40 per cent. Although the protocol on right of residence and establishment was signed in 1986, few states ratified it, restrained by the effects of privatisation of parastatals and the mass retrenchments that followed the streamlining of personnel in the public sector, and other conditions relating to structural adjustment programmes on the domestic labour market (Ojo, 1999).

In almost all countries in the region, national interests and national immigration laws have overridden the laws, regulations, policies and strategies of regional organisations. Even so, intra-regional migration has been sustained in spite of several regional and national contradictions on laws and regulations, protocols of different regional organisations and national policies. Where national interest and community aspirations conflict, the former invariably prevails to the disadvantage of immigrants. Several countries have enacted a series of laws that in effect restrict 'foreigners', including nationals of community states, from participating in certain kinds of economic activities. As economic conditions worsened, and unemployment among nationals in the receiving countries intensified, immigrants were targets for reprisals through expulsion.

Before, and remarkably after, the formation of sub-regional economic unions, expulsions and deportations remain policy measures commonly directed at so-called illegal migrants. Examples of expulsions of non-nationals have been recorded in Sierra Leone (1968), the Côte d'Ivoire (1958,

1964), Ghana (1969), Chad (1979), Uganda (1972), Zambia (1971, 1996), Equatorial Guinea (1974), Zaire (1970, 1973), Kenya (1977, 1978–81, 1984–85), Senegal (1967, 1990), Cameroon (1967), Guinea (1968), Nigeria (1983, 1985), Liberia (1983), Gabon (1995), Republic of South Africa (1994, ongoing). Such expulsion of so-called aliens from some member states negates the *raison d'être* for establishing these communities.

Perhaps the most dramatic mass expulsion was the estimated 2 million illegal aliens from Ghana under its Aliens Compliance Order of 1969. This trend did not abate in the 1970s and 1980s despite protocols on free movement of nationals of union or community countries. In East Africa, about 50,000 Asians were expelled from Uganda in 1972. The collapse of the East African Community also triggered a wave of expulsions of 'aliens'. Between 1979 and 1985, Kenya expelled several Community workers and nationals of Tanzania and Uganda and their families (Oucho, 1995).

In recent times, as border disputes between Ethiopia and Eritrea took belligerent proportions, each country expelled nationals of the other country from its territory. This development also generated refugees and the internal displacement of thousands of persons in both countries whose nationals hitherto lived (sometimes tenuously) as kith and kin. This aptly illustrates how breakdown in co-operation, even bordering on integration, between countries and the politics of border disputes, can have devastating effects on a population. The expulsion of Ethiopian officials from Assab and Massawa by Eritrea prompted Ethiopia to expel several thousand Eritrean teachers, technicians and professionals, initially from the northwest province and, after intensification of hostilities over the disputed territory, from Addis Ababa. While the dispute and fighting continued, the wave of expulsions and displacements intensified.

THE ROLE OF CORE COUNTRIES IN SUB-REGIONAL ECONOMIC GROUPINGS

Because economic unions are often dominated by the economies of a single country, migrants have typically moved to a limited number of countries within the unions—Republic of South Africa in SADC, Gabon in UDEAC, Côte d'Ivoire in CEAO, Nigeria in ECOWAS and Congo in CEPGL. Such a situation often sparks xenophobic reaction among nationals of the dominant countries against so-called illegal aliens, including those from member states of sub-regional economic unions, as well as mistrust and suspicion of dominance by nationals of smaller countries. Expulsions and deportations are common measures directed at illegal migrants.

Nigeria

In early 1983 and mid-1985, the Nigerian Government revoked Articles 4 and 27 of the Protocol on Free Movement of Persons to expel between 0.9

and 1.3 million illegal aliens, mostly Ghanaians, in spite of the fact that Nigeria was the main driving force behind the establishment of ECOWAS, and its main financier. The implementation of the second phase of ECOWAS Protocol in July 1986 coincided with the implementation of the structural adjustment programme in Nigeria. Another 0.2 million illegal aliens were expelled in June 1985 as the economic crisis deepened. Aliens are usually scapegoats when governments are confronted with economic and political teething problems. Apart from the deteriorating economic situation in Nigeria, the Government's expulsion order of January 1983 derived partly from a fear of possible effects of large numbers of undocumented aliens on voting patterns, violence and civil disorder during the bitterly contested general election later that year. This made immigrants targets of hostility from the native population. They were blamed for a range of economic, social and political problems.

Gabon

In recent years, thousands of immigrants entered Gabon from Burundi, Rwanda, former Zaire and Congo under irregular situations to look for work. War and political instability in these countries forced thousands more as refugees to Gabon where they hoped to secure a better life and greater security. However, unemployment increasingly posed a challenge in Gabon, and in 1991 a presidential decree was issued to safeguard jobs for nationals in response to rising urban unemployment. Since then, the policy of 'Gabonising' the labour force has been pursued with vigour. In September 1994, the Government enacted laws requiring foreigners to pay residence fees or leave the country by mid-February 1995. The fee varied according to the foreigner's country of origin and was criticised as being arbitrary and discriminatory: higher for the poor African and much lower for French nationals. At the end of the deadline, about 55,000 foreign nationals were expelled from the country while 15,000 legalised their residency (Le Courrier, 1997).

Republic of South Africa

Majority rule was assured in 1994. The democratisation process was followed by an influx of migrants from various parts of the region—Nigeria, Senegal, Sierra Leone, Zaire, Kenya and Uganda. Some nationals of these countries had earlier clandestinely entered the Republic's at that time nominally independent homelands during the period of apartheid. The numbers were small and included two major categories—those who entered without proper documentation, and others who overstayed the legal residency (Adepoju, 1995).

The black population later vented their anger against immigrants from other African countries. They, and some politicians, called for the arrest and deportation of so-called illegal immigrants—fellow Africans, including those from countries that hitherto had sheltered South African freedom fighters, especially members of the ruling ANC party. In 1994, the Government expelled about 91,000 'illegal' immigrants, mostly (75 per cent) Mozambicans. Others had come from Nigeria, Sierra Leone, Ethiopia and Zambia. There was a dramatic increase in the number of illegal aliens expelled in the previous three years under apartheid rule (293 in 1990 and 83,109 in 1992). By 1996, deportation of illegal immigrants rose to 181,230, up from 157,695 in 1995. Thousands of the estimated 300,000 Zimbabweans living in South Africa illegally are deported every month (Mfono, 1998; Adepoju, 1998a).

Locals accused so-called illegal immigrants of being involved in criminal activities, taking scarce housing and jobs from locals, working for very low wages thereby undercutting the workers' dream of higher wages and better working conditions, exploiting local girls by marrying them solely to obtain residence permits, and so on. To counter these allegations, the Government promised to overhaul the whole system and introduce new forge-proof passports and identity cards. In addition, 'marriages of convenience' would be more closely policed, and employers who hired illegal immigrants would be penalised (*The Economist,* 4 March 1995).

But root causes of the problems can be traced to the wide disparity between incomes in the RSA and those of her neighbours—members of SADC. Measured by income per capita, RSA is 35 times more affluent than the other 11 member states of COMESA combined, and accounts for two-fifths of the gross national product of all SSA. Moreover, per capita income in RSA is 37 times that of Mozambique (*The Economist,* 2 September 1996). Even when RSA erected electric barbed fences along its borders with Mozambique to control the influx of immigrants, desperate migrants continued to risk entry into RSA. Meantime, RSA is undertaking a regularisation drive for undocumented migrants and legislation to curb illegal immigration. But these are short-sighted strategies: in the long run, the security of RSA lies not in these measures but in helping to stimulate the economic growth of neighbours which it helped to destabilise over the past two decades.

In 1994, the ANC Government initiated plans in conjunction with the National Union of Mine Workers to grant voting rights at local and national elections, and later citizenship, to migrant workers. Residence status was granted to 90,000 former Mozambican refugees, and about 124,000 nationals of SADC countries (especially from Lesotho) who had been living in the country since 1986. Another 51,000 miners were also exempted from the provisions of the 1996 Aliens Control Act (Mfono, 1998). By the end of August 1999, about 300,000 Mozambican immigrants and refugees who entered the country between 1985 and 1992 were to be granted permanent residence.

Côte d'Ivoire

Côte d'Ivoire has always been a major country of immigration in the West African sub-region because of its vast and varied natural resource endowment, diversified and modernised export agriculture and plantation economy, efficient infrastructure, and modern industries. Most migrants originate from the Sahelian zone, especially Burkina Faso, Mali, Niger and the poorer coastal countries of Guinea, Togo and Benin. The country's domestic labour force is small and about a quarter of its waged labour force are foreigners. The country's first post-independent president, ignoring the arbitrary borders drawn by colonial powers, encouraged immigration from the country's poor neighbours. Immigrants from Burkina Faso, Nigeria, Liberia, Senegal and Ghana flooded the plantations clandestinely and did menial jobs shunned by the local population. They brought their families and were allowed to marry cross-culturally, settle and vote.

Immigrants constituted 17 per cent of the total population in 1965, 22 per cent in 1975, 28 per cent in 1988 and 25 per cent in 1993. By 1995, there were 4 million immigrants in a population of 14 million (Toure, 1998). The Government's liberal immigration policy over three decades has now been jeopardised by political expediency. The new president played the ethnic card by abrogating the foreigner's right to vote (*Financial Times*, 12 September 1995). The economic downturn and increasing unemployment among young nationals were also used to justify recent government policy to register and issue special identity cards to foreigners, a development widely viewed as aimed at deporting (now classified) illegal immigrants.

The trend set in motion in Côte d'Ivoire is slowly taking root in other parts of the region. In March 1999, Ghana also required all aliens resident in the country to register and be issued with identity cards. Immigrants were suspicious of this move, recalling the antecedents, three decades earlier, of the 1969 Alien Compliance Order that culminated in the expulsion of all non-Ghanaians. Perhaps the most celebrated misuse of the ethnic identity card is the example of Zambia whose first post-independent president of twenty-nine years has been declared a non-Zambian and an illegal person in the country.

CHALLENGES AND PROSPECTS

Emerging Trends in the Context of Sub-regional Economic Unions

The traditional countries of immigration in the sub-regional economic unions are Nigeria, Senegal, Côte d'Ivoire, and Ghana in ECOWAS; Senegal and Côte d'Ivoire in CEAO; Gabon, Cameroon and Congo in UDEAC; and South Africa, Botswana and Zimbabwe in SADC. But the tide has changed in recent years. Deteriorating economic conditions, huge external debt and the biting effects of structural adjustment programmes have rendered these traditional immigration countries increasingly incapable of accommodating the influx of migrants. As the economic crisis has worsened, some immigration countries have become labour-exporting countries: Zambia, and increasingly Zimbabwe, Kenya, Ghana and Senegal. Nigeria has also joined the league of labour-exporting countries. Most of its emigrants during the last decade have been highly skilled professionals who moved to prosperous countries of the North in response to the deepening political crisis and economic deterioration in Nigeria.

Diminished opportunities for employment and the failure of sub-regional economic unions to generate adequate opportunities for intra-regional migration of labour, and to absorb the rapidly increasingly labour force, have led African migrants, especially young people, to adopt more daring methods to enter countries of the North, which have tightened their border controls. Movements are more clandestine and spontaneous involving more risky passages and trafficking via diverse transit points. Some enter the host countries clandestinely as tourists or students and later work and live there without officially changing their status. Others travel via intermediate countries such as Gambia, Cape Verde or Guinea to obtain false documentation for a fee en route to Spain, Portugal, Italy, or Libya, invariably via another country, giving rise a multi-polar and multi-dimensional migratory path. While some continue with the traditional two-step move from a village to a coastal city and then to Europe, many others pursue varied itineraries through Sahelian or coastal African cities to reach the ultimate destination, Europe (Findley, 1997). Morocco, Algeria, Tunisia, Turkey and Greece have become transit routes for the illegal entry of Africans to Europe.

Clandestine migrants, who initially migrate as businessmen, students or tourists, employ a variety of tactics to stay on at the destination, living with friends and working in the 'underground' sector. The deteriorating political and economic situation in SSA has reinforced the resolve of emigrants to sidetrack official channels of immigration in countries of the North. This has given rise to irregular migrations through various channels and routes, including trafficking in migrants by organised syndicates. Female migration as a family survival strategy has also increased. At the same time, what was once regarded as brain drain from the region is gradually being transformed into brain circulation within the region, and commercial migration is replacing labour migration in some parts of the region.

Trafficking in Illegal Migrants

Although statistics are difficult to obtain, it is now evident that trafficking in illegal migrants, hitherto a rare phenomenon, has increased as young people become involved in daredevil ventures to gain entry into Europe. Individual stowaways engage in life-threatening ventures hidden on board ships to southern Europe, and recently to as far as East Asia and Australia. Unscrupulous agents also exploit desperate youths with promises of passages from West Africa to Italy, Spain and France via, for instance, Dakar and Las Palmas. Most of these youths become stranded in Dakar; others who get through are apprehended and deported on arrival or soon afterwards. The point to be stressed here is that the first leg of the migration, from home country to Senegal, the transit country, has been facilitated by the ECOWAS protocol on free movement of Community nationals.

Traffickers in children and young girls to Equatorial Guinea and Gabon from southeastern Nigeria and from Togo to Côte d'Ivoire's farms and plantations have been intercepted in recent years. But perhaps the most pathetic case is that of two young Guinean stowaways, boys aged 14 and 15 years, whose bodies were found frozen and crushed in the landing gear of the Belgian aircraft on arrival in Brussels. They had stowed away from Conakry after a stopover in Mali. Several women trafficked to Italy from Nigeria ostensibly to work as domestic servants but ended up in the sex industry have been deported. Between September 1999 and March 2000, about 340 young women who had been trafficked by organised syndicates were deported from Italy and are being rehabilitated.

From Brain Drain to Brain Circulation

The migration of highly skilled African manpower has its antecedents in the 1960s, when African countries engaged in unprecedented educational expansion (Fadayomi, 1996). Emigration was spurred by a combination of economic, social and political factors. In the 1970s, highly qualified and experienced workers in trades and professions emigrated from Zimbabwe, Zambia, Senegal, Ghana and Uganda to RSA and to countries outside Africa. Since the 1980s, emigration to Europe, North America and the oil-rich countries of the Middle East has increased. It has been estimated that SSA lost 30 per cent of its highly skilled nationals between 1960 and 1987, mostly to the European Community. Between 1986 and 1990, an estimated 50,000 to 60,000 middle and high-level African managers emigrated in response to deteriorating socio-economic and political conditions in the region (*IOM News*, March 1996: 7).

As political and economic crises continue to adversely affect conditions in the traditional countries of immigration within the region, the lure of Botswana and RSA waxes strong and highly-skilled professionals, pressured to leave their countries by uncertain economic conditions, have found a new RSA and the booming economy of Botswana attractive destinations (Adepoju, 1991; 1995). What was once a brain drain from the region is being gradually transformed into brain circulation within the region (Logan, 1999).

The tempo of migration to RSA has increased since the demise of apartheid and spectacular political transformation in the country. The immigrants were mostly skilled professionals—teachers, university professors, doctors, lawyers, nurses and engineers—a situation that set them aside from traditional immigrants from the satellite states of Lesotho,

Swaziland, Botswana, Malawi and Mozambique, who were mostly unskilled mine workers and farm labourers. Zairian traders and students followed in 1991–94 as their country's economy, polity and society virtually collapsed. While part of the skill circulation is in response to the buoyant economies of Botswana and the new opportunities in independent South Africa, the admission of RSA into SADC meant that nationals of the Community, especially from Zambia and Tanzania that had barred their people from emigrating to apartheid South Africa, could, and do, migrate in regular situations, unlike the underground clandestine migrations of the apartheid period.

Increasing Female Migration

The traditional male-dominated long-term and long-distance migratory streams in the region are becoming increasingly feminised. Until recently, migration was sanctioned only for male members of the family. Some of the changes being observed involved rising levels of female education and independent female migration. Professional women from Nigeria, Ghana, and to some extent Tanzania, now engage in international migration, often leaving their spouses behind to care for the children. Female nurses and doctors have been recruited from Nigeria to work in Saudi Arabia, and some have taken advantage of bigger pay packages in the US where they work for a spell in order to accumulate savings to tide them over harsh economic conditions at home. Others migrate with their children to pursue studies abroad as the educational system in Nigeria has virtually collapsed (Adepoju, 1996b). Female migration is indeed a manifestation of the pressure on African families—women, like men are migrating as a survival strategy. As jobs became tighter during the 1980s and as remittances thin out, many families increasingly have relied on women and their farming activities (Findley, 1997). The failure of the domestic economy to provide employment opportunities has been aggravated by the effects of structural adjustment policies. Women have also entered the labour market to supplement meagre family income. In Côte d'Ivoire, for instance, female migration from Burkina Faso has intensified in spite of looming economic crisis in the traditional receiving country. The explanation is to be found in the fact that women generally cluster in the informal commerce sector which is less affected by economic crisis than the waged sector where most male migrants are engaged as either agricultural labourers or as white collar workers in the services sector.

From Labour to Commercial Migration

In contrast to traditional migration across contiguous countries which are also members of sub-regional economic unions, migrants from francophone west Africa are exploring non-conventional destinations with limited linguistic, cultural and colonial ties: initially to Zambia, and when the economy of that country collapsed, increasingly to RSA. They are also moving to European countries such as Italy, Portugal, Germany, Belgium and Spain. Finding the situation of immigrants in Europe increasingly intolerable, with local residents and the media becoming increasingly apprehensive and xenophobic, and anti-immigration political parties increasingly vocal and popular, some immigrants have crossed the Atlantic to the US in search of greener pastures, mainly as petty traders (Ebin, 1996). Post-apartheid waves of immigrants from Senegal, Nigeria, Sierra Leone and so on, to RSA, consisted mostly of street vendors and traders trying to tap the relatively affluent market of the new Republic (Bouillon, 1996).

The Future of Regional Integration

Africa needs regional integration to enhance intra-regional trade and mobility of factors of production, especially labour. In the process, several aspects have to be addressed. African countries are small in population size, economy and market size. Intra-African trade remains miniscule in spite of the concentric nature of economic groupings. Inter-country infrastructure facilities are weak. Thus, for instance, the unharmonised transport systems, different railway track systems and rules and regulations that change across frontiers, limit trade, especially for landlocked countries that must transport goods to coastal harbours for export and import. Inter-state border disputes and wars are endemic and political support for sub-regional organisations is waning.

The multiplicity of sub-regional economic unions has resulted in duplication of efforts and poor financial support. Economic downturn during the last two decades has eroded employment opportunities for a variety of skills in migrant receiving countries, thereby intensifying the pressure for potential migrants to find alternative destinations. Political leaders have to address the constraints on growth of these economic unions, and appropriately harmonise the diverse unions, especially the national laws and regional and supra-national treaties dealing with labour migration.

The political landscape, especially the transition to democracy, the socio-political effects of structural adjustment programmes and the endemic ethnic conflicts, have to a large extent dampened the lingering optimism that the region would enter the twenty-first century less distressed than in the 1980s, a period popularly regarded as the lost decade for the region. Since no meaningful development can take place in conditions of conflict, SSA governments have to strengthen the democratisation process and improve the quality of governance to ensure a greater and more effective participation of people in the development process. Already civil wars in Liberia, and later in Sierra Leone and Guinea-Bissau, have tested the resolve of the sub-region's political leaders to the limit and almost tore ECOWAS apart. The divide between francophone and anglophone members of the group deepened and nearly fractured the peacekeeping role of ECOMOG, composed initially of soldiers from the anglophone countries of ECOWAS. Furthermore, the civil war in the Democratic Republic of Congo (DRC) almost fractured SADC, which it joined in 1998. Although SADC ruled out the possibility of intervening on the side of its new member, three member countries— Namibia, Zimbabwe, Angola—pitched their military support for the leadership of the DRC, while Uganda and Rwanda supported the rebels. Thousands of migrants and refugees criss-crossed neighbouring countries in search of security, employment and safe haven: several thousand others remained internally displaced.

Economic recovery and improved living conditions and survival for the poor in SSA depend crucially on successful resolution of the on-going economic malaise without which effective and sustainable development is but a mirage. But this goal is not in sight. The debt overhang has dramatically reduced the capacity of SSA governments to mobilise resources for development: alleviation of poverty and debt relief, among others, are crucial for the future economic development of the region and in influencing all forms of migration, especially irregular and illegal. Governments should also redirect their huge military and security expenditure to much-needed socio-economic development. As experience shows for several countries (Togo, Zaire, Liberia, Burundi, Rwanda, Sierra Leone, Somalia, Sudan), the absence of peace and stability discourages investment and leads to capital flight. At the same time, lack of economic alternatives prompts emigration, both regular and irregular.

A major development issue during the next decade is the productive employment of the millions of educated young people who will scramble for work in the formal sector, or join the lengthening queue of potential emigrants, ready to migrate clandestinely to do any kind of odd jobs anywhere, but increasingly outside their countries. African countries should therefore provide their nationals with adequate information on conditions in receiving countries, especially for potential emigrants to countries having or likely to have a significant potential migrant population such as Lesotho, Burkina Faso, Mali, Senegal, Zaire, Ghana, etc. regarding rules and regulations guiding entry, residence and employment abroad.

Experience shows that wherever spectacular differentials exist, migratory flows, in regular but increasingly in irregular situations, are directed from the poorer impoverished countries to the more affluent ones. Thus, in spite of the strict immigration policies of the countries of the North, it is certain that the pressure for labour migration in search of jobs abroad will intensify for the millions of people in SSA who will enter the labour market annually. The xenophobic reaction to immigrants especially in France and Germany reinforces the feeling that immigrants from African countries are unwanted and must be returned to their countries. Accordingly, thousands have been expelled. It is in this light that the Abuja treaty of 1993 to set up an African Economic Community by 2025 to facilitate intra-regional labour mobility was most timely. Sub-regional and regional bilateral and multi-lateral co-operation unions have the potential to greatly influence the flow of labour migration. Sub-regional economic unions that provide in their agreements for free flow of skilled labour and rights of establishment in member countries, could facilitate intra-regional labour mobility and promote self-reliant development in the region.

CONCLUSION

Unlike Europe that used integration for prosperity and strength, Africa needs regional integration for survival and to generate employment for its teeming population. African countries are small in population size, economy and market size. The economic entities are not viable as producers, consumers and trading partners. Indeed, intra-African trade is miniscule; five per cent of export trade, in spite of the myriad of economic groupings. Africa's markets are fractured, and fiscal and monetary policies are distorted. These have been compounded by economic downturn during the last two decades, deteriorating basic social services—health, education and transport—and declining per capita consumption. The weak political support for, and rivalry between, sub-regional unions and the non-ratification and implementation of protocols, are ominous signs that these regional groupings have thus far functioned poorly and in turn failed to stimulate growth and generate opportunities for the millions of young people eager to work in the region, but equally determined to risk entry into the countries of the North clandestinely.

The existence of overlapping economic groupings strains the limited resources of their members; they also compete with one another in objectives and operations. This situation poses several problems, including those relating to the harmonisation of goals and strategies, duplication, divided loyalty, fragmentation and lack of co-ordination in, for instance, trade liberalisation and labour mobility (Asante, 1990). Multiplicity of economic groupings and dual membership of states in sub-regional economic groupings with conflicting objectives all too often result in inability to implement protocols in the agreements.

For these reasons, and also as a result of deepening poverty, unemployment and socio-economic insecurity, migration in irregular situations will become more visible in the region in the future. Some migration that would otherwise take place internally is likely to become replacement migration in urban areas and within member countries of the sub-regional unions, and sequentially emerge as undocumented migration across borders to the relatively more prosperous countries.

Increasingly, political and economic crises are triggering migrant labour to new destinations outside the traditional labour-receiving countries of the sub-regional economic unions. As political and economic crises intensify, both refugee flows and undocumented migration are increasing in both quantum and impact. Structural adjustment and the current economic downturn are also accelerating emigration. A significant proportion of women—single and married—now emigrate alone in search of secure jobs in countries of the region and also developed countries. Such female migration is likely to intensify as a result of fluctuating socio-economic conditions in the region. The extent to which regional economic unions are able to create employment opportunities for such migrants to be absorbed within the region has implications for, amongst others, the emerging trend in trafficking of females into sex industries in the countries of the North.

In spite of membership in sub-regional economic unions, inter-state border disputes and wars are rampant (Eritrea and Ethiopia; Togo and Ghana; Nigeria and Cameroon). There is also a general reluctance to surrender national sovereignty to supra-national, regional economic organs. Realising that peace and political stability are essential ingredients for development, the various sub-regional economic unions are pursuing peace efforts amongst warring factions. To this end, peace treaties were signed in Togo in July 1999 to end the fratricidal war in Sierra Leone. The fragile peace treaty for DRC signed in Zambia and several regional efforts to end the Ethiopian/Eritrean war are signs that these organisations are working hard to restore peace and stability to the region and address one of the root causes of migration, refugees and internal displacements of the population.

In the prolonged process of establishing the African Common Market and African Economic Community, the sub-regional co-operation unions are expected to serve as building blocks in a functionalist and gradualist approach. Potentially, economic integration in the region offers a long-term prospect for stimulating intra-regional labour mobility if the right policies are pursued. Persistent political unrest and the fragmented, weak national economies of the region make regional and sub-regional economic groupings most pertinent. Ratification of the memorandum to set up an African Common Market by the year 2025 is a landmark on the road to all-African regional integration. Since many countries are ambivalent to the principle of free movement, and are reluctant to modify domestic laws and administrative practices, it is necessary to harmonise national laws which conflict with regional and sub-regional treaties. Efforts at promoting regional integration and co-operation must also address the right of residence and establishment of migrants and obligations of the host countries.

REFERENCES

Adekanye, J. 'Bayo, (1998), 'Conflicts, loss of state capacities and migration in contemporary Africa', in Reginald Appleyard (ed.) (1998), *Emigration Dynamics in Developing Countries*, vol. 1: Sub-Saharan Africa, Aldershot: Ashgate, pp. 165–206.

Adepoju, A. (1983), 'Undocumented migration in Africa: trends and policies', *International Migration*, **26** (2), 204–17.

Adepoju, A. (1991), 'South-North migration: the African experience', *International Migration*, **29** (2), 205–22.

Adepoju, A. (1995), 'Emigration dynamics in Sub-Saharan Africa', *International Migration*, Special Issue: Emigration Dynamics in Developing Countries, **33** (3 and 4), 315–90.

Adepoju, A. (1996a), 'The links between intra-continental and inter-continental migration to and from Africa', in A. Adepoju and T. Hammar (eds) (1996), *International Migration to and from Africa: Dimensions, Challenges and Prospects*, Dakar: PHRDA and Stockholm: CEIFO, pp. 13–37.

Adepoju, A. (1996b), 'Population, poverty, structural adjustment programmes and quality of life in Sub-Saharan Africa', PHRDA Research Paper No. 1, Dakar: PHRDA.

Adepoju, A. (1998a), 'The role of regional economic communities in the politics of migration in African countries', in Pontifical Council for the Pastoral Care of Migrants and Itinerant People, *Migration at the Threshold of the Third Millennia*, Rome: The Vatican, pp. 197–209.

Adepoju, A. (1998b), 'Emigration dynamics in Sub-Saharan Africa', in Reginald Appleyard, (ed.) *Emigration Dynamics in Developing Countries: Vol 1: Sub-Saharan Africa*, Aldershot: Ashgate, pp. 17–34.

Afolayan, A.A. (1998), 'Regional integration, labour mobility, clandestine labour migration and expulsion of illegal immigrants', paper presented at the Regional Meeting on International Migration in Africa at the Threshold of the 21st Century, Gaborone, 2–5 June.

Asante, S.K.B. (1990), 'Regional economic cooperation and integration: the experience of ECOWAS', in P.A. Nyong'o (ed.) (1990), *Regional Integration in Africa: Unfinished Agenda*, Nairobi: Academy Science Publishers, pp. 99–138.

Bouillon, A. (1996), 'La nouvelle migration Africaine en Afrique du Sud. Immigrants d'Afrique Occidentale et Centrale à Joannesburg', paper presented at Colloque Systèmes et Dynamiques des Migrations Internationales Ouest-Africaines, IFAN/ORSTOM, Dakar (3–6 December).

Ebin, V. (1996), 'Négociations et appropriations: les revendicatiions des migrants Sénégalais à New York', paper delivered at Colloque Systèmes et Dynamiques des Migrations Internationales Ouest-Africaines, IFAN/ORSTOM, Dakar (3–6 December).

Fadayomi, T.O. (1996), 'Brain drain and brain gain in Africa: causes, dimensions and consequences', in A. Adepoju, and T. Hammar (eds), *International Migration in and from Africa: Dimensions, Challenges and Prospects*, Dakar: PHRDA and Stockholm: CEIFO, pp. 143–59.

Findley, S. (1997), 'Migration and family interactions in Africa', in A. Adepoju (ed.), *Family, Population and Development in Africa*, London and New Jersey: Atlantic Highlands, Zed Books, pp. 109–38.

Kennes, W. (1999), 'African regional economic integration and the European Union', in D.C. Bach (ed.), *Regionalisation in Africa: Integration and Disintegration*, Oxford: James Currey, pp. 27–40.

Logan, B.L. (1999), 'The reverse transfer of technology from Sub-Saharan Africa', *International Migration*, **37** (2), 437–63.

Le Courrier (ACP), Reportage (1997), *Gabon*, **165**, (September-October): 15–18.

Mfono, Z.N. (1998), 'International migration in South Africa in the 1990s', Migration Country Profile presented at the Regional Meeting on International Migration in Africa at the Threshold of the XXI Century, Gaborone, 2–5 June.

Nnoli, O. (1998), 'Ethnicity, ethnic conflict and emigration dynamics in Sub-Saharan Africa', in Reginald Appleyard (ed.), *Emigration Dynamics in Developing Countries: Vol 1: Sub-Saharan Africa*, Aldershot: Ashgate, pp. 206–63.

Ojo, O.B.J. (1999), 'Integration in ECOWAS: successes and difficulties', in C.D. Bach (ed.), *Regionalisation in Africa: Integration and Disintegration*, London: James Currey Publishers, pp. 119–24.

Oucho, J.O. (1995), 'Emigration dynamics in Eastern African countries', *International Migration*, Special issue: Emigration Dynamics in Developing Countries, **33** (3 and 4), 391–434.

Schmeidl, S. (1996), 'Hard times in countries of origin', in A.P. Schmid (ed.), *Migration and Crime*, Milan: ISPAC, pp. 43–60.

Toure, M. (1998), 'Country report: Côte d'Ivoire' Migration Country Profile presented at the Regional Meeting on International Migration in Africa at the Threshold of the XXI Century, Gaborone, 2–5 June.

5. The Economics of Illegal Migration for the Host Economy[1]

Barry R. Chiswick

INTRODUCTION

The worldwide growth in international migration in recent decades has been accompanied by an increase in what is variously called 'irregular migration', 'undocumented migration' or 'illegal migration'. That is, there has been an increase in the number of persons living in the higher-income countries who have either entered the country in violation of that country's laws, or who have done something to violate a condition of legal entry. The latter may arise from staying longer than permitted, or from working in spite of a visa that prohibits or limits working, such as a tourist, student or temporary worker visa.

This increase in illegal migration has occurred in countries that have generous legal immigration programmes, such as the US which accepts nearly one million legal immigrants each year. At the other extreme, it has also occurred in island countries that have virtually no legal migration, such as Japan. There is every reason to believe that illegal migration from the developing countries of the 'South' to the high income countries of the 'North' (including Australia) will intensify in the coming decades if present policies continue. This chapter explores some of the basic principles and issues related to the economics of illegal migration for the host economy. Its purpose is to stimulate further discussion and thought on these issues.

In exploring issues having to do with the supply and demand for illegal migrant workers, it is assumed that the migration is motivated purely by economic factors, leaving refugee and asylee illegal migration for another time. The chapter considers why illegal migrants tend to be low-skilled workers, and assesses their impact on the distribution of income in the host economy, and the use of income transfers. It concludes with a discussion on the political economy of illegal migration, or why enforcement seems incomplete.

THE SUPPLY AND DEMAND FOR ILLEGAL MIGRATION

Consider two countries, A and B, where country A has higher real wages for workers of a given level of skill because of its more advanced technology, greater capital stock per worker, greater human capital embodied in its workers, greater abundance of natural resources per worker, and a political/legal system more conducive to economic growth. Assume that legal barriers prohibit the migration of workers from B to A, and that even if there were no legal barriers migration could not take place because the costs of moving are high and the wage differential between A and B is small for workers of the same level of skill. Now consider a situation in which the costs of migration and resettlement (including information costs) decline, wages in A increase, or those in B decrease.[2] The rate of return to investment in migration has increased. If the rate of return exceeds the individual's interest cost of funds, that is, the person's discount rate, there is an economic incentive to migrate.

In a world with no legal barriers to migration, enough migration would occur until the rate of return declines to the discount rate, that is, until there would be no economic gain for the person at the margin from moving from B to A. A wage differential between A and B could persist only to the extent that the present value of the stream of wage differences equals the present value of the full cost of migration borne by the individual. This is represented in Figure 5.1, with a migration level of m_0 and a wage differential of d_0.

With the existence of legal barriers to mobility, however, a rate of return in excess of the discount rate can persist. This is represented by the larger wage differential d_1 in Figure 5.1. This larger wage differential need not persist indefinitely, however, because in the long run the movement of other factors of production (e.g. capital and entrepreneurship) and free trade in goods, could bring about 'factor price equalisation'. In the absence of these latter adjustments, at the margin there may be large economic rents to be had from migrating (the wage differential d_1-d_2) even though it is against the law. Illegal labour migration is therefore a response to disequilibrium in international labour markets brought about by barriers to the unrestricted movement of factors of production, including labour.

The supply of illegal migrants can be thought of as a rising function of the wage differential, with a greater supply forthcoming the lower is the cost of migration, the lower the probability of apprehension and the lower the penalty if apprehended. For some countries in close proximity, such as Mexico and the US, wage differentials are large and increasing and the costs of illegal migration have decreased over time. The incentives for illegal migration have increased. The extent of illegal migration therefore depends, in part, on the degree of enforcement along the border and in the interior of the destination country.

Figure 5.1 Supply and demand for migrant workers

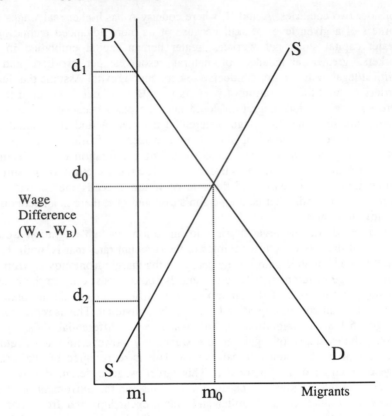

Notes:
1. m_0, d_0:   Equilibrium number of migrant workers (m_0) and wage difference (d_0)
2. m_1, d_1:   Number of migrant workers and wage difference if migration limited to m_1
3. d_2 - d_1:   Economic rent to be had from illegal migration when legal migration limited to m_1.

This illegal flow can then be imperfectly regulated by raising and lowering the cost of illegal migration to the potential migrant by varying the extent of enforcement. The greater the amount of resources devoted to enforcement and the greater the penalties if illegal migration is detected, the lower is the supply of illegal aliens to the destination. This enforcement can occur at the frontier (border enforcement) or in the interior.

The expected penalty from being detected can be thought of as the probability of detection and the value of the penalty if detected, including the disruption costs from deportation. If illegal migrants were risk neutral they would be just as sensitive to a 10 per cent increase in the probability of being apprehended as they would be to a 10 per cent increase in the penalty. If, as seems more realistic, they are risk averse, a 10 per cent increase in the probability of apprehension would have a greater deterrent effect than a similar increase in the penalty. However, apprehensions without penalties, or penalties without apprehensions, have no deterrent effects.[3]

The demand by employers for illegal alien workers arises from the difference in wages paid in the labour market to legal workers and the reservation wage of illegal aliens, the lowest wage needed to induce them to migrate illegally. The demand for illegal alien workers can be reduced by lowering their productivity or by raising the cost of hiring illegal alien workers. Penalties against employers who 'knowingly' hire illegal aliens, referred to as 'employer sanctions', are a mechanism to reduce illegal alien employment by raising the hiring costs to employers (Chiswick, 1986, 1988a).

The obvious question that arises is, why are there barriers to the free movement of people for employment across international boundaries?[4] This question becomes increasingly relevant as international barriers to the free trade in market goods and capital have been declining.[5] There are several reasons why nation-states limit the free movement of people. While it is recognised that an individual has a human right to emigrate from his/her country of origin, it is also recognised that there is no right to immigrate into any particular country. That is, countries have the right to regulate the number and characteristics of international migrants who enter their country. Governments do this, in part, to influence the impact of migration on the host country's culture and demographic characteristics. Some countries have ideologies or mythologies that emphasise diversity or heterogeneity (such as the US); others have ideologies or mythologies that emphasise homogeneity (such as Japan).[6] Many countries, for example, the UK, Ireland, Germany and Japan, give preference to immigrants with a similar cultural, historical, or ancestral background as the dominant population of the host country. This may be done because it facilitates economic and social integration, to assist culturally close individuals, as a mechanism for preserving or maintaining the host country culture, or for broader cultural or ideological reasons, including xenophobia.

There are, however, political and economic reasons as well for nations to control entry. On the political side, immigrants may change the political balance of power, and thereby implicitly or explicitly change the distribution of property rights and the distribution of income by aligning themselves with what would otherwise be a minority of the population. To oversimplify, imported goods do not vote, but 'imported' people do vote, or at least have political influence.

There are also economic arguments for restrictions on immigration into high income countries (Chiswick, 1982). One issue is the 'absorptive capacity' of the economy. To what extent does immigration impose externalities on the host population? Consider, for example, a situation in which immigrants add to congestion and thereby impose costs on others that the immigrants themselves do not pay. These costs may be simple congestion costs (e.g. crowded streets and highways slowing down traffic), or the costs of more pollution and fewer trees; or they may involve the rising marginal cost of adding to the increased social overhead capital needed by a larger population. These costs may outweigh the benefits from the larger labour force that pushes outward the country's production possibility frontier.[7]

Other economic costs may arise if immigrants, or subsets of immigrants, make use of public income transfers that raise their total income (transfers plus labour market earnings) above their level of productivity.[8] This is more likely to occur for low-skilled immigrants. This would tend to reduce the net income after paying taxes and receiving transfers of the native population of the immigrant receiving country.

Finally, political and economic factors are intertwined. Migrants may have positive effects on some segments of the population and negative effects on others. For example, low-skilled immigration would change the distribution of income by lowering the wages of all low-skilled workers and raising the earnings of high-skilled workers and the return to the owners of land and capital. If the gainers are diffused, but the losers are concentrated, or have political power, the latter may be more effective politically, and pressure the political process to reduce migration. If the gainers are concentrated or otherwise have political power which the losers lack, there would be political pressure to increase migration, whether legal or illegal.

THE SKILLS OF ILLEGAL ALIENS

A general characteristic of illegal alien workers in developed economies is that they tend to be lower skilled than legal permanent immigrants and the average worker in the destination labour market (Chiswick 1983, 1984, 1988b). This is due, in small part, to immigration laws. The immigration laws of many of the receiving countries give some preference to high-skilled professionals, technical workers, and managers (executives). Yet, this tilting of legal immigration in favour of the highly skilled is too minor to account for the preponderance of the low-skilled workers in the illegal alien population.

Part of the answer is in the formality of labour markets. In highly formal labour markets that require educational credentials, occupational licences or union membership, it is more difficult for an illegal migrant to mask his or her illegal status. Educational credentials and occupational licences are more common in high-skilled jobs than in low-skilled jobs. Hence, illegal migration is relatively less attractive, when comparing opportunities in the origin and destination, for workers in the origin with educational credentials and occupational licences. For very low-skilled workers this is less of a problem.

The most important explanation, however, may have to do with the expected temporary nature of much illegal migration. Because of concerns regarding apprehension and deportation, many potential illegal migrants would view their stay at the destination as being subject to involuntary interruptions. Moreover, since the probability of apprehension and the costs of deportation would increase if there were more members of the family in an illegal status, there is an incentive to leave family members at the origin. This would increase the number of trips back and forth, and decrease the likelihood of uninterrupted long-term or permanent working spells at the destination.

Investments in human capital, including destination language skills, labour market information, and on-the-job training, as well as union membership and occupational licensing, have many elements that are country-specific. Expectations of short or interrupted stays at the destination would decrease incentives for investing in destination-specific human capital, as would upward job mobility that increased the probability of being detected. Moreover, the destination specific human capital that is acquired would depreciate in value during periods back home. Furthermore, investments made at the origin before migration, or during sojourns at home, would depreciate in value while at the destination. These considerations imply that temporary migrants, whether guest workers or illegal aliens, would make fewer human capital investments specific to the destination than would otherwise comparable permanent immigrants.

There is a general complementarity between internationally transferable human capital and destination-specific human capital, each enhancing the productivity of the other (Chiswick and Miller, 1999). Lower returns from destination-specific human capital will lower incentives for investment in internationally transferable skills. Hence, illegal migrants will tend to have lower skill levels than legal permanent migrants and the native population at the destination. One implication of this analysis is that investments in destination-specific skills would increase, and so too would their earnings, the greater the expected permanence of their stay, either because of a decline in the enforcement of immigration law or because of the receipt of an amnesty. Yet, even with an increase in their investments in human capital after an amnesty, most illegal migrants remain relatively low-skilled workers engaged in low-wage jobs with relatively flat earnings profiles.

THE IMPACT OF ILLEGAL MIGRATION

The low skill levels of illegal migrants have implications for their impact in the labour market. They compete with low-skilled native-born workers for the lower-skilled jobs and compete with low-income native-born families in the low-income housing market and for public income transfers (Chiswick, 1982, 1992; Altonji and Card, 1991). The larger the stock of illegal migrants at the destination, the greater the intensity of this competition in the labour market, the housing market and the market for public income transfers, and hence the lower the level of economic well-being among the native-born poor. It is the low-income native-born (and legal immigrant) population that pays the highest economic price from low-skilled illegal migration. On the other hand, a greater supply of low-skilled workers, whether illegal or legal migrants, increases the wages of high-skilled workers and the return to capital (Chiswick, 1982). This follows from the principle of complementary in production: a greater supply of one factor of production increases the productivity of other complementary factors.

It is often said that one of the benefits of illegal migrant workers is that they do the jobs that native workers will not do. These are the dirty, dangerous, dull and difficult low-skilled jobs. By implication, it is 'important' that these jobs be done. The relevant question is: 'At what wage rates will native workers do these jobs?' It is to be expected that undesirable jobs, that is, those with less favourable non-pecuniary characteristics, will command a higher wage in the labour market than desirable jobs requiring the same level of skill. At a sufficiently large wage differential, native-born workers will be indifferent between undesirable and desirable jobs. With the increase in wealth and marginal tax rates in developed countries in the post-war period, there has also been an increase in the wage differential that would be needed to induce workers to be indifferent between undesirable and desirable jobs.

If employers have to pay the cost of attracting native-born workers to the less desirable jobs, they will have an incentive to invest in making these jobs less undesirable. A cleaner, safer, more pleasant workplace would emerge. Moreover, employers will invest in substituting capital for the now more expensive labour to reduce the amount of labour that employers demand for these jobs. Finally, some of these jobs will disappear from the destination labour market, either not be done at all or to be exported to other countries. The goods and services that are worth producing will be produced, even if production methods and market baskets differ due to the higher cost of low-skilled labour.[9]

Sectors of the economy that are particularly active in the illegal alien labour market have identifiable characteristics. These tend to be sectors employing low-skilled labour that need not have host-country skills (including knowledge of the destination country's language), that are characterised by unstable employment or in which high job turnover has low costs, that tend to be outside the formalised sectors of the economy, and that tend to be viewed as offering 'undesirable' job characteristics.

Illegal migrants tend to have low skill levels, leave their family members in the country of origin, and return when their employment opportunities deteriorate for cyclical, seasonal or other reasons. As a result, they tend to make much less use of the broad range of government benefits, including schooling for their children and health care for family members, than lawful permanent immigrants with the same level of skill and earnings. This raises an interesting public policy dilemma. It is clearly politically and socially undesirable to have a segment of the population living outside the law and denied the law's full protection, including social welfare or social security benefits. A 'solution' is therefore necessitated.

One extreme policy is to remove illegal migrants from the country, that is, have wide-scale round-ups and deportations of illegal migrants (Chiswick, 1988a). While this would have a favourable effect on the low-income native-born population, it raises a host of civil liberties issues. There are some things that governments in liberal democracies cannot do politically, and one of these is draconian measures toward deporting illegal migrants.

Another extreme policy, at the other end of the spectrum, is to grant illegal migrants legal status through an amnesty programme (Chiswick, 1988a), a policy also not without its problems. Workers whose presence was not desired in the first place find their status regularised. This does not solve the problem that, for whatever reason, their presence in the labour market was not wanted by the legal system. Moreover, it does not deter the inflow of illegal migrants after the amnesty is granted. Once an amnesty is granted it creates expectations that if the illegal migrant pressures once more become intense, amnesties will be given again in the future. This lowers the cost or increases the benefits of illegal migration, encouraging additional illegal flows.

Furthermore, with legal status, the former illegal migrant has new rights to income transfers, is more likely to bring dependent family members to the destination, and is less likely to return to the origin if and when employment opportunities decrease in the destination due to seasonal, cyclical or other, perhaps random, reasons. In addition, the availability of these benefits tends to decrease the incentives for working, and hence reduces the supply of labour from the beneficiaries of amnesty. Then, the low-skilled illegal migrant worker who contributed more to the public treasury than he or she took out in benefits may become a net cost when these same low-skilled migrants are given legal status (Chiswick, 1982).

It is perhaps because the two extremes of deportation and amnesty have such undesirable implications that a middle ground 'solution' of 'benevolent ambiguity' is often grudgingly tolerated (Chiswick, 1988a; Hillman and Weiss, 1999). Under this approach there is strict enforcement of immigration law at the border, but minimal enforcement in the interior—neither massive deportations nor formal amnesties. Sanctions against employers who knowingly hire illegal aliens may exist in principle, but because of employer objections due to the enforcement burden placed on them, and, in some countries, civil liberties arguments, they are not vigorously enforced.[10] There is a form of de facto but not de jure amnesty for those who are established in the destination. The employment of illegal aliens is tacitly tolerated, but they receive fewer income transfers and are less likely to bring dependent family members. Hence, although they have adverse labour market effects on the wages of low-skilled natives, they are likely to contribute more to the economy than they take in the form of wages and transfer benefits—or at least contribute more than they would if they had legal status. In a static model this scenario has its own pragmatic appeal.

The 'benevolent ambiguity' approach will have its appeal in diverse settings. It is the approach adopted in the US which experiences large flows of illegal alien workers primarily from Mexico, a very low income country that has difficulty creating employment for its expanding youth labour force and which shares a 2,000-mile-long border that for geographic and political reasons is difficult to seal. Yet, similar problems, and seemingly similar solutions, are being adopted in other liberal democracies. Although the level of illegal migration flows are much smaller than in the US, the island nations of Japan and Australia, and Canada which has relied on the US as a protective barrier, are finding that in the modern era, oceans and the geographic space of other countries offer limited but not complete immunity from illegal immigration.

In a dynamic setting, however, there are problems. Incentives are created for the continued growth of an illegal alien workforce, with increasing numbers developing a permanent attachment and bringing in dependent family members. To avoid the development of a population living outside of, or on the margins of, the legal system, pressures increase for the awarding of de jure amnesty, with expanding economic, social and political rights.

The emergence of a legal population of the same ethnic origin as streams of illegal migrants makes it more difficult to control illegal migration. First, it makes it easier for illegal migrants to mask their illegal identity. They have an enclave that makes it easier to live and work while avoiding detection. Second, as a result of kinship ties, ethnic solidarity and ethnic politics, a vigorous enforcement of immigration law at the border and in the interior becomes politically that much more difficult. The legal population becomes a political advocate for reduced enforcement and for the awarding of amnesty and economic and social benefits.

CONCLUSION

Illegal migration flows are seductive. The low-skilled workers come providing 'needed' labour services for employers unwilling or unable to offer higher wages and more attractive job opportunities to those with legal rights to work or to reduce their demand for low-skilled labour. Although initially illegal migrants seem like unsanctioned temporary or guest workers, with the passage of time their attachment increases and their use of government transfers and services also increases. They compete with low-skilled native-born workers in the labour market, the housing market and for public income transfers. It is the low-income native-born population that pays the greatest price for the presence of illegal migrants. With the passage of time, measures to combat their presence become more difficult to implement, particularly if a significant legal population of the same ethnicity develops. Some processes are much easier to stop or reverse in their early stages before they have become established, and this is an important characteristic of illegal migration.

NOTES

1. The first draft of this chapter was written while I was the John M. Olin Visiting Professor, Center for the Study of the Economy and the State, Graduate School of Business, University of Chicago. An earlier version was presented at the OECD Seminar on Preventing and Combating the Employment of Foreigners in an Irregular Situation, The Hague, 22–23 April 1999, and the International Expert Meeting on Irregular Migration: Dynamics, Impact and Policy Options, Jerusalem, 29 August–2 September 1999.

2. The immediate costs of migration, for example, the airline or bus ticket, and the time involved in this transportation mode are generally a minor part of the total cost of international migration. The greater part of the cost involves leaving familiar places and people, the cost of resettling in the new location where the language skills, labour market skills, information and networks acquired in the origin have little or no value and new investments must be undertaken. Indeed, that is why there is a tendency for international migrants to select destination countries, or locations within the destinations, that minimise these costs, other variables being the same. This results in the appearance of chain migration and the formation of immigrant/ethnic concentrations or enclaves. It is not that immigrants are any more 'clanish' than natives, but they seek a mechanism for minimising resettlement costs. These less tangible costs, along with high discount rates due to low incomes, may explain why seemingly large international and inter-regional wage differences can persist over time.

3. It has been said that the US government policy of focusing on enforcement along the border with Mexico, with a virtual abandonment of interior enforcement, has the effect of increasing the number of apprehensions while imposing few penalties on those apprehended along the Mexican border. The result of this policy of apprehension with minimal penalties has been little deterrent effect. A de facto amnesty in an irregular status is granted most illegal aliens who penetrate the border and do not commit felonies or seek to leave and re-enter the US.

4. For an overview of arguments for freer movement of persons across international borders, see Ghosh, 1997.

5. It should be noted that barriers to international migration have decreased in some regions. The free mobility of labour among citizens of the member states within the European Union is one example.

6. For a comparison of immigration issues in the US and Japan, see Chiswick, 1998.

7. On the other hand, economies of scale and immigrant contributions to the financing of collective goods (e.g. national defence) would argue for larger immigration.

8. Throughout this chapter public transfers refer to welfare, social insurance, social security, educational and medical benefits received from the government and non-profit (non-government) organisations.

9. When asked recently what I would do if illegal alien gardeners disappeared from the Chicago labour market, I replied that there would be a variety of responses: paying higher wages to attract similarly skilled or higher-skilled native-born workers, switch from labour-intensive flower beds to less labour-intensive grass lawns, plant slower growing varieties of grass, brick over part or all of the garden, prefer a house with a smaller lawn, and let the grass grow longer, among other alternatives. Thus, substitutions come in the form of using different types of labour inputs, substitution of capital for labour, use of a different technology, and substitution among consumption goods. Similar substitution possibilities exist for other market goods and services.

10. Employer sanctions may be viewed as a tax on the employment of illegal aliens. One alternative is to have a low-skilled guest worker programme in which a fee is levied on employers using the certified guest workers, as in the US–Mexico Bracero programme (for farm labourers) in the mid-twentieth century. While this approach legalises the status of otherwise illegal aliens, their experience of working in the US will make it more difficult to get them to leave when their contracts expire. Moreover, once in the US they have an incentive to leave their guest worker employer to work illegally. Raising the legal minimum wage serves to make illegal alien workers more attractive for employers. Subsidies to forms of capital that substitute for low-skilled workers, thereby lowering the demand for low-skilled workers, are difficult to target and harm the economic status of low-skilled native-born and legal immigrant workers.

REFERENCES

Altonji, Joseph and David Card (1991), 'The Effects of Immigration on the Labor Market Outcomes of Less-Skilled Natives', in John Abowd and Richard Freeman, (eds), *Immigration, Trade and the Labor Market*, Chicago: University of Chicago Press, pp. 201–34.

Chiswick, Barry R. (1982), 'The Impact of Immigration on the Level and Distribution of Economic Well-Being', in Barry R. Chiswick, (ed.), *The Gateway: U.S. Immigration Issues and Policies*, Washington: American Enterprise Institute, pp. 289–313.

Chiswick, Barry R. (1983), 'Illegal Aliens in the United States Labor Market', in Burton Weisbrod and Helen Hughes (eds), *Human Resources, Employment and Development*, vol. 3, *The Problems of Developed Countries and The International Economy*, London: Macmillan, pp. 346–67.

Chiswick, Barry R. (1984), 'Illegal aliens in the United States labor market: analysis of occupational attainment and earnings', *International Migration Review*, **18** (3), Fall: 714–32.

Chiswick, Barry R. (1986), 'The Impact of Illegal Aliens and the Enforcement of Immigration Law', in Robert J. Thornton and J. Richard Aronson (eds), *Forging New Relationships Among Business, Labor and Government*, Greenwich, CT: JAI Press, pp. 105–18.

Chiswick, Barry R. (1988a), 'Illegal immigration and immigration control', *Journal of Economic Perspectives*, **2** (3), Summer: 101–15.

Chiswick, Barry R. (1988b), *Illegal Aliens: Their Employment and Employers*, Kalamazoo, MI: Upjohn Institute.

Chiswick, Barry R. (1992) Review of 'Immigration, Trade and the Labor Market', *Journal of Economic Literature*, **30** (1), March: 212–13.

Chiswick, Barry R. (1998), 'The Economic Consequences of Immigration: Application to the United States and Japan', in Myron Weiner and Tadashi Hanami (eds), *Temporary Workers or Future Citizens? Japanese and U.S. Migration Policies*, New York: New York University Press, pp. 177–208.

Chiswick, Barry R. and Paul W. Miller (1999), 'Immigration Earnings: Language Skills, Linguistic Concentrations and the Business Cycle', Working Paper No. 152, George J. Stigler Center for the Study of the Economy and the State, University of Chicago.

Ghosh, Bimal (1997), *Gains from Global Linkages: Trade in Services and Movements of Persons*, New York: St Martins Press.

Hillman, Ayre L. and Weiss, Avi (1999), 'A theory of permissible illegal immigration', *European Journal of Political Economy*, **15**, pp. 585–604.

6. The Business of International Migration

John Salt

THE NEW CONTEXT

The last quarter century has seen the study of international migration come of age. Perhaps it should be no surprise that the growth in academic interest should parallel the ascent of migration issues within the international political agenda. Today we are more than ever aware of the complexities of our subject and the need for interdisciplinary approaches, while at the same time appreciating the importance of providing policy-related information and advice. Looking back, we can see how new issues have emerged. Asylum, for example, was hardly considered relevant when the first major international academic conference on international migration took place in 1979. Even in the 1980s some migration scholars refused to accept that the movement of the highly-skilled, associated with the globalisation of corporate activity, was really international migration at all. Today, there are many who would argue similarly against the pendular cross-border movements currently endemic in Central and Eastern Europe (CEE): this is not migration, they would say. But as we look into the twenty-first century, I would argue that we need to look for new expressions of international migration and new ways of conceptualising and understanding them.

European migration vocabulary has become rich in novel terms: 'transit migration', 'incomplete migration', 'migrant trafficking', 'petty trading', 'labour tourism', and others. Central and Eastern Europe and the former Soviet Union, a region of controlled emigration and limited immigration under Communism has, since 1989, become a highly complex migration field. New ethnically-based migrations are a visible manifestation of older nationalisms and minorities and recall patterns of migration stopped by the descending Iron Curtain in the late 1940s.

These eastern novelties supplement the legacy of half a century of immigration in Western Europe which has seen even the former Mediterranean migrant fountains of Iberia and the classical lands become poles of attraction. The result of these developments has been the creation of a new European international migration regime that is part of an evolving global mobility framework which challenges our traditional thinking about the concept of migration.

Such challenges have increasingly become a feature of debates about immigration in North America and Australasia which have traditionally adopted a different starting point from those in Europe. In the 1990s in Australia, Canada and the US, the contribution of migrants to economic development was more likely to be stressed. Underlying much of the discussion about immigration in these countries is the question of their ability to compete for skills in the world's 'migration market'. Put simply, how can immigration best help the Australian and North American economies? Such a debate has hardly started in Europe.

In this chapter I suggest that we need new ways of conceptualising migration and to argue that it is now a global business. To begin with, we need to unpack what we mean by migration.

THE NATURE OF MIGRATION

When we use the term 'migration', it is not immediately clear what is meant. Traditionally, it has been associated with some notion of permanent settlement, or at least long-term sojourn. In reality, it is a sub-category of a more general concept of 'movement', embracing a wide variety of types and forms of human mobility, each capable of metamorphosing into something else through a set of processes which are increasingly institutionally driven. What we then define as migration is an arbitrary choice, and may be time-specific.

Let us look at some of these movements. The concept of permanent migration, for example, is epitomised in the idea of new lands of opportunity, perhaps typified by Australia. But today what we mean by 'permanent' is no longer clear; where it occurs for the most part it does so indirectly, as a development of previous temporary migrations, mainly through family reunion and family formation. Indeed, most 'permanent' settlement today may be associated with return migration to their home countries by former labour migrants and by certain ethnic and national groups such as German *Ausseidler*, Ingrian Finns, Bulgarian Turks, Pontion Greeks, and Romanian Magyars.

Most voluntary migration in recent decades has featured temporary labour migrants, yet this is an enormously diverse group, including au pairs and domestic servants, agriculture, construction and manufacturing workers, hotel, catering, and cleaning staff. Many of them are seasonal, others are frontier workers, or perhaps they are highly skilled corporate secondees. Transit migrants are a 1990s innovation and predominantly an Eastern European phenomenon: people who enter the territory of a state in order to travel on to another. Many of them, however, are unable to do so and their presence has turned Poland, Hungary and other countries in the region from corridors into vestibules.

Young people are traditionally mobile. Students are normally admitted for limited time periods. They are little studied but, as we shall see, very large in number and increasingly touted for their cheque books. Many in their teens and twenties backpack as working holidaymakers, perhaps in pursuit of experience and language training to further their career development.

During the last few years, asylum seekers and others fleeing war situations have dominated policy attention. Some of them are accepted as genuine refugees, others on humanitarian grounds, such as ELR in the UK, or given some form of temporary protected status, as with many fleeing from former Yugoslavia.

Possibly growing in number are migrants who have placed themselves in an irregular position, mostly after entering the host country legally. Clandestine entry is more likely where there are extensive land borders or long and difficult coastlines close to sources of potential immigrants. Many have placed their destinies in the hands of traffickers and human smugglers.

There are numerous other international movers whose status easily blends into that of migrant: cross-border commuters, labour tourists and petty traders, perhaps engaged in incomplete migration, a state of being in which most of their livelihood is derived from frequent short-term visits to other countries. The new migration space in Central and Eastern Europe and the former Soviet Union is replete with such novelties.

Finally, the mobility spectrum must take some account of the vast numbers of tourists and business travellers. Not only may they take on the characteristics of temporary migrants, but in sustaining a global network of travel infrastructure they help reduce the friction of distance which ultimately makes migration easier for everyone. For many of them, brief trips abroad are fact-finding missions which ultimately lead to longer-term moves; for others, business travel is a substitute for two or three-year corporate secondment.

It is important that these diverse groups are not seen as discrete, since one type of migration or journey may be transposed into another. For example, an overseas student may marry and stay on; an asylum seeker be given leave to remain; or a landed immigrant fail and go home. It does not therefore make sense to think in terms of rigid categories, nor to place 'migration' at some defined point on the mobility continuum. Migration streams, seen as mobility streams, are dynamic and pliant, involve different types of people and motivations, have different roles and methods of insertion into host societies, and are influenced and managed by different agencies and institutions. They present, and result from, wide-ranging business opportunities.

MIGRATION AS A BUSINESS

Traditionally, international migration has been conceived of as a relationship between, on the one hand, an individual or household moving for purposes of permanent settlement or work and, on the other, a government acting as gatekeeper for entry into a country and acquisition of its citizenship. Most explanatory theoretical frameworks are based on this notion. However, not only have many existing migration theories proved to have low predictive power because of the inherent complexities of the phenomena they seek to explain, but they are manifestly unable to cope with the dynamism inherent in new contemporary movements.

These inadequacies have led to several attempts at re-evaluating and restructuring the existing theoretical basis of international migration. For example, the comprehensive review of Massey et al. (1993) emphasised the importance of distinguishing between theories to explain the initiation of migration flows and those to explain their development and continuation. More recently, Skeldon (1997) has shown how migration theories generally have evolved to take into account changing economic, social and environmental concerns, as new problems have required new approaches and new solutions. He and others (for example, Salt, 1992) have also indicated the need to link internal and international migration conceptually. One reason for this is the development of a set of institutions that operate at a range of geographical scales and which powerfully affect flows of labour, goods, finance and services in the modern economy at both national and international levels.

For those who have studied the subject over the last quarter century, one thing stands out: international migration is inevitable. It can be managed by states but not controlled by them. To the simple dichotomy of individual and state must be added the myriad of institutions which have become part of this management process. Today, international migration can also be regarded as a diverse international business, with a vast budget, providing hundreds of thousands of jobs world-wide, and managed by a set of individuals, agencies and institutions, each of which has an interest in developing a sector of the business. From this perspective, migration may be analysed in contractual terms.

Such a reconceptualisation has important consequences for researchers and policymakers. For the former, it requires the creation of new theoretical frameworks for analysis. In particular, it begs an understanding of all the vested interests involved. For governments, it raises questions about the nature and effectiveness of their regulatory mechanisms and policies. Often these are still framed largely in terms of a contractual relationship between migrants and the state. If migration is a business, then policymakers and managers need to adopt a business regulatory approach.

The migration business may be thought of as a system of institutionalised networks consisting of organisations, agents and individuals, each of which stands to gain some form of remuneration from international movement. In other words, there are vested interests in the promotion of migration. Even government departments have an interest in 'talking up' the problem in order to increase their budgetary allocations. While it is possible to identify some of these actors, current knowledge of their precise role, and of how much they gain economically from migration, is so far limited. There is much research to be done on the characteristics and motivations of the institutions involved. We need to know their aims and objectives, and how they function; who owns them, their size and scales of operation. It means going beyond a simple 'institutions' approach to one which emphasises business objectives.

Figure 6.1 The global migration business

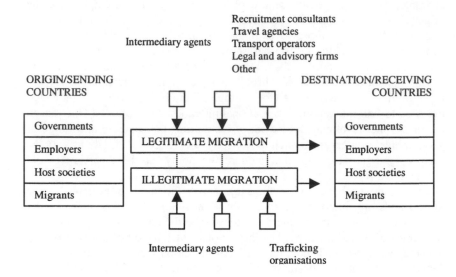

Let us identify the major players in this global migration business (Figure 6.1). At both origins and destinations there are governments, employers, host societies and the migrants themselves (actual and potential). Each have their reasons for supporting a given level of migration and for increasing movement in both short and long terms. Connecting them are streams of migrants, managed by a string of intermediary institutions designed in whole or in part to encourage and help people move. These institutions include recruitment and travel agencies, transport operators, legal and advisory firms, and others, all of whom make a profit out of migration, all of whom are ultimately involved in organising, even encouraging, human movement. Governments have a dual role. They are both institutional actors and systems managers.

The global migration business is not homogeneous. Most obviously, it may be divided into a legitimate (legal/regular) and an illegitimate (illegal/irregular) component, each of which may be further subdivided, be differently valued, and represent a particular business niche. To understand why migration occurs means studying the operation of the institutions which manage and control movement within these businesses. In order to do this I have chosen four generic migration business types: public, private, informal and irregular or illegitimate.

MIGRATION AS A PUBLIC BUSINESS: THE GOVERNMENT PERSPECTIVE

National Economies

The governments of those countries which have become net exporters of labour have a strong vested interest in promoting emigration, in the form of remittances and savings returned to their economies. For example, in 1997 remittances to Indonesia totalled £3.1 billion: in its current circumstances a sum that size is a godsend. In these circumstances, labour can be viewed as a commodity to be traded like any other. Using World Bank and national statistics, estimates have been made of the total amount of money remitted in private transactions by individuals (Keely and Tran, 1989; Russell and Teitelbaum, 1992). The estimates should be regarded as minimum since they are based only on officially recorded private transactions. In 1991, the figure was around £44.4 billion, more recent estimates (Martin, private communication) put it under £37.5 billion; still a lot of money. The total US aid figure at the same time—£32 billion—puts it into perspective. In consequence, sending governments have developed policies and procedures designed to maximise income from remittances, including encouragement for individual migrants, as well as the development of packages of skills for turnkey projects.

China has around 130 million surplus rural workers, and its overmanned state industrial enterprises laid off 9 million workers in 1996 alone. The Chinese government desperately wants to export as much of this unemployment as possible, and to this end strongly encourages emigration. It is now providing training facilities specifically designed to make its citizens more marketable as foreign labour. So far it has set up over 160 institutions specifically for this, 140,000 people have been trained, passed examinations, and gone to work abroad (Gao, 1998). It is not clear how many of these persons were unemployed prior to training; intuitively the expectation would be few of them. Nor are these numbers likely to make much of a dent in the overall labour surplus in China. Nevertheless, they represent a significant business investment by the Chinese government.

An infrastructure designed to help nationals abroad is a part of the process. Some sending governments have set up special ministries/units which have their own staffs and budgets (and therefore have an interest in increasing numbers) for this purpose. The Philippines Overseas Employment Administration is an example. Such a policy is partly out of social concern, but it is also a way of maximising the return of remittances by formalising procedures between governments, of encouraging more labour emigrants, and developing a more congenial client (sending country)–customer (destination country) relationship and thus a better environment for business.

Alternatively, the threat of refusing to control strong emigration pressures may be used: the best recent example is probably that from the Soviet Union in 1991, voiced by its deputy prime minister. He suggested that the removal of exit controls would release 20 million Russians into the rest of Europe (unless sufficient aid was forthcoming to keep them at home!). The prediction appears to have been the result of an opinion poll undertaken in 1990. Had the source been recognised—instead of just accepted—it would quickly have become clear that the fears were groundless. Opinion polls may indicate stated preferences, but are not a safe basis for making valid inferences about intentions and actions. But in the migration business all sorts of marketing ploys might be expected.

In due course, shortages of skills may also encourage sending countries to explore the migration market. The usual method is some kind of return of talent programmes, perhaps using embassy facilities to allow companies to recruit expatriates back into the home country: for example, some years ago UK employers were aided by UK missions in the US to attract back highly skilled Britons who had been part of the 'brain drain'. Whatever the rationale, the overall result is that the state becomes an active institution in the promotion and management of migration.

Destination country governments and governmental institutions also have an interest in promoting foreign immigration where it can be seen to be in the interests of economic growth. They have developed institutional apparatuses designed to maximise the benefits stemming from the immigration of those groups deemed to contribute most economically. An immigration market has developed within which states compete for high-quality human resources. Australia and Canada have for decades had a skill-based component in their immigration programmes upon which more emphasis has recently been placed. Since 1990, the US too has become more concerned about the quality of its intake. The 1990 Immigration Act sharply increased quotas of persons with the highest level skills, including corporate transferees. The first report to Congress in 1995 of the Commission for Immigration Reform stressed the importance of skill-based immigration in helping US businesses to compete in the global economy.

Students—Another Type of Public Business

Students provide an example of a migration public sector niche market. The provision of tertiary education internationally is now a major business and source of income, both directly (through fees received in destination countries) and indirectly (establishment of links) (Baker et al., 1996). The latest collated statistics enumerate 759,360 foreign students enrolled at the tertiary level in just 10 selected OECD countries. World-wide, an estimated 1.5 million students are studying overseas. That foreign students are big business is apparent for individual institutions. Between 1991 and 1995, overseas student numbers at University College London (UCL) rose from 1,289 to 1,716, their aggregate fees from £7.2 million to £11.4 million, about five per cent of the College budget.

In 1985, Australia changed its international student policy from an 'education for aid' to an 'education for trade' focus, a change which decreased the number of subsidised and sponsored international students but encouraged the recruitment of fee-paying overseas students by Australian education institutions. It has been estimated that foreign students represent a 0.5 per cent addition to the country's labour demand, and 0.25 per cent to labour supply. More important, though, is the overall economic impact. The Department of Employment, Education and Training calculated the value of the education export industry at $A1.1 billion in 1992, ranking it seventh in export earnings. Competition is growing. Australia is currently promoting the fact that its foreign students have an easier time working in part-time jobs than they would in the US. It is now using the economic crisis in South East and East Asia to highlight its colleges' relative cost advantages which have grown more pronounced after Asian currency devaluations against the US dollar and the British pound.

Foreign students in the US are estimated to have contributed £4.2 billion to the country's economy in 1993 (Institute of International Education, 1994, quoted in Skeldon, 1997). The 458,000 foreign students in the US in 1997 were estimated to have contributed more than £4.4 billion to the American economy in that year. Canada, with 95,000 foreign students, had plans to set up 25 educational information centres at Canadian consulates by 2000 in order to attract more, described by one marketing specialist with the Canadian government as a 'new spin in marketing activities' (Ruddick, 1997).

MIGRATION AS A PRIVATE BUSINESS: THE CORPORATE SECTOR

Conceptualisation of migration as movement, and the need to think of that movement as constituting an international business, applies to the acquisition and deployment of high-level skills. An example of a legitimate migration business is that dealing with corporate expatriation. It involves the international transfer of professional, managerial and technical staff between company locations world-wide, aided by a set of legal, relocation, counselling and advice institutions. The business is enormous. It is also extremely dynamic. We can only understand the migration processes which constitute it through the lens of corporate business organisation.

Numbers of corporate migrants are not great. For the UK, perhaps a quarter of a million coming into and going during the last ten years. But qualitatively the high levels of skill involved give them a significance not warranted by the numerical size of the movement alone. Some idea of that importance can be gained by the amounts that companies are prepared to spend in seconding their staff around the world. A few years ago we attempted to estimate how much companies invested in corporate relocation, the bottom line of which also serves as an indicator of the profit to be derived from staff transfers. The study analysed the cost to UK companies of seconding staff to three destinations for three-year periods, based on their relocation packages (Table 6.1). Relating these results to the number of corporate transfers per year suggests that transnational corporations in the UK are spending about £4.2 billion per year on moving their highly-skilled staff. To put the figure in perspective, the annual UNHCR budget is around £625 million. By any stretch of the imagination this is big business, driven by corporate needs in a global economy, aided by a panoply of agencies and institutions designed for the purpose.

Table 6.1 The net annual cost of a three-year international secondment

	Frankfurt	Los Angeles	Singapore
Employee's earnings			
£30,000 per annum	£56,300	£44,000	£75,300
£50,000 per annum	£87,600	£73,500	£102,000

The nature of migration business can best be understood in terms of corporate aims and structures, and their interaction with the careers of their staffs. The relationship between corporate requirements and career development systems can be seen in the following example of a migration chain within one company (Figure 6.2). It is in effect a vacancy chain, consisting of a series of related moves which in this case took eight months to complete. At first sight, the chain was precipitated by the closure of an office in Bahrain. However, this event was known in advance and its consequences fed into career planning. The Bahrain man had a lateral (non-promotional) move to a neighbouring part of the region in which he was a specialist. In turn, the company wished to move the Dubai occupant to Taipei in a planned promotion career move. Meanwhile, back in London a new unit was being created in which a vacancy occurred requiring skills held by, among others, the man in Milan. He was due for a move anyway as part of his career development. The ensuing Milan vacancy was suitable for the man in Taipei whose career had been mainly in the Far East and who was ready for European experience. What really triggered the chain? Office closure in the Middle East? Creation of a new unit in London? Rather surprisingly, perhaps, career development thinking focused on the need to move the man in Milan because he had been there long enough and required new experience. Therein lay the trigger, and events in Bahrain and London were brought into a pre-existing train of thought and not the other way round.

Figure 6.2 The corporate migration chain

What we see here is an illustration of the commonplace that migration involves the physical movement of human beings. At any one time large international companies are involved in complex networks of corporate secondment which are extremely expensive. I argued earlier that this movement occurs at various points on a mobility continuum. From time to time developments occur that shift 'types' of movement along this continuum, such as the introduction of new ways of working, or changes in technology. In fact, the highly skilled are best thought of as repositories of expertise which is almost infinitely divisible. Movement of their expertise may or may not involve a physical move by an individual. If it does involve a physical move, then the duration away may range from days to years.

Evidence from some modern business organisations suggests that companies are moving from highly-skilled migration in its traditional sense (for example, overseas assignments or contracts for periods of a year or more) to multiple strategies for acquiring and moving expertise. Such strategies will combine different forms of physical movement of staff and also include transmission or acquisition of knowledge without a physical presence being required at the destination: moving the mind without the body.

These premises suggest that migration for extended periods by the highly skilled is but one element in a much broader geography of the movement of expertise. Acceptance of such a view raises a new set of issues. It may be hypothesised that the costs of acquiring highly-specialised expertise encourage employers to contract for it on an 'as-you-need' basis, leading to the evolution of a highly-skilled internationally mobile elite, with very specialised skills, employed on a sub-contractual basis for limited periods. In short, expertise may be acquired in new and different ways: through shorter secondments or even business travel; by local acquisition; or through the use of new information technologies and international networking.

The speed and dense network of modern air travel have made it much easier to disseminate global expertise. Intuitively, it might be expected that the high costs of expatriation and of foreign recruitment would be obviated by increased levels of business travel, which would substitute for migration. Migration studies have traditionally eschewed consideration of short-term visits within mobility regimes, but there is empirical evidence that migration, secondment, short-term assignments and business visits are increasingly substitutable. We cannot therefore divorce the migration of expertise from its related package of movements.

An alternative strategy is through localised acquisition of expertise, rather than by physical transfer or distant recruitment in the external labour market. Localisation may be achieved directly through overseas branches and wholly-owned subsidiaries, indirectly through collaboration with foreign partners on an equity-sharing or non-equity basis, or through international or local consultancy firms. The implications are that as trans-national corporations (TNCs) become more decentralised and multidivisional they will make less use of their internal labour markets in assembling expertise at various international locations. The role of short-term mobility of key staff, including consultants, and of telecommunications, is likely to increase correspondingly. Migration is thus only one component in an integrated corporate mobility regime.

The application of information technology (IT) presents employers with a third set of options to communicate and transfer expertise. Although low-skilled migrant labour usually must be physically present to perform tasks, the highly-skilled contribute knowledge that, traditionally, either is transferred directly (decisions or advice) or requires a physical presence (collaboration). Because new IT supports both direct transfer of knowledge and collaboration among multiple, geographically dispersed actors, it has the power to reduce the growth of physical mobility amongst the highly-skilled.

The consequences of such movements of expertise in a European network of around 40 states and a global network of 200, have barely begun to be considered. The indications are that they can only be studied in an integrated analytical framework embracing all types of mobility.

MIGRATION AS AN INFORMAL BUSINESS

A rather different type of migration business has developed in Central and Eastern Europe where what was in many respects an international migration vacuum a decade ago, has been filled with an anthill of intense, short-term trans-border movements.

Tourist Workers and Tourist Traders

Associated with the informal economies in CEE are the various types of tourist traders and tourist workers. Almost by definition these are uncounted and uncountable, though some estimates have been made. One suggestion is that 20–25 million border crossings are made annually within the CEE region and between there and Western Europe by small business tourist traders, and that 600–700,000 persons from CEE countries are engaged in tourist working in Western Europe, compared with 300,000 legally employed contract workers (Morawska, 1999). Both tourist traders and tourist workers make multiple crossings annually. What both types are doing is earning their wages in high-income countries while spending them in their lower-cost home states. The income they generate for their home countries is an important element in the overall process of economic transformation.

Informally employed tourist workers satisfy an increasing demand in Western Europe 'for undocumented, cheap and dispensable labour for construction work, personal services and small shops and for buyers and sellers of contraband merchandise' (Morawska, 1999: 9). Informalisation of the economies of CEE countries has also occurred, frequently in association with employment abroad. A study in Poland suggested that 25–30 per cent of wages in a sample of private firms in 1995 were paid informally outside the state welfare and fiscal system (Bak, 1995, quoted by Morawska, 1999). The uncertainty in such forms of employment was tempered by many of those involved seeking temporary work sojourns abroad. Such short-term labour migration has thus become an integral part of household survival strategies. It also constitutes a substantial business element for economies in transformation.

Tourist workers from Eastern Europe and the CIS are in growing demand in the more economically advanced CEE countries, finding jobs in agriculture, handicrafts, services, and small garment manufacturers: one estimate is that 700–800,000 come to Poland each year and that such workers make up about twenty to twenty-five per cent of the employees in private Polish firms (Bak, 1995). Overall, it has been estimated that border and bazaar commerce in 1996 constituted over a quarter of Poland's entire trade with its eastern neighbours, and that the value of goods purchased by Ukrainian tourist-traders alone represented nearly 50 per cent of the value of Poland's official exports to that country (Bak and Kulawczuk, 1996).

Official short-term contract workers are another group in CEE countries coming from further east, mainly from the western parts of the former USSR. In 1997 there were reckoned to be over 25,000 of them in the Czech Republic, 15,000 in Hungary and 12,000 in Poland, their employment dependent on the continuing flexibilisation of the economies of those countries.

The Warsaw Bazaar

The mechanisms by which these movements occur can be illustrated by the example of the Warsaw Bazaar, studied by Okolski (1995). The bazaar, located at a stadium site in the centre of the city, is a large market where foreigners, as well as Poles, come to buy and sell goods and find occasional employment. Set up spontaneously in 1989 by petty traders, it has since become highly organised, with wholesale activities as well as a large number of retail outlets run by citizens of many countries. Goods are no longer smuggled through the Polish border by tens of thousands of false tourists, but as a rule come from newly established Poland-based small plants, the operation of which is highly internationalised, but whose employees are often irregular migrants. Each day the market is visited by 20–30,000 persons, around 60 per cent of whom are foreigners. Its estimated turnover in 1995 was £21 billion, with an export value of £220 million—1.5 per cent of the total value of all goods exported from Poland and 8.5 per cent of expenditures made in Poland by all foreign citizens. To put this in context, in 1995 only four Polish firms recorded higher exports. The bazaar employs over 6,500 persons, of whom at least 3,000 are foreign, but it is estimated that its multiplier effect provides 60,000 jobs.

What we have here is a migration system that functions as a complex international business. Now of considerable importance to the Polish economy, it has been allowed to grow from almost completely informal beginnings, entirely migrant centred, to a largely formalised operation supported and encouraged by the authorities. The migrations associated with it can be explained almost entirely in terms of its structure, evolution and institutional behaviour.

MIGRATION AS AN ILLEGITIMATE BUSINESS: TRAFFICKING IN HUMAN BEINGS

The darker side of the migration business is trafficking in human beings, a process which threatens to create a new geography of international movement. It must be recognised, however, that for some asylum seekers traffickers represent their only hope of escape. In these circumstances, traffickers might appear as 'white knights'. Traffickers increasingly determine the choice of migrants' destination countries and the routes taken. Their channelling of migrants reflects their use of local knowledge, of key locations, and their wider intelligence of international weaknesses in regimes of migration control. Knowledge of the trafficking business is currently sporadic, largely anecdotal and often highly sensitive (Salt and Hogarth, 2000).

Trafficking is increasingly perceived to be a business of considerable complexity. The term 'trafficking' itself is now frequently used in connection with the illegal and exploitative employment of those who are trafficked, usually involving debt bondage. This business includes many who are forced to work in sweatshops for extremely low pay, after being misled about the conditions they would face. More often it is used in connection with the trafficking of women and children for purposes of sexual exploitation. Indeed, recent literature on trafficking, together with public concern, is dominated by this subject. 'Human smuggling' is a term that is increasingly used to describe the nefarious actions of those whose trafficking roles are mainly confined to helping migrants cross borders illegally. In practice, it is doubtful if this terminological distinction between trafficking and smuggling is very useful, though there is an important conceptual distinction between a focus on the employment at destination (as in debt bondage) and one on the means by which migrants are assisted to move.

Trafficking: Its Importance, Size and Scale

The illegal trafficking of migrants is widely recognised to be a major international problem. In addition to security issues, the problem of trafficking is also one of human rights. Migrants who are trafficked may be exploited by being charged extortionate prices for their journey, having their money and belongings stolen, having their identities stolen (passports and other travel documents, identity cards, etc.), and being trapped into debt bondage. They may also be subject to inhuman conditions and to physical abuse, sometimes resulting in death.

It is uncertain how large a business trafficking is, how much money it generates, and how many people it employs. Nevertheless, it is on its way to becoming an established branch of well-organised international gangster syndicates, according to one estimate bringing in an annual income of about $US5 to $US7 billion, and perhaps as profitable as drug-smuggling (Widgren, 1994). To individual migrants, the costs of trafficking vary enormously depending on their nationality, ethnicity, and on the means of transport employed and the distances involved. The total annual business of trafficking Chinese to the US in the early 1990s was estimated to be worth some $US3 billion to the traffickers (*Far Eastern Economic Review*, 8 April 1993, as cited in Skeldon, 1994).

There are almost insuperable difficulties in assessing how many migrants are trafficked, though the usual starting point is the incidence of irregular and undocumented migration. Police evidence in practically all Western European States suggests a growth in stocks of illegal aliens working and residing in these countries (Expert Group of the Budapest Group, 1996). Statistics on border apprehensions seem to confirm the trend, although they may reflect increased vigilance rather than more transgressions. Despite attempts such as the Budapest process, which aims to manage flows of irregular migrants, and suggestions that some forms of irregular migration are now better controlled (for example, asylum seekers), it is anticipated that unless efficient counter-measures are established there will be a continued increase in inflows into Europe outside legal channels.

There is evidence to suggest that traffickers are behind a substantial proportion of irregular migration, though how much can, at best, only be guessed. Where estimates of the extent of illegal border crossings organised by traffickers have been made, it is likely that they have undercounted the problem because of a reliance on statistics of border apprehensions. One of the few attempts to estimate the scale of trafficking in Europe is that of Widgren (1994). He suggested that approximately 15–30 per cent of those managing to reach their destinations in Western European countries in 1993 used the services of traffickers during some part of their journey, the proportion being slightly higher for asylum seekers (20–40 per cent), resulting in a trafficked total of 100,000 to 220,000 persons. Evidence from Central and Eastern European states, in replies to anti-trafficking surveys, suggests similar proportions (Expert Group of the Budapest Group, 1995).

There is limited statistical information on numbers of illegal migrants apprehended while being trafficked across borders (IOM, 1998). A major problem is in distinguishing trafficked and non-trafficked illegal migrants and also accounting for the fact that one individual may attempt a border crossing several times, resulting in multiple counting. Where data are collected, presentation of the results may be partial in that only selected nationalities (perhaps the ten largest) are recorded (Lederer, 1997). Furthermore, there are few data which allow trends in numbers to be identified.

The limited trend evidence presents mixed results on whether trafficking is growing. Even where the source used is identical, revisions from year to year in the data may make for differences in trends. Federal border data for Germany for the period 1990–96 suggest that trends in apprehensions for illegal migrants as a whole, those engaged in trafficking, and numbers of individual migrants trafficked show some differences. Apprehensions of illegal immigrants peaked in 1993 then fell in each succeeding year. In contrast, numbers of cases of trafficking which were relatively low in the early 1990s, peaked in 1993, fell back in 1994 but rose in 1995 and 1996. However, the numbers apprehended as traffickers, which also peaked in 1993, fell in 1994, rose in 1995, but fell in 1996, suggesting that latterly the number of traffickers per case was falling and therefore that one trafficker per case was becoming more common (Bundesministerium des Inneren, 1997). It appears then that in 1996 an individual trafficker was responsible for more migrants. Numbers of trafficked migrants also peaked in 1993, fell in 1994, and have risen every year since. Thus in 1995 and 1996, numbers of illegal migrants recorded were falling, numbers of cases of trafficking were rising, numbers of traffickers apprehended fell in 1996 while numbers of trafficked individual migrants rose throughout. In 1997, the situation may have changed: the number of illegal migrants in the first six months of 1997 rose by 30 per cent compared with the previous year. In contrast, cases of trafficking during the same period fell by 6 per cent while the number of migrants trafficked who were apprehended rose by 17 per cent (Severin, 1997). These statistics would appear to suggest that the number of migrants per trafficking operation was continuing to rise, and that the trafficking business was expanding.

One interpretation of these figures is that trafficking in migrants was becoming relatively more important and the process more efficient, although the poor quality of many of the data and the effort expended by the authorities in apprehending and charging illegal entrants mean that such a conclusion must be approached with caution. Some support for this interpretation, however, comes from US enforcement data: trends in numbers of 'smugglers of aliens located' fell from 21,901 in 1990 to 13,458 in 1996, but at the same time numbers of 'aliens located who were smuggled into the US' rose from 71,049 to 122,233 (INS, 1997).

Many references can be found to the sums of money paid to traffickers. Most of the information is 'event related', i.e., it refers to individual cases. It is difficult to come up with anything approaching a set tariff since the sums paid vary according to the level of service provided. As might be expected, the costs are positively related to distance (Table 6.2). Hence trafficking to the US costs more than to Europe. For similar destinations, however, there may be sharp differences in amounts paid: one study found a range from $3,000 to $30,000 (Smith, 1997). In some cases, prices are known for individual services including fraudulent documentation, transport, guided border crossing and job brokering. Examples include $4,000 transport to Lithuania (IOM, 1997), fraudulent documentation and other initial expenditures, $600 to $1,500 for migrants trafficked from the Dominican Republic (IOM 1996), and $1,500 for obtaining a US visa (*News*, 14 April 1997).

Although resort to trafficking varies for different national and ethnic groups, by gender and by sector of employment, studies consistently show trafficking's increasing importance in flows of irregular migrants. Around 40 per cent of transit migrants interviewed in Turkey were without a valid document and almost all of them arrived with the aid of traffickers. One-third, mainly Iranians, ethnic Turks from Iraq, and Africans, were planning to use traffickers to help them reach their final destinations (IOM, 1995). Findings of the German Border Police suggest that more than 60 per cent of the foreigners who illegally entered Germany in 1995, most of them from and via Central and Eastern Europe, were guided by trafficking organisations (Ternes, 1996). An estimated 2,000 of the 19,000–25,000 foreigners currently working as prostitutes in Italy had used the services of traffickers (IOM, 1996). A similar story applies to the case of Chinese irregular migration into Central and Eastern Europe (IOM, 1995).

While it would appear that trafficking is organised, often highly so, there is less evidence that 'organised crime' *per se* is heavily involved. For the most part it appears that the main operators are more likely to be conventional criminal groups than internationally organised crime syndicates. It appears that trafficking is a business with relatively low entry costs and one that can be carried out by small-scale entrepreneurs. The primary motivation is that of high profits and low risks (Lederer and Nickel, 1997). The major exception would seem to be the Chinese Triads (IOM, 1995), Italian Mafia (Global Survival Network, 1997), and, perhaps, Vietnamese in Germany diversifying from their main activity of cigarette smuggling (Spiegel, 1996).

Table 6.2 The cost of trafficking

Destination / Route Taken	Price ($US per person)
Europe, via	
Bulgaria-Europe	4,000
Greece-France, Italy, Germany	800–1,200
Turkey-Greece	1,400
Hungary-Slovenia	1,500
Kurdistan-Germany	3,000
North Africa-Spain	2,000–3,500
Sri Lanka-Turkey	4,000
Pakistan-Turkey	4,000
Dominican Republic-Europe	4,000–10,000
Dominican Republic-Australia	5,000
China-Europe	10,000–15,000
Afghanistan / Lebanon-Germany	5,000–10,000
Iraq-Europe	4,100– 5,000
Iran-Europe	5,000
Palestine-Europe	5,000
US, via	
China-New York	35,000
China-US	30,000
Middle East-US	1,000–15,000
Pakistan-India-US	25,000
Mexico-Los Angeles	200–400
Canada, via	
Iran, Iraq	10,000
Venezuela-Canada	1,000–2,500
Ireland, via	
Africa-Ireland	5,000
Eastern Europe-Ireland	3,000
Others	
China-Argentinia	30,000
Arab sates-UAE	2,000–3,000
Philippines-Malaysia, Indonesia, Taiwan	3,500

Source: See text.

Trafficking: A Business Model

What follows here is an attempt to go beyond the headline concept of trafficking, based as it is mainly on anecdote, and presented either as a purely criminal activity or as an unfortunate human drama, and produce a hypothetical model of trafficking constituted as a business (Figure 6.3) (Salt and Stein, 1997). This should be regarded as merely a first attempt and needs to be revisited frequently as information becomes available. For example, there is a need to incorporate return movements more fully into the model.

The model presents trafficking as an intermediary system in the global migration business, facilitating movement between origin and destination countries. It is not meant to be a description of actual trafficking organisations, nor does it assume any particular size of operation. It is an attempt to understand how such organisations operate and the functions described in the model are intended to be applicable both to large and small-scale trafficking syndicates. Some large trafficking organisations may encompass all aspects of the model; other, smaller ones, may operate in only part of the system described.

Throughout, the trafficking system involves a number of elements, in particular the planning of smuggling operations, information gathering, finance and a set of specific technical and operational tasks. There are clear inputs and outputs to the system. The main inputs are the migrants themselves and the principal object of trafficking is to transport them from origin to destination countries. Trafficking organisations act as conduits for these migrants. The final output of the system is the insertion of a migrant into some element of the labour market or society of the destination country; in other words, migrants settled 'in place'. The inputs and outputs are linked by various trafficker roles, guided along geographical routeways, connecting a set of transit countries. Sometimes borders or gateways into particular countries may be temporarily blocked (for example, because of increased border security) requiring the rerouting of migrants via some other transit country.

The trafficking process itself is divided into three consecutive stages: first, the process of mobilisation by which migrants are recruited in origin countries; second, the requirements en route as migrants are transported from origin to destination countries; and third, the processes by which migrants are inserted and integrated into destination countries. Centralised systems of planning and management may exist, particularly with large-scale organisations, and there may be parallel businesses, such as trafficking in drugs, stolen goods, or money-laundering.

Figure 6.3 The trafficking business

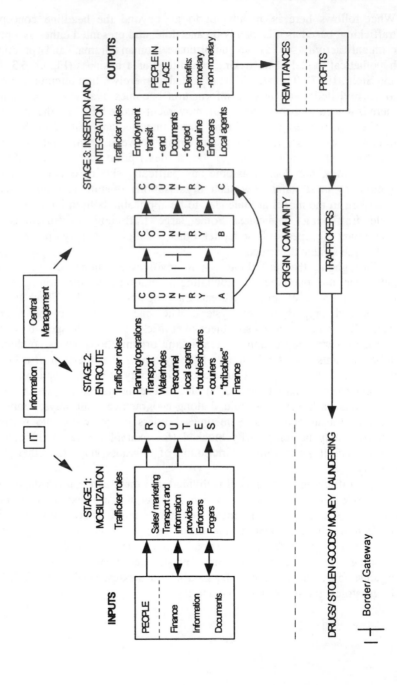

Critical to the survival of trafficking operations are systems of information-gathering. Some information is specific, such as that on travel documents necessary to produce forgeries or knowledge of when border control staff numbers will be low, of who will be on duty, of how well specific borders are policed and when. More general information includes which countries are the easiest targets, the best way of exploiting asylum procedures, or which routes and means of transport are the most reliable. In all such cases it is necessary to have systems and people in place to collect the relevant information, and who are able to use it to the best advantage sometimes at short notice. For example, trafficking agents are known to have rented flats on the sea front at Bari, Italy, from where they were able to watch the directions taken by coastguards going out on patrol. They then signalled to their boats offshore to come in via a different direction.

The model also includes a set of functional tasks or 'trafficker roles', including the provision of adequate financing, transport, information, documentation and forged documents. Each of these functions may be further subdivided into specific technical and operational tasks, for example, the production of counterfeit money, obtaining stolen travel documents, the adaptation of vehicles to hide aliens, and the transport of aliens across borders. This separation of tasks is an important method of survival in and of itself for trafficking operations. By a clear division of labour, and by carefully defining individual and group tasks, the organisation as a whole is protected so that if criminal investigations or mistakes occur only small elements of the organisation are exposed.

Understood as a business, trafficking is, like legitimate businesses, adept at circumventing systems designed to control it. As some avenues close others are opened up. The business is remarkably responsive to change and always seems to remain one or several steps ahead of those seeking to control it. National authorities often have to agree on concerted action, and this takes time, so that relative to the ability of governments to control them, traffickers demonstrate greater flexibility, organisation and speed of response. This means that unless the operational systems of trafficking are properly understood, and the interests involved in the process and contradictions of migration policies directly confronted, countries may lose control of their borders.

CONCLUSION

The last two decades have seen a substantial extension to the migration lexicon. New types of movement have challenged the narrowness of traditional thinking about what constitutes a migration. We must now come to grips with a paradox: the vast majority of people do not migrate nor do they wish to; increasing numbers of people are moving internationally. At the same time, the sheer complexity has presented almost unfathomable dilemmas for states wishing to develop effective migration policies. Several of these have been brought home to me forcibly in the last two years while working with the Council of Europe to develop a continent-wide migration management strategy, for example, how to persuade an origin state to take back those of its citizens who have entered another state illegally.

What is suggested in this chapter is an approach, not a panacea. Its main message is to suggest that these movements, including those which we have always assumed to be international migration, can be considered as the component parts of a world-wide industry, consisting of a series of businesses where it is possible to identify vested interests which seek to develop, manage and promote migration flows. To explain why, where and how people move needs an understanding of those interests. By extension, policy measures to deal with their consequences need to focus on them and not the migrants.

Analysis of the business of international migration therefore supplements attempts at explanations based on individual preference and choice. It allows us to consider the degree to which movement of the individual is organised, how choices are constrained, and how people's behaviour may adapt to or side-step rules of practice. It helps us to understand the two-way relationship which exists between migrants and those who govern the business. In this scheme of things we may conceive of migrants as products, commodities and consumers. The trick will be not to lose sight of the fact that, first and foremost, they are people.

REFERENCES

Bak, M. (1995), *Nieformalny Rynek Pracy*, Warsaw: Oficyna Naukowa.
Bak, M. and P. Kulawczuk, (eds) (1996), *Informal sector in foreign trade*, Warsaw: Institute for Private Enterprise and Democracy.
Baker, M., F. Robertson, A. Taylor, and L. Doube, (1996), *The Labour Market Effects of Overseas Students*, Canberra: Bureau of Immigration, Multicultural and Population Research.
Bundesministerium des Inneren, (1997), *Texte zur inneren Sicherheit*, Vol. II/1997.
Expert Group of the Budapest Group (1995), *Report of the Expert Group on the Five Themes Selected for Examination by the Budapest Group*, Third Meeting by the Budapest Group, Zurich, 14–15 September 1995.
Expert Group of the Budapest Group (1996), The Need for Reinforced Co-operation Between All European States to Tackle Illegal Migration: An Evaluation of the Implementation of the Recommendations of the 1993 Ministerial Conference and of the Role of the Budapest-process, General report by the Expert Group of the Budapest Group, Ljubljana, 13–14 June 1996.
Gao, G. (1998), *People's Republic of China: Country Report*, Meeting on International Migration and Labour Markets in Asia, Tokyo, Government of Japan, OECD, ILO.
Global Survival Network (1997), *Crime and Servitude: An Exposé of the Traffic in Women for Prostitution from the Newly Independent States*, a report in collaboration with the International League for Human Rights, Washington, DC: Global Survival Network.

Institute of International Education (1994), *Open Doors 1993–94*, Report on International Educational Exchange.

IOM (1995), Chinese Migrants in Central and Eastern Europe: The Cases of the Czech Republic, Hungary and Romania, Migration Information Programme, Budapest, pamphlet.

IOM (1997), The Baltic Route: The Trafficking of Migrants Through Lithuania, Migration Information Programme, Budapest, pamphlet.

IOM (1998), Analysis of Data and Statistical Resources Available in the EU Member States on Trafficking in Humans, Particularly in Women and Children, for Purposes of Sexual Exploitation, unpublished paper.

Keely, C. and B.G. Tran (1989), 'Remittances from labor migration: evaluations, performance and implications' *International Migration Review*, **23** (3).

Koser, K. (1998), 'Negotiating entry into 'fortress Europe': the migration strategies of 'spontaneous' asylum seekers', in P. Muus (ed.), *The Exclusion and Inclusion of Refugees in Contemporary Europe*, Utrecht: ERCOMER.

Lederer, H.W. (1997), 'Migration und Integration in Zahlen, ein Handbuch', in *Auftrag der Beauftragten der Bundesregierung für Ausländerfragen*, European Forum for Migration Studies, Bamberg.

Lederer, H.W. and A. Nickel (1997), *Illegale Ausländerbeschäftigung in der Bundesrepublik Deutschland*, Forschungsinstitut, Abteilung Arbeits und Sozialforschung, Friedrich-Ebert-Stiftung.

Massey, D.S., J. Arango, G. Hugo, A. Kouaouci, A. Pellegrino, J.E. Taylor (1993), 'Theories of international migration: review and appraisal', *Population and Development Review*, 20 (4): 699–751.

Morawska, E. (1999), 'Trans-national migration in the enlarged European Union: a perspective from east Central Europe', Forthcoming in: *Robert Schuman Centre Working Papers*, European University Institute, Florence, Italy.

Okolski, M. (1995), Report to the OECD From the SOPEMI Correspondent for Poland, OECD: Paris.

Okolski, M. (1997), 'Incomplete Migration—a New Form of Mobility in Central and Eastern Europe: the Case of Ukrainian Migrants', paper given at Pultusk Conference, Poland, 11–13 December 1997.

Ruddick, E. (1997), 'Report to the OECD From the SOPEMI Correspondent for Canada', OECD, Paris.

Russell, S.S. and M. Teitelbaum (1992), 'International Migration and International Trade', *World Bank Discussion Papers 160*, Washington.

Salt, J. (1992), 'The Relationship Between International and Internal Labour Migration', in A. Champion and A. Fielding (eds), *Migration Processes and Patterns: Volume 1, Research Progress and Prospects*, London: Belhaven.

Salt, J. and J. Hogarth, (2000), *Trafficking in Europe: a Review of the Evidence*, Report to the International Organisation for Migration, Geneva.

Salt, J. and J. Stein (1997), 'Migration as a business: the case of trafficking', *International Migration*, 35(4): 467–94.

Severin, K. (1997), 'Illegal Einreise und internationale Schleuserkriminalität. Hintergründe, Beispiele und Massnahmen', *Aus Politik und Zeitgeschichte*, B46/97, 7: 11–19.

Skeldon, R. (1994), 'East Asian Migration and the Changing World Order', in W.T.S. Gould and A.M. Findlay (eds), *Population Migration and the Changing World Order*, Chichester: John Wiley & Sons.

Skeldon, R. (1997), *Migration and Development. A Global Perspective*, Harlow: Longman.
Der Spiegel, (1996), 'Mauer des Schweigens', **1**, pp. 56–7.
Smith, P.J. (ed.) (1997), *Human Smuggling: Chinese Migrant Trafficking and the Challenge to America's Immigration Tradition*, Washington, DC: CSIS.
Ternes, E. (1996), 'Report to the OECD From the SOPEMI Correspondent for Germany', OECD: Paris.
US Immigration and Naturalisation Service (1997), *Statistical Yearbook of the INS*, Washington DC: US Government Printing Office.
Widgren, J. (1994), 'Multilateral co-operation to combat trafficking in migrants and the role of international organisations', 11th IOM Seminar on Migration, October, Geneva.

7. The Dangers of Diaspora: Orientalism, the Nation State and the Search for a New Geopolitical Order

Ronald Skeldon

CONCEPTUAL BACKGROUND

Global patterns of population migration have changed markedly during the last half century, and so too have the ways we have thought about that migration. While real transformations in the migration system might have provided the context for new ideas, much of the shift reflects undercurrents of thinking in the social sciences in general. From narrowly focused models of migration that attempted to explain the causes and consequences of population movement, there has been a shift towards more qualitative, even introspective, interpretations. The almost overwhelming concern with internal migration of the 1960s has given way to the almost equally overwhelming concern with international migration of the 1990s. The words 'internal migration' have been virtually replaced by 'population redistribution', and in the area of international migration the word 'diaspora' has come to prominence. Elsewhere I have examined the transition in interpretations in international migration from assimilation through multiculturalism to diaspora (Skeldon, 1998). In this chapter I engage critically with the term itself.

To say that 'diaspora' has almost come to displace 'migration' by those studying the international movements of people over the last decade is but a slight exaggeration.[1] As the word literally means a scattering of peoples, the use of diaspora appears perfectly legitimate. Like so many words, however, it comes with a 'baggage' of nuances and implications, and one does not necessarily have to be a postmodernist to wish to deconstruct it into its various meanings. Until its recent incorporation into migration literature, the use of diaspora in the English language was primarily associated with the Jewish peoples who had been banished from their homeland and lived 'in diaspora'. Diaspora was also applied to other groups such as the Armenians or the Palestinians who had also been expelled from their homelands and lived scattered around the world. Peoples living in 'exile' was thus an integral part of the concept of diaspora together with the image of the migrant as victim.

Yet the implications of diaspora, as currently used, extend far beyond expulsion and victimisation to incorporate the idea of transnational communities that have evolved to such an extent that they have come to question the fundamental building block upon which the modern world has been constructed: the nation-state. Mass migration in an era of widely available, cheap and rapid communications has allowed the creation of 'deterritorialised' groups which owe allegiance to no single state but operate in transnational space with identities of their own. These communities are an integral part, it is argued, of the process of globalisation or, in the words of Appadurai (1996), 'modernity at large'. The separate ethnic communities in destination societies, promoted by the liberal policies of multiculturalism, identify primarily with co-ethnics rather than with the citizens of their chosen destination. The interaction with co-ethnics extends back across boundaries to areas of origin and outwards to other destinations and, in this way, the integrity of the nation-state is called into question.

The use of diaspora can be seen as part of the search for a new global order now that the Cold War certainties of a bi-polar world have been swept away. Identities and loyalties join economic factors at the centre of discussions of the consequences of human migration with security issues writ large. The origin and destination of the flows take on a geopolitical significance: do migrant communities in destination states act in the interests of origin states to destabilise the former if that is seen to be in the interests of the latter? Weak fundamentalist regimes may be able to exercise political advantage through diasporic networks. Conversely, dissident emigrant groups might be manipulated by their host societies to achieve advantage in origin states.[2] Thus the diaspora underlies the geopolitics of the new international relations.

However, such recent thinking may have become overly focused on the situation at one point in time rather than appreciating the nature of the dynamic process that is migration: the concept of diaspora, despite having brought undeniable insight, lacks the dynamic connotations of migration. Perhaps more importantly, there has been a 'fetishization' (*sic*) (Mitchell, 1997) diaspora which has suspended critical judgement and led to the assumption of homogeneity of flow, to an almost 'orientalist' interpretation that diasporas are coherent, monolithic entities. They are separate from the nation-state, deterritorialised forces of outsiders (or exiles) that are a threat to the identity of the insiders. I will examine critically this idea in the context of one migrant group that is now most commonly seen to have created a diaspora: the Chinese. Together with the British, the Indians, the Jews and a few other smaller groups, the Chinese have created a truly global network of communities, an 'ungrounded empire' (Ong and Nonini, 1997), and are now commonly seen to be in diaspora (for example, Wang and Wang, 1998).

OF DIASPORAS AND THE CHINESE

To apply diaspora to a dynamic, entrepreneurial people such as the Chinese does not at first appear intuitively obvious. Only a tiny minority of the Chinese as a whole live outside China and, with the exception of the arguably fading aspirations of a *Kuomingtang* government-in-exile in Taiwan, they have not been expelled from their homeland. Also, as Taiwan was an inalienable part of China, whether they had ever been truly expelled from their homeland was a moot point.

The migrations of the nineteenth and early twentieth centuries produced a global network of overseas Chinese communities, concentrated in the *Nanyang*, or the countries of South East Asia, where Chinese settlement dates back 'long before recorded history' (Reid, 1996: 17), but spreading to North, South and Central America as well as the Caribbean, southern Africa, Europe and Australasia. The Chinese truly were 'scattered' around the world.

However, there was more to the idea of the Chinese diaspora than simply a scattering of peoples. Implicit in the concept of communities-in-exile is the assumption that peoples are not assimilated into the societies of destination: they retain their distinct identities ready for the day when they can return home. This fits well with the Chinese concept of migration that considers that no self-respecting Chinese will leave home permanently but travels as a 'sojourner'.

Generally speaking, no Chinese will leave his home to seek his fortune at a distance unless he is in some way driven to do so ... No Chinese leaves his home not intending to return. His hope is always to come back rich, to die and be buried where his ancestors are buried (A.H. Smith cited in Purcell, 1965: 30).

From the point of view of the destination society, the sojourner does not wish, or is not allowed, to assimilate into that society. With the exposure of the myth of the American 'melting pot', that the assimilation of migrants from different cultural backgrounds to some new American norm was not occurring, the term diaspora came to prominence. Perhaps the first use of the term applied to the Chinese in this context was in an article by Lyman published originally in the mid-1970s (Lyman, n.d.). The designation 'sojourner' to the Chinese dates from much earlier: the classic exposition on the sojourner by Siu dates to the early 1950s but he traces its roots back much earlier (Siu, 1952–53).

OF CHINESE AND CHINESE MIGRANT GROUPS

One of the consequences of according such importance to transnational linkages within migrant groups in the concept of diaspora is that the diaspora community is seen as fairly homogeneous. The ties within the migrant group that extend across states should be stronger than those across different groups within the state, either at origin, or especially at destination. That such conditions may not always, or even ever, hold has done little, thus far at least, to diminish the attraction of the idea of diaspora.

Information on international migration comes primarily with reference to nation-states. Thus, our data refer to the number of Mexicans in the US, Pakistanis in the UK, Greeks in Australia and so on. While some national migrant groups are certainly more homogeneous than others, particular issues arise when the Chinese are considered and the 'Chinese diaspora' may imply a unity of migration that is more apparent than real.

National identity assumes some commonly accepted criteria that make one national population distinct from another. The 'idea' of the nation is, however, quite recent in history, dating from late eighteenth century Europe, and is constantly changing (Hobsbawm, 1990). It is a concept that has been diffusing throughout the developing world as countries newly independent from colonial empires struggled to establish some kind of common identity from the often artificial creations of colonialism. The ideas of common nation identities are diffusing at precisely the same time, however, as global forces, including increasing migration, are acting to erode national identities in favour of international values. China, never a colony, has nevertheless been profoundly affected by forces of modernisation and by questions of national identity in the twentieth century. In the words of Lucien Pye, contemporary China is not so much a 'civilization pretending to be a state but rather an empire claiming to be a nation-race' (cited in Dikotter, 1996: 599).

It is not, however, simply the so-called 'minority' peoples within China who need to be brought within a common identity, but also the Han peoples themselves. Although they are of one racial group and come from a common Confucian heritage with a virtually identical written script, there are significant differences among them in terms of spoken language, diet and folk culture. Variously termed 'ethnic groups', 'sub-ethnic groups', 'speech groups', or the Chinese word 'bang', the issue of ethnic divisions within the Han majority remains one of the intriguing research questions within China and is of direct relevance to the study of the Chinese diaspora. Wang (1988: 1) has argued, somewhat enigmatically, that the Chinese have never had a concept of identity but only a 'concept of Chineseness, of being Chinese and of becoming un-Chinese'. In terms of an identity based on place of origin, there is little between this broad sense of 'Chineseness' and the local family unit to which an individual belongs.

The critical questions as far as this chapter is concerned are the following: first, whether there is a truly Chinese diaspora or whether there are a series of separate diasporas based on specific place of origin of the groups concerned; second, whether any juxtaposing of the various Chinese groups with non-Chinese peoples in overseas destinations has forged a new composite sense of Chineseness; and third, whether the diaspora experience of the Chinese has forged new identities and, if so, whether these have expression in the structure and function of the diaspora communities.

OF IDENTITIES, SETTLERS AND SOJOURNERS

In 1990, and excluding Hong Kong and Macau, it was estimated that there were just over 30 million Chinese outside China and Taiwan (Poston, et al., 1994). A very significant proportion of that 30 million had, however, been born in overseas destinations and belonged to families which had been established overseas for several generations. In 1990, just over 85 per cent of the Chinese overseas were in Asian countries and were dominated by the long-established communities in Indonesia, Thailand, Malaysia, Singapore and the countries of Indo-China. The identity of the South East Asian Chinese has already been the focus of much attention, for example, Cushman and Wang (1988), Lim and Gosling (1983), Reid (1996) and Suryadinata (1997) to name only the major overview studies. Their minority status in all countries except Singapore in a region where China is one of the dominant powers has lent a certain geopolitical cachet to the debate: whether the Chinese overseas see themselves primarily as Chinese or as citizens of the states in which they live. If the former, do they then represent some kind of security threat to their host societies? This complex issue is not central to the current discussion but suffice to say here that there is little evidence of the Chinese overseas acting either as agents of Chinese expansionism or as active promoters of change back in China.

Whether the Chinese see themselves primarily as Chinese or as citizens of other countries appears a non-issue as they clearly can be both at the same time. Although the terms 'Irish overseas' or 'Scottish overseas' are not commonly used, the fact that citizens of the US, Canada or Australia of Irish or Scottish descent are proud of their heritage and become misty-eyed on St Patrick's or St Andrew's night in no way detracts from their American, Canadian or Australian citizenship. Migrants of European descent were always seen to be settlers: the 'Scottish emigrant', 'the Irish settler', and so on. Yet many European settlers did go home, and continue to go home. In the latter part of the nineteenth and the early twentieth centuries, the peak period of migration from across the Atlantic, about twenty per cent of Scandinavians and just under 40 per cent of English and Welsh returned home: between 40 and 50 per cent of Italians returned during the early twentieth century (Baines, 1991: 39; Nugent, 1992: 35). During the time of free migration from China to North America before the imposition of the exclusion acts, the incidence of return for Chinese, at around 47 per cent, was clearly comparable with that of Europeans (Chan 1990: 38). The contrast between a Chinese sojourner system and a European settler system is thus over-simplified as there were European sojourners and Chinese settlers. Transnational circulation, as implied in the concept of diaspora, is an integral part of all international migration systems.

Today, large numbers of Americans, Canadians and Australians of European descent return to their countries of origin upon retirement and these settler societies have become important countries of emigration. For example, between 1947 and 1991, fully one fifth of the 5.1 million settlers who arrived in Australia left. In addition, another 380,340 Australia-born left the country (Hugo, 1994: 43). One interesting indicator of the implications of this type of movement is that Australia pays, every year, more than $A22 million in pensions to British settlers to Australia alone who have since left the country. Thus, the transnational linkages implied in the concept of diaspora have profound financial implications for countries of origin and destination. The fact that those European migrants had 'double identities' did not appear to have prejudiced the emergence of strong independent states with identities in their own right.

Thus, the Europeans were sojourners as well as settlers, just as the Chinese were settlers as well as sojourners. Of the 30 million Chinese overseas, the vast majority live in long-established communities in South East Asia with, almost certainly, generally lower rates of return migration to China than those of European settlers to overseas destinations back to Europe. The principal reasons for this were the often disturbed political and economic conditions within China until the late 1970s, and the relative poverty of China compared with overseas destinations.

There was return nevertheless. Although emigration from China virtually ceased from 1949 until after the implementation of the reforms in 1979, the return of overseas Chinese was welcomed and encouraged, particularly when they faced persecution as in Indonesia in 1959–60 and in 1967. It has been estimated that between 1949 and 1966 almost 500,000 overseas Chinese returned, some 94,000 in 1960 alone from Indonesia (Fitzgerald, 1972: 69), but this number represented less than 10 per cent of the Chinese overseas of the time.

MIGRATION FROM CHINA

The above discussion draws attention to the fact that the transnational linkages of a Chinese diaspora may certainly have been no more, and were likely to have been less, than in European migratory flows. As already noted, there was little migration from China for about thirty years between 1949 and 1979. The most significant outflows were to Hong Kong in 1960 and during the second half of the 1970s (Skeldon, 1986). Immediately after World War II there was little international migration of any Chinese people as few destinations were prepared to accept them. The settler societies of Australia, Canada and the United States only modified their immigration laws to accept Asians from the mid-1960s and the colonies that were soon to emerge as independent countries of South East Asia had essentially closed their borders to further Chinese migration. Those ethnic Chinese who could prove that they had been born on British-administered territory were an exception and this gave rise to a small but significant flow from the New Territories of Hong

Kong to the UK (Watson, 1975). This flow, too, was gradually reduced after the passage of the 1962 Immigration Act of the UK.

By the 1970s, the US, Canada (and later Australia) emerged as principal destinations for the migration of the Chinese (Skeldon, 1996). The movement began from peripheral parts of China in the 1960s, from Hong Kong and Taiwan, and, after the reforms of 1979, came to incorporate China itself. While growth in movement out of these Chinese areas is marked, and the numbers are quite significant, perhaps more notable is the fact that they are small compared with the base population of China itself. However, any attempt to relate migration from China with the population of China is meaningless as the migrants come from a series of very small parts of that vast territory. One of the principal source areas in the western part of the Pearl River delta in Guangdong province is Siyi, or the four districts of Taishan, Kaiping, Xinhui and Enping. The population of the Siyi in the early 1990s was some 3.6 million, with about 1.8 million migrants and their descendants from that area living overseas and another 1.1 million in Hong Kong, Macau and Taiwan (data cited in Christiansen, forthcoming). In one part of Fujian province, in Changle District, up to half the population of particular villages is estimated to be living overseas, with, in the one extreme case of Houyu, an astonishing 80 per cent of the population now living in New York and its environs (Hood, 1998: 33). Diasporas indeed, if on a local scale!

The regional origins of migration from China have long been recognised. The vast majority of migrants from China come from just three provinces in the south of the country—Guangdong, Fujian and Zhejiang—and from a relatively small number of areas within those provinces. The principal migrant groups from southwest to northeast along the coast are: Hainanese from the eastern part of Hainan island; Cantonese or Yue-speaking peoples from around the Pearl River delta: Teochiu (Chiu Chow or Chaozhou), or southern Min-speaking peoples from coastal areas of eastern Guangdong and the western border of Fujian; Hakka from inland areas of eastern Guangdong and southwestern Fujian; Hokkien, also a southern Min language, from coastal areas around Xiamen in Fujian; Hokchiu and Hokchia, northern Min-speaking peoples from areas around Fuzhou also in Fujian; and Wu dialect speakers of the areas around Wenzhou and Qingtian County in coastal Zhejiang. Of these language groups, only the Hokkien and Teochiu speak dialects of the same language, the others being mutually unintelligible. Even the Taishan dialect of the Cantonese of the Siyi can be understood only with difficulty by speakers of standard Cantonese.

In addition to these areas of origin must be added Hong Kong and Taiwan, which have dominated recent migration streams to North America and Australasia, particularly of business and investor migrants. While Hong Kong is predominantly Cantonese, and migration from mainland China to Taiwan has traditionally been dominated by migrants from Fujian, the ethnic composition of both areas is more complex, especially since the immigrations from China post-1949.[3] Unfortunately, data on movements from these two origins are rarely available by ethnicity. Even the more detailed studies of Hong Kong emigrants, such as those coordinated by Skeldon (1994), contain little information on sub-groups among Hong Kong migrants. The Shanghainese, for example, a small group compared with the total population of Hong Kong, accounting for 10 to 16 per cent of the population, are known to have built up an extensive business network out of the city far more important than their mere numbers would suggest (Wong, 1988).

The above origins should not imply that no migration takes place or has taken place from other parts of China. There was a substantial movement of labour out of Shangdong, for example, to Europe to serve as auxiliaries during World War I, involving nearly 100,000 men (Summerskill, 1982), and from Shandong, Hebei and Henan to South Africa between 1904 and 1907 to work in the gold mines, involving over 60,000 men (Yap and Man, 1996: 111–35). Neither of these flows from northern provinces of China gave rise to long-term settlement and, with only a few exceptions, all the labourers were repatriated at the end of their contracts. This migration from northern China was in complete contrast to the movements from Zhejiang to Europe, and from Canton to South Africa, which gave rise to permanent communities. The Cantonese, in fact, showed little inclination to volunteer for work on the goldfields, showing why the recruiters turned to northern sources of supply. The northern Chinese and those from the Chinese heartland have not been part of any sustained Chinese diaspora although, in recent years, northerners from Heilongjiang have been moving into the Russian Far East and Mandarin-speaking students and technocrats from all parts of China have been going overseas as China joins the global community.

Although the actual situation can be exceedingly complex, certain flows from specific origins in China are often associated with specific destinations. The movement of ex-farmers from the New Territories of Hong Kong to the UK has already been mentioned. Originally concentrated in the largest cities, these migrants, given their trade of running Chinese restaurants and 'takeaways', set up 'branches all over' the country to serve a dispersed market (Baker 1994). Over 40 per cent of the movement towards Thailand was made up of Teochius and some 90 per cent of rural Chinese in Cambodia came from that area. Hakka dominated the migration to western Sarawak and the domination of particular language groups to specific destinations was a characteristic of Chinese agricultural colonisation throughout South East Asia (Hill, 1988: 125–6).

Until the mid-1960s, migration to North America, in its transitions of free immigration through exclusion, was dominated by Cantonese villagers from the western Pearl River delta, most notably from the Siyi, and especially from Taishan, and from the Sanyi, or the three districts of Panyu, Nanhai and Shunde, plus the county of Zhongshan (Lai 1998; Ng, 1998). Included among the Cantonese were Hakka-speakers, also from the Pearl River delta. The greater part of recent illegal Chinese migration into the US, perhaps some 200,000 in 1991–93 alone, has been from one specific area of Fujian, Changle County (Hood, 1998: 33). Unlike movements to South East Asia, North America and Australasia which were dominated by peoples from Guangdong and Fujian, migrants from Zhejiang, particularly from Qingtian and Wenzhou, went primarily to destinations in Europe.

Thus, migration out of China has been made up of flows from highly localised origins to specific destinations that at first might not seem to fit easily with the idea of an overarching 'Chinese diaspora'. It is not simply in terms of origin that the diversity among Chinese migrants is to be found, but also in occupation. From the Chinese coolie or laundryman of the nineteenth century to the entrepreneur promoting a special brand of Chinese capitalism of today, stereotypes have tended to characterise Chinese migration. That coolies, laundrymen and entrepreneurs were, or are, significant components of the migration flows is not in question but composition of the flows was much more complex depending upon the type of migration, whether recruited as indentured servant or moving as a 'free migrant', and the destination involved. While certainly the nature of the migration usually meant that the migrants moved through urban centres, many engaged in rural activities. Recruitment for plantations in Hawaii or Thailand, small-holder market gardening in Thailand and subsistence agriculturalists in Sabah were all important activities of Chinese overseas.

Again the ethnic dimension is important. The Teochius appear to have pioneered the introduction of sugar cultivation in Thailand just as the Hainanese attempted to introduce a cotton plantation system into that country in the nineteenth century (Hafner, 1983: 34) and the 'ethnically homogeneous Chinese middleman group' in the Malayan Peninsula in more recent years was a Hokkien group (Landa, 1983). Cantonese were pepper planters in Sibu district in Sarawak (Hill 1988; 126).

One of the most ethnically diverse destinations of Chinese migration is Singapore. There the different dialect groups were associated with different occupations, specialisations that were reinforced by their concentration in specific districts of the city (Cheng, 1985: 89ff). There, in the early part of this century, the Hokkien dominated commerce and trade, the Teochiu 'were more represented in agriculture than in commerce' and the Cantonese were famous for manufacturing furniture, leather goods, soya sauce, clock and watch repairing, tailoring, goldsmithry and jewellery. The Hakkas were involved in pawnbroking and in dealing in Chinese medicines and herbs as well as moving into the textile trade. The Hainanese dominated the coffee-shop trade and later catering and bakery businesses. Their relatively late arrival and isolation in Singapore led them to invest heavily in the education of the next generation, which saw a 'rather high proportion of Hainanese academicians, graduates, professionals and prominent civil servants' in more recent years (Cheng, 1985: 97). Road transport, including bicycle, motor-cycle and the taxi business were dominated by Hokchias. Thus, in common with so many migrant groups around the world, place of origin becomes associated with occupational specialisation. Migration is a critical factor in the segmentation of labour markets.

The existence of these distinct flows should not detract from the very real changes that have occurred in volume and composition and in the nature of the communities of origin and destination over time. For example, the rise of Chinese nationalism from the beginning of this century and the later introduction of Communism provided common ideological glosses for all China, and the gradual erosion of the latter under the reforms may see the re-emergence of regionalism as seen upon the demise of Socialism in other parts of the world. Under Communism, however, there was little migration out of China and its resurgence after the reforms of 1978 may both reinforce and be reinforced by that regionalism. Much depends upon what occurs in the destinations of the migration and there, too, significant and divergent changes have occurred.

THE CHINESE AS SETTLERS: THE HISTORICAL DIMENSION

Chinese migrants, as emphasised above, were not all sojourners: they became settlers and, depending upon the situation, assimilated to varying degrees with the indigenous populations. In some parts of South East Asia, Thailand and Cambodia, for example, that assimilation became virtually complete. In other areas, from the eighteenth century, an 'intermediate' culture was created that was neither indigenous nor Chinese. Skinner (1996), in an exemplary analysis, examines this 'creolisation' of Chinese societies in three different contexts, Java, the Straits Settlements of the Malayan Peninsula and the Philippines in their Peranakan, Baba and mestizo variants, respectively. While each of these three variants was descended from Hokkien migrant groups, the critical factors in whether intermediate societies were to emerge revolved around the nature of the host society and the barriers to assimilation. Even barriers themselves, however, did not necessary determine the outcome. Where these were formidable, as in the cases of more orthodox islamic societies in Makasar, Aceh and Madura, Chinese might convert in order to obtain access to highly valued ends, essentially women, high social status and economic opportunities (Skinner, 1996: 74). In these areas their children were assimilated into the local indigenous culture and no intermediate cultures emerged.

Significant changes in the nature of these intermediate societies occurred from the late nineteenth century. In the migration system the critical difference was the participation of increasing numbers of Chinese women which led to a ethnically 'purer' Chinese groups, the *totok*. Space does not permit full justice to be given to the sophistication of Skinner's analysis, but from that time on, there became less need for Chinese migrants to assimilate into intermediate communities, and tensions rose between the latter and the new *totok* groups. The policies of the dominant colonial power in each area were also significant to the types of communities to crystallise as were the attitudes of the Chinese groups to the new nationalism emerging in China. In the Philippines, the mestizo Chinese merged with indigenous groups to produce the new Filipino nationalism; in the Straits Settlements, the *baba* were absorbed into broader Chinese communities; and in Java, only the *peranakan* survived as an identifiable separate cultural group, very different from its Chinese origins and equally different from the *totok* Chinese.

The significance of Skinner's analysis for the theme of a Chinese diaspora is to reinforce the very different outcomes that can emerge from Chinese migration. Skinner's three cases all had a common origin in Hokkien settlement but because of a complex matrix of local, regional and global factors, generated three very different sets of outcomes. Adding other ethnic Chinese groups to the equation, whether Cantonese or Techiu, yet further complicates the picture.

THE 'NEW' CHINESE SETTLERS

The inclusion of the 'new' migrations from Chinese origins from the 1970s onwards truly reveals the heterogeneous nature of the Chinese diaspora. The new migrant flows consist much more of the highly educated, and of families, than the old labour movements of the nineteenth and early twentieth centuries, even if temporary labour movements are being promoted by state and provincial authorities. There are large numbers of students going overseas to continue their studies and settlers to Canada, Australia and the US. There is also considerable illegal movement from China to North America, Australasia and Europe of a type not dissimilar to earlier migrations.

The recent migration appears to be mainly from traditional areas of outmovement in Guangdong, Fujian and Zhejiang provinces. Hong Kong and Taiwan together with South East Asian countries are, however, among the major sources of the new migration with the original ethnic origin of the migrants an unknown. Whether that origin would be meaningful is also unknown as a Hong Kong or Singaporean identity may be of greater importance than a Shanghai or Hokkien origin. Also, the new migration out of Hong Kong is very different from the 1950s movement out of New Territories villages.

Significant numbers of the settlers to North America and Australasia, however, appear to return home after establishing residence and/or citizenship in destination countries. The head of household only may return, leaving his family at the destination where the children are established in a school system less pressured than in Hong Kong, Singapore or Taiwan. These household heads may essentially commute across the Pacific at regular intervals creating transnational systems of circulation that give substance to the idea of diaspora as a transnational community. Where only household heads are involved this circulation has been termed the 'astronaut' phenomenon, and where both parents return to continue their work in origin areas, the children left at the destination are known as 'parachute' kids (Skeldon, 1994; Pe-Pua, et al, 1996).

Chinese communities in North America, Australasia and in Europe have become increasingly heterogeneous, divided by language, origin, political persuasion, class and legal status (Wong, 1987; Chen, 1992; Benton and Pieke, 1998). Yet within this heterogeneity new ethnicities and identities are being manufactured (Kwong, 1997). In the face of a new and hostile environment, no matter whether that hostility is real or perceived, common Chinese solidarity is emphasised. To the outsider, the migrants, irrespective of background, are 'all Chinese'; to the insider, a common Chinese front is in the best interests of self-protection. Thus, the commonality of 'Chineseness' as a racial category, promoted by both outsiders and insiders for very different reasons, can obscure real and significant differences within the Chinese communities.

The Chinese migrants to Europe have been portrayed as the 'first Europeans' (Christiansen, 1998) in the sense that they moved to Europe rather than to any single European state and seldom comprehended the differences among European nations. However, there were enough factions among them, and there were Chinese groups that had virtually no contact one with the other, that it is difficult to see them as a single ethnic group. The communities in North America and Australasia similarly appear to be becoming increasingly heterogeneous. The direction of future change will depend to a large extent on the relative openness of all these communities to intermarriage. Changes equivalent to those observed by Skinner in the historical experience of Chinese communities in South East Asia can surely be expected in the destinations of Chinese migration today. The outcomes are likely to be multiple, depending upon factors internal to the Chinese migrant community, factors in the host community and policies implemented by the host country. Multicultural policies, for example, may have different outcomes from policies of a more assimilationist bent.

That there has been a Chinese diaspora in the sense of a spreading of Chinese peoples around the world is beyond doubt, although its impact has been various. Diaspora appears to imply some form of uniformity, of a single great wave of oriental peoples that may threaten other societies. That wave is made up of many separate and distinct parts. To include them all as if they were part of a single migration is extremely deceptive. While accepting the real transformation of the global migration system through the incorporation of Asian and Latin American groups, it is equally important to be aware of the differences among and within those groups, the Chinese among them. These differences include those of background and place of origin in China, and differences that evolve in the destination areas themselves as the Chinese groups are transformed by and transform their host societies. There has perhaps been a Chinese diaspora but, more meaningfully, there has been a varied and complex migration of Chinese peoples.

THE DANGERS OF DIASPORA

It is not just the complexity of the migrant flows themselves that is the sole issue, but the diversity of outcome. Clearly, assimilation of Chinese peoples *has* taken place; new identities *have been*, and *are being*, created; and there *are* significant differences in terms of type, composition and origins of flows from such a vast country of origin as China. The Chinese diaspora is thus highly fractured. Diaspora gives the impression of unity, of a significant transnational force that can challenge the primacy of the state. Certainly, the potential role of minorities among the migrants to transform the state can never be discounted. Returned students schooled in different ways may provide a challenge to aged leaderships (Skeldon, 1997), but the diaspora as a unitary force seems very much in doubt.

Whether the Chinese diaspora is a typical example of the genre is clearly pertinent to the argument. That most 'classic' of diasporas, the Jewish diaspora, too, seems to have become transformed with the creation of the homeland in the state of Israel. The very availability of a choice of whether to return or not has thrown into high relief the issue of how assimilated to destination cultures Jewish peoples have become. Jewish Americans will clearly remain American Jews but whether they will wish to associate themselves with the state of Israel is another issue, particularly when that state itself is becoming increasingly heterogeneous through the very process of the in-gathering of the exiles. With time it may not just be Europe that experiences a 'vanishing diaspora' (Wasserstein, 1997).

In the US too, if recent research reported in *The Economist* (3 July 1999) is to be believed, assimilation of the new migrants is taking place just as was the case with old migrants. Intermarriage and language acquisition appear to be occurring as they always did. In 1900, the proportion of new immigrants who spoke English was around 25 per cent, yet this did not prohibit the US from emerging as the most powerful nation state in the world. In 1990, more than 76 per cent of immigrants spoke English with 'high proficiency' within 10 years of arriving and, by the third generation, a third or more of Latino and Asian women were marrying outside their ethnic group.

The argument of this chapter is essentially that diaspora may be but a transient phase in the whole process of the transformation of the global migration system *and* in our thinking about that system. The dangers of diaspora are not so much directed towards the future viability of the state as many multiculturalists and postmodernists appear to believe. Rather the dangers of diaspora lie in implications of interpretation: of an oversimplification of the process of migration; of a static approach to a dynamic process; of a reiteration of the classic fear of the outsider and of the 'other'. Diaspora is an orientalist interpretation in the sense that it stereotypes the migrant, obscuring or ignoring differences among migrant groups that are in any way distinct from the host group. Conversely, it can be seen as a counter-orientalist interpretation in the sense that it can attempt to impose a unity on diverse groups to give the impression of strength in the face of powerful host states. While the concept of diaspora has indeed provided insight into the process of population movement and adaptation, the time is perhaps now ripe to revert to the use of the more prosaic but less ideologically laden term, 'migration'.

NOTES

1. For examples of the current usage of 'diaspora' in migration studies see Cheng and Katz (1998), Cohen (1997), Van Hear (1998), Kotkin (1993), Chaliand and Rageau (1995) and the journal *Diaspora: A Journal of Transnational Studies*.
2. Recent work on migration and security included Weiner 1993, and Teitelbaum and Weiner, 1995.
3. For a discussion of ethnicity in Hong Kong, see Guldin, 1997.

REFERENCES

Appadurai, Arjun (1996), *Modernity at Large: Cultural Dimensions of Globalization*, Minneapolis: University of Minnesota Press.

Baines, Dudley (1991), *Emigration from Europe 1815–1930*, London: Macmillan.

Baker, Hugh D.R. (1994), 'Branches all over: the Hong Kong Chinese in the United Kingdom', in Ronald Skeldon (ed.), *Reluctant Exiles? Migration from Hong Kong and the New Overseas Chinese*, New York: M.E. Sharpe, pp. 291–307.

Benton, Gregor and Frank N. Pieke (eds) (1998), *The Chinese in Europe*, London: Macmillan.

Chaliand, Gerard and Jean-Pierre Rageau (1995), *The Penguin Atlas of Diasporas*, Harmondsworth: Viking Penguin.

Chan Sucheng (1990), 'European and Asian immigration into the United States in comparative perspective', in Virginia Yans-McLaughlin (ed.), *Immigration Reconsidered: History, Sociology and Politics*, New York: Oxford University Press, pp. 37–75.

Chen Hsiang-Shui (1992), *Chinatown No More: Taiwan Immigrants in Contemporary New York*, Ithaca, NY: Cornell University Press.

Cheng Lim-Keak (1985), *Social Change and the Chinese in Singapore*, Singapore: Singapore University Press.

Cheng, Lucie and Marian Katz (1998), 'Migration and the diaspora communities', in Richard Maidment and Colin Mackerras (eds), *Culture and Society in the Asia-Pacific*, London: Routledge, pp. 65–87.

Christiansen, Flemming (1998), 'Chinese identity in Europe', in Gregor Benton and Frank N. Pieke (eds), *The Chinese in Europe*, London: Macmillan, pp. 42–63.

Christiansen, Fleming (forthcoming), *Chinatown, Europe*, Richmond, Surrey: Curzon Press.

Cohen, Robin (1997), *Global Diasporas: An Introduction*, London: UCL Press.

Cushman, Jennifer and Wang Gungwu (eds) (1988), *Changing Identities of the Southeast Asian Chinese Since World War I*, Hong Kong: University Press.

Dikotter, Frank (1996), 'Culture, "race" and nation: the formation of national identity in twentieth century China', *Journal of International Affairs*, **49** (2): 590–605.

Fitzgerald, Stephen (1972), *China and the Overseas Chinese: A Study of Peking's Changing Policy, 1949–1970*, Cambridge: Cambridge University Press.

Guldin, Gregory E. (1997), 'Hong Kong ethnicity: of folk models and change', in Grant Evans and Maria Tam Siu-Mei (eds), *Hong Kong: The Anthropology of a Chinese Metropolis*, Richmond, Surrey: Curzon, pp. 25–50.

Hafner, James A. (1983), 'Market gardening in Thailand: the origins of an ethnic Chinese monopoly', in Linda Y.C. Lim and L.A. Peter Gosling (eds), *The Chinese in Southeast Asia, volume 1. Ethnicity and Economic Activity*, Singapore: Maruzen, pp. 34–5.

Hill, Ronald D. (1988), 'Notes on Chinese agricultural colonization in Southeast Asia', *Erdkunde*, **42**: 123–35.

Hobsbawm, Eric J. (1990), *Nations and Nationalism Since 1780*, Cambridge: Cambridge University Press.

Hood, Marlowe (1998), 'Fuzhou', in Lynn Pan (ed.), *The Encyclopedia of the Chinese Overseas*, Singapore: Archipelago Press, pp. 33–5.

Hugo, Graeme (1994), *The Economic Implications of Emigration from Australia*, Canberra: Australian Government Publishing Service.

Kotkin, Joel (1993), *Tribes: How Race, Religion and Identity Determine Success in the Global Community*, New York: Random House.

Kwong, Peter (1997), *Forbidden Workers: Illegal Chinese Immigrants and American Labor*, New York: New Press.

Lai, Him M. (1998), 'The United States', in Lynn Pan (ed.), *The Encyclopedia of the Chinese Overseas*, Singapore: Archipelago Press, pp. 261–73.

Landa, Janet T. (1983), 'The political economy of the ethnically homogeneous Chinese middleman group in Southeast Asia: ethnicity and entrepreneurship in a plural society', in Linda Y.C. Lim and L.A. Peter Gosling (eds), *The Chinese in Southeast Asia. Volume 1. Ethnicity and Economic Activity*, Singapore: Maruzen, pp. 86–116.

Lim, Linda Y.C. and Gosling, L.A. Peter (1983), *The Chinese in Southeast Asia*, 2 volumes, Singapore: Maruzen.

Lyman, Sanford M. (n.d.), 'The Chinese Diaspora in America, 1850–1943', in Sanford M. Lyman (ed.), *The Asian in North America*, Santa Barbara: ABC-Clio Press, pp. 11–24.

Mitchell, Katheryne (1997), 'Different diasporas and the hype of hybridity', *Environment and Planning D, Society and Space*, **15** (5): 533–53.

Ng Wing Chung (1998), 'Canada', in Lynn Pan (ed.), *The Encyclopedia of the Chinese Overseas*, Singapore: Archipelago Press, pp. 234–47.

Nugent, Walter (1992), *Crossings: The Great Transatlantic Migrations, 1870–1914*, Bloomington: Indiana University Press.

Ong, Aihwa and Donald Nonini (eds) (1997), *Ungrounded Empires: The Cultural Politics of Modern Chinese Transnationalism*, London: Routledge.

Pe-Pua, Rogelia, Coleen Mitchell, Robyn Iredale and Stephen Castles (1996), *Astronaut Families and Parachute Children: The Cycle of Migration Between Hong Kong and Australia*, Canberra: Australian Government Publishing Service.

Poston, Dudley, Xinxiang Michael Mao and Mei-Yu Yu (1994), 'The global distribution of the overseas Chinese around 1990', *Population and Development Review*, **20** (3): 631–45.

Purcell, Victor (1965), *The Chinese in Southeast Asia*, second edition, London: Oxford University Press.

Reid, Anthony (ed.) (1996), *Sojourners and Settlers: Histories of Southeast Asia and the Chinese*, St Leonards, NSW: Allen and Unwin.

Siu, Paul C.P. (1952–53), 'The sojourner', *American Journal of Sociology, ***58**: 34–44.

Skeldon, Ronald (1986), 'Hong Kong and its hinterland: a case of international rural-to-urban migration', *Asian Geographer*, **5** (1): 1–24.

Skeldon, Ronald (ed.) (1994), *Reluctant Exiles? Migration from Hong Kong and the New Overseas Chinese*, New York: M.E. Sharpe.

Skeldon, Ronald (1996), 'Migration from China', *Journal of International Affairs*, **49** (2): 434–55.

Skeldon, Ronald (1997), *Migration and Development: A Global Perspective*, London: Harlow.

Skeldon, Ronald (1998), 'From multiculturalism to diaspora: changing identities in the context of Asian migration', in Eleanor Laquian, Aprodicio Laquian and Terry McGee (eds), *The Silent Debate: Asian Immigration and Racism in Canada*, Vancouver: Institute of Asian Research, University of British Columbia, pp. 213–26.

Skinner, G. William (1996), 'Creolized Chinese Societies in Southeast Asia', in Anthony Reid (ed.), *Sojourners and Settlers: Histories of Southeast Asia and the Chinese*, St Leonards, NSW: Allen and Unwin, pp. 51–93.

Summerskill, Michael (1982), *China on the Western Front*, London: Michael Summerskill.

Suryadinata, Leo (ed.) (1997), *Ethnic Chinese as Southeast Asians*, Singapore, Institute of Southeast Asian Studies.

Teitelbaum, Michael S. and Myron Weiner (eds) (1995), *Threatened Peoples, Threatened Borders: World Migration and U. S. Policy*, New York: Norton

Van Hear, Nicholas (1998), *New Diasporas: The Mass Exodus, Dispersal and Regrouping of Migrant Communities*, London: UCL Press.

Wang, Gungwu (1988), 'The Study of Chinese Identities in Southeast Asia', in Jennifer Cushman and Wang Gungwu (eds), *Changing Identities of the Southeast Asian Chinese Since World War II*, Hong Kong, Hong Kong University Press, pp. 1–21.

Wang Ling-Chi and Wang Gungwu (eds) (1998), *The Chinese Diaspora: Selected Essays*, 2 volumes, Singapore: Times Academic Press.

Wasserstein, Bernard (1997), *Vanishing Diaspora: The Jews in Europe Since 1945*, London: Penguin Books.

Watson, James L. (1975), *Emigration and the Chinese Lineage: The Mans in Hong Kong and London*, Berkeley: University of California Press.

Weiner, Myron (ed.) (1993), *International Migration and Security*, Boulder, CO: Westview Press.

Wong, Bernard (1987), 'The Chinese: New Immigrants in New York's Chinatown', in Nancy Foner (ed.), *New Immigrants in New York*, New York: Columbia University Press, pp. 243–71.

Wong, Siu-Lun (1988), *Emigrant Entrepreneurs: Shanghai Industrialists in Hong Kong*, Hong Kong: Oxford University Press.

Yap, Melanie and Dianne L. Man (1996), *Colour, Confusion and Concessions: The History of the Chinese in South Africa*, Hong Kong: Hong Kong University Press.

8. International Migration and Globalisation: an Investigation of Migration Systems in Pacific Asia with Particular Reference to Hong Kong

Allan M. Findlay[1]

INTRODUCTION

Contemporary trends in international migration are inextricably linked to complex economic and social processes associated with the globalisation of production and consumption. Globalisation has brought about changes in the nature of production processes which in turn have affected the organisation of labour and labour migration. Using secondary data for the four Asian dragon economies and primary survey data from Hong Kong, this chapter explores the effects of globalisation on investment, trade, production and migration linkages.

There is nothing new in claiming that migration is linked to wider economic trends (Jones, 1990: 209; Castles and Miller, 1993). However, it is difficult to determine precisely how labour migration is linked to evolving global economic systems. In this chapter the position taken is that contemporary globalisation processes are not only historically unprecedented, but have the power to transform migration systems in the 'massive shake-out' of societies and economies that is taking place (Held et al., 1999). By contrast, most popular conceptions of migration trends over time, such as 'migration transition theory', depend on a diffusionist view of development and offer an inadequate conceptualisation of the links between globalisation and migration.

In order to examine the links between global economic restructuring and labour migration, this chapter progresses from a review of key questions arising from the research literature relating to the hypothesis of the 'migration transition' to examination of data sets collected for the Asian dragon economies in the mid-1990s. The conclusions from this analysis are then investigated in more depth with reference to primary survey data from

Hong Kong. Migration to and from Hong Kong in the 1980s and 1990s is shown not only to be inextricably linked to trends in global markets, but also to be rooted in the changing regional division of labour. Mobility implications of economic restructuring are investigated in terms of different categories of labour, including low-wage production staff moving within China as well as international skill exchanges linking China's Special Economic Zones to Hong Kong and the rest of the world economy.

GLOBALISATION AND THEORIES OF MIGRATION CHANGE

Globalisation has involved the widening, deepening and acceleration of global connections. Greater inter-connectedness has resulted from a wide range of technological developments and has been evident in many spheres of life from the economic to the social and from the political to the cultural. Although most academics agree that a greater intensity of links is evident around the globe, there is considerable debate about the meaning and nature of these connections (Leyshon, 1997; Dicken et al., 1997). Debate is especially strong in relation to international migration because its economic significance cannot be separated from its cultural impact.

While many different interpretations can be offered of the links between migration and economic development (Skeldon, 1997), this chapter focuses on just two for the sake of simplicity and clarity. The first position might be represented as viewing technological advances and national economic development as leading to a progressive internationalisation of trade, investment and migration flows. From this perspective the development path of individual states involves them in engaging in international migration as part of their progression towards having increased their global economic reach. This perspective on development anticipates increased regional and international economic integration over time and the emergence of global markets. Several variants have been identified relating to how globalisation proceeds within this 'model' (Stalker, 2000). The extreme case is that of the emergence of a 'borderless' global economy which eventually undermines the power of the state as well as producing new global divisions of labour (Ohmae, 1990, 1995).

It is possible to see how neo-liberal economic views (see for example Fields, 1994) within this school might view migration as only one of many signs of increasing internationalisation flowing from the early stages of a Rostowian model of sustained economic development (Rostow, 1960). Migrant labour is seen primarily as a factor of production whose location is not fixed, but which can be shifted by the migration process in response to the needs of the market. Within this model, labour should flow in the opposite direction to capital. The equilibrating effect of market forces shapes labour migration flows as part of a process operating in favour of a levelling out of regional wage differentials.

The argument has been spelt out in more detail by advocates of what has come to be termed 'migration transition theory'. For example, Pang (1993: 300) notes that 'rapid growth has expanded not only trade and investment but also labour flows'. The linkage between these processes is interpreted as causal, one with migration being a dependent variable linked to a country's development status. Thus:

> at very low levels of development, a country neither sends nor receives significant numbers of migrant workers. ... As a country's per capita income rises and its trade and information links with the rest of the world expand, there is likely to be an increase in the country's net outflow of people. ... At some point, however, the rate of increase in the net outflow of workers slows down because the net attractions of staying home increase with the growth of the economy. ... As the country industrialises, there may be a return flow of nationals working abroad and the country itself becomes attractive to foreign workers. (Pang, 1994, 84–6)

The patterns of labour supply and demand described above have often been taken as an explanation for the emergence of regional migration systems during the course of development, with the largest flows being between proximate countries experiencing conditions of uneven development (Jones, 1990). For example, Birks and Sinclair (1980) interpreted the rapid economic growth of the Arab oil economies as being responsible for a massive new labour demand which was supplied by neighbouring labour-surplus economies. As the supply from proximate states dried up, so the migration system evolved to require flows from more distant states. This interpretation of migration leads to the expectation that over time regional systems of international migration both appear and disappear in relation to unevenness in patterns of economic growth and related regional inequalities in the supply and demand for labour.

Pang (1994), added many caveats to his migration transition model, but others including most economists concerned with Pacific Asian migration were less cautious. Fields (1994) for example concluded that the demand-led shift in certain Pacific Asian labour markets produced higher wages, and as this occurred:

> those who previously were willing to emigrate were no longer willing to do so; they either returned home or stayed at home. Firms tried to mitigate wage increases in several ways: by importing labour...by shifting to labour saving, labour augmenting technologies and/or by moving overseas. ... The net effect was rapidly improving earnings opportunities in the home countries, hence the migration transition. (Fields, 1994: 26)

Other academics have offered legitimacy to transition theory, identifying turning points and migration transitions in a large number of countries in Pacific Asia (Alburo, 1994; Park, 1994; Lim, 1996) the more critical engagement is found in Skeldon's (1994) views on Hong Kong.

If Pang introduced terms such as 'turning point' and 'migration transition' in a *descriptive* capacity and later enhanced their application, imbuing them with *explanatory* value, others have gone further in developing a *predictive* dimension. For example Kim (1996: 303) argues that 'increasing economic integration will lead to migration transition for many Asian countries', and proposes three different types of migration sequence over time. The *predictive* nature of the migration-development link becomes evident in statements such as 'over the longer run, the successive exploitation of low-cost labour, down the hierarchy of demographic and industrial transition, through trade and investment will certainly enable many Asian countries to pass through migration transition' (Kim, 1996: 315).

Although the simplicity of the migration transition thesis is attractive, and the scale of its legitimation by other researchers rather remarkable, this chapter argues that it is fundamentally flawed. Not only does the model not apply to the migration experiences of most countries, but it has not been specified in such a way as to identify the fundamental conditions linking migration events to other aspects of power relations governing the advance of globalisation.

An alternative theorisation of the links between globalisation, migration, trade, investment and production is offered by adopting a transformationalist standpoint (Findlay et al., 1998; Held et al., 1999). The transformationalist position sees globalisation as an essentially contingent historical process. The existence of a global system is not taken as evidence of global convergence. Instead, globalisation has involved a highly structured set of interwoven processes organised on a hierarchical basis. Central to the functioning of the global system have been a small number of global cities. Friedmann (1986) identified three—New York, London, and Tokyo—which he claimed commanded the apex of the global system of international investment flows—but whose ability to sustain a global reach was only sustained through lower order global cities such as Hong Kong and Singapore (Knox, 1996). The relations between these control centres of the global system has been the subject of much recent geographical research.

Hierarchical power relations operating at a global level, rather than economic factors working at a local spatial level, have had an ever-increasing influence on patterns of international migration. Thus, for example, global cities need certain types of low-wage service workers in order to thrive and remain competitive. The ability of global cities such as Hong Kong and Singapore to formulate city-specific immigration policies may have operated significantly in their favour in contrast with global cities located in larger states where labour requirements have been hampered by the need to conform to national immigration policies 'out of sync' with the needs of global cities (Findlay et al., 1996).

This chapter contends that migration trends in Pacific Asia cannot be analysed separately, one economy from another. Instead, migration transformations over time need to be understood in relation to global linkages that are changing the terms of production and reproduction within geographically specific labour markets. It has become important to theorise migration in relation to global power hierarchies, as organised through global cities, and to consider how labour flows to or from a country may relate to the location, sphere of influence and functions of these places. This approach is applied first in relation to some secondary data for the four Asian dragon economies and then in more detail using primary survey data for Hong Kong.

LABOUR MIGRATION, TRADE AND INVESTMENT: HONG KONG, SINGAPORE, KOREA AND TAIWAN IN THE MID-1990s

Selected indicators of economic and demographic growth presented in Table 8.1 show that the economic context of immigration to these states was one of rapid economic expansion fuelled by very high levels of investment. The dragon economies enjoyed high export growth in the mid-1990s when foreign investor confidence rode high (McKibbin, 1998). At the same time, demographic forces meant that these societies were expanding only slowly in terms of population numbers, with fertility rates well below replacement level (2.1). Significant improvements in health have raised life expectancies producing an ageing effect in their population structures. Stagnant demographic regimes have combined with boom economic circumstances to generate a context favourable to significant labour immigration.

Two issues are raised by Table 8.1. First, what patterns of migration, trade and investment have been stimulated by the economic prosperity of the dragon economies? Second, what would one anticipate to be the effects of the economic crisis of 1997/98 on migration flows? Figure 8.1, taken from data collated by Findlay et al. (1997), provides some answers to the first question. It maps annual migration flows of 10,000 persons or more to the four Asian dragons in the mid-1990s. Inevitably the map is imperfect since it shows only legally recorded intra-regional labour migration. Significant numbers of clandestine migrants as well as refugees and asylum seekers are omitted from the map. Bearing these problems in mind, at least two important deductions can be reached. First, in line with both the migration theses presented above, it is clear that the four dragons drew very large numbers of workers from other states within Pacific Asia during the early and mid-1990s. Second, the pattern of migration was not governed purely by geographical propinquity and disparities in labour market opportunities. This apparently contradicts aspects of the transition hypothesis. Selective structuring of flows is evident. Regional experts will not be surprised to note that South Korea received large numbers of in-migrants from Japan (some of them of Korean ethnicity) but not from North Korea. Taiwan was strongly linked to Thailand but not to Vietnam. Hong Kong received many more migrants from the Philippines than from the People's Republic of China (PRC). Singapore attracted large numbers of Thais but few migrants from Kampuchea. Clearly, political and cultural factors strongly influenced migration patterns; it was not labour market factors alone which were at work in moulding the migration map. But there was much more to the migration system than these unremarkable statements might suggest, and a useful starting point in exploring the structuring of the system is to consider how Figure 8.1 compares with the pattern of investment and trade flows in the region.

Table 8.1 Indicators of economic and demographic growth in the Asian dragon economies: 1994–98

	Real GDP growth (% p.a.)[a]			Investment growth (% p.a.)[b]			Total fertility rate	Female life expectancy[c]
	1994	1996	1998	1994	1996	1997	1998	1998
Hong Kong	5.4	4.7	−5.5	22.9	13.7	20.7	1.1	82
Singapore	10.3	6.9	1.5	10.7	20.1	n.a	1.7	80
S. Korea	8.4	7.1	−5.5	13.7	9.4	−16.6	1.7	76
Taiwan	6.5	5.7	4.8	5.7	2.4	10.9	1.7	78

Sources: a. World Bank (1998)
b. IMF (1998)
c. Population Reference Bureau (1999)

Garnier (1996), Cheng et al. (1998) and others have described the changing position of the dragon economies in the world economy as one involving a switch from being manufacturing based to becoming high value service economies, each with its own sphere of influence in terms of controlling international flows of trade and investment within the region relative to the global chain of production. The pattern of trade flows in the mid-1990s was one linking the region strongly with the US. Rather than being deeply integrated in a mesh of inter-regional flows of imports and exports, each of the dragons was linked to the US as either the largest, second of third largest trading partner. South Korea and Hong Kong had strong two-way trade links with Japan, and Japan was one of the leading sources of imports of all the dragons. In addition to strong linkage to US and Japan, some limited linkages existed between Hong Kong and Taiwan. Intra-regional trade links were also highly selective, with each dragon being strongly tied to only one specific hinterland (e.g. Singapore to Malaysia; Hong Kong to China, etc.).

Figure 8.1 Annual legal migration flows of 10,000+ persons to the Asian dragons, 1993/94

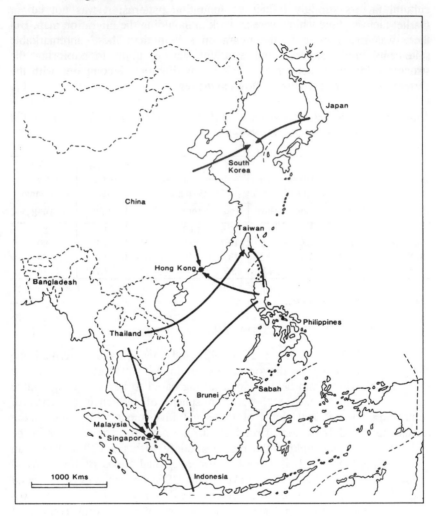

The main picture to emerge is that of a hierarchically structured trade system which dominantly links the dragon economies to the major actors controlling global capital in Pacific Asia—namely the US and Japan. This coincides with the view of O'Loughlin and Anselin (1995: 157) who conclude that there was no evidence of regional trade blocks emerging in Pacific Asia during the 1980s or early 1990s. Although the volume of inter-regional trade grew dramatically, so too did the volume of global trade. As with migration, so also trade flows appear to have been shaped more by fundamental global economic forces than by regional economic integration.

Table 8.1 depicts the strength of investment in dragon economies during the mid-1990s, a significant part of which was foreign direct investment. The two largest sources of foreign inward investment to the four dragon economies were in every case Japan and the US. Just as interesting as the patterns of inward investment were the linkages created by outward investment flows from the dragon economies. The largest single foreign investment outflows link Singapore to Malaysia, and Hong Kong to China. These flows reflect the transfer of labour-intensive manufacturing from these high-wage global cities to lower-wage locations in nearby dominated labour markets. Korea and Taiwan's largest outward investment flows were towards the US, reflecting the cost of accessing new technologies and the desire to penetrate lucrative western markets (ESCAP, 1993). Outward investment from the dragons to neighbouring economies also grew in the 1990s, but it neither came to dominate pre-existing flows, nor contribute to significant regional economic integration. Indeed, investment flows have been highly selective, often structured in such a way as to link a dragon economy to only one dominated foreign labour market.

In relation to the second question raised above—the effect of the Asian economic crisis on migration patterns—Table 8.1 shows that the crisis reversed economic growth trends in Hong Kong and South Korea, resulting in a modest decline in GDP in 1998 of 5.5 per cent. GDP growth rates in Singapore plunged but remained positive, whereas economic growth in Taiwain actually led to an expansion of GDP of 4.8 per cent in 1998. While the effect of the economic crisis in dragon economies was significant, the economic ramifications on Thailand and Indonesia were enormous. Initially it was feared that the crisis would stimulate significant return flows of migrants, and while some return occurred from Malaysia and Thailand (Pillai, 1998; Chalmwong, 1998), early evidence from the dragon economies is very different (Table 8.2).

Table 8.2 Impact of the economic crisis on migrant stocks in the dragon economies*

	Pre-crisis 1997 (000s)	Mid-late 1998 (000s)
Taiwain	230	246
Hong Kong	460	523
Singapore	450	420
Korea	286	233

*Estimates of the Scalabrini Migration Research Center (1999) and as reported by the Hong Kong SAR Immigration Office (1999)

During 1998, Taiwan's migrant stock appears to have increased. Hong Kong's stock also grew significantly, according to the data of the Hong SAR Immigration Office. Of the dragon economies, only Korea experienced a serious reduction in migrant numbers during 1997/98. It also experienced a revival of interest in emigration of Koreans. However, Park (1998) notes that Korean firms have also faced difficulties in hiring local workers to undertake jobs held previously by migrants. With economic recovery in 1999, it seems likely that the government will reconsider its policies on foreign workers.

This brief overview of migration, trade and investment flows points to a remarkably consistent picture of the position and function of the dragon economies in the global economic system. They are located within the world economy as primary satellites of the global capitalist system, and their different roles are determined by their functions as second and lower-order global city regions rather than as nodes within a strongly integrated local regional system. The economic crisis of 1997/98 involved some critical economic adjustments within the region, but it did not stimulate mass repatriation of migrants from the dragon economies. On the contrary, in Taiwan and Hong Kong migration stocks continued to grow throughout the crisis.

This interpretation of the relation between labour movements, trade and investment leads to certain expectations about the nature and behaviour of migration within the system. First, one would expect a duality to be evident in the composition of migration to states such as Hong Kong and Singapore. Immigration flows would increase first amongst low-cost service workers drawn into dangerous, difficult and undesirable jobs in the booming economies of the Asian dragons. A second significant migrant flow would be of highly-skilled professionals, managers, and service providers linking the dragon economies to other parts of the global urban hierarchy. Furthermore, if modes of social regulation are of any significance in influencing how international migration impacts on society and culture in particular places, then one would anticipate that the geography of international flows would be uneven. A country's migration policies would selectively structure which societies and cultures are construed as suitable sources for different categories of low-wage labour migration, and also operate to exclude immigration from other places deemed as inappropriate migrant origins.

THE TRANSFORMATION OF PRODUCTION, TRADE AND MIGRATION LINKS IN HONG KONG

The context of Hong Kong's changing economic position within the world economy has been researched by Henderson, 1991; Brohman, 1995; Murphy; 1995; and Eng, 1997. Manufacturing employment in Hong Kong declined from 42 per cent of the total workforce in 1984 to only 17 per cent a decade later (Figure 8.2). This reflected change in opportunities presented by the opening up of China after 1978, comparative wage levels in Hong Kong and China, and new legislation introduced after 1980 which allowed labour-intensive tasks to be relocated from Hong Kong to neighbouring provinces in China. In global terms, the attraction of producing goods in a very low-wage environment such as China's Guangdong province was very great, while at the same time being able to oversee manufacturing and marketing operations from Hong Kong as a major world city. The result was not only significant investment into and through Hong Kong, but economic expansion of Hong Kong's service sector throughout the 1980s and 1990s. By the early 1990s more than three million persons were employed in China in firms financed from Hong Kong or networked in some close way with Hong Kong-based businesses and their partners (Federation of Hong Kong Industries, 1993). De-industrialisation of Hong Kong occurred at an astounding pace with manufactuing jobs tumbling from over 800,000 in 1989 to 440,000 just five years later. However, this economic restructuring did not result in mass unemployment. Growth of employment in the service sector more than compensated for the downturn in manufacturing, reflecting the way in which Hong Kong has prospered on account of its economic involvement with its neighbour, Guangdong province.

Figure 8.2 Trends in sectoral employment, Hong Kong, 1984–97

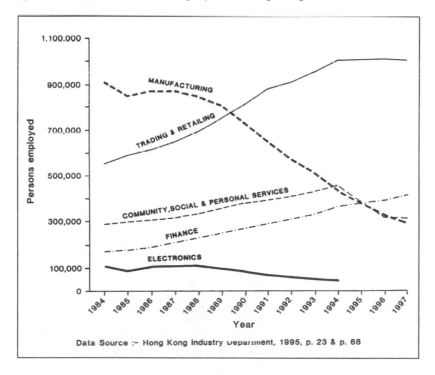

By the mid-1990s Hong Kong was also able to boast merchandise exports greater than those of Taiwan or South Korea and almost twice the value of those from Australia. The prosperity associated with their economic transformations saw Hong Kong's GDP per capita increase strongly and consistently throughout the 1990s until the economic crisis of 1997–98 (Table 8.1). This fuelled demand for labour migrants to fill a range of low-wage service sector jobs such as domestic helpers and construction workers for Hong Kong's new airport.

Tables 8.3 and 8.4, drawn from statistics issued by the Hong Kong Immigration Department, show that the largest annual inflows of immigrants have been from the Philippines and other parts of China. Table 8.3 shows substantial stocks of immigrants from the US, Canada, Thailand and the UK. Asian origins accounted for 47 per cent of migrants in 1986 and 55 per cent in 1996, and that nearly all the growth was due to increased immigration from the Philippines, the dominant source of Hong Kong's domestic maids. An ever-strengthening tie has developed between these two labour markets based on Hong Kong's demand for low-wage service workers from a non-Chinese labour source (Li et al., 1998). Other migrant origins which have grown rapidly in recent years are those associated with global capital such as Canada, Japan, Australia and the US, although the Canadian and Australian immigrant stocks may include some Hong Kong-born return migrants. Skeldon et al. (1995) estimates that such return migrants represent a small proportion of the total inflow from these destinations. The polarisation of migrant wages is evident in Table 8.4 which shows that expatriates from the US, UK and Japan are more than twice as likely as the Hong Kong population to command a monthly income of over HK$30,000. By contrast, migrants from Thailand or Indonesia were more likely than any other group to earn less than HK$15,000 per month.

Table 8.3 Number of foreign nationals in Hong Kong at year end, 1986–96 (selected countries)

Year	1986	1990	1994	1996
Total Number	168,400	227,600	368,500	438,200
Top 10 countries				
Philippines	36,800	61,200	115,500	128,800
United Kingdom	16,000	16,400	23,700	25,500
India	15,300	17,000	19,500	22,000
USA	14,000	19,300	29,900	34,700
Malaysia	10,100	11,700	13,800	14,300
Thailand	9,900	14,300	23,800	24,800
Australia	8,400	12,000	18,700	21,200
Japan	7,500	10,600	17,600	21,800
Canada	8,100	13,000	24,700	30,600
Indonesia	—	—	19,700	31,600

Source: Adapted from Findlay et al. (1997)

There is little convincing evidence in Hong Kong of a significant increase in intra-regional migration as a share of the total migrant stock. By contrast, some migration flows have grown dramatically in size (absolute and relative) and these are links which seem compatible with the emergence of a new dualistic pattern of immigration to Hong Kong, one of the key global cities within Pacific Asia.

Table 8.4 Household income of selected migrant groups in Hong Kong, by place of birth of head of household (HK$ per month), 1996

Birthplace	Less than 15,000 (HK$) (%)	More than 30,000(HK$) (%)
Australia	6.1	82.5
USA	7.3	79.1
UK	7.3	78.5
Japan	7.6	70.4
Canada	10.8	70.2
Hong Kong	32.9	30.6
Philippines	39.5	30.2
Thailand	61.6	17.0
Indonesia	62.7	15.5

Source: Hong Kong 1996 by-census

MIGRATION AND THE ELECTRONICS INDUSTRY: A HONG KONG CASE STUDY

In order to research production and migration linkages in more depth, a sample survey of Hong Kong electronics companies was conducted by the author in 1996. Electronics is Hong Kong's second largest manufacturing industry in terms of employment, gross output, and export earnings. Throughout the 1970s and 1980s, market demand grew rapidly for new consumer goods in the electronics sector such as calculators and television games. In the 1980s, most labour-intensive aspects of production were relocated in southern China. Foreign investors in the electronics sector restructured their operations in Hong Kong, turning it into the regional centre for marketing, design, testing, and packaging of electronics products (Henderson, 1991). Meanwhile, local manufacturers expanded the network of producer relationships involving partners in southern China. Thus, although employment in the manufacturing of electronic goods in Hong Kong fell dramatically in the 1990s, the export of electronic parts and components through Hong Kong grew at an annual average rate of 18.7 per cent between 1980 and 1994. Restructuring of the electronics industry in Hong Kong has thus been shaped by its specific geo-economic linkages within China and is therefore likely to have distinctive effects on labour migration to and from Hong Kong.

Electronics is a sector whose growth and success owes much to adaptive strategies and flexible organisation. Large numbers of technically-sophisticated small companies produce components within a production chain co-ordinated by foreign TNCs. A significant number of endogenous firms network to produce electronic goods under their own brand names (Hong Kong Government Industry Department, 1995a). Compared with other sectors attracting foreign inward investment, electronics has the largest workforce employed in the offices and factories of foreign firms. Not only are there more foreign staff employed within this workforce than in any other sector, but international information/technology flows have been more important than practically anywhere else (Hong Kong Government Industry Department, 1995b). Like other sectors in manufacturing, it has seen a rapid fall in its Hong Kong-based workforce since the late 1980s (Figure 8.2), from around 110,000 in 1988 to only 46,000 in 1994. Numbers of employees per establishment have also declined from 57 to 39 over the same period. These data seem to show a sector experiencing every sign of very rapid re-organisation and restructuring.

The 1994 survey by Findlay et al. (1996) of large foreign-owned companies in Hong Kong showed that foreign staff were used extensively by companies financed by Japanese inward investment, and to a lesser extent by American and European firms. The larger the company the greater the use of expatriates who were employed specifically to maintain 'control' functions within the organisation. A second survey (questionnaire and in-depth interviews) was undertaken in 1996 with 60 small and medium-sized Hong Kong-based companies (owned by Hong Kong investors or with global headquarters in Hong Kong).[2]

Table 8.5 Main sources for Hong Kong businesses of material/components and main markets for major products

Location	Main sources (n=60) (%)	Main markets (n=60) (%)
Hong Kong	26 (43.3)	18 (30.0)
China	15 (25.0)	11 (18.3)
Other parts of the world	27 (45.0)	52 (86.7)

Note: More than one location was stated by some respondents

Table 8.5 indicates the main sources of raw materials and components of these companies and the primary markets to which the main products were sold. Sources and markets are divided into three categories: Hong Kong;

People's Republic of China (PRC); other foreign sources and markets. While this is a crude geographical typology, it nonetheless serves to distinguish between 'localised' production and consumption, the global production chain and a production chain grounded specifically in the cultural, economic, and political context of the PRC. The relative unimportance of China, both as a source of raw material and components, and also as a market for the Hong Kong electronics industry, is evident from Table 8.5. In terms of sourcing, most companies were linked to a global production chain either via other Hong Kong firms or through companies located in the rest of the world. Companies were strongly export-oriented, in particular being linked to European and US markets. Only about ten per cent of firms produced exclusively for Hong Kong and China. Although the survey's focus was on small- and medium-sized companies, most of the companies surveyed could legitimately claim to be part of a global production chain, oriented towards western markets.

Table 8.6 Hong Kong companies' strategies to cope with increases in market demand/workload in the last five years

Coping strategies	Frequency	per cent (n=53*)	Cross-tabulations with employment of immigrant staff in Hong Kong (significance of chi-square test)
Employ more staff in China	33	62.3	n.s.
Investment in machines	24	45.3	p<.05
Relocate to China	21	39.6	p<.05
Staff in China asked to work additional hours	20	37.7	n.s.
Subcontracting	19	35.8	n.s.
Employ more staff in Hong Kong	18	34.0	p<.05
Staff in Hong Kong asked to work additional hours	10	18.9	n.s.
Do not accept extra orders	4	7.5	n.s.

* The number of valid cases excludes companies which had not experienced any increase in demand for their products or increase in workload during the last five years.

Note: More than one strategy was sometimes reported

The survey revealed considerable changes in labour organisation practices. Table 8.6 shows that by far the most popular strategy in situations of rapidly rising demand during the five years prior to the survey was for companies to employ more staff in associated production units in China. This response was given by over 62 per cent of companies, being twice as popular as increased staffing in Hong Kong (34 per cent of companies) and also more likely than investment in extra machinery (forty-five per cent of the sample). About forty per cent of companies claimed that increased demand for their products had directly contributed to their decision to relocate manufacturing activities to China in the last five years (Table 8.6), and 90 per cent had a production base in China or had subcontracted work to plants in China. This figure is comparable with estimates made by other authors (Hobday, 1995). Plants were located mainly in southern and coastal regions designated by the Chinese government as Special Economic Zones (SEZs) (e.g. Shenzhen). The survey revealed that in all cases the shift of production to China took place after 1981, half the companies having done so in the 1990s. For most companies, the shift to China for production was accompanied by a decline in manufacturing units in Hong Kong.[3]

A major aspect of flexibility described by the interviewees concerned how production was organised. Relocation of production to China meant that flexibility could be achieved either 'internally' within the company's Hong Kong operations, or 'externally' within their associated production units in China. In both cases, flexibility in production was achieved through the use of shifts or extension of working hours (Table 8.6). However, such flexibility was more likely to involve the workforce the Chinese factories than in Hong Kong, since Chinese employees were reported to be generally more willing to work unsociable hours and for a longer duration than those in Hong Kong. Furthermore, labour regulations in China were perceived to be less stringent than those in Hong Kong, thus allowing employers to enforce 'flexibility' in the organisation of working hours. It seems that flexibility from the employers' perspective effectively equated with the Chinese workers' greater vulnerability to exploitation.

It was also not uncommon for staff numbers in the plants in China to vary according to market demand. Seasonal fluctuations were often reported. The workforce in these plants consisted both of those who were in the more stable 'core' (managers, technicians and some of the less-skilled workers) and also of those who were considered to be more 'peripheral' (Short, 1996: 241). Despite the fact that some of the workers were recruited only to deal with seasonal surges in orders, most of the managers who were interviewed maintained that it was not their company's policy to employ staff only for short duration. In other words, companies did not set out to recruit 'temporary' staff, but employees would opt to leave when there was not enough work, since the wages of most of the production workers were tied to the number of working hours.

'External' flexibility in production was also achieved through the use of sub-contractors (Table 8.3). In most cases, the company's relationship with their Chinese associates was similar to a sub-contracting arrangement. Some firms also subcontracted to other companies in Hong Kong which had production facilities in China. Usually the contractor was responsible for all costs involved in production, including the purchase of materials and machines. Subcontracting was therefore particularly advantageous to small companies which were not able to make a large or risky capital commitment and preferred to concentrate resources on other activities such as sales and marketing, or research and development.

Table 8.7 Change in size of Hong Kong operations and the use of immigrant staff

Change in number of staff in Hong Kong during the last three years	Immigrant staff in Hong Kong		
	None (%)	At least one (%)	TOTAL (%)
No significant changes	19 (57.6)	14 (42.4)	33 (100)
Number has been falling	6 (54.5)	5 (45.5)	11 (100)
Number has been rising	2 (15.4)	11 (84.6)	13 (100)
TOTAL	27	30	57

Chi-square = 6.9, df = 2, $p<.05$

One might have anticipated that economic restructuring, involving the de-industrialisation of Hong Kong and a switch to more flexible production systems, would have brought an end to immigration. To test this hypothesis, companies were asked if they used non-Hong Kong staff in their Hong Kong operations, including any Chinese-born people who had migrated from China during the previous ten years. Perhaps surprisingly, half the companies surveyed employed immigrant non-Hong Kong staff in their Hong Kong operations (Table 8.7). The vast majority were recent legal immigrants from China. Some 15 per cent of companies also employed skilled immigrants from other parts of the world. Most of the recent Chinese immigrants occupied junior posts. The immigrant labour had been recruited through the normal channels in Hong Kong and their immigrant status was often reported to be irrelevant to their appointment. Only a very small number of mainland Chinese immigrants had been brought to Hong Kong by their employers. In 1994, the Hong Kong Government introduced a scheme which allowed the entry of up to 1,000 professionals and managers who were graduates of 36 key higher education institutions in China. Two of the companies interviewed had utilised this scheme to bring in engineers from China. It was necessary to import Chinese engineers because of the lack of young Hong Kong-born technical experts. The relocation of manufacturing to China, a strategy which responded to local shortages of low-wage labour in Hong Kong, had actually been partially responsible for creating a shortage of skilled labour in Hong Kong. Some of the more experienced Hong Kong engineers and managers had been transferred to plants in China or had chosen to set up their own companies. Moreover, because little manufacturing remains in Hong Kong, young engineering graduates trained in Hong Kong had less practical work experience in production.

To further explore the relationship between flexibility and the use of immigrant staff in Hong Kong, the questionnaire data were analysed in greater depth. Chi-square tests on cross-tabulations showed that three of the coping strategies reported earlier were significantly related to the employment of non-Hong Kong staff (Table 8.6). The first was the relocation of production to China to cope with increased market demand which was associated with a higher tendency to use mainland Chinese in the Hong Kong workforce. While no simple explanation for this unexpected finding can be identified from the empirical data, it is interesting that certain company characteristics seemed to be associated with the use of immigrant labour. For example, those companies which had used relocation as a strategy to cope with increases in market demand, and which had also employed Chinese immigrants in Hong Kong, apparently had a larger workforce in both Hong Kong and in China. This may suggest that while some companies had shifted manufacturing to China in response to increases in production costs in Hong Kong, others might have done so because local labour shortages in Hong Kong had hindered expansion during periods of growth. For the latter group of companies, although their production facilities in China had helped solve the problem of low-wage labour shortages in Hong Kong, they had *also* chosen to employ Chinese immigrants in Hong Kong to maintain aspects of their Hong Kong-based activities.

Two other coping strategies were found to be significantly associated with the use of immigrant staff. These were the employment of more staff in Hong Kong and increased productivity through investing in machines during periods of increased market demands (Table 8.6). While some coping strategies, such as subcontracting, could be undertaken as short-term responses to cyclical changes in market demand, the purchase of machines involved capital investment which was usually made for more long-term benefits. The employment of more staff in Hong Kong could be either a temporary or a longer-term strategy, although it seems to be a relatively permanent arrangement since both the interviews and questionnaires revealed that companies were unlikely to employ Hong Kong staff on a temporary basis. These two strategies were therefore probably used to cope with a more steady increase in demand. Analysis of company size indicated that companies that had used these two strategies were much more likely to have experienced an expansion in their workforce in Hong Kong in the three years previous to the study, and they also tended to be slightly bigger than the companies which had not used these strategies. This further suggests that the use of immigrant labour was related to company growth during a period when there was an overall shortage of local skilled labour in Hong Kong. As Table 8.7 verifies, this relationship is statistically significant.

What generalisations can be drawn from these empirical findings? Global economic forces have been responsible for a substantial restructuring of Hong Kong's manufacturing base. Many production activities have been relocated to neighbouring sites within China outside the territory of what since 1997 has been labelled SAR Hong Kong. Despite this flow of investment capital from Hong Kong, immigration has continued to grow. Some 300,000 legal immigrants entered Hong Kong from China alone in the ten years prior to the survey work.

The survey suggests that electronics companies did not respond in the same fashion to changes in their environment. Some smaller companies externalised their production because this was the only viable option to survive soaring property and labour costs. This group of companies found that flexible adjustment of working hours for staff in China was less costly and more efficient than maintaining a flexible workforce in Hong Kong. These companies were more likely to be involved in the manufacturing of low-end electronic products. Their workforce in Hong Kong could be kept small because all or most of the production processes could be handled by associated factories in China. In contrast, other companies used externalisation as part of a package of measures to cope with growth in market demands. For these companies, while measures such as flexible working hours or subcontracting to other manufacturers could cope with short-term increases in demand, more sustained growth required additional strategies such as automation and expansion of workforce both in China and in Hong Kong. For companies following this strategy (including both small and large companies), expansion of the workforce in their Hong Kong operations implied taking on further immigrant employees. In terms of wider theory, what the research seems to show is the possibility of flexible accumulation alongside high rates of employment growth and the continued use of immigrant labour. The findings are in harmony with Dicken's (1993) claim of globalisation operating through a spectrum of organisational forms, with so-called 'flexible' working practices being employed by different organisational forms for quite varied reasons. While the resultant net changes in the labour market, both in Hong Kong and China have been striking, they have not brought an end to immigration of labour to the smaller-scale manufacturing units remaining in Hong Kong. In this case, flexible regimes of accumulation do not seem to have proved inimitable to continued labour migration. This contrasts strongly with generalisations about migration-production linkages developed by other analysts in a West European context (Fielding, 1993; 1997).

At other sites in the production chain the restructuring of Hong Kong's electronics industry has had quite different labour mobility implications. For example, the general shift of manufacturing from Hong Kong to southern China (of which the survey reports only one small part) has had significant impacts on migration both within China and from Hong Kong to China.

Millions of persons are believed to have moved from other parts of China into the Special Economic Zones since the open-door policy was introduced in 1979. The population in Shenzhen grew by 20 times from 1979 to 1991 (Leung, 1993). Chang (1996) suggests that the 'floating' migrant population crossing into Guangdong province in 1990 was no less than four million. The 1990 Census in China recorded 3.29 million migrants in Guangdong province (a higher proportion than any other province in China), although these figures exclude migrants of less than one year's residence as well as illegal movers (He, 1992). This therefore gives credibility to some of the higher estimates of the stock of migrant workers in Guangdong province (Liu, 1995). Whatever the precise figures, the important point is that these Special Economic Zones of Guangdong province have become a pole of attraction for mass migration within China as a result of foreign direct investment, much of which is controlled from Hong Kong. Part of this flow is accounted for by the type of 'small' Hong Kong electronics companies covered in the survey.

Recruitment agencies were mentioned in many interviews with company managers. They were seen as an important means of selecting and organising migrant labour. The agencies were state-run organisations instrumental in promoting the geographical mobility of elements of the Chinese population. The concentration of most export-oriented manufacturing facilities in China's Special Economic Zones quickly absorbed local labour supplies and pushed up local labour costs. As a result, it was necessary for employers to turn to other provinces for labour, usually for less skilled tasks. In some cases, technical expertise (e.g. junior engineers) was brought in from more developed cities such as Shanghai. Usually, local recruits were preferred to deal with local government, such as in liaison work with customs and tax offices. The use of state-run intermediary agencies to recruit workers allowed the Chinese government some control over population flows. Further regulations were exercised through the requirement that internal migrants obtain permission for relocation from authorities at both places of origin and destination (Laquian, 1989). The use of large numbers of internal migrants in production was so common in the companies included in the interviews, that provision of staff accommodation was considered normal.

If recruitment agencies channel low wage migrant labour from other provinces of China to the Special Economic Zones, Hong Kong companies are responsible for organising a very different type of flow: professional and technical workers from Hong Kong to China (Tang, 1994). Two-thirds of the companies in our survey reported frequent (at least once a month) visits undertaken by their Hong Kong based employers or senior employees to associated plants in China. In some cases, these staff made such journeys regularly every week. Almost half the companies also reported more permanent deployment of their Hong Kong personnel to affiliated factories in China. Whilst spending most of their time in China, these staff also travelled frequently to their Hong Kong offices. The number of persons transferred from Hong Kong to China ranged from one to 36, with a median of two to three per company. According to the General Household Survey conducted in 1992 (Hong Kong Census and Statistics Department, 1992), no less than 64,200 Hong Kong residents had worked in China in the previous year. For those companies in the survey which had transferred staff from Hong Kong to China, the age and sex compositions of such staff were similar to those identified in the General Household Survey (Table 8.8). The typical staff deployed were men in their 30s or 40s.

Table 8.8 Age and Sex of Hong Kong residents working in China

Total No of persons who had worked in China at some point during the previous 12 months	Oct–Dec 1989	Apr–Jun 1992
	24,600	64,200
Age: 15–19	200	300
20–29	10,600	13,700
30–39	16,400	23,700
40 49	11,800	17,000
50 and over	6,600	9,500
Male	39,700	55,600
Female	5,900	8,600

Source: Hong Kong Census and Statistics Department, 1992

The Hong Kong staff who made frequent trips or who were posted to China were mostly in management positions. Many, particularly among those Hong Kong based staff who travelled frequently to plants in China, were engineers. Table 8.9 summarises the functions fulfilled by these staff. An obvious difference between the frequent travellers and the more permanent transferees concerned overall control of the Chinese branch plants. This may be explained by the fact that many of the visits made by Hong Kong-based staff were undertaken to subcontracting firms in China which were not owned by the companies surveyed. In these cases, the trips were made mainly for trouble shooting, corporate communication or other reasons related to production, including the provision of technical expertise, supervision of production and quality control. Permanent deployment of Hong Kong staff was far less likely to be motivated by the need for corporate communication or technical expertise, although the need to supervise and control the quality of production was still important. The relative insignificance of technical expertise as a reason for permanent staff transfer reflected the fact that the factories were often involved in low-end production steps, such as assembly work, which did not require advanced technology. The interviews also revealed that some companies were prepared to use mainland Chinese

engineering graduates from famous universities since their wage demands
were lower than those paid to Hong Kong engineers working in China.

Table 8.9 Main functions of Hong Kong staff deployed to China

Functions	Hong Kong staff based in China n=27* (%)	Hong Kong-based staff who travelled frequently to China n=39* (%)
Overall control of the China plant	21 (77.8)	15 (38.5)
Supervise production	17 (63.0)	20 (51.3)
Train Chinese staff	14 (51.9)	15 (38.5)
Trouble shooting	12 (44.4)	23 (59.0)
Provide technical expertise	10 (37.0)	22 (56.4)
Quality control	14 (51.9)	19 (48.7)
Control accounts	10 (37.0)	14 (35.9)
Corporate communication	7 (25.9)	19 (48.7)
Public relations	6 (22.2)	9 (23.1)
Sales and marketing	4 (14.8)	7 (17.9)

*n equals the number of companies with such staff who answered the questions on functions.

Note: More than one function was sometimes reported.

The case study has shown that new patterns of investment, global
production and international migration are intimately linked. Global cities
such as Hong Kong act as centres for the management of international capital
and production as organised by large transnational companies. They also host
the headquarters of smaller companies which belong to global production
chains. Both these types of global linkage are associated with flows of
capital, commodities and labour. But these flows are organised in a highly
structured hierarchical fashion, reflecting transformative power relations at
work in the global economy. In the case of the Hong Kong electronics
industry this has meant a mass relocation of production to China and the
associated reorganisation of migration to meet the needs for low-wage
labour, managerial control between production site and headquarters in Hong
Kong, and international linkage to consumer markets in other parts of the
world. Patterns of economic reproduction as well as production in Hong
Kong have also been transformed in recent decades, including the addition to
Hong Kong's labour force of many low-wage service staff, mainly from the
Philippines.

CONCLUSION

This chapter has sought to explore some of the linkages between production
regimes and migration processes. The case study of Hong Kong's electronics
sector has helped illustrate how economic development has produced

transformations in the organisation of labour and the production chain which have affected migration at many different scales. Some of these have been mapped in Figure 8.3 in terms of production-migration relationships involving the global city of Hong Kong.

Figure 8.3 The hierarchy of skill exchange in Hong Kong industry

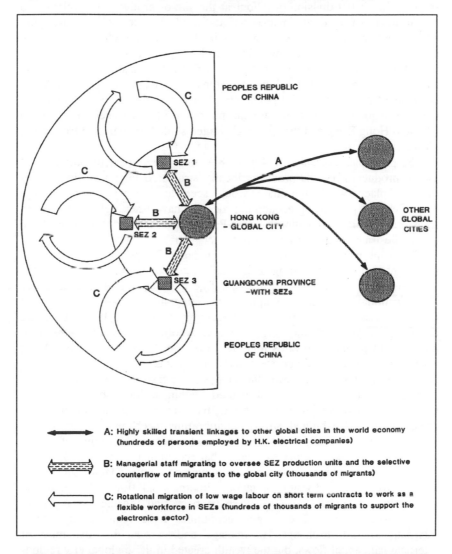

A: Highly skilled transient linkages to other global cities in the world economy (hundreds of persons employed by H.K. electrical companies)

B: Managerial staff migrating to oversee SEZ production units and the selective counterflow of immigrants to the global city (thousands of migrants)

C: Rotational migration of low wage labour on short term contracts to work as a flexible workforce in SEZs (hundreds of thousands of migrants to support the electronics sector)

Three levels of relations are represented in Figure 8.3: those linking Hong Kong to the rest of the global economy and especially to other global cities; interactions between company headquarters in Hong Kong and production units located in the Special Economic Zones (SEZs) of Guangdong province; and flows into the SEZs from other parts of China. With each level in this hierarchy, specific types of labour flow would be expected. In terms of migration and production linkages in China, the characteristics of skill transfers are postulated to be governed by at least three processes. These include: first, the nature of labour organisation within the production process; second, the spatial division of labour at the site of production in relation to that in interconnected labour markets; and third, the need for certain highly skilled migrants to move between sites in the production chain to facilitate control, information exchange and technology transfer. In terms of migration–production linkages not only is there the transfer of Hong Kong staff to China, but migration flows into Hong Kong might also be expected to be shaped by its position as a global city. In terms of the electronics industry, the two major types of flows are the migration of low-waged labour from China to Hong Kong and the very high-waged skilled immigration from other global cities.

The principles presented in Figure 8.3, that hierarchical organisation of global production chains produces locally structured migration linkages at different places within the chain, would seem to have wider applicability. The effects of globalising economic processes have been highly selective in transforming migration patterns across Pacific Asia in the 1990s, as has been amply illustrated in the earlier part of this chapter.

The empirical material which has been presented points to at least two important conclusions relating to globalisation and migration theory. First, there seems to be strong evidence to refute the view that as global forces power national economic development, net emigration initially increases and then decreases until it is replaced by net immigration (Kim, 1996: 306). The dragon economies are not discrete entities whose development paths have driven them primarily towards regional interdependence. Nor has the Asian economic crisis inevitably caused migration systems to shrink in all states or in a uniform fashion. Instead, the analysis suggests that globalisation of economic systems has been structured within a hierarchy of unequal relationships. Flows of migration, trade and finance within the Pacific Asia region have not exhibited strong equilibrating mechanisms operating to remove market inequalities. Second, it would appear that mobility of capital and labour are inherent aspects of the global economic system, with the flows which result being highly structured and governed by many factors, including a distinctive spatial division of labour. International flows of capital and labour do not appear, however, to have been tied together in a precise deterministic fashion. The dragon economies have required high level international skill exchanges to manage and monitor the dynamics of international capital flows, but the wealth created in these global city regions has also generated a differential demand for low-wage service labour drawn selectively from certain countries of origin deemed to be culturally appropriate. Both these types of migration flow have helped maintain the attractiveness of dragon economies as sites of global control (Boyle et al. 1996).

The evidence presented in this chapter concerning employment patterns in the electronics industry has illustrated how the spatial division of migrant labour linked to a global city region involves not only the city itself but also its hinterlands through the physical and human resources which it controls. Since labour migration is an integral and necessary part of these economies' ongoing transformation, it seems inevitable that the patterning, organisation, and scale of labour migration to the four Asian dragon economies will continue to develop and change. Future changes will reflect the evolving power relationships exercised by these places within global financial and production systems, with further migration transformations resulting from the ongoing reorganisation of global capital. High levels of low-wage and significant levels of highly-skilled migration will remain a prerequisite for success of the dragon economies in the foreseeable future if they are to maintain their powerful global positions.

NOTES

1. The Economic and Social Research Council of the UK funded some of the work on which this chapter is based (Award No. L324253026). I am grateful to my colleagues Huw Jones and Lin Li who contributed to many aspects of the research on which this chapter is based. It was much improved as a result of helpful comments on an earlier draft by Charles Keely and Barry Chiswick.
2. Technical details of the sampling procedure and definitions used in the survey are reported in Findlay et al. (1997).
3. Further details of how flexibility was operationalised in different types of firms have been reported elsewhere (Findlay and Li, 1997).

REFERENCES

Alburo, F.A. (1994), 'Trade and turning points in labour migration', *Asian and Pacific Migration Journal*, 3: 49–80.
Birks, J. and S. Sinclair (1980), *International Migration and Development in the Arab Region*, Geneva: ILO.
Boyle, M., A. Findlay, E. Lelievre, and R. Paddison (1996), 'World cities and the limits to global control: A case study of executive search firms in Europe's leading cities', *International Journal of Urban and Regional Research*, 20 (3): 498–517.
Brohman, J. (1995), 'Postwar development in the Asian NICs: does the neoliberal model fit reality?', *Economic Geography*, 71: 107–30.
Castles, S. and M.J. Miller, (1993), *The Age of Migration*, Basingstoke: Macmillan.
Chalmwong, Y. (1998), 'The impact of the crisis on migration in Thailand', *Asian and Pacific Migration Journal*, 7: 297–312.
Chang, S.D. (1996), 'The floating population: an informal process of urbanization in China', *International Journal of Population Geography*, 2: 197–214.

Cheng, Y., M. Wong, and C. Findlay (1998), 'Singapore and Hong Kong' in R. McLeod and R. Garnaut (eds), *East Asia in Crisis*, London: Routledge, pp. 162–78.

Dicken, P. (1993), 'The Changing Organisation of the Global Economy', in R. Johnston (ed.), *The Challenge for Geography*, Oxford: Blackwell, pp. 31–53.

Dicken, P., J. Peck and A. Tickell (1997), 'Unpacking the Global', in R. Lee and J. Wills (eds), *Geographies of Economies*, London: Arnold, pp. 158–66.

Eng, I. (1997), 'Flexible production in late industrialisation: the case of Hong Kong,' *Economic Geography*, **73**: 1–25.

ESCAP (1993), *Economic and Social Survey of Asia and the Pacific 1993*, New York: United Nations.

Federation of Hong Kong Industries (1993), *Hong Kong's Industrial Investment in the Pearl River Delta*, Industrial and Research Division, Federation of Hong Kong Industries.

Fielding, A. (1993), 'Mass Migration and Economic Restructuring', in R. King (ed.), *Mass Migration in Europe*, London: Belhaven, pp. 7–18.

Fielding, A. (1997), 'The effects of Economic Restructuring on the Populations of Western Europe's Cities and Regions', in H.H. Blotevogel and A.J. Fielding (eds), *People, Jobs and Mobility in the New Europe*, Chichester: Wiley, pp. 297–304.

Fields, G.S. (1994), 'The migration transition in Asia', *Asian and Pacific Migration Journal*, **3**: 7–30.

Findlay, A.M. and F.L.N. Li. (1997), 'Economic Restructuring, Flexibility, and Migration: Hong Kong's Electronics Industry in the Global Economy', Research Paper 97/2, Centre for Applied Population Research: University of Dundee, Dundee.

Findlay, A.M., F.L.N. Li, J. Jowett, and R. Skeldon (1996), 'Skilled international migration and the global city', *Transactions, Institute of British Geographers*, **21**: 54–65.

Findlay, A.M., H. Jones and G. Davidson (1997), *Migration Transition or Transformation of Asian Dragon Economies*, Research Paper 97/5, Centre for Applied Population Research: University of Dundee: Dundee.

Findlay, A.M., H. Jones and G. Davidson (1998), 'Migration transition or transformation of Asian dragon economies', *International Journal of Urban and Regional Research*, **22**: 643–63.

Friedmann, J. (1986), 'The world city hypothesis', *Development and Change*, **17**: 69–83.

Garnier, P. (1996), 'International trade in services', *Asian Pacific Migration Journal*, **5**: 367–97.

He, J. (1992), 'China's Migration Regions, *1953–1990'*, APRU Discussion Paper 92/3 Department of Geography, University of Glasgow: Glasgow.

Held, D., A. McGrew, et al., (1999), *Global Transformations*, Cambridge: Polity Press.

Henderson, J. (1991), 'The political economy of technological transformation in the Hong Kong electronics industry', in K.Y. Chen, M. Nyaw and T.T.C. Wong (eds), *Industrial and Trade Development in Hong Kong*, Centre of Asian Studies, Hong Kong: University of Hong Kong, pp. 57–115.

Hobday, M. (1995), *Innovation in East Asia: The Challenge to Japan*, Aldershot: Edward Elgar.

Hong Kong Census and Statistics Department (1992), *Special Topics Report No. X.*, Hong Kong.

Hong Kong Government Industry Department (1995a), *Survey of External Investment in Hong Kong's Manufacturing Industries*, Hong Kong.

Hong Kong Government Industry Department (1995b), *Hong Kong's Manufacturing Industries*, Hong Kong.

IMF (International Monetary Fund) (1998), *International Financial Statistics Year Book 1998*, Washington, DC: IMF.

Jones, H. (1990), *Population Geography*, London: Paul Chapman.

Kim, W.B. (1996), 'Economic interdependence and migration dynamics in Asia', *Asian and Pacific Migration Journal*, 5: 303–18.

Knox, P. (1996), 'Globalization and the world city hypothesis', *Scottish Geographical Magazine*, 112: 124–6.

Laquian, A. (1989), 'Megacities in China', in E. Brennan (ed.), papers for the XXIst International Population Conference Session 13: Megacities: Trends, Issues and Policies, International Union for the Scientific Study of Population: Liege, pp. 211–24.

Leung, C.C. (1993), *The Lessons of East Asia: Hong Kong—A Unique Case of Development*, Washington, DC: World Bank.

Leyshon, A. (1997), 'True stories? Global dreams, global nightmares and writing globalization', in R. Lee and J. Wills (eds), *Geographies of Economies*, London: Arnold, pp. 133–46.

Li, F.L.N., A.M. Findlay and H. Jones (1998), 'A cultural economy perspective on service sector migration to the global city', *International Migration*, 36: 131–58.

Lim, L. (1996), 'The migration transition in Malaysia', *Asian and Pacific Migration Journal*, 5: 319–37.

Liu, Y. (1995), 'Labour migration of China', *ASEAN Economic Bulletin*, 12: 299–307.

McKibben, W. (1998), 'Internationally mobile capital and the global economy', in R. McLeod and R. Garnaut (eds), *East Asia in Crisis*, London: Routledge, pp. 227–44.

Murphy, A. (1995), 'Economic regionalisation and Pacific Asia', *Geographical Review*, 85: 127–40.

Ohmae, K. (1990), *The Borderless World*, London: Collins.

Ohmae, K. (1995), *The End of the Nation State*, New York: Free Press.

O'Loughlin, J. and Anselin, L. (1995), 'Geo-economic competition and trade bloc formation', *Economic Geography*, 71: 131–60.

Pang, Eng Fong (1993), 'Labour migration to the newly industrialising economies of South Korea, Taiwan, Hong Kong and Singapore', *International Migration*, 31: 300–13.

Pang, Eng Fong (1994), 'An eclectic approach to turning points in migration', *Asian and Pacific Migration Journal*, 3: 81–92.

Park, Y. (1998), 'The financial crisis and foreign workers in Korea', *Asian and Pacific Migration Journal*, 7: 219–34.

Pillai, P. (1998), 'The impact of the economic crisis on migrant labour in Malaysia', *Asian and Pacific Migration Journal*, 7: 255–80.

Population Reference Bureau (1999), 'World Population Data Sheet 1999', Washington, DC: PRB.

Rostow, W.W. (1960), *The Stages of Economic Growth*, Cambridge: Cambridge University Press.

Scalabrini Migration Center (1999), *Asian Migration Atlas*, Manila: SMC.

Short, J.R. (1996), *The Urban Order*, Oxford: Blackwell.

Skeldon, R. (1994), 'Turning points in labour migration: the case of Hong Kong', *Asian and Pacific Migration Journal*, 3: 93–118.

Skeldon, R. (1997), *Migration and Development*, Harlow: Addison Wesley Longman.

Skeldon, R., J. Jowett, A.M. Findlay, and L. Li (1995), 'An Assessment of Available Data Sources for the Analysis of the Trends in Migration', in R. Skeldon (ed.), *Emigration from Hong Kong*, Hong Kong: Chinese University Press, pp. 79–110.

Stalker, P. (2000), *Workers without Frontiers*, Geneva: ILO.

Tang, K.Y. (1994), 'Hong Kong's Economic Relations with China', in OECD (ed.), *New Economic Partners: Dynamic Asian Economies and Central and Eastern European Countries*, Paris: OECD, pp. 41–60.

World Bank (1998), 'World Development Report', Washington, DC: World Bank.

9. The Impact of Immigration on the Ageing of Australia's Population[1]

Peter McDonald and Rebecca Kippen

A STATEMENT OF THE ISSUE

In 1998, just over 12 per cent of Australia's population was aged 65 years and over. Population projections indicate that this percentage is likely to at least double in the next 40 years. This trend has given rise to concerns about the capacity of the Australian economy in the future to support the older members of the Australian society. In particular, an older population implies increased costs for aged pensions and health and aged care services.

As part of the response to this future situation, it has been suggested that the country should reduce the extent or speed of ageing through changes to immigration policy. The argument is that, as immigrants are younger on average than the Australian population, an increase in the level of immigration would reduce the ageing of the population. To strengthen the case, it has also been suggested that the immigration programme should recruit persons who are younger than the immigrants that enter Australia now. The call is for more and younger immigrants who have skill levels at least equal to those of immigrants at present. In addition, proponents of this position sometimes claim that immigrants have higher fertility than the Australian average, so that higher immigration would increase Australia's birth rate and, hence, reduce ageing of the population.

The counter argument is that immigration makes only a marginal difference to the ageing of the population because, in the longer term, immigrants themselves grow old. Larger immigration leads to larger numbers of older people, with little impact on population age structure. In other words, immigration is an inefficient response to the ageing of the population and a belief in immigration as a solution may draw our attention away from the social and economic reforms necessary as we face an ageing future. In addition, proponents of this position sometimes argue that, rather than importing high fertility immigrants, there is a need to support childbearing and childrearing in Australia so that the fertility rate stops falling.

Public debate about these two points of view has waxed and waned over the past 15 years, rising again in the past 12 months. The aim of this chapter is to examine the validity of the propositions that underpin these arguments.

WHY IS OUR POPULATION AGEING?

As fertility and mortality rates fall, populations age. In Australia, as in other advanced industrialised countries, fertility and mortality rates have been falling for more than a century. In 1870, 42 per cent of Australia's population was aged less than 15 years and 2 per cent was aged 65 years and over. In 1998, 21 per cent was aged less than 15 years and 12 per cent was aged 65 years and over. Thus, ageing is not a new phenomenon. Being an outcome of increased control over both childbearing and death, ageing for the last century has generally been welcomed, so why is it that ageing has now become a major concern?

The sudden emergence of ageing as an issue is indicated by the lack of concern expressed about ageing in the 1975 Report of the National Population Inquiry (the Borrie Report). Indeed, the ageing of the population received only passing mention in this, the most comprehensive report on Australia's population ever undertaken, and no mention at all in the concluding chapters related to policy.

Ageing has recently emerged as an issue because fertility and mortality have both fallen since the mid-1970s to a greater extent than was envisaged in the Borrie Report. As birth and death rates have fallen in Australia, the speed and the future level of population ageing have increased sharply. The year 1973 was the last year of recorded statistics available at the time of writing of the Borrie Report. If birth rates were the same at each age today as they were in 1973, there would have been 40 per cent, or 100,000, more births in 1998. If death rates at each age were the same today as they were in 1971–76, there would have been 60 per cent, or 78,000, more deaths in 1998. These are remarkable changes within a short period of time. One hundred thousand fewer people each year at the young end of the age structure and almost 78,000 more people each year at the old end of the age structure are the reasons ageing of the population has emerged as a policy issue.

In addition, ageing will be rapid in the second, third and fourth decades of the twenty-first century because, in those years, the large post-war, baby-boom generation will be in the older age groups. In this sense, rapid ageing of the population is the product of a sustained period of high fertility rates (1946–1975) followed by a sustained period of low fertility rates (1976 onwards). That the extent of ageing in 2020, for example, is related to births up to 75 years earlier indicates that population ageing is a long-term process. Even projections of population 50 years into the future may fall short of measuring the full impact of ageing.

RESEARCH AND OPINION ON THE ISSUE: 1983–98

Ageing, and the possible impacts of immigration on ageing, emerged as policy considerations in the early 1980s, when new official projections based on assumptions of sustained low fertility and lower mortality rates showed that ageing was likely to be more rapid and more severe than the Borrie Report had indicated. Discussion of the issue in the 1980s and early 1990s has been reviewed extensively by Young (1994) and our analysis draws on her work.

The issue of immigration and ageing was addressed in a joint study by the Committee for the Economic Development of Australia (CEDA) and the Department of Immigration and Ethnic Affairs (DIEA). In 1983, the main authors of this study wrote that the 'younging' effect of immigration was regarded as an 'uncontroversial fact' (Norman and Meikle, 1983: 15). By 1985, the same authors had become more ambivalent, writing in the final report that differences between projected age distributions were 'not great, despite the large differences between the migration assumptions' and, on the same page, 'immigration adds disproportionately large numbers to the younger age groups' (Norman and Meikle, 1985: 84). As Young (1994: 56–7) reports, however, the technical work carried out for this study generally concluded that the impacts of immigration upon ageing were minimal. This result was confirmed during the 1980s by each new publication of the official projections made by the Australian Bureau of Statistics.

Despite this technical work, based on the Executive Summary of the CEDA/DIEA Report, newspapers reported the study's finding that 'the mean age of the Australian population can be reduced by increasing the number of migrants'. This position was backed by the Minister for Immigration, Mr Hurford, who wrote in 1985 that 'migrants help our economy by reducing the average age and the costs associated with the greying of Australia' (*The Age*, 17 July 1985). Then, in 1986, the Migration Committee of the Government's National Population Council, reported that, 'by adding younger people, immigration retards demographic ageing' (National Population Council 1986: 25). In 1987, the Minister for Immigration, Mr Young, said that '(w)ithout immigration we would experience an accelerated ageing of the population, a steep increase in welfare payments and therefore higher taxation' (Young, 1987).

Thus, the belief that immigration has a substantial retarding effect on ageing continued despite the empirical evidence available at the time demonstrating that this was not the case.

More empirical work was carried out in 1988 by the Committee to Advise on Australia's Immigration Policies (CAAIP). The Committee's report concluded that massive levels of immigration would be required to retard ageing (Centre for International Economics, 1988: iv).

In the report, *Australian Immigration: A Survey of the Issues,* published by the Bureau of Immigration Research in 1990, University of Adelaide demographer, Graeme Hugo, concluded:

> Claims, therefore, that the immigration program can retard the overall ageing of the population which is occurring must be treated with suspicion...Young has made a definitive demographic refutation of claims that immigration can have anything more than a slight retardation effect on the ageing of the Australian population. (Hugo, 1990: 49–50)

In the second half of the 1980s, the ANU demographer, Christabel Young, conducted a number of studies on the impact of immigration upon ageing. These studies concluded that large-scale immigration was not a sensible response to the ageing of the population (Young, 1988, 1989). Her most important study of the issue was *Australia's Ageing Population—Policy Options* (Young, 1990). Added to her previous empirical research, this report was highly influential in challenging the view that immigration could substantially retard population ageing. Following the publication of this report, official sources became much more circumspect about statements regarding immigration and ageing. For example, the December 1991 final report of the Population Issues Committee of the National Population Council, *Population Issues and Australia's Future,* stated that 'while the level of immigration will affect the relative size of the labour force at any particular time, its impact will be transitory unless the size of the intake were to continue to increase' (National Population Council, 1991: 30). The Chair of the Population Issues Committee, Professor Glenn Withers, as Commissioner of the Economic Planning Advisory Council (EPAC), said in 1992:

> With respect to immigration, its use as a major instrument for response to demographic ageing would require substantially increasing levels of migration over time. It should be no surprise that migrants themselves do age and do bear children, so that the net effects of a given migration intake on ageing and on dependency ratios are more muted than might otherwise be thought. (EPAC, 1992: 12)

A later EPAC study concluded:

> Even the most ambitious migration programs, by historical standards, would not eliminate a substantial increase in age dependency ratios. The ageing of the population structure must therefore be addressed directly through effective retirement income policies, health care reform, support for the disabled, etc. (Clare and Tulpule, 1994: 17)

Young (1994: 54–6) also documents the shift away from the view that immigration can substantially retard ageing. This shift became evident in publications of the Department of Immigration and Ethnic Affairs during the early 1990s and was complete by 1999 when the Department stated that '[e]xtensive research has concluded that immigration is a very inefficient means of reducing the impact of ageing' (DIMA, 1999: 10).

The notion that ageing can be substantially retarded by immigration has also been dismissed recently by a group of four academic writers with a long history of immigration research:

> In the 1980s, immigration was advocated as a means of alleviating or 'solving' the ageing of the population—as the median age of immigrants is lower (by around five years) than that of the Australian population in general. In the 1990s, a more conservative view has gained ground and ABS projections now[2] show that ageing of the population is only slightly more pronounced without overseas migration. (Castles et al., 1998: 33–4)

AGAINST THE FLOW? ALVARADO AND CREEDY

During the 1990s, Jose Alvarado, an economist working in the Department of Premier and Cabinet in Victoria, and John Creedy, a professor of economics at the University of Melbourne, conducted research on migration, ageing and future social expenditure (Alvarado and Creedy, 1996). The study was commissioned by the Bureau of Immigration, Population and Multicultural Research, but was published after that organisation had been abolished. The results of this work have also recently been published in two books (Alvarado and Creedy, 1998; Creedy, 1998). While these works are recently published, a great deal of the input data underlying the projections made by Alvarado and Creedy dates back to the 1980s.

The work of Alvarado and Creedy is most notable in that it goes beyond demographic outcomes to measure the economic benefit arising from a reduction in the proportion of people at older ages. The measure employed is the ratio of public social expenditure to gross domestic product (Box 9.1). In their 1996 report the authors make the general theoretical proposition that:

> Large inflows of people with higher fertility and a younger age structure than the native population can retard the process of population ageing and therefore the growth in the ratio of social expenditure to GDP. (Alvarado and Creedy, 1996: 42)

They then go on to conclude from their own research that 'the results of the study suggest that immigration can retard population ageing to some extent' (1996: 42), but in their final conclusion they state that:

> Projections (of future social expenditure) appear to be more sensitive to changes in productivity growth, participation and unemployment rates than to changes in immigration levels. (Alvarado and Creedy, 1996: 44)

Indeed, all studies of past and potential future social expenditure conclude that increases in the various categories of social expenditure are explained very largely by changes in demand per head and by changes in provision and not by demographic changes (Johnson, 1999).

Box 9.1 Alvarado and Creedy's approach to the estimation of future social expenditure due to ageing

Creedy and Taylor (1993) obtained estimates for 1988 of the annual dollars per head of population spent by Commonwealth and State Governments for seven areas of social expenditure. The data were obtained from information published in 1990 by the Commonwealth Department of Community Services and Health. The seven areas of expenditure were the aged pension, other assistance to aged people, unemployment benefit, other social security, health, education, and employment programmes. The unique feature of this data set was that it provided public social expenditure according to the age group of the person upon whom the money was expended. The total social expenditure per head for each age group across these seven categories provided a measure of the relative social cost of persons in each age category. For example, the total for a person aged 70–74 years was A$8,325 compared to $2,870 for a person aged 16–24 years. That is, social monies expended by government on the older person were almost three times higher than social monies expended on the younger person.

Having obtained these estimates, Alvarado and Creedy applied them to estimates of the future population by age group. That is, they assumed that the relative costs by age remain unchanged into the future, or, in terms of the example, that the older person will continue to cost almost three times the younger person. They also estimate future levels of gross domestic product (GDP) so that the estimated future levels of social expenditure can be compared with future levels of GDP.

The study has many limitations: the population is not divided by sex, it does not consider potential changes in household composition, it includes only recurrent expenditure and not capital expenditure, it does not consider private expenditure or substitution between private and public expenditure, some areas of social expenditure are not included, and no allowance is made for feedbacks between the growth of social expenditure and the growth of GDP. Also, it does not allow for variation in future social expenditure costs and relative costs by age. If older people of a given age in future are more likely to have their own source of income as opposed to the aged pension (almost certainly the case), the method used by Alvarado and Creedy will overestimate the aged pension component of social expenditure. On the other hand, health expenditure per capita at each age has been growing, especially at older ages (Badham, 1998) and, if this trend were to continue, the Alvarado and Creedy method would underestimate future health expenditure. Finally, the input data used by Alvarado and Creedy are dated. In particular, fertility has fallen below, and can be predicted to fall even further below, the level assumed by Alvarado and Creedy.

Alvarado and Creedy are cautious in their conclusions and do not call for a large-scale increase in the level of immigration. Despite this, it appears that their work has been the basis of a resurgence of the argument that large-scale immigration can keep the population young.

THE ISSUE REBORN: 1999

The following quotations are representative of the resurgence of the view that immigration is the answer to the ageing of our population:

> Labour knows that immigration can help keep our population young. (Kim Beazley, Leader of the Opposition, Address to the Global Foundation Luncheon, 3 August 1998)

> The prospect of a static, greying population is why the Premier, Mr Jeff Kennett, has joined the Australian Chamber of Commerce and Industry and the Federal Opposition in the chorus of voices calling for an increase in Australia's migrant intake. (Editorial, *The Age*, 9 March 1999: 16)

> Mr Sciacca said greater immigration, properly targeted, provided the best solution to securing the future for Australia's growing ageing population. (*The Australian*, 19 February 1999: 1)

> The answer is not to veto a long-term immigration program, condemning Australia to slowing population growth, an ageing population and worsening employment prospects. (Editorial, *The Australian*, 4 August 1998)

The average reader would be forgiven for concluding from these statements that increased immigration can stop our population growth rate falling and can keep our population young, both literally and figuratively. The reappearance of these views is all the more remarkable because there has been no new research to suggest that they are anything but misleading. The fact is that nothing will keep Australia's population young and nothing will stop the fall in our population growth rate, short of our fertility rate rising to peak, baby-boom levels; an extremely unlikely scenario. In this report we confirm the finding of *all* previous empirical studies that substantial ageing of our population in the next 30 years is inevitable.

A REVISIONIST VIEW: GLENN WITHERS AND 'A YOUNGER AUSTRALIA'

In 1999, Glenn Withers, Professor of Public Policy at the Australian National University, published what he called 'a revisionist view' in his paper, 'A Younger Australia?' (Withers, 1999). As the quotations above indicate, until recently, Withers and the committees or organisations that he headed were consistent in their support of the view that immigration could have only a marginal impact upon ageing of the population. In the last year, however, Withers has promoted the opposing viewpoint:

> Immigration has helped keep Australia younger in the past. But some demographers assert it cannot do so in the future, a view accepted by Government and used as a justification for lower immigration. This paper argues that the Government view and its demographic underpinnings are wrong. Once

deficiencies in conventional demographic methodology are allowed for, a much more significant impact of immigration is describable. These corrections involve migrant composition, projecting migration rates not levels, properly calculating dependency ratios and incorporating budget costs. (Withers, 1999: 1)

Immigration is also good for our society. An ageing society is not a creative and vibrant society. A younger Australia can be. Fortunately, Australia's population has not yet reached age profiles like Japan or Germany. But two decades from now a dramatic change is forecast: the ratio of the elderly to those of working age will double and the share of social expenditure in GDP will rise from the current 12 per cent to 25 per cent or more. Migration, in conjunction with other policies, can play a key role in moderating this. (Withers, 1998)

The statement that immigration has kept Australia's population young in the past is largely false. Australia's population has been kept young in the past by the previous higher levels of fertility and mortality (ABS, 1998: 29). The title, 'A Younger Australia?', and the reference in the above quotation to a 'younger Australia' are also very misleading. These words suggest that immigration may make Australia younger than it is now. Withers contrasts the prospect of a future old population with a young and vibrant alternative that allegedly results from changes to immigration policy. His numbers show, however, that what he really means is that immigration may make Australia a little younger than it might otherwise be, that is, still considerably older than it is now. The potential for the literal interpretation of Withers's words was confirmed by Michelle Grattan in the *Sydney Morning Herald* (23 April: 17) when she reported that Withers challenged the recent orthodoxy that population ageing is inevitable. That is, his words have given the impression to a senior journalist that population ageing is not inevitable when it surely is.

Withers' 'A Younger Australia?' is not based upon new research. Instead, its primary sources are the studies by Clare and Tulpule, and Alvarado and Creedy, to which we have already referred. These studies have been dated by the changes to Australia's demography in the past decade.[3] However, even allowing for the fact that these studies are not based upon recent demography, as quoted above, both studies concluded that the impact of immigration on ageing was considerably less than the impact of changes in social policy. Both concluded that there was no substitute for prudent social and economic planning to meet the needs of our future ageing population. Clare and Tulpule (1994: 17) call for effective retirement income policy, health care reform and support for the disabled. Although Withers may agree, he does not draw this conclusion in his recent paper, instead focusing only upon immigration as a response to ageing. Withers also provides a negative image of older people as 'conservative and resistant to innovation' (1999: 4). In contrast, in the context of population ageing, the OECD (1998) stresses the importance of fostering a positive approach to older people. Indeed, the OECD emphasises the importance of reversing the trend to early retirement partly through the promotion of a more positive attitude by employers to older workers.

Withers, following Creedy and Alvarado, refers to the potential to reduce ageing through changes in the composition of immigrants. The first compositional aspect to which he refers is a shift to a younger intake of immigrants, increasing the proportion aged under 30 years from 60 per cent to 80 per cent.[4] Using recent data, we examine the potential for a younger age structure of immigrants in detail later in the chapter. In doing so, we show that the alternative age distribution of immigrants used by Alvarado and Creedy and implicitly by Withers is implausible. Withers also states that Alvarado and Creedy model the impact on age structure of increasing the share of immigrants coming from non-English speaking backgrounds (NESB) to 75 per cent, the logic being that NESB migrants have higher fertility. In fact, this is a misinterpretation of what Alvarado and Creedy have done. They do not consider (or recommend, as Withers implies) a change in the ethnic composition of the immigration intake.

Most population projections, including the official projections made by the Australian Bureau of Statistics and those made in the studies of Young and Alvarado and Creedy, assume that immigration in the future will be a constant number (e.g. 100,000 per annum) rather than a constant percentage of the population size (e.g. one per cent per annum). Withers argues against this approach quoting Clare and Tulpule (1994: 12): 'the assumption of fixed levels of migration is likely to be increasingly misleading the greater the period for which projections are made, at least in the presence of a growing population base.' In fact, the past 50 years of Australian immigration do not support their case. The trend line for the number of net migrants over the past 50 years is almost flat at an average of around 80,000 per annum, while the trend line for annual migration as a percentage of the population has been sharply downwards. In this chapter, we follow the conventional approach. In the end, a percentage of population translates into some number and the feasibility of the proposed intake would be judged by the feasibility of that number. Population projections made by the United Nations Population Division (United Nations Population Division, 1998) make use of an annual rate of net migration but the rate falls over time as the population increases.

Finally, Withers places major store on Alvarado and Creedy's projections of social expenditure relative to GDP. While the Alvarado and Creedy study is valuable, being the only study of its type, its limitations are great (see Box 9.1). Other careful research is underway on the impact of ageing upon particular aspects of social expenditure. We await the outcomes of those studies.

THE REAL QUESTIONS

The popular debate on immigration and ageing has been polarised between those who claim that immigration has such a large effect upon ageing that it can keep our population young (or much less old) and those who argue that immigration has no worthwhile or appreciable impact on ageing. The two most detailed empirical research studies conducted in Australia on immigration and ageing both concluded that the reality lies between these two extremes. Both show that substantial ageing of the population is inevitable, but both also conclude that immigration can have some effect in retarding ageing.

Christabel Young concluded:

> While an annual net migration of 50,000 compared with zero annual net migration has some effect in retarding the ageing of the population, each additional 50,000 has progressively less effect. (Young, 1990: 65)

Alvarado and Creedy concluded:

> Higher levels of immigration retard the growth of the social expenditure to GDP ratio...Under a scenario of 40,000 immigrants, the ratio of social expenditure to GDP is projected to grow 29 per cent between 2011 and 2031 (because of ageing of the population), but with 170,000 immigrants the rate of growth of that ratio is projected to fall to 22 per cent over the same period. (Alvarado and Creedy 1996: 43)

The primary difference between the conclusions of the two studies is that Young argues that the first 50,000 net migrants have the greatest impact on slowing population ageing whereas Creedy and Alvarado suggest that it is large inflows of the order of 170,000 that can retard ageing. Thus, the real questions about ageing and immigration are:

- How much do differing levels of immigration change the speed and level of ageing?
- How much of a change in ageing due to immigration is beneficial from the perspective of efficiency?

Official wisdom seems to follow the Alvarado and Creedy argument that it is very large-scale immigration that retards ageing:

> [M]assive levels of immigration would be needed to have any appreciable impact on the proportion of the population that is aged. (DIMA, 1999: 10)

> Demographers have already shown that only an effective doubling of our immigration program would have an appreciable impact [on ageing of the population]. (Phillip Ruddock, Minister for Immigration and Multicultural Affairs, quoted in *The Australian*, 4 August 1998: 3)

We have demonstrated elsewhere that if we literally want to keep our population young, that is, if we want to maintain the proportion of the population aged 65 years and over at its present level, then impossibly large immigration intakes would be required (McDonald and Kippen, 1999a: 12–13). On the other hand, in support of Young's conclusion, we demonstrate below that the largest and demographically most efficient impact of immigration on ageing occurs with the first 50,000 net migrants and that the impact reduces significantly with each additional 50,000 net migrants.

As Young (1994: 20) noted, the relative impact on ageing of additional immigrants is partially dependent upon the level of fertility. Essentially, as fertility falls, the number of immigrants that makes an appreciable difference increases. Since 1990, when Young's study was completed, fertility in Australia has fallen. Alvarado and Creedy's study is also based on dated demographic information. In this chapter we address the two questions above in light of the most recent demographic trends.

A STANDARD POPULATION PROJECTION

In the next sections of the chapter we examine the impacts on Australia's population age structure of differing future levels of fertility, mortality and migration. To enable meaningful comparisons to be made, we make use of a standard population projection. The standard projection involves the following assumptions:

- Fertility (technically, the Total Fertility Rate or TFR) falls from 1.76 children per woman in 1998 to 1.65 children per woman by 2008. After this, fertility remains constant at 1.65 births per woman.
- Mortality follows a trend consistent with the official projections made by the Australian Bureau of Statistics (ABS, 1998). Under this trend, expectation of life at birth increases by about ten years over the twenty-first century.
- Annual net migration is set at 80,000 persons per annum, roughly the average of the past eight years (76,000) and of the past 50 years.
- The age distribution of 'net migrants' is set at the average applying for the years 1994–97.
- Immigration and emigration have no impact on the levels of fertility and mortality of the population.

The standard projection essentially represents a continuation of current demographic trends. This projection leads to Australia's population stabilising at 24–25 million people and zero population growth (McDonald and Kippen, 1999a: 4–9).

After examining the impacts on ageing of varying levels of fertility and mortality from those assumed in the standard, we examine the impact of altering the three migration assumptions by varying the level of annual net migration, the age structure of migrants and the fertility level of migrants.

AGEING AND VARIATIONS IN FERTILITY AND MORTALITY

Figure 9.1 shows the impact on ageing during the twenty-first century of different levels of fertility while maintaining the other assumptions of the standard projection. The figure shows the proportions of the population that would be aged 65 years and over under different assumptions about fertility. The result is that variations in fertility make very little difference to ageing in the next 25 years, but beyond that time, the differences between the projections in terms of population ageing begin to increase and become substantial in the second half of the twenty-first century. This reiterates the point made earlier that, in considering ageing of the population from the perspective of population policy, projections longer than 50 years are required. The path of fertility in the next 25 years will be an important determinant of ageing in the twenty-first century. In the long-term, each fall of 0.2 in the TFR produces a rise of about 2.8 percentage points in the proportion of the population aged 65 years and over. Thus, for example, a rise in fertility from the level of the standard (1.65 births per woman) to the level consistent with long-term replacement of the population (about 2.05 births per woman) would reduce (in comparison with the standard) the projected proportion of the population aged 65 years and over by 5.6 percentage points.

Figure 9.1 Percentage of the population aged 65+ under different TFR assumptions, Australia, 1998–2098

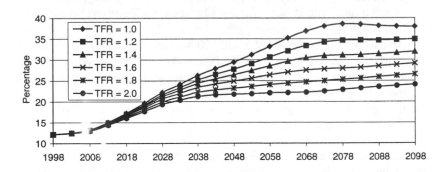

Figure 9.2 shows the impact on ageing over the twenty-first century of two different assumptions about future mortality while maintaining the other assumptions of the standard projection. The first assumption is that mortality

will follow the standard assumption in which expectation of life at birth increases by about ten years over the twenty-first century. The second is a more optimistic assumption that expectation of life will increase by 20 years over the twenty-first century. The second assumption, while being much more optimistic than the official ABS projection, is more in keeping with past trends in changes in expectation of life; expectation of life has increased by about twenty years in the past century and by five years in the last two decades. The conclusions drawn from Figure 9.2 mirror those for changes in fertility; differing levels of mortality have only a very small impact on ageing in the next 25 years, but the impact becomes considerably greater in subsequent years. In the long-term, an additional ten years in expectation of life would add about eight percentage points to the proportion of the population aged 65 years and over. Thus, our population could be considerably older than current projections suggest if mortality rates fall more than is conventionally assumed. Such a fall would probably imply increased control over cancer mortality.

Figure 9.2 Percentage of the population aged 65+ under different mortality assumptions

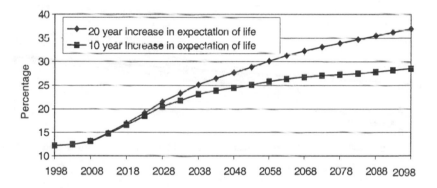

These results are given to provide perspective to the following analysis of the impact of different levels and compositions of migration upon ageing. No reasonable variation in the level of immigration from the standard can produce anything as large as an eight percentage point change in the proportion of the population aged 65 years and over, yet a plausible change in future mortality does produce that change. This perspective has been largely ignored in Australian studies of ageing.

AGEING AND VARIATIONS IN THE LEVEL OF MIGRATION

Given the fertility and mortality levels of the standard, the impact upon ageing of differing levels of annual net migration is as shown in Figure 9.3. The conclusions here are quite different to those for variations in fertility and mortality. The impact of immigration on ageing in the first 25 years from 1998 is somewhat larger than the impacts of varying levels of fertility and mortality. Because immigrants, on average, are relatively young upon arrival in Australia, they have not had time to age in the first 25 years of the projection. Beyond 25 years, however, the impact of immigration on ageing tends to be much less than the impacts of potential changes in fertility and mortality, as shown in Figures 9.1 and 9.2. Figure 9.3 also indicates that substantial ageing of the population will occur over the next 30 years whatever the level of annual net migration.

Figure 9.3 Percentage of the population aged 65+ under different annual net migration assumptions

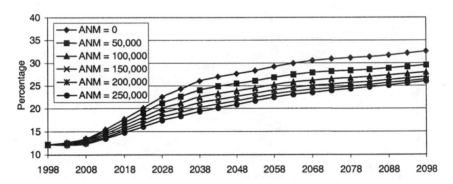

Most importantly, Figure 9.3 shows that, at all points in time, the impact of immigration on ageing is subject to diminishing returns. Each additional 50,000 immigrants has a smaller impact on ageing. Between zero and 50,000 annual net migration, the 50,000 migrants would reduce the proportion of the population aged 65 years and over in the year 2098 by 3.0 percentage points. However, between 200,000 and 250,000 annual net migration, the additional 50,000 migrants would reduce the proportion aged by only 0.5 percentage points. That is, the impact upon ageing of the first 50,000 migrants is six times the impact of the fifth 50,000. On the other hand, each additional 50,000 migrants would produce the same addition to the total population (6.7 million people in 100 years).

The addition of 6.7 million people merely to change the aged proportion by less than half a percentage point is a very inefficient approach to modifying Australia's population age structure, evoking images of the sledgehammer and the walnut.

The efficiency of immigration in this regard may be quantified with an index of efficiency (Box 9.2).

Box 9.2   An index of efficiency: reductions in the proportion of the population aged 65+ versus absolute population increase

A change in the assumptions about future migration leads to a change in both population size and age structure. Essentially, there is a trade-off between a reduction in ageing of the population and an increase in the size of the total population. The index of efficiency measures the population increase resulting from the migration changes required to reduce the proportion of the population aged 65 years and over by one percentage point. For example, a shift in annual net migration from zero to 50,000 would reduce the proportion aged 65+ by 3.05 percentage points by the year 2098. The same change would produce an increase in the total population over the same period of 6.72 million. Hence:

$$\frac{\text{Index of}}{\text{efficiency}} = \frac{\text{Population increase due to change}}{\text{Reduction in percentage aged 65+}} = \frac{6.72 \text{ million}}{3.05} = 2.2 \text{ million}$$

This means that, with this change in the level of migration, a one percentage point reduction in the aged population can be obtained at the cost of an addition to the size of the total population of 2.2 million people. An efficient change would be one that minimised the increase in the population for each one percentage point reduction in the proportion of the population aged 65 years and over.

Table 9.1 shows this index for different future levels of annual net migration. The table clearly shows that the level of efficiency falls off very rapidly as the level of annual net migration increases. This is particularly the case in the longer term, that is, over a century rather than over 50 years. Those who promote very high immigration as an approach to population ageing usually focus on the impact of immigration in the first 30–50 years. The table shows the importance of taking a longer term view.

The results in Table 9.1 confirm the finding of Christabel Young that small-scale immigration makes the most important and efficient contribution to retardation of ageing. Use of increasingly larger scale immigration to retard ageing is very inefficient.

The central conclusion from Figures 9.1, 9.2 and 9.3 is that substantial ageing in Australia over the next few decades is absolutely inevitable and no reasonable change of course in the demographic components will prevent this from happening. Indeed, over the next 30 years, the demographic components operative during that time will have little bearing on the proportion of the population aged 65 years and over. However, variations in the paths of fertility and mortality over the next 30 years will have major impacts after 2028. As shown above, there is a case that the first 50,000 to 100,000 migrants have a worthwhile impact on reducing the ageing of the population (see also, McDonald and Kippen, 1999a, 1999b).

Table 9.1 Efficiency of changes in the level of annual net migration in relation to population ageing

Increment to net migration	Incremental reduction in 65+ per cent (percentage points)[a]		Efficiency index (millions)[b]	
	2048	2098	2048	2098
0– 50,000	2.2	3.0	1.5	2.2
50,000–100,000	1.6	1.5	2.1	4.3
100,000–150,000	1.2	0.9	2.7	7.2
150,000–200,000	1.0	0.6	3.4	10.7
200,000–250,000	0.8	0.5	4.2	14.9

Notes:
a. Each successive 50,000 increment to net migration would add a constant 6.72 million people to the total population by 2098. These increments would be added to the 13.90 million to which the population would fall in 2098 if there was zero annual net migration. The reductions in the proportion of the population aged 65+ are incremental reductions from the 27.7 per cent (32.6 per cent) that would result by 2048 (2098) if annual net migration was zero.
b. See Box 9.2

AGEING AND VARIATIONS IN THE AGE STRUCTURE OF THE IMMIGRANTS

Alvarado and Creedy have analysed the impact on ageing of a younger migrant intake. They assume an alternative age structure of immigrants, with 80 per cent of immigrants being aged less than 30 years compared with the 60 per cent that applied at the time they were making their projections. Their results showed that the younger age structure of immigrants could reduce the proportion of the population aged 65 years and over by about 1.6 percentage points by 2051 (Alvarado and Creedy, 1998). More importantly, they pointed out that this reduction was much more efficient (in terms of additions to the total population) than an increase in the migration intake level.

Alvarado and Creedy's alternative immigrant age structure involves an implausible shift in the ratio of persons aged 0–9 to persons aged 30–39, considering that the former are likely to be offspring of the latter. The suggested change has the number of children aged 0–9 years per adult aged 30–39 years increasing from 0.7 to 2.4 (Table 9.2).

Table 9.2 Children and parents: Alvarado and Creedy's alternative age structure of immigration compared with the actual intake

	Numbers aged 0–9	Numbers aged 30–39	Ratio of 0–9 to 30–39
Actual immigration intake (Average of 1988/9–1992/3)	19,190	26,613	0.72
Alvarado and Creedy	30,708	12,906	2.38

However, it is possible to define younger immigrant age structures that are more plausible. We have defined two alternative possibilities. The first of these involves increasing both the percentages of children aged 0–14 years and the percentages in the ages that would be the parents of these children (Age Structure 2 in Appendix 9.1). To achieve this result, preference would need to be given in the migration intake to persons who had children. The second younger alternative concentrates net migration in the 15–29 ages (Age Structure 3 in Appendix 9.1). This would involve a greater preference for persons at these ages (a greater emphasis upon age than upon skill, for example).

Table 9.3 Efficiency of variations in the level, age structure and fertility of immigrants in relation to retardation of population ageing

	Reduction in 65+% (percentage points)[a]		Efficiency index (millions)[b]	
Change to annual net migration	Year			
	2048	2098	2048	2098
Level change	1.1	0.9	2.4	5.7
Age structure 2	0.6	0.7	0.3	1.0
Age structure 3	0.8	0.8	0.5	1.4
Fertility change	0.4	0.8	1.0	1.6
Level and age 2	1.9	1.7	1.6	3.6
Level and age 3	2.2	1.8	1.5	3.9
Level and fertility	1.6	1.9	2.0	3.9
Age 2 and fertility	1.0	1.5	0.6	1.3
Age 3 and fertility	1.2	1.6	0.7	1.6
Level, age 2 and fertility	2.4	2.7	1.5	3.1
Level, age 3 and fertility	2.7	2.7	1.5	3.3

Notes:
a. Reduction from the proportion of the population aged 65+ in the standard projection.
b. See Box 2

The impacts upon ageing of these alternative migrant age structures are very small. Compared with the standard, the shift to Age Structure 2 would reduce the proportion aged 65 years and over by only 0.6 percentage points by 2048 and by 0.7 percentage points by 2098. The corresponding falls related to the use of Age Structure 3 are 0.8 by 2048 and 0.8 by 2098. However, as indicated by Alvarado and Creedy, the changes in age structure are much more efficient in achieving reductions in ageing than changes in the level of migration (Table 9.3). Nevertheless, given the difficulty involved in redefining the migration programme to provide either a preference for families with children, or to those aged 15–29 years, the small reduction in ageing related to these changes is unlikely to be worthwhile. In addition, the changes required would probably mean a reduction in the skill level of the intake.

AGEING AND VARIATIONS IN THE FERTILITY OF IMMIGRANTS

More controversial than choosing immigrants on the basis of their age is choosing them on the basis of their likely fertility. Alvarado and Creedy divided the Australian population into two groups, those born in English-speaking countries including Australia and those born in non English-speaking countries. Their methodology contains some errors[5] but they concluded that 'the birthplace composition of immigrants has a negligible effect on the projections' (Alvarado and Creedy, 1996: 44). Alvarado and Creedy do not recommend that we should change the ethnic composition of the migrant intake in order to reduce population ageing.

Projections of Australia's population show that the impact of higher immigrant fertility on the course of population ageing is likely to be negligible. Under the assumptions of the standard projection, net migrants would require a TFR of 2.60 in order to reduce the proportion of the population aged 65 years and over in 2048 by one percentage point. A two percentage point reduction would require immigrant fertility to be 3.63 births per woman and a three percentage point reduction would require immigrant fertility of 4.76 births per woman.

In fact, immigrants to Australia from high fertility countries tend to be selective of the persons in those countries who have relatively low fertility. Also, a high proportion of Australia's immigrants come from countries with low fertility such as the United Kingdom and New Zealand. Consequently, the overall level of immigrant fertility is very close to that of the Australian average (Abbasi-Shavazi, 1998). Thus, much higher fertility among immigrants to Australia would imply a considerable shift in the source countries of the migration intake. This would be difficult to achieve while maintaining a non-discriminatory and a high-skills policy for the selection of immigrants. Furthermore, fertility is falling in almost all countries where the fertility rate is above two children per woman so that, by the middle of the twenty-first century, it can be expected that there will be very few countries with fertility rates above two children per woman. There is a high degree of impracticality associated with this approach to lowering the ageing of the population.

COMPARATIVE AND CUMULATIVE IMPACTS ON AGEING OF DIFFERENT IMMIGRATION OPTIONS

To summarise the potential impacts of immigration upon ageing, we now compare the impact upon ageing and the relative efficiency of four changes to the migration assumptions of the standard. The four changes are:

- increasing the level of the annual net migration from 80,000 to 120,000
- changing the age of net migrants to Age Structure 2
- changing the age of net migrants to Age Structure 3
- changing the fertility of net migrants from 1.65 to 2.00

In addition, we examine the impacts of combinations of these changes. The results are shown in Table 9.3.

The largest impact of immigration upon ageing is produced in the final combination in the table. In this case, the proportion aged 65 years and over would be reduced compared to the standard projection by only 2.7 percentage points at the cost, by 2098, of an additional 3.4 million persons for each of these percentage points. That is, the population would be larger than the standard by 9.2 million people. This is a very large number of additional people when the aim is merely to reduce the proportion aged 65 years and over from 28.5 per cent (the result for the standard projection in 2098) to 25.8 per cent. Indeed, the population aged 65 years and over would be 1.7 million people larger under this three-assumption combination than under the standard assumptions. Added to this is the impracticality of making the age structure of immigrants substantially younger than it is now or of choosing immigrants who would have higher fertility than the Australian average.

Finally, all the reductions in the proportion of the population aged 65 years and over shown in Table 9.3 are small compared with the changes that would be brought about by potential movements in fertility and mortality. A change of 0.1 in the Total Fertility Rate would change the proportion aged 65 years and over by 1.4 percentage points by 2098, and a change in expectation of life of two years would change the proportion aged 65 years and over by 1.6 percentage points. These are small changes in fertility and mortality but they have impacts as large or larger than some major changes in migration.

AUSTRALIA'S CHANGING AGE STRUCTURE

In the previous section, projections were considered in which migration assumptions had been varied. The impacts upon ageing observed were not impressive. However, the impact upon ageing of a shift in the net migration intake from zero to 80,000 (the assumption of the standard projection) reduces the proportion aged 65 years and over in 2098 by almost four percentage points. Thus, it can be concluded that the first 80,000 net migrants make a substantial contribution to the reduction of ageing of the population. This result is related to the changing nature of Australia's age structure that, in turn, is the product of our past fertility and mortality rates.

The past and future of Australia's age structure can be characterised in fundamental demographic terms. In 1971, our age structure, following a period of high fertility, had the shape of a pyramid except for a small irregularity arising from low fertility during the Depression. The pyramid is the classic shape of a population that is growing. As fertility has fallen, our age structure is moving towards a beehive shape, the shape that results from a combination of below-replacement fertility and levels of net migration that would lead to at least zero population growth. However, our future age structure depends on the future course of the demographic components. There are two main possibilities. The zero-growth, beehive shape, will be maintained across the twenty-first century if the fertility level remains around 1.6 to 1.7 births per woman and net migration is in the region of 80,000 per annum. Higher levels of immigration within a range that is reasonable will ultimately only add people to the population and make little difference to the age structure. This is why the projections considered in Table 9.3 yielded unexciting results.

The other main possibility for Australia's future age structure is a shift to a coffin-shaped age structure, resulting from zero net migration and a lower level of fertility. This is the classic shape of a population that is declining in size. Its age structure is much older than that of the beehive. The beehive-shaped age structure has a relative concentration of people in the working ages, while the coffin-shape implies substantial falls in the absolute size of the labour force.

The change in our age structure from 1971 and the two alternative future age structures are shown in Figure 9.4.

The ageing of Australia's population represents a fundamental, historical demographic change. The shift from a pyramid-shaped age structure is likely to occur only once in our history. A return to the pyramid shape would require a return to the fertility of the 1960s; twice as high as the present level of fertility. This seems extremely unlikely. From a population policy perspective, our choice now is between the beehive-shaped age structure and the coffin-shaped age structure. The beehive shape is clearly the superior option (McDonald and Kippen, 1999a, 1999b).

Figure 9.4 Beehive and coffin scenarios, Australia, 1971–2098

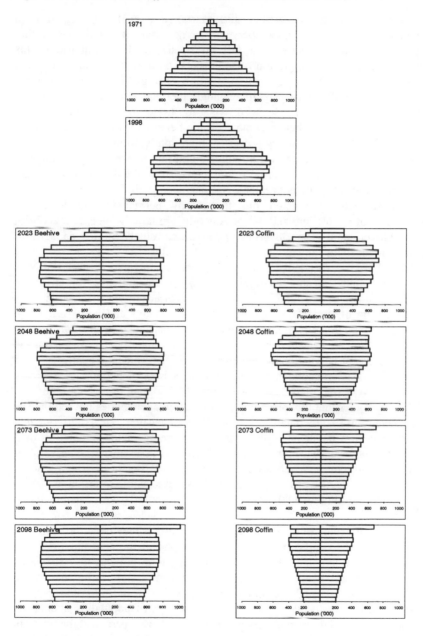

CONCLUSION

Given current trends in fertility and mortality, annual net migration to Australia of at least 80,000 persons is necessary to avoid spiralling population decline and substantial falls in the size of the labour force. This level of annual net migration also makes a worthwhile and efficient contribution to the retardation of population ageing. Levels of annual net migration above 80,000 become increasingly ineffective and inefficient in the retardation of ageing. Those who wish to argue for a higher level of immigration must base their argument on the benefits of a larger population, not upon the illusory 'younging power' of high immigration.

The effects upon ageing of a younger immigrant intake or higher migrant fertility are very small. Furthermore, implementation of either measure would be problematic. They are not realistic options.

It must also be pointed out that many permanent and long-term movements of people into and out of Australia are largely outside the control of the Government. The Government has an extremely limited capacity to prevent or accelerate any movement out of Australia.

Also, there is little control possible over movements into Australia of New Zealanders and of spouses and fiancés of Australians. Finally, the Government has only a limited degree of control at present over movements into Australia of students, temporary business entrants and holiday makers. Thus, even though a government may aim for a particular level of annual net migration, the actual level achieved may be substantially removed from the target because of population movements outside governmental control.

Paul Johnson, an economist at the London School of Economics, recently provided a very important message in regard to population ageing (Johnson, 1999). He argues that the 'problem' of population ageing does not require the implementation of draconian or extraordinary measures. He points out that Australia is in a better position to deal with ageing of the population than almost any other OECD country. Given Johnson's assessment, and given that very high immigration levels are ineffective and inefficient in bringing about changes in the ageing of the population, it is not sensible to argue for large-scale immigration (above 80,000 net per annum) on the basis of its impact on ageing.

Substantial ageing of the population of Australia is inevitable over the next 30 years. No reasonable shift in our demography in the next three decades can change this outcome. Through prudent long-term policies in the areas of income support, health and service provision and retirement from employment, and through the promotion of positive attitudes to older people, Australia will be well-placed to meet the challenge of population ageing. At the same time, demographic trends in the next 30 years will be vital in determining the shape of Australia's age structure beyond 2030. With zero immigration and lower fertility, the ageing of our population will continue apace after 2030: the coffin scenario. Ageing of the population can be substantially retarded beyond 2030 through combinations of fertility and immigration which guarantee at least zero population growth: the beehive scenario.

NOTES

1. This chapter was originally commissioned as a research paper for the Department of Immigration and Ethnic Affairs. The authors are grateful to the Department for allowing its publication here.
2. ABS projections, including those in the 1980s, have always shown this result. Indeed, as we indicate below, as fertility has fallen ABS projections show an increasingly larger impact of immigration upon ageing.
3. Withers (1999: 5) uses the 1996 official ABS projections in his Table 2. The 1998 official projections that assume lower levels of fertility are readily available.
4. In 1997–98, 67 per cent of the 'net' migration intake was aged less than 30 years, not 60 per cent. The 1998–9 figure was 71 per cent.
5. For example, they assume that second generation non-English speaking background (NESB) persons who are already living in Australia at the commencement of the projection period have Australian or English speaking background (AESB) demography during the projection period, but second generation NESB persons, born to immigrants who enter the country after the projection has commenced, have NESB demography. There are also errors in the way that NESB mortality rates have been estimated.

APPENDIX

9A.1   Alternative age structures of Australian net migration

Age group	Age structure 1 (Australia 1994–97)		Age structure 2		Age structure 3	
	Males %	Females %	Males %	Females %	Males %	Females %
0–4	3.2	2.8	5.0	5.0	3.0	3.0
5–9	3.6	3.5	5.0	5.0	3.0	3.0
10–14	3.7	3.6	4.0	4.0	3.0	3.0
15–19	7.4	7.8	6.0	6.0	9.0	9.0
20–24	6.9	7.9	7.5	7.5	10.0	10.0
25–29	4.9	7.1	9.0	9.0	12.0	12.0
30–34	5.1	5.7	4.0	4.0	3.0	3.0
35–39	3.9	4.0	4.0	4.0	2.0	2.0
40–44	3.0	2.6	2.0	2.0	1.5	1.5
45–49	2.0	1.6	1.0	1.0	1.0	1.0
50–54	1.2	1.2	1.0	1.0	1.0	1.0
55–59	1.1	1.3	0.5	0.5	0.5	0.5
60–64	1.2	1.0	0.5	0.5	0.5	0.5
65–69	0.7	0.6	0.3	0.3	0.3	0.3
70–74	0.4	0.4	0.2	0.2	0.2	0.2
75+	0.2	0.3	0.0	0.0	0.0	0.0
Total	48.5	51.5	50.0	50.0	50.0	50.0

REFERENCES

Abbasi-Shavazi, M. (1998), 'The fertility of immigrant women in Australia', *People and Place*, 6 (3): 30–38.

ABS (Australian Bureau of Statistics) (1998), *Projections of the Populations of Australia States and Territories, 1997–2051,* (Cat. No. 3222.0), Canberra: Australian Bureau of Statistics.

Alvarado, J. and J. Creedy (1996), *Migration, Population Ageing and Social Expenditure in Australia*, Canberra: Department of Immigration and Multicultural Affairs.

Alvarado, J. and J. Creedy (1998), *Population Ageing, Migration and Social Expenditure*, Cheltenham: Edward Elgar.

Badham, J. (1998), 'Future financial impact of the current health financing system', *Australian Health Review*, 21 (4): 96–110.

Castles, S., W. Foster, R. Iredale and G. Withers (1998), *Immigration and Australia: Myths and Realities*, Sydney: Allen and Unwin.

Centre for International Economics (CIE) (1988), 'The relationship between immigration and economic performance', Consultant's Report for the Committee to Advise on Australia's Immigration Policies, *Immigration. A Commitment to Australia*, Canberra: AGPS.

Clare, R. and A. Tulpule (1994), *Australia's Ageing Society*, Canberra: AGPS.

Creedy, J. (1998), *Pensions and Population Ageing*, Cheltenham: Edward Elgar.

Creedy, J. and P. Taylor (1993), 'Population Ageing and Social Expenditure in Australia', *Australian Economic Review*, July–September, 56–68.

DIMA (Department of Immigration and Multicultural Affairs) (1999), *Population Flows: Immigration Aspects*, Canberra: DIMA.

EPAC (Economic Planning Advisory Council) (1992), 'Economic and Social Consequences of Australia's Ageing Population – Preparing for the 21st Century', Canberra: AGPS.

Hugo, G. (1990), 'Demographic and spatial aspects of immigration', in M. Wooden, R. Holton, G. Hugo, and J. Sloan, *Australian Immigration: a Survey of the Issues*, Melbourne: Bureau of Immigration Research.

Hurford, C. (1985), Letter to the editor, *The Age*, 17 July.

Johnson, P. (1999), 'Ageing in the 21st Century: Implications for Public Policy', paper presented to the Conference on Policy Implications of the Ageing of Australia's Population organised by the Productivity Commission and the Melbourne Institute of Applied Economic and Social Research, Melbourne, 18–19 March.

McDonald, P. and R. Kippen (1999a), 'Population Futures for Australia: the Policy Alternatives', Vital Issues Seminar, Parliamentary Library Seminar Series, Canberra: Department of the Parliamentary Library.

McDonald, P. and R. Kippen (1999b), 'Ageing: the Social and Demographic Dimensions', paper presented to the Conference on Policy Implications of the Ageing of Australia's Population organised by the Productivity Commission and the Melbourne Institute of Applied Economic and Social Research, Melbourne, 18–19 March.

National Population Council (Migration Committee) (1986), *The Australian Population: Options and Scenarios*, Canberra: Department of Immigration and Ethnic Affairs.

National Population Council (Population Issues Committee) (1991), 'Population Issues and Australia's Future: Environment, Economy and Society', Final Report, Canberra: AGPS.

National Population Inquiry (1975), 'Population and Australia: A Demographic Analysis and Projection', 2 volumes, Canberra: AGPS.

Norman, N. and K. Meikle (1983), 'Immigration—The Crunch Issues for Australia', Information Paper IP8 CEDA Research Department, Melbourne: CEDA.

Norman, N. and K. Meikle (1985), *The Economic Effects of Immigration on Australia*, Volume 1, Melbourne: Committee for the Economic Development of Australia.

OECD (1998), Maintaining Prosperity in an Ageing Society, Paris: OECD.

Ruddock, P. (1999), 'Labor's "Peas and Thimbles" Immigration Policy', Media Release, Minister of Immigration and Multicultural Affairs, 19 February.

United Nations Population Division (1998), *World Population Prospects: The 1998 Revision, Volume 1, Comprehensive Tables*, New York: United Nations Secretariat.

Withers, G. (1998), 'The Power of People', *CEDA Bulletin*, October: 19–20.

Withers, G. (1999), 'A Younger Australia?', Discussion Paper No. 63, Public Policy Program, Canberra: Australian National University.

Young, M. (1987), 'Economics of Immigration', News Release, Minister of Immigration, 22 April 1987.

Young, C. (1988), 'Towards a population policy. Myths and misperceptions concerning the demographic effects of immigration', *Australian Quarterly*, **60** (2): 220–30.

Young, C. (1989), 'Australia's population. a long term view', *Current Affairs Bulletin*, **65** (12): 4–11.

Young, C. (1990), *Australia's Ageing Population—Policy Options*, Melbourne: Bureau of Immigration Research.

Young, C. (1994), 'Beliefs and realities about the demographic role of ageing', *Australian Quarterly*, **66** (4): 49–74.

10. International Migration and the Nation-State in Asia

Stephen Castles[1]

INTRODUCTION

Since the mid-1970s, there has been a substantial increase in international migration within Asia and between Asia and other world-regions. Temporary and permanent mobility of various types of persons have developed, including low-skilled workers, highly-skilled personnel, family reunion, settlers, refugees and asylum-seekers. Slower-developing Asian countries have become sources of migrant labour, while fast-growing economies have become labour recruiters. This chapter will not attempt to summarise these trends, since many overviews are available.[2] Rather, the central question to be addressed is: *to what extent is growing international population mobility likely to have significant effects on the nation-state in East and South-East Asia?* The focus will be on immigration countries because of the difficulty of covering both immigration and emigration issues in a single paper.[3]

This immediately raises the question of the characteristics of the nation-state in East Asia, and indeed whether it is appropriate to talk of this political form at all. My position on this (which is developed in more detail below) is that processes of nation-state formation have been important in most countries throughout the post-colonial period. Political leaderships have been concerned not only with building institutional frameworks for governance, but also with defining who belongs to the nation and with developing concepts of national identity. This clearly has important consequences for attitudes towards migration and settlement.

Although there is a long history of migration and ethnic diversity in many areas of East Asia, most of the current migratory flows are of fairly recent origin. It is therefore difficult to make balanced judgements on the effects of such migrations on the nation-state. Nonetheless, in the interests of good public policy it is important to begin thinking about possible impacts as early as possible. To do this, it is useful to draw on four types of analysis:

- An examination of some important characteristics of the modern nation-state and how these are being changed by globalisation (and specifically by international migration).
- Analysis of how highly-developed Western countries have been affected by their experiences of immigration since 1945.
- A discussion of differences in the characteristics of nation-states in East and South East Asia compared with Western models.
- A review of available information on experiences of migration and settlement in East and South East Asia.

Each of these topics really needs a major study on its own, so my treatment here is necessarily brief and general, with just a few examples to illustrate analytical points.

THE NATION-STATE AND GLOBALISATION

The contemporary international political system comprises about 200 states, each of which is supposed to have sovereignty over a specific territory demarcated by internationally agreed boundaries. According to historians, the development of the modern state began with the 1648 Treaties of Westphalia, which ended a long period of war in Europe (Held et al. 1999: 45–9). In the centuries which followed, new elements were added to the state through democratic revolutions, the rise of nationalism, and struggles for inclusion by women, workers and other previously excluded groups. Some important characteristics of the modern nation-state around the middle of the twentieth century can be summed up as follows:

1. State *sovereignty* over a specific territory. The legitimate government of a state was not meant to be answerable to any outside power with regard to its laws and policies within its borders. This implied mutual respect of territorial sovereignty by other such entities within a world of nation-states.
2. State *autonomy* in controlling its own economy, culture, and environment and society. The state could invoke a wide range of powers in various areas. These were based on varying notions of the division of responsibilities with the private sphere and civil society, and were not subject to external scrutiny.
3. State *control over its borders*. The state had final control of all flows across the borders, whether of capital, commodities, cultural artefacts or people.
4. *The rule of law, democracy and citizenship* as indicators of political legitimacy. The democratic revolutions of the eighteenth, nineteenth and twentieth centuries established the principles of constitutionally

guaranteed rights for citizens and democratically-elected law-making bodies.

5. The linking of the *state* as a political community with the *nation* as a cultural community, and thus the linking of *citizenship* with *nationality*. Democracy made it necessary to define exactly who could be a citizen, with all the rights and duties this implied. Citizenship was linked to membership of the nation, seen as a cultural community, whose members were held together by bonds of solidarity, based on shared history, values and traditions. However, since the great majority of nations were the result of amalgamation or incorporation (often by conquest) of diverse ethnic groups, the shared identity was often the result of suppression of minority identities—sometimes leading to resistance and separatist movements. Two principles existed for defining membership of the nation: *ius soli* (literally: law of the soil), according to which anyone born in a territory could belong; and *ius sanguinis* (literally, law of the blood), according to which belonging was based on descent from an existing citizen.

6. The emergence of the *welfare state*. Struggles by labour and social movements established the principle that full participation in nation-states required basic minimum economic, social and educational standards. The need to secure mass loyalty, especially during the World Wars and the Cold War, forced states to take responsibility for guaranteeing such standards. State sovereignty and autonomy played a crucial part in making it possible to regulate labour markets and provide social services—even in countries with strong ideologies of private enterprise such as the US.

These characteristics obviously form an ideal type, and, moreover, correspond with the *western* nation-state. In their historical evolution, western nation-states expanded by destroying the sovereignty of other states through conquest and colonialism. The principle of respect for sovereignty did not apply to non-western states, nor even to weaker European neighbours in many cases. Democracy, prosperity and inclusion in the metropole was based on repression, exploitation and racism in the colonies. It is only since 1945 that decolonisation has created the conditions for proliferation of the nation-state model to other regions. However, as will be argued below, many non-western countries are in the process of adopting many of the characteristics mentioned here.

The paradox is that at the very moment when the nation-state has become a global norm, it is being challenged by the forces of globalisation. An important recent work on *Global Transformations* argues that:

> Globalisation may be thought of initially as the *widening, deepening and speeding up of worldwide interconnectedness* in all aspects of contemporary social life, from

the cultural to the criminal, the financial to the spiritual. (Held et al., 1999: 2) (emphasis added)

The key characteristic of globalisation is the rapid increase in *cross-border flows* of all kinds: finance, trade, people, ideas, drugs, pollution, global warming, media products and so on. The key organising structure for all these flows is the *transnational network*, which can take the form of the transnational corporation, the global market, the international governmental organisation, the international non-governmental organisation, or the global criminal syndicate. The key tool is *modern information and communications technology*, especially the Internet but also improved telephone system and relatively cheap air travel. The rise of the global 'network society' (Castells, 1996) is empirically verifiable because we can measure the increase in 'extensity, intensity, velocity and impact of the flows and networks' (Held et al., 1999: 16). On all these indicators, global interconnectness is growing rapidly.

Globalisation affects the nation-state in many different ways.[4] Although economic globalisation is the most obvious aspect, it is important to realise that the cultural, social, political and environmental aspects of globalisation are equally important. In the context of this chapter, the main focus is on migration as a mediating force of globalisation, which affects each of the key characteristics of modern nation-states outlined above:

1. Sovereignty: if international legal regimes and human rights principles can now lead to intervention by the so-called 'international community' (as in Kosovo and East Timor in 1999), then the principle of respect for national sovereignty laid down in the 'Westphalian system' has clearly lost its sanctity. International human rights conventions may lay down rights for migrants and other non-citizens, which signatory states are obliged to implement—even if this contradicts existing national law (Soysal, 1994). In fact, immigration countries have been reluctant to sign international conventions on the rights of migrants,[5] but general international norms on human rights, freedom of movement, labour standards, and protection of the family can also reduce national sovereignty in this area.

2. Autonomy: today global politics are regulated by 14,000 international treaties, which are implemented by 260 international governmental organisations (Held et al., 1999: 53). States have found it impossible to control a transnational process like international migration through national institutions. In Europe, there are trends to regional regulation through the Schengen Agreement and the European Union. In Asia, the first step in this direction was taken through the Bangkok Declaration on Irregular Migration signed by 19 governments in April 1999. Migration is monitored by the International Organization for Migration (IOM), the International Labour Organization (ILO) and the Organization for

Economic Cooperation and Development (OECD). The United Nations High Commission for Refugees (UNHCR) organises the movement and reception of refugees. Bilateral or multilateral co-operation between sending and receiving countries is also developing. Such co-operation helps regulate migration, but also creates norms and rights for the migrants.

3. Border control: the ever-increasing cross-border flows and the transnational networks which generate and regulate them can no longer be effectively controlled by nation-states. This applies as much to mobility of people as it does to movements of capital, commodities or ideas. Most states welcome visitors and students, and favour international labour markets for highly-skilled personnel, yet seek to limit flows of manual workers, family members, and asylum-seekers. Such distinctions are hard to enforce, and millions of persons move irregularly, aided by a transnational 'migration industry' consisting of recruiters, labour brokers, travel agents—working both legally and illegally.

4. The rule of law, democracy and citizenship: globalisation may undermine democracy because more and more of the vital decisions that affect citizens are no longer made at the national level, but rather by intergovernmental organisations, transnational corporations and global markets. There are as yet no mechanisms for citizen control of such bodies. Immigration affects citizenship in another way: where there are large numbers of foreign residents, the population becomes split into citizens and non-citizens. This undermines the principle of political inclusion crucial to democracy. Often this is also a class split, for resident non-citizens tend to have low-status jobs and poor social conditions. The result is a divided society, where conflict may increase—which is also harmful to democracy.

5. The state/nation or citizenship/nationality link: globalisation leads to new forms of identity and loyalty that can transcend national boundaries. In the long run, democratic states tend to integrate immigrants by offering them and their children citizenship. However, the failure of assimilation policies and the growth of ethnic communities mean that the new *citizens* are often *not nationals* (in the sense of sharing the dominant culture). The emergence of multicultural societies creates major challenges to national identities. Institutions are likely to change in response to diverse values and needs (Castles and Davidson, 2000). The recent trend to development of transnational communities is a further challenge to the nation-state: modern forms of transport and communication make it possible for immigrants and their descendants to maintain long-term links with the ancestral homeland or with diaspora groups elsewhere (Basch et al., 1994; Cohen, 1997). Thus the idea that a state must be based on a relatively homogeneous nation is becoming increasingly difficult to sustain.

6. Globalisation has had negative effects on welfare states in many places. The power of global capital to invest where production costs are lowest has led to growing unemployment and to fiscal crises in old industrial countries. However, despite ideologies of privatisation and individual responsibility, welfare expenditure has not fallen significantly as a proportion of GDP. Strong welfare states may serve as both an incentive to migration, since immigrants hope to gain benefits if they cannot find jobs, and as a mechanism of closure to migration, since governments are unwilling to take on potential financial burdens (Bommes and Halfmann, 1998). However, it is hard to measure these conflicting effects in practice, and western welfare states continue to have high immigration despite efforts at restriction.

Such changes appear as threats to many people, giving rise to various forms of resistance. Where this is backward-looking, and based on idealised notions of nations and nationalism, the result may be conservatism, racism and fundamentalism. A more useful stance is to try and promote the beneficial aspects of globalisation, such as greater cultural openness and the potential for better living standards through economic growth, while seeking to combat current tendencies to greater inequality, social exclusion and disempowerment of certain regions and groups. The point is that globalisation is in itself neither good nor bad. It is simply the latest stage in the integration of the world economy which began with the rise of capitalism and modernity. As such it would be futile to try to stop or reverse globalisation; rather the task is to tame it and build a global civil society. Increasing population mobility is an integral part of globalisation, and has the potential to weaken nationalism and to create more open multicultural societies. However, immigrants are often the visible scape-goats for social groups which feel threatened by globalisation; hence the increase in racism in many areas in recent years (Castles and Davidson, 2000).

HOW IMMIGRATION HAS AFFECTED WESTERN NATION-STATES

It is impossible in the space available here to summarise the research on how immigration and increased cultural diversity has changed the nation-state in Western Europe, North America and Oceania.[6] Instead, I will present some very general conclusions based on my own previous work (Castles et al., 1984; Castles, 1986; Castles et al., 1992; Castles and Miller, 1998; Castles and Davidson, 2000).

The starting point for a comparative analysis is that virtually all western countries experienced large-scale immigration after 1945. Yet countries like the US, Australia, the UK, France, Germany and Sweden had quite different historical models for nation-building and dealing with ethnic difference.

Moreover, types of migration varied considerably: temporary labour migration in many Western European countries, permanent settler migration in North America and Oceania, post-colonial migration in France, the UK and the Netherlands. The receiving countries therefore had quite different expectations of the outcomes of immigration: the 'guestworker' recruiting countries did not envisage any substantial settlement; the permanent settlement countries wanted new citizens, but expected them to come mainly from the same countries as the existing population or to be willing to undergo cultural assimilation; and the post-colonial labour importers wanted certain groups but not others to settle and assimilate. This led to widely varying policies on such matters as residence and settlement, family reunion, social and political rights, and naturalisation and citizenship. However, on one matter, all receiving country governments seem to have concurred: they believed they could control immigration and manage cultural difference, so that no major changes in national identity and political institutions would take place.

Half a century on, it is possible to see that this core belief was mistaken: in every case immigration led to permanent settlement and formation of ethnic communities or minorities. Immigrants became incorporated into society not simply as individuals, but also as groups with specific positions in segmented labour markets and partially-segregated neighbourhoods. New forms of culture, religion and social life have changed life-styles and identity for majority populations as well. Community relations became an important issue, and in many places extreme-right racist movements became significant political players. This situation has presented major challenges to national identity and political institutions, as can be seen clearly through long-drawn-out public debates, the politicisation of issues of immigration and difference, and repeated changes in citizenship laws in most countries.

In recent years, globalisation has led a new volatility and diversity in migration movements. This coincides with general tendencies to settlement and community formation by the earlier post-war migrants. As a result, trends to policy convergence have emerged in western immigration countries. For instance, the marked differences between Germany's temporary labour recruitment policy and Australia's permanent immigration have declined. Both countries now have a variety of entry types, with varying frameworks to manage them. Citizenship is perhaps the most important area of convergence. In 1999, Germany finally took a major step away from *ius sanguinis* and towards making immigrants and their children into citizens. Australia has moved away from a system of privilege for British immigrants and acceptance of immigrants as citizens only on the condition of assimilation. Today it has one of the most open citizenship models of any country in world: any legal settler can quickly become a member of the political community without a requirement for cultural adaptation. Until recently, there were strong trends towards multiculturalism in many highly-developed immigration countries including Australia, Canada, the US, the UK, Sweden and the Netherlands. Along with other European countries, Germany and France had strong reservations, but were engaged in public debates about the need for change. Since the mid-1990s, multicultural policies have been modified, restricted or renamed in several countries. The reform momentum has diminished, although a return to assimilationist or exclusionary policies has not taken place either.

Overall, the most striking similarity between western countries is that immigration led to the emergence of a culturally-diverse society. In each case this development was unexpected, and occurred despite official policies designed to prevent it. Three main reasons for continued immigration and trends to settlement can be identified:

1. Principles of human rights and legal protection (even for non-citizens) which made large-scale deportation of immigrants impossible.
2. The strength of welfare states, which gave social rights to non-citizens on the basis of employment or residence, thus creating an incentive to remain even when labour market conditions were poor.
3. The importance of social networks in the migration process: once a movement got under way, it became self-sustaining through the mutual support of migrants and the activities of various types of agents (both informal and commercial) who organised migration, job-finding and settlement. The social character of the migration process is a major factor undermining government policies based on economic or political considerations.

Once this outcome became clear, each country had to change its rules on immigration, settlement and citizenship. Bauböck (1996) argues that this is due to inherent characteristics of democratic civil societies, which make it extremely difficult to limit immigration and prevent settlement once migratory movements have got under way. Multicultural societies and major changes in national identity and citizenship seem to be the inevitable outcomes of globalisation and immigration. The question is: do these conclusions also apply to immigration countries in Asia?

ASIAN EXPERIENCES OF NATION-STATE FORMATION

Are contemporary Asian nation-states similar enough to their Western counterparts to allow valid comparisons? It is my argument that there are important differences but also significant similarities, which do allow a comparative approach (for overviews see Davidson and Weekley, 1999; Castles and Davidson, 2000, Chapter 8).

A first difference lies in the historical context of nation-state formation. In Western Europe, this took place over several centuries through two simultaneous processes. One was the dissolution of feudalism and the growth of towns, where the new social category of the citizen emerged. Struggles for emancipation from feudal rule gave rise to the principles of the rule of law, individual rights and equality of treatment for all citizens. The other process was the territorial extension and centralisation of the state, which provided the conditions for building a national culture. These two processes were the basis for the development of democracy and the modern universalistic state. As the French historian Renan put it, the long historical trajectories gave citizens 'time to forget' past cultural heterogeneity and to develop a common national consciousness (Renan, 1992).

By contrast, the nation-state and citizenship are fairly recent creations in Asia. Colonialism often brought together previously separate and diverse cultural groups and imposed new boundaries on them. Absolutist or feudal rule was not overthrown by democratic struggles, but rather overlaid by colonial authority. Anti-colonial movements embraced Western ideas of nationalism and democracy, and the post-colonial political entities adopted the institutional forms of the nation-state: parliament, elections, separation of powers and a modern legal system. Yet these principles were often quite superficial. The process of change took place very quickly and under external influences, so there was no 'time to forget' past social and cultural differences. Western ideas of individualism and universalism gained some support among the new middle classes, but did not replace more traditional principles of consensus, hierarchy, group-solidarity and family-based authority.[7]

A second difference is the degree of societal and cultural diversity. There are many differences between Western European countries, but there is also a shared history and culture based on Judeo-Christian values, notions of rationality deriving from the eighteenth century Enlightenment, and constant interaction and migration. By contrast, the diversity within and between Asian countries is often much greater. Some countries have a wide range of ethnic groups and languages, and may be home to Muslims, Christians, Hindus and members of other religions. Social and political variations may also be great, with widely differing economic frameworks and forms of government in close proximity to each other.

An important distinction is between those countries which were colonised by western powers and those which were not. In the first group we find South Asia, Indochina, nearly all the states in the Malay peninsular and Indonesia. In the second we find China, Japan, Korea and Thailand. The distinction is not rigid—China was dominated by western countries from the mid-nineteenth century, and all the non-colonised states were strongly influenced by the encounter with the West. In addition, Japanese colonialism brought about major changes in Korea and China. Nonetheless, those states which did become part of western empires have much greater historical continuity with regard to borders, culture and identity than do those that were colonised. This is linked to another distinction: that between relatively monocultural countries and those marked by considerable diversity. China, Japan and Korea are each dominated by a single ethnic group, which sees unitary cultural identity as a major source of strength. In fact, each of these countries does have significant ethnic minorities, but they have been largely marginalised and disempowered. Most countries of South East Asia have historical traditions of diversity, based on the incorporation of a range of ethnic groups, as well as on migration for purposes of trade, work, religion and social contact. This pre-existing diversity was complicated under colonial rule through the recruitment of new groups to serve as labourers and traders: Chinese and Indians in Malaya, Chinese in the Dutch East Indies and so on. Building nations on the basis of such diversity has been a major challenge, which has been further complicated by new types of migration.

Another important difference lies in the international context for nation-state formation. In the West, nation-states developed in the period of ascendancy of this new form. Political struggles sought to replace the older absolutist state with the new model, which rapidly proved itself superior to its absolutist predecessor as a framework for industrialisation, administration and integration of new social groups. The initial context for nation-state formation in Asia after 1945 was decolonisation and the Cold War, with Western powers exerting considerable economic and political influence (Berger and Borer, 1997). Rather than developing in parallel with industrialisation and modernisation, the nation-state was adopted as a ready-made framework, which was then supposed to act as a motor for economic and social development. The most successful Asian economies (Japan and the 'tiger economies') developed variants of what came to be known as the 'developmental state' (Castells, 1998: 206–309) Since the mid-1970s, the context has gradually shifted due to the end of the Cold War and the acceleration of globalisation. Asian states now have the contradictory task of trying to merge diverse groups into cohesive populations and to develop a common national identity at the very moment when globalisation is undermining such efforts.

However, there are also important similarities between Western and Asian nation-states. The most obvious one lies the very fact that the nation-state model has been adopted in most Asian countries. Moreover, this has taken place in a context of modernisation and industrialisation which is bringing about major social and cultural changes. Even though the historical trajectory and cultural context differ from the West, the adoption of broadly similar institutions and legal frameworks implies the possibility that Asian states may react in similar ways to the political challenges posed by immigration and settlement.

The post-colonial states of Asia had to find ways of defining who belongs to the nation and building a national consciousness. This problem posed itself in different ways in the multi-ethnic states of South East Asia compared with the relatively homogeneous states of East Asia, yet in both cases the trend has been to emphasise ethnic origins and to establish the principle of *ius sanguinis*. Under European colonial rule, the *ius soli* principle had been established in British possessions, while a mixture of *ius soli* and *ius sanguinis* was the rule in French and Dutch colonies.[8] This conferred citizenship (or subject status) in the colonising state, which facilitated migration to Britain, France and the Netherlands after independence. The new states generally changed their citizenship principle to *ius sanguinis*. Citizenship by descent seemed a way of integrating diverse groups into the nation and creating a common culture. Countries like Indonesia, the Philippines and Malaysia used their education systems and mass media to develop national languages and national consciousness.

However, nationalist ideologies on the common descent and traditions of the people were problematic in states with diverse cultures, often leading to differential policies towards minorities. In Malaysia, for example, special affirmative action policies were introduced to protect Malays, who feared economic marginalisation at the hands of the large ethnic Chinese minority. In Indonesia, with its enormous cultural and religious diversity, official ideologies on national unity sometimes served as a cloak for domination by the largest group, the Javanese. Singapore, by contrast, maintained the *ius soli* principle as a way of integrating the different groups into its new multi-ethnic society. However, differential immigration and naturalisation rules seem to favour immigrants of Chinese ethnicity.

Countries like China, Japan and the Republic of Korea faced different issues. The high degree of homogeneity made it possible to base new state structures on notions of unique national traditions, even if their continuity had been interrupted by war and occupation (in the case of Japan), colonisation (Korea) and the Communist Revolution (China). Ethnic minorities had little weight. The Chinese Government did develop special policies to improve integration of 'national minorities', while Japan largely ignored the situation of indigenous and immigrant minorities for many years. The *ius sanguinis* principle is very strong in East Asian states. For instance, according to Yoshino, Japanese people tend to see themselves as a distinct 'racial' community with a unique and unchanging national character and culture. It is regarded as impossible for foreigners to ever share these qualities (Yoshino, 1992).

In virtually all the countries of South East and East Asia, it is extremely difficult for immigrants to become citizens. In the relatively monocultural states, the principle of a closed national community with membership by descent makes naturalisation very unusual. But even in multi-ethnic South East Asia, group loyalties based on ethno-religious belonging are seen as crucial, and the idea that foreigners could become nationals is quite alien. Thus the idea of national closure implicit in the nation-state model has actually become stronger in Asian countries than was the case in Europe when post-1945 migration started. It will be very hard for the new waves of immigrants to settle and become citizens.

However, there are other important factors that might lead one to expect changes in ideas and rules on naturalisation over time. The rule of law, democracy and citizenship are central aspects of the nation-state. Many Asian countries have adopted these principles, although actual implementation varies: Japan has all the characteristics of a modern democracy; the Republic of Korea, Taiwan, the Philippines and Thailand have made substantial steps in this direction; while other countries lag behind in important areas. Overall, the gradual development of democratic institutions and attitudes is a force for change. The growth of the middle classes as a result of industrialisation and social change provides the basis for a wide range of civil society organisations, that demand reform and recognition of human rights. Of course, the middle classes are often still relatively weak and have an ambivalent position between authoritarian leaders and emerging working classes. Nonetheless, there are tendencies to increasing political confidence, as shown particularly through democratic movements in a number of countries. Moreover, Asian states put increasing weight on participation in international organisations and agreements, which lay down basic rights, such as fair legal process, prohibition of various types of discrimination, and protection of refugees, indigenous peoples and minorities.

Finally, it is necessary to examine the role of welfare systems. As discussed above, they played an important part in encouraging immigration and settlement in Western countries. In general, the welfare state is far less developed in Asian immigration countries, due in part to the recentness of industrialisation and in part to the continuing emphasis on the role of the family in providing for social needs. However, public provision for education and health care has developed strongly in the last thirty years, and is considered one of the major factors in social development in many countries (World Bank, 1998: 76). The rapid demographic shift to lower fertility and an ageing population in Japan and the newly industrialising countries makes social policy reform increasingly urgent. A widespread response to the Asian Crisis of 1997–99 was the call for social safety-nets to cushion the impact of economic change and unemployment.

The differences in Western and Asian nation-state formation may be summarised as follows:

- Long historical struggles to develop the nation-state and citizenship in the West, compared with a fairly recent process and strong external influences in Asia.
- Widespread acceptance of individualism and universal rights in the West, compared with competition of such principles with other value systems in Asia.

- Higher degree of cultural, religious and social diversity within and between Asian countries compared with Western countries.
- Formation of the Western nation-state in the period of ascendancy of this model, compared with Asian nation-state formation under conditions of globalisation.

The similarities can be summarised as:

- The introduction of the nation-state model, which makes it necessary to define membership of the nation and to develop national culture and consciousness.
- The need to define membership of the nation according to criteria of birth on the territory (*ius soli*) or descent from a national (*ius sanguinis*). The Asian preference for *ius sanguinis* makes it very hard for immigrants and their descendants to become citizens.
- Trends to introduction of the rule of law, democracy and citizenship, which make it hard to deny human rights and fair legal process to immigrants.
- Trends to growth in public provision for education, health and social welfare.

HOW IMMIGRATION IS AFFECTING ASIAN NATION-STATES

As noticed above in the Western examples, permanent settlement and development of multicultural societies were facilitated by three main factors: principles of the rule of law and human rights even for non-citizens; incorporation of immigrants into welfare systems; and the effect of social networks in maintaining the migration process despite changed official policies. The question is whether similar factors exist or are likely to arise in Asian immigration countries. If this is not the case, governments may be able to control immigration and prevent settlement. But if, as the above discussion suggests, it is difficult for increasingly democratic states to stop immigration (once it has started) and to prevent settlement, then they had better start planning for multicultural societies.

Which of these two scenarios is most probable cannot be resolved on a theoretical level. Indeed, a full empirical answer is likely to take twenty years or more. However, it is useful to look at some of the trends of the last two decades and see where they are pointing. In view of the complexity of the issues, it is possible to give only a few examples on some key topics.

Controlling Migration

Since the mid-1980s, rapid economic growth and declining fertility have led to considerable demand for migrant labour in such countries as Japan, the

Republic of Korea, Hong Kong, Taiwan and Singapore. Malaysia and Thailand have both emigration and immigration. Throughout the fast-growing 'tiger economies', migrant workers took on the '3D jobs'—dirty, dangerous and difficult—that nationals could increasingly afford to reject. By 1996 there were an estimated 5 million migrant workers in Asia (OECD, 1998: 46). The Asian Crisis of 1997–99 led to some reduction in labour migration and attempts to repatriate migrants from several countries, but the overall number does not appear to have fallen significantly. Refugee movements within Asia have a longer tradition, with very large movements after the Vietnam War, and many smaller movements since, such as the flow from Myanmar to Thailand.

Asian governments treat labour migrants as temporary workers, with very limited rights. Most states have rigid rules to prevent unwanted migration and to restrict length of stay. There are strict visa requirements and often severe punishments for illegal migrants or persons who employ them. Several countries admit only highly-skilled personnel and reject manual workers. Despite this, illegal migration is very frequent. This often takes the form of tourist visa-holders who overstay their permits, but there is also a great deal of smuggling of undocumented workers over borders. The number of illegal migrants may well exceed the number of legal migrants (Lim and Oishi, 1996; OECD, 1998: 45).

A few examples may help illustrate the situation. By 1995, there were 533,000 registered foreign workers in Malaysia, of whom 253,000 were from Indonesia and the rest from mainly Bangladesh, the Philippines and Thailand (Huguet, 1995: 525). Estimates of irregular workers were as high as 1.2 million in 1993, making up 16 per cent of the total 7.4 million employed workers (Lim, 1996: 321). In 1997, in response to the Asian Crisis, the government announced plans for mass deportations of irregular workers, now claimed to be as numerous as 2 million. Apprehensions of illegal entrants increased, but it soon became clear that the authorities were unable to completely prevent illegal entry, since the coastline is long and hard to control. An amnesty was introduced to encourage irregular workers to leave without penalties. The costs and logistical problems involved were considerable, and it became clear that it would be impossible to expel all illegals in this way (Kassim, 1998). Poor economic conditions in Indonesia led to increased migration pressures, while Malaysian employers sought to retain workers in industrial and plantation jobs which were not attractive to local workers. Overall, it seems that only about 200,000 foreign workers were repatriated in 1998. At the same time, plantation employers were claiming that they could not get labour and the Government authorised the hiring of an additional 100,000 workers (Stahl, 1999).

From the mid-1980s, Taiwan experienced labour shortfalls and illegal immigration. In 1992, a foreign labour policy was introduced permitting recruitment of migrant workers for occupations with severe labour shortages.

Duration of employment was limited to two years. In January 1996, there were 200,000 legal foreign workers and up to 250,000 illegals. Workers came mainly from Thailand (68 per cent), the Philippines (25 per cent), Malaysia (3.5 per cent) and Indonesia (3.2 per cent). Most recruitment is carried out by labour brokers, who charge workers up to US$3000, the equivalent of 4–6 months' wages. Despite rigid regulations, including prohibition of job-changing, the authorities appear to have lost control of movements. Many workers stay on illegally after two years, or change jobs to get higher wages, and to escape repayments to brokers (Lee and Wang, 1996).

South Korea was a major source country for workers migrating to Gulf oil countries in the 1970s, but rapidly became a labour importer due to rapid economic growth in the 1980s (Martin, 1991). By 1996, there were an estimated 211,000 foreign workers in Korea of whom 130,000 were irregular (OECD, 1998: 132). Government policies allow entry only of highly-skilled workers; unskilled migrants are barred. In 1992, the Industrial and Technical Training Program (ITTP) was introduced to provide trainees for manufacturing industries suffering from labour shortages. The initial one-year period of training was extended to two years in 1993 and three years in 1996. This is in fact often a form of labour recruitment, and some 30 per cent of the trainees have actually left their training places to take up irregular employment. Many irregular workers are paid low wages and lack basic rights. About forty per cent of irregular workers are Chinese citizens, often of Korean ethnic origin. The increase in irregular foreign workers has become an issue of public concern in Korea (Kang, 1996; OECD, 1998: 131–3).

In 1996, the estimated stock of foreign nationals in Japan was 1.4 million, of whom 283,000 were irregular workers (OECD, 1998: 129). Recent labour migration to Japan began in the late 1980s with legal entry of women to work as 'entertainers'. They were followed by men entering irregularly to take up unskilled jobs in construction and manufacturing, due to high labour demand during the 'bubble economy' period. In 1990, it was decided not to allow entry of unskilled workers. However, schemes were introduced to recruit trainees (some 45,000 by 1996) and *Nikkeijin* (workers of Japanese ancestry from Brazil and Peru—211,000 in 1996) (OECD, 1998: 130).[9] Illegal immigration continues in response to demand for low-skilled labour for '3-D jobs'. The low birthrates, ageing population and high education levels of the Japanese population make it likely that demand for such labour will continue. Official policy is to move labour-intensive workplaces overseas through foreign direct investment, but there are limits to this: jobs in construction, health services, aged care and similar areas cannot be exported. Since the Japanese state clearly has the institutional capacity to control entries, it is hard to escape the impression that a certain level of irregular labour migration is tacitly accepted. In response to increased unemployment since 1997, the authorities have organised regular control campaigns and crackdowns on illegal foreigners, but the numbers arrested during any one campaign average only 200 to 300–less than 1 per cent of illegal migrants (Komai, 1998).

An important general reason for loss of government control over migration is the role of 'migration networks': informal linkages between migrants, their families and their communities of origin, which help to organise migratory movements and sustain them once they have got under way. These play a substantial role in both migration and settlement (Boyd, 1989; Hugo, 1994; Castles and Miller, 1998: 25–7). This is linked to another significant feature of Asian labour migration: the major role played by the 'migration industry'. Much recruitment of migrant workers within Asia is organised by migration agents and labour brokers. Governments and employers in receiving countries find it easier to rely on such intermediaries than to organise movements themselves. Authorities of labour-sending countries have found themselves powerless to stop or control the frequently exploitative activities of the industry. Martin (1996: 201) estimates that migrants typically pay fees equal to 20–30 per cent of their first year's earnings. For the whole of Asia, the labour broker industry could be worth US$2.2 billion per year. While some agents carry out legitimate activities, others indulge in illegal practices, such as tricking women into prostitution, or smuggling human cargoes over borders.

Overall, it appears that Asian states are finding it increasingly difficult to maintain strict border control. The contradiction between strict immigration rules and growing irregular movement has a number of causes:

- Difficulty in controlling movement across long land or sea borders, especially in regional migration systems with long traditions of mobility.
- Lack of institutional capacity to develop effective systems for monitoring and control.
- Government toleration of irregular movements due to labour demand and employer pressure.
- The role of migration networks and the migration industry in organising and sustaining migratory movements despite government policies.
- At a more general level we can link ineffective immigration control to the porosity of borders resulting from globalisation. Since some flows are wanted (e.g. tourists, skilled or business migration), it is hard to completely close the door to those which are not.

Settlement and Community Formation

Relatively little research has been done on the extent to which intra-Asian migratory movements since the 1980s are leading to permanent settlement. This is partly due to the recentness of such developments and partly due to conventional perceptions that put a taboo on the theme of settlement. Asian governments do not expect or want settlement to occur, and therefore tend to ignore the phenomenon, a very similar situation to some western countries 30 years ago. Until recently, academic researchers have also paid little attention to this topic, showing how social scientists are often influenced by national preconceptions on immigration and cultural diversity. However, the situation is beginning to change, and a new generation of researchers is beginning to present evidence of complex patterns of family reunion and settlement.[10]

Research in Japan by Komai (1995; 1998) finds tendencies to international marriages, family formation, residential concentration and the building of ethnic communities. Ethnic places of worship, businesses, associations and media are beginning to emerge. There is evidence of socio-economic marginalisation and differentiation linked to recession and economic restructuring. Differing employment patterns are often linked to varying legal status: legal workers (especially immigrants of Japanese ethnic origin from Latin America—*Nikkeijin*) find jobs in large enterprises, while undocumented workers are displaced to small enterprises or informal-sector jobs. Another significant trend is the weak but gradually improving situation of immigrants with regard to various civil, political and social rights (Kondo, 1998). About half the foreign residents are long-standing residents, mainly of Korean origins. Many were born in Japan; some are even third or fourth generation Japanese residents who remain non-citizens due to the strict application of *ius sanguinis*. However, legal changes in 1992 led to a gradual rise in naturalisations from 6,794 in 1990 to 14,495 in 1996 (OECD, 1998: 261).

Mori (1997: 155) argues that immigrant workers have become heavily concentrated in certain sectors or occupations, causing structural dependence on irregular workers. This could encourage employer pressure for regularising such workers, which could in turn reinforce trends to settlement. He also finds strong tendencies to long-term settlement, and shows how public authorities are gradually including foreign residents—even irregular workers—in health, education and welfare services (ibid.: 189–206). Most recently, a range of social integration programmes for foreign workers and their families have been introduced. These include the establishment of Employment Service Centres for foreign workers as well as the provision of education for children of foreign nationals on equal terms with native Japanese (OECD, 1998: 131). There are clear parallels here with the way the welfare state helped stabilise immigrant populations in Western Europe.

However, as Komai (1998) shows, the differences between Japan and Western European countries are also marked. Labour migration to Japan started in a short-term boom, which soon gave way to recession; there is no parallel to the long 1945–73 boom which provided the conditions for structural incorporation of immigrants in the economies of Western European countries. Moreover, the immigrant share in the population is only 1 per cent—very low compared with other industrialised countries. Komai points out that Japanese people have generally accepted immigrants with little hostility. There are no campaigns of racist violence against them. Yet this may well be because of the small numbers, for ethnocentrism is strong in Japanese society. Although there are NGOs working to support immigrants, and there has been some discussion of improved naturalisation rules and political rights, it seems unlikely that immigrants will become a significant political factor in the foreseeable future (see also Weiner and Hanami, 1998).

Similarly, research by Azizah Kassim (1998) shows trends to long-term settlement by immigrants in Malaysia. Her fieldwork over a long period in squatter settlements around Kuala Lumpur has documented processes of community formation and examined their economic and social causes. She shows that basing policies on the assumption that the use of migrant workers is temporary, when they in fact meet long-term structural needs, leads to non-compliance with official policies on the part of both employers and immigrant workers. The result is that regulations are often ignored and become unenforceable. For instance, regulation of wages for legal contract workers gives them protection, but prevents job-changing to gain better conditions. It may actually be more beneficial to work illegally. Similarly, the failure to plan for the housing needs of immigrants has led to squatter settlements, which have encouraged ethnic concentration and community formation. Recent official policies of preventing illegal entry and deporting illegal workers cannot be adequately enforced. This leads to an expectation of future changes in rules, which may encourage illegal entry and residence.

Overall, Kassim's work confirms the impression that labour migration leads to settlement and community formation, whatever the original intentions of both migrants and policymakers. However, the social and cultural position of immigrants in Malaysia is highly complex and changing rapidly. First, movement to Malaysia takes place in the framework of regional migration systems that have deep historical roots. Migrants to Malaysia do not have to adjust to a single dominant culture, but rather to find their place in an already complex ethnic mix. Some Indonesian and Filipino migrants are culturally very close to Malays.[11] In such circumstances, ethnicity can easily become politicised. Second, large-scale labour migration to Malaysia has started at a very early point in the country's transition from a rural to an industrial economy (Lim, 1996). This means that Malaysia has simultaneous patterns of in- and out-migration of differing ethnic and socio-economic groups. If policies do eventually shift to recognition of migrant rights and the emergence of new ethnic communities, then some type of multiculturalism seems likely.

Only two examples have been presented in this section. Clearly there are important differences. Japan is a highly-developed country with strong institutional structures. It is also one of the most monocultural countries in Asia. This provides a very different context for immigration than Malaysia with its less-developed (but fast-growing) economy, its lower institutional capacity for regulating immigration and the labour market, and its high degree of cultural diversity. Malaysia also has a much larger volume of immigration relative to population. Yet both countries share some characteristics: the apparent inability to prevent irregular labour migration, the growing structural dependence on foreign labour, and the emergence of trends to settlement and community formation. Ethnic relations issues have long been highly politicised in Malaysia, and recent developments have exacerbated this situation. Issues of immigration and ethnicity are less significant in Japan, but public concern does seem to be increasing. Is it possible to generalise from these two cases to other Asian immigration countries? I believe that similar tendencies are to be found in many places. However, much more detailed research is needed on these matters.

MANAGING ETHNIC DIVERSITY IN ASIAN IMMIGRATION COUNTRIES

At the beginning of post-1945 migration processes, Western nation-states based their policies for managing ethnic diversity on varying historical experiences of nation-formation. There were two main approaches: exclusion of immigrants from membership of the national community and citizenship; or cultural assimilation of immigrants as a precondition for membership and citizenship. Western countries had to modify these policies as a result of their experiences. They found that once immigration had been started (usually for economic purposes), it was extremely difficult for democratic countries to stop further entries and to prevent the development of culturally-diverse societies. The trend is now towards citizenship and full membership of society, without prior cultural assimilation. In some cases (Australia, Canada, US, Sweden, etc.), this has led to multiculturalism as a model for national identity and citizenship. In other cases (France, Germany) such developments are less explicit. The Western experience indicates that a 'best practice model' for managing immigration and ethnic diversity would contain the following elements:

- A non-discriminatory immigration policy, which does not discriminate on criteria of national origins, race, ethnicity, religion or culture, although it may select according to economic, social and humanitarian criteria.
- The right to family reunion for both economic and humanitarian entrants.
- Access to most civil, political and social rights for legally resident non-citizens.
- Educational and social measures to combat specific forms of disadvantage faced by immigrants.
- Easy access to citizenship for immigrants and their children.

- Acceptance of cultural maintenance and community formation by immigrants.
- Measures to combat racism and ensure social justice for immigrants.
- Acceptance of the role of immigration in nation-building.

Asian nation-states have varying models for dealing with ethnic diversity. Major differences exist between countries which underwent Western colonisation and those which did not; and between culturally diverse countries and relatively monocultural ones. It might be expected that new forms of immigration would lead to modification of pre-existing approaches. Theoretical analysis of the characteristics of the modern nation-state leads to the hypothesis that trends to acceptance of the rule of law, democracy and human rights will make it more difficult for Asian nation-states to prevent settlement and to insist on cultural assimilation of immigrants. If this theoretical hypothesis is borne out by empirical research, then it is likely that Asian immigration countries will become more culturally diverse, and will, in the long run, tend to adopt multicultural policies.

There are already signs that Asian immigration countries are finding it increasingly difficult to control their borders. Powerful economic and social factors are leading to irregular migration movements, which states are unwilling or unable to control. Similarly, there is evidence of trends to long-term settlement and community formation in some immigration countries. Again, the economic and social dynamics of migration processes often seem to override official policies which are based on unrealistic theories and methods. However, there is as yet little evidence that Asian governments are modifying their models for dealing with ethnic diversity. In general, the following principles are entrenched:

- immigrants should not be allowed to settle;
- foreign residents should not be offered citizenship except in exceptional cases;
- national culture and identity should not be modified in response to external influences.

Thus there is no sign as yet that dominant Asian ideas on national identity and citizenship are beginning to undergo the type of changes that we observed as a result of immigration in the Western examples. The question is: does this lack of change in policies for managing ethnic diversity indicate simply that the migration process is at a much earlier stage than in Western countries, or does it indicate a fundamental and lasting difference between Western and Asian nation-states?

Large-scale entries to Asian immigration countries started about thirty years later than in the Western countries. Major shifts in Western policies on national identity and citizenship came only after 25–40 years of immigration and settlement. Thus Asian countries could theoretically still follow this trajectory. On the other hand, as shown above, there are important differences (as well as similarities) in the characteristics of Asian nation-states. These may well result in different outcomes from Western countries. It may be possible to maintain existing approaches to ethnic diversity, especially in countries with relatively low acceptance of human rights and legal guarantees even for non-citizens.

It is impossible to come to any clear conclusion on this important question at the present time and with the existing level of information. It would be very important to carry out detailed research on these matters in all Asian immigration countries. This might help to avoid some of the painful conflicts and unplanned changes which have been experienced elsewhere.

NOTES

1. This chapter is based on a paper presented at the *Conference on International Migration into the 21st Century* at the University of Western Australia, 29 November—1 December 1999. I thank Reg Appleyard and Ron Skeldon for their comments on the draft paper. An earlier version was presented at the Asia Pacific Migration Research Network, International Symposium on New Trends in Migration in the Asia Pacific and Consequences for Japan, 24–6 September 1999, Waseda University, Tokyo.

2. See for instance Castles, 1998; Castles and Miller, 1998, Chapter 6; and the quarterly *Asian and Pacific Migration Journal*.

3. Interesting analyses of the effects of emigration on the nation-state in the case of the Philippines are contained in a special issue of the *Philippine Sociological Review* (1996, vol. 44: nos.1–4), see Aguilar, 1996 and Blanc, 1996.

4. It should be noted that the above analysis does not imply that globalisation is to be equated with a general reduction in the power of states. Rather, as the nexus between territory and sovereignty is undermined by globalising forces, new forms of governance emerge at the national, regional and global levels, with the military and economic power of the dominant states still playing a decisive role. A system of 'polyarchy' is emerging, marked by a diffusion of forms of political authority and types of political actor (Held et al., 1999: 50). In this system the nation-state is just one level of power among others. Yet democracy and citizenship is still concentrated almost exclusively at the nation-state level. With a few exceptions (such as the European Parliament), there are no bodies elected by citizens at the supranational level. Thus citizen rights and democracy appear to be excluded from the emerging institutions of global power.

5. The 1990 United Nations Convention on the Rights of Migrant Workers and Members of their Families has been ratified by only a few emigration countries; the record on ratification and implementation of ILO Conventions 97 and 143 is also poor.

6. There is a huge literature on immigration to Western countries and the changes this has brought about for their societies and nation-states (see for instance Bauböck, 1994; Kymlicka, 1995; Bauböck et al., 1996; Habermas, 1996; Bader, 1997; DeWind et al., 1997; Bauböck and Rundell, 1998; Joppke, 1999).

7. For analyses of democratic movements and the role of the middle classes in Asia, see Rodan, 1996: Laothamatas, 1997.

8. See above for definitions of *ius soli* and *ius sanguinis*.

9. The difference should be noted between the German policy of immediate citizenship for returning 'ethnic Germans' and the Japanese policy of giving labour market rights but not citizenship to *Nikkeijin*.

10. Several papers presented at the APMRN International Symposium on New Trends in Migration in the Asia Pacific and Consequences for Japan, 24–26 September, Waseda University, Tokyo, provided micro-studies of community formation and ethnic relations issues in Japan. These did much to question the conventional wisdom that immigration will not lead to settlement nor undermine homogeneity in that county. The papers are being published in a special issue of the *Asian and Pacific Migration Journal*. The UNESCO-MOST Asia Pacific Migration Research Network (APMRN) carries out research in 13 countries, and is dedicated to examining long-term social and political consequences of migration. Contact: apmrn@uow.edu.au

11. This points to the continuity of historical patterns of mobility in the Malay 'maritime world'. Such international migrants may have greater cultural affinity to the receiving population than do many internal migrants within the multi-ethnic archipelago of Indonesia.

REFERENCES

Aguilar, F.V.J. (1996), 'The dialectics of transnational shame and national identity', *Philippine Sociological Review*, 44 (1–4): 101–36.

Bader, V. (ed.) (1997), *Citizenship and Exclusion*, London: Macmillan.

Basch, L., N. Glick-Schiller and C.S. Blanc (1994), *Nations Unbound: Transnational Projects, Post-Colonial Predicaments and Deterritorialized Nation-States*, New York: Gordon and Breach.

Bauböck, R. (ed.) (1994), *From Aliens to Citizens: Redefining the Status of Immigrants in Europe*, Aldershot: Avebury.

Bauböck, R. (1996), 'Social and cultural integration in a civil society', in R. Bauböck, A. Heller, and A.R. Zolberg (eds), *The Challenge of Diversity: Integration and Pluralism in Societies of Immigration*, Aldershot: Avebury, pp. 67–131.

Bauböck, R. and J. Rundell (eds) (1998), *Blurred Boundaries: Migration, Ethnicity, Citizenship*, Aldershot: Ashgate.

Bauböck, R., A. Heller and A.R. Zolberg (eds) (1996), *The Challenge of Diversity: Integration and Pluralism in Societies of Immigration*, Aldershot: Avebury.

Berger, M.T. and D.A. Borer (eds) (1997), *The Rise of East Asia: Critical Visions of the Pacific Century*, London and New York: Routledge.

Blanc, C.S. (1996), 'Balikbayan: a Filipino extension of the national imaginary and of state boundaries', *Philippine Sociological Review*, 44 (1–4): 178–93.

Bommes, M. and J. Halfmann (1998), *Migration in nationalen Wohlfahrtstaaten: Theoretische und vegleichende Untersuchungen*, Osnabrück: Universitätsverlag Rasch.

Boyd, M. (1989), 'Family and personal networks in migration', *International Migration Review*, 23 (3): 638–70.

Castells, M. (1996), *The Rise of the Network Society*, Oxford: Blackwell.

Castells, M. (1998), *End of Millennium*, Oxford: Blackwell.

Castles, S. (1986), 'The guest-worker in Western Europe: an obituary', *International Migration Review*, **20** (4): 764–78.

Castles, S. (1998), 'New migrations in the Asia-Pacific region: a force for social and political change', *International Social Science Journal*, (156): 215–28.

Castles, S. and A. Davidson (2000), *Citizenship and Migration: Globalisation and the Politics of Belonging*, London: Macmillan.

Castles, S. and M.J. Miller (1998), *The Age of Migration: International Population Movements in the Modern World*, London: Macmillan.

Castles, S., H. Booth and T. Wallace (1984), *Here for Good: Western Europe's New Ethnic Minorities*, London: Pluto Press.

Castles, S., M. Kalantzis, B. Cope and M. Morrissey (1992), *Mistaken Identity: Multiculturalism and the Demise of Nationalism in Australia*, Sydney: Pluto Press.

Cohen, R. (1997), *Global Diasporas: An Introduction*, London: UCL Press.

Davidson, A. and K. Weekley (eds) (1999), *Globalisation and Citizenship in the Asia-Pacific*, London: Macmillan.

DeWind, J., C. Hirschman and P. Kasinitz (1997), 'Everything old is new again? Processes and theories of immigrant incorporation', *International Migration Review (Special Issue: Immigrant Adaptation and Native-Born Responses in the making of Americans)*, **31** (4): 1096–112.

Habermas, J. (1996) *Die Einbeziehung des Anderen: Studien zur politischen Theorie*, Frankfurt am Main: Suhrkamp.

Held, D., A. McGrew, D. Goldblatt and J. Perraton (1999), *Global Transformations: Politics, Economics and Culture*, Cambridge: Polity.

Hugo, G. (1994), *Migration and the Family*, Vienna: United Nations Occasional Papers Series for the International Year of the Family, no. 12.

Joppke, C. (1999), 'How immigration is changing citizenship: a comparative view', *Ethnic and Racial Studies*, 22: 629–52.

Kang, S.D. (1996) 'Typology and conditions of migrant workers in Korea', *Asian and Pacific Migration Journal*, **5** (2–3): 265–79.

Kassim, A. (1998), 'The case of a new receiving country in the developing world: Malaysia', paper presented at the UN Technical Symposium on International Migration and Development, The Hague.

Komai, H. (1995), *Migrant Workers in Japan*, London: Kegan Paul International.

Komai, H. (1998), 'Migrants in Japan', paper present at the UN Technical Symposium on International Migration and Development, The Hague.

Kondo, A. (1998), 'From "Monoethnic" State to Cultural Pluralism in Japan', Stockholm: Centre for Pacific Asia Studies at Stockholm University, Occasional Paper 38.

Kymlicka, W. (1995), *Multicultural Citizenship: A Liberal Theory of Minority Rights*, Oxford: Clarendon.

Laothamatas, A. (ed.) (1997), *Democratization in Southeast and East Asia*. Singapore: Institute of Southeast Asian Studies.

Lee, J.S. and S.W. Wang (1996), 'Recruiting and managing of foreign workers in Taiwan', *Asian and Pacific Migration Journal*, **5** (2–3): 281–301.

Lim, L.L. (1996), 'The migration transition in Malaysia', *Asian and Pacific Migration Journal*, **5** (2–3): 319–37.

Lim, L.L. N. and Oishi (1996), 'International labor migration of Asian women: distinctive characteristics and policy concerns', *Asian and Pacific Migration Journal*, **5** (1): 8–116.

Martin, P. (1996), 'Labor contractors: a conceptual overview', *Asian and Pacific Migration Journal*, **5** (2–3): 201–18.

Martin, P.L. (1991), 'Labor migration in Asia: conference report', *International Migration Review*, **25** (1): 176–93.

Mori, H. (1997), *Immigration Policy and Foreign Workers in Japan*, London: Macmillan.

OECD (1998), 'Trends in International Migration: Annual Report 1998', Paris: OECD.

Renan, E. (1992), *Qu'est-ce qu'une nation? et autres essais politiques*, (introduced by J. Roman) Paris: Presses Pocket, Agora.

Rodan, G. (ed.) (1996), *Political Oppositions in Industrialising Asia*, London: Routledge.

Soysal, Y.N. (1994), *Limits of Citizenship: Migrants and Postnational Membership in Europe*, Chicago and London: University of Chicago Press.

Stahl, C. (1999), 'International migration in East Asia: trends and policy issues', paper presented at the Asia Pacific Migration Research Network International Symposium on New Trends in Migration in the Asia Pacific and Consequences for Japan, 24–26 September 1999, Waseda University, Tokyo.

Weiner, M. and T. Hanami (eds) (1998), *Temporary Workers or Future Citizens? Japanese and U.S. Migration Policies*, New York: New York University Press.

World Bank (1998), *East Asia: the Road to Recovery*, Washington: World Bank.

Yoshino, K. (1992), *Cultural Nationalism in Contemporary Japan*, London: Routledge.

11. Caribbean Geopolitical Imperatives and Citizenship in American Immigration Policy and Practice

Anthony P. Maingot

INTRODUCTION

There is already enough scholarship to establish the study of international migration as a major field. The implication of this is that we do not need to keep reinventing the wheel. We should rather attempt to deepen our understanding of some of the significant attempts at conceptualising the field in a comparative manner. Such an attempt is the IOM/UNFPA project on Emigration Dynamics in Developing Countries (Appleyard, 1998, 1999). Utilising a flow model designed by Nasra Shah, those studies probed the economic, political, and demographic patterns operating in sending countries. This author utilised a slightly modified version of that model in presenting findings for migration from the Caribbean, specifically from Haiti and the Dominican Republic (Maingot, 1999). My purpose here is to return to that modified model (Figure 11.1), and attempt to provide a more 'reflective' analysis of segment 7 ('Receiving Countries') as it impacted and continues to impact segment 4 ('Sending Country Policies'). In so doing, I have added another variable to the model: geopolitics and the nature and rates of naturalisation, i.e. citizenship. The 'Receiving Country' under analysis is the US.

The justification for limiting the focus is that the history of changes in US immigration law, and its impact on migration from the Caribbean, has been amply recorded. Similarly, the history of illegal migration into the US is also broadly analysed and debated. As distinct from these two aspects, however, the role of geopolitics in the process, while certainly studied,[1] is less well known. It has to be given significant causal weight, not only because of its past role but, even more so, because its potential future role. In the Caribbean, the unsettled cases of Cuba, Haiti, and even Puerto Rico come to mind. From the mainland, more and more Colombians and Venezuelans are arriving in South Florida. Potential future crises will not have the same geopolitical context as the situations dealt with here, i.e. the special imperatives of the Cold War. Cold War geopolitical imperatives tended to override domestic fears and prejudices about class and ethnicity. Consequently, geopolitics were crucial in creating new diasporas and their social networks. Once networks were established, the naturalisation process became a key step in the assimilation process, though not necessarily involving acculturation. Citizenship has become a form of protection because it allows participation in the metropolitan political system, taking advantage of the benefits and avoiding the penalties of not being a citizen.

Hispanics increasingly see citizenship as a major resource even though traditionally, they have had very low rates of naturalisation. Once naturalised and politically mobilised, they are becoming a factor in changing the nature of the flow from sending to receiving countries (see Figure 11.1). Just how important citizenship is remains an empirical question. Alexander DeConde has persuasively argued that US foreign policy is still very much an Anglo-American concern and the history of that concern has often been tainted with racism and ethnocentrism (DeConde, 1992). If that has been so in foreign policy, it has also been with attitudes towards naturalisation. Throughout most of US history, writes Rogers M. Smith, 'lawmakers pervasively and unapologetically structured U.S. citizenship in terms of illiberal and undemocratic racial, ethnic, and gender hierarchies.' (1997:1). It is warranted, therefore, to ask whether the present liberal *apertura* can be accepted as a permanent change in US attitudes. We begin with a reflection on basic US attitudes towards immigration and naturalisation.

IMMIGRATION POLICIES: BY DESIGN OR 'DERIVED'?

Is the US immigration problem just another of the many difficult issues confronting decision-makers and citizens alike, or is it a special problem? Certainly in terms of persistence it has the features of a special problem; each US generation seems to need (though perhaps not to relish) the debate over the principles and implications of immigration. Like the 'race problem', it appears to be an integral part of the larger complex of persistent problems the US democracy carries over from generation to generation.

If the immigration question is another one of the ongoing complex of issues, why has there never been anything approximating a consensus on the precise nature of the problem, let alone a possible resolution of it? Consensus is used here to mean legitimacy: the belief by at least a working majority in the essential appropriateness—if not full righteousness—of a particular policy. Is the US any closer today to such a consensus than it has been in prior periods of serious debate on the issue—the 1890s, the 1920s and the 1950s? Surely one could argue that there have been periods of substantial consensus on that other American question—race. Whatever their private feelings and prejudices, society and its political and judicial representatives have slowly but surely been giving shape to a civil rights thrust that can be slowed down but not reversed.

The argument in this chapter is that no such legitimising consensus appears likely on the immigration issue. A comparison with the race problem reveals fruitful insights. One can do no better than turn to Gunnar Myrdal for guidance. Myrdal was convinced that the US had developed 'the most explicitly expressed system of general ideals in reference to human interrelations' of any Western society (Myrdal, 1944: 3), the 'American Creed' in his phrase. Both blacks and immigrants appeal to this creed in their disputes and claims over rights and privileges. Here the two problems of race and migration show a similarity: both groups and their supporters appeal to the American Creed specifically, and to the conflicting values of the majority white society generally. This is very important because the common appeals produce similarities in the manner in which arguments, claims, and grievances are articulated and in the mechanisms utilised for their redress. The American Creed is used to legitimise utilisation of the whole gamut of legal and political avenues for redress.

Once the similarity is established, however, the differences begin to reveal themselves more clearly. Perhaps a closer review of these differences will throw some light on the lack of consensus on the immigration problem. This is so because, in a fundamental way, these differences reflect the attitudes and postures of the white majority to the race problem and the immigration problem, respectively. The black–white relationship has a firm moral infrastructure and the resulting dilemma has a heavy content of historical guilt. The immigration dilemma, while also ideologically related to the American Creed, is more political and secular. Placing immigration within a context of social policy rather than moral dictates, engenders the good sociological analysis or court brief. This issue is hard pressed, however, to produce the righteous moral indignation of a Harriet Beecher Stowe's *Uncle Tom's Cabin*. At no time has the immigration question produced the poignancy of a Richard Wright's, *Black Boy*, or the passion of a James Baldwin's, *The Fire Next Time*. The kind of excruciating and guilt-laden response of a Norman Podhoretz, 'My negro problem, and ours', has been absent from social discourse about immigration policy. 'Special feelings about color', confessed Podhoretz (1963), 'are a contagion to which White Americans seem susceptible even when there is nothing in their background to account for the susceptibility'. The collective guilt of a nation indicates that racism is not yet conquered, even while a system of egalitarian ideals expressed in the American Creed is explicitly embraced, as Myrdal noted. This historical guilt—part of the underpinnings of US black–white relations—is lacking in the immigrant problem. These special feelings are reserved for the only group in the US mosaic that did not come voluntarily, that cannot identify historically with a single particular country, language, or religion.

Figure 11.1 A model for conceptualising emigration dynamics

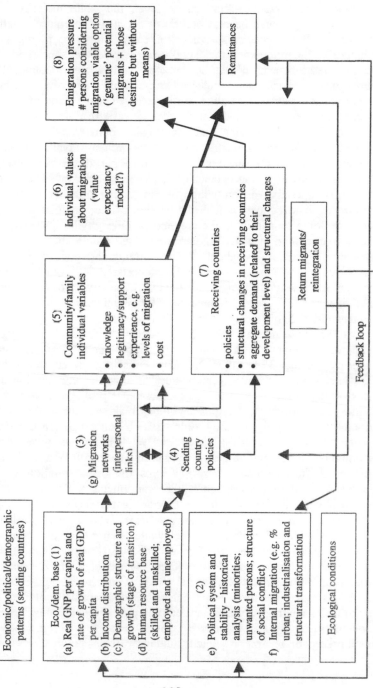

205

Immigrants and immigration, on the other hand, were conceptualised quite differently. At a practical, immediate level, the white majority's interest seldom stretched much beyond a concern about the foreigner's right to be here in the first place, the privilege of entry. Since the immigrant came voluntarily, the immigrant was supposed to have the special feelings of gratitude and satisfaction. At a broader and more ideological level, immigrants were subsumed under an overarching view of nation-building. Immigrant and native born alike were perceived to be parts of an ongoing process in which, as Frederick J. Turner (1920: 281–2) put it, self-determination, self-restraint and 'intelligent democracy' were creating something new and original. The well-researched travails of each new immigrant group as they attempted to become a part of the experiment warns us against too ready an acceptance of this widely held view. The belief in an earnest, co-operative nation-building—like Turner's theory of frontier—is more myth than reality. Through the process of the self-fulfilling prophesy, nation building lent itself to the creation of other myths. In the process of ethnic bargaining, which accompanied the immigration process and integration, perceptions about various immigrant contributions to US democracy and society were very important.[2] In other words, the battleground was that of power, and the task at hand was to gain membership in the community as a competitor. But immigrants had a chance at membership quite different to African Americans.

Because the American Creed is appealed to concerning immigrants, the immigration problem has a moral dimension, but one of moral accountability rather than of moral obligation. No moral consciousness constantly activates the white majority's sense of guilt. Lacking this, the immigration dilemma takes on the dimensions of a high-order secular problem. It is a matter of politics—trade-offs, concessions and deal making—rather than of moral principle. Immigration is a high order issue because it has a moral content that appeals to the American Creed, and yet it is secular, given shape and direction by an ongoing process of bargaining, nationally and internationally. This means that contemporary opponents of 'open' migration, such as George J. Borjas (1999), pitch their arguments on instrumental, not intrinsically moral grounds. 'Heaven's Door', as Borjas calls the US, is not to be closed, only to be restricted in terms of 'quantity' and 'quality' of entrants.

The overriding concern in the white majority's attention to the immigration problem has been limited historically to periodic attempts to achieve politically acceptable procedural justice at a given time. This is different from the pursuit of a general policy of equality of human beings that transcends space and time. Power interests, not historical guilt, provide the key to understanding why immigration policy produces periodic reviews and revisions of policy and procedure, rather than an overriding consensus on moral precept or general principle to guide admissions policy over time.

Illegal immigration and refugee issues are problems like other immigration issues requiring politically acceptable policies that involve deal making and compromise. They are also more unpredictable than many immigration issues because they have intensified the moral appeals to the American Creed. While more complex and having a larger moral content, refugee and illegal migration have not been converted into a new American dilemma. They remain secular political issues, even if more complex points of political and legal philosophy and procedure are involved, including international relations.

Unlike the case of American preoccupation with race relations, or more specifically, what US whites, until recently, called the 'Negro problem'. there has not been fundamental agreement among US scholars or social commentators on the need to study and document the nature of geopolitics, ethnicity, and citizenship in the process of immigration and acculturation in the US. Fortunately, not all US scholars have felt this way, because there is a need to understand the parallel developments of cultural pluralism and social pluralism. The former describes the retention of ethnicity as an organising principle within groups; the latter scrutinises the stratification system, the structure of inequality.

The first major systematic exposition of the concept of social pluralism was that of Furnivall (1939) in his study of what is today Indonesia. Furnivall's fundamental thesis is that the plural society was not created by fiat, by a series of policies; rather, historical circumstances, including an evolving economic system, dictated policy. 'The plural society', he wrote, 'was not planned; it happened'. It happened because the values and institutions of the society are not shaped by one group. No one group monopolises power; none has social economic, or political predominance. 'The plural society', he noted, 'is in fact held together only by pressure exerted from outside by the colonial power; it has no common social will' (Furnivall, 1945: 168).

Certainly no one would argue that Furnivall's plural society model fits the US precisely. Yet in a very fundamental Furnivallean way, the US was not planned, 'it happened'. It happened because after the initial consensus on an open door, on the value of not having an explicit or institutionalised immigration policy, there never was a single policy that could be agreed on, much less implemented. There was, rather, unplanned and incremental growth of territory and population.[3] Agreement on essential aspects of state sovereignty, control over state borders and the right of exclusion, grew even more slowly internationally and in the US, immigration laws, such as they were, tended to follow population movements; they neither caused them, nor, indeed, totally controlled them.

Other factors, such as economic cycles, were more important. As early as 1926, Harry Jerome hypothesised that, with few exceptions, immigration increased with prosperity and decreased in depressions. Emigration tended to follow an opposite course. Economics, however, has certainly not been the dominant factor at all times. Indeed, as will be argued here, it receded in importance at critical junctures. International politics and geopolitics, especially foreign wars, also shifted immigration flows and policy. The exemption of Western Hemisphere citizens from both restrictive 1924 and 1952 quotas in US law, for instance, responded to both specific national politics as well as foreign policy needs. By the time limits were set on Western Hemisphere immigration (the 120,000 ceiling of 1965), events of the Cold War had created new conditions that made that ceiling totally unrealistic. The architects of refugees from Communist countries had no way of predicting where those refugees would come from. Geopolitics of the Cold War drove immigration policy and practice in the US.

Changing geopolitical desiderata forced flexibility and shifts in immigration policy and practice. While reforms in immigration policy had taken place every quarter century, after 1965 the pace of immigration reform picked up considerably (Fix and Passel, 1994: 10). Geopolitics also explains the repeated presidential vetoes of restrictive immigration legislation passed by a US Congress more focused on domestic concerns. Both reflected the different constituencies operating in US politics, with the executive showing more susceptibility to pressures from urban immigrants than the legislature (Fuchs, 1968; Roney, 1981; Fix and Passel, 1994).

By the mid-twentieth century the US had become a complex, socially and culturally plural society. Even the most restrictive of policies could not control immigration. The finding of Roney (1981: 321–2), that between 1953 and 1965—a period of strict quotas and emphasis on control over immigration flows—only 35 per cent of all immigrants admitted to the US were quota immigrants, is significant. Four-fifths of the nonquota admissions during that period were nonquota immediate relatives of US citizens or natives of Western Hemisphere countries. Additionally, hundreds of thousands were admitted or permitted to stay through special legislation. When the Immigration and Nationality Act of 1965 established a seven-category preference system based on the principle of family unification, and to a lesser degree, skills, it was merely giving legal status to an existing sociological reality.

To understand the growth of US social pluralism in all its unplanned and uncontrolled dimensions, it is not adequate to ask whether all who wanted to come in, did. The key question is rather whether large numbers of those whom the restrictionists of the early 1920s and 1950s and other periods wanted to keep out, were kept out. After entry, how many immigrants became citizens and, thus, direct activists within the debate on immigration?

Observers of past periods of restrictive immigration policy assumed that policy would indeed restrict the flows. They misread the real dynamics of the flows. Writing in the early 1950s, Kuznets and Rubin (1954: ch. 4), for instance, took note of the free market play between capital and labour, but worried that wars and restrictive legislation would curtail not only immigration, but also the health patterns of US population growth. Their conclusion was less than prophetic:

> Indeed, the change in the whole climate of international relations has been so drastic that it is hard to imagine a return to the unprecedentedly wide and free movement of people in the world. ... [No longer would they] take advantage of better opportunities and contribute markedly to the growth of their country of destination. (Kuznets and Rubin (1954)).

In fact, history records that during the two decades after the 1965 legislation, immigration to the US reached levels equal to those of 1900–10 (between 8 and 9 million). A telegraphic listing of the causes of increased immigration since 1965 reinforces the notion of an unplanned social plural society: (1) the removal of national origins quotas and increase in the ceiling of legal immigration by the 1965 amendments to the Immigration and Nationality Act; (2) refugee flows in the Cold War context due to events in Cuba, other countries in the Caribbean, Central America, and Indochina; and (3) the large increase in illegal immigration due to unilateral ending of temporary labour programmes and changes in access to immigrant visas.

The first cause—the 1965 Act—can be said to have been planned; it responded to pressures of the new emphasis on civil rights with the US system and to older themes of ethnic political constituencies that helped elect John F. Kennedy. In other words, liberalised immigration policy was a direct beneficiary of shifts in national politics. However, even the 1965 legislation did not have the outcomes in either the numbers or origins of immigrants predicted by Congressional proponents. Causes two and three were well nigh impossible to anticipate and plan for. How could those who in 1965 set a limit of 17,400 refugees per year predict that continued Cuban and then Vietnamese flows would produce hundreds of thousands of refugees? Additionally, who could predict that Britain, for instance, would no longer welcome West Indians just at the time when the 1965 amendments opened the doors of the US to these West Indians? The result was a shift in destination of West Indian migrants and an unanticipated change in the number and source of immigrants following the 1965 Act in the US.

The inner contradiction between an assertion of an American Creed and the existence of social pluralism (which assumes precisely the absence of a such collective will or consensus) becomes evident. A resolution might be found in the admission that major portions of the American Creed itself have been flexible and malleable, a product of ongoing bargaining. Each generation, confronted with different problems, assesses the situation and interprets the Creed. In this process, intellectuals play a significant role.[4] 'The writing of American history', wrote Higham (1962: 10), 'has always had ... an intimate relation to history in the making. To examine the two together is to see the United States in terms of its evolving consciousness of itself'. In this process, the interpretations of the role of immigration—written, as Fuchs

(1982) notes, largely by Anglo-Saxon Protestants—have emphasised the exact opposite from the historical guilt evidenced toward the Negro problem: a not-undeserved sense of pride in US largesse with foreigners. Potter puts the issue in historical perspective:

> Historically, equality of opportunity was a particularly apt form of equalitarianism for a new, underdeveloped frontier country. ... The best economic benefit which the government could give was to offer a person free access in developing underdeveloped resources for his own profit, and this is what America did offer ... equality of opportunity did become the most highly sanctioned form of equalitarianism in the United States. (Potter 1962: 215)

The principle of equality of opportunity, especially when produced by guilt and fear, might operate to create a consensus on certain problems. Immigration is not one of them. Short of saying 'all are welcome' or 'none is welcome', opportunities become the result of political bargaining combined with innumerable and thus unpredictable events, geopolitical contingencies being of particular importance among the latter. As long as access to opportunity is not mostly restricted on the basis of nationality, bargaining can go on about the meaning of equality of opportunity and the place of immigration in specific time circumstances remains a matter of political policy, not moral dictate.

Given unpredictability, immigration policy has been reactive historically. This reactive nature of US policy is evident in the broad sweeps of ideology regarding immigration and ethnic assimilation. Gordon (1964), for instance, admits that Anglo-conformity is probably still the strongest implicit theory of assimilation in the US; yet he masterfully delineates three major philosophies or 'goal systems of assimilation' in US history up to 1960. Data show that, regardless of whether the dominant integration ideology was 'Anglo-conformity', 'melting pot' or 'cultural pluralism', to use Gordon's terms, the flow of immigrants continued. In fact, by the 1960s the US had a population and society that, prodded by the right combination of issues, was ready to enter another ideological phase, that of ethnic revitalisation.

The shift in ideologies indicates how an initially dominant majority group adjusted to new circumstances as pressure from the new immigrant groups, as well as rethinking among intellectual leaders of the majority groups, pressed for changes. To be sure, changes did not reflect fundamental shifts in overall power relationships, but they do reflect the role of conflict and competition in US life as new actors (i.e. citizens) join the fray.[5]

Far from creating a consensus, the US immigration problem has tended to draw responses from a wide number of different groups with varied interests. Not only is there no solid, ongoing foundation of affected morality or historic guilt to cement the transition from one ideological phase to another, there is also the regionalisation of the problem. The historic concentration of ethnic immigrant groups in a few states means that groups agitate in different geographical areas, even though, in the final analysis, they all end up lobbying in Washington (Fuchs, 1968; Mathias, 1981).

In such a milieu, what are the prospects for immigration policy on the one hand and racial justice on the other? Because of a lack of consensus on policy, expanded immigration is probable, but an increased perception of ethnic and racial justice is not. While the ideology of ethnic revitalisation may suit the Cuban immigrant well, for instance, there is some evidence that the same ideology might be counterproductive to the native black ethnic group, as Kilson (1976) warned decades ago. The ideology of ethnic revitalisation merely adds new elements to the existing process of bargaining in the system. In the US, the search for a consensus on immigration policy at the turn of the millennium takes place within a context of criss-crossing allegiances, interests and values characteristic of the era of ethnic revitalisation at home and significant geopolitical change abroad. Crucial issues of rights (individual and societal), of national identity, of nationhood (sovereignty and national security), all perfectly legitimate in their own right, contribute to the ongoing lack of consensus regarding immigration policy.

The dynamic interaction between geopolitical considerations and immigration has been quite evident in the Caribbean. Several cases illustrate how the 'immigrant experience', that is, the flow from movement to settlement to political entitlement (citizenship), has contributed to keeping immigration policy rolling and as far as ever from anything approximating a consensus.

US GEOPOLITICAL IMPERATIVES AND CARIBBEAN MIGRATION

It is hardly a controversial argument that Puerto Rican migration to the US was welcomed by decision makers on both sides of the divide. As the fundamental *Economic Study of Puerto Rico*, done by the US Department of Commerce in 1979 noted, neither the capital intensification of the industrialisation process of Operation Bootstrap, nor the traditional agricultural sector could absorb sufficient labour. 'It was the emigration to the mainland that served as the "safety valve" for the growing labor force' (vol. I: 4). Safety valves do not exist in a vacuum. In the Caribbean, from the early 1950s, what was being sought was safety from communism. The academic literature on this point has survived the test of time (C. Wright Mills, 1950; Senior; 1951, Maingot, 1994). Less well known is that the same policies ensuring a safety valve for Puerto Rico were also applied to the Dominican Republic. As Table 11.1 shows, both cases dovetailed chronologically into the case of Cuba. All three had a similar source: US Cold War geopolitical strategies. In short, concern over the Cuban Revolution's spreading influence in the area led the US to override issues of race, ethnicity and class to open 'Heaven's Door' to many. Puerto Ricans were not immigrants since they have been US citizens since 1917. Cubans fell under the category of refugees after 1959 and were given special attention. Dominicans have been immigrants. Their case deserves special attention.

Table 11.1 Migration to the United States from the Hispanic Caribbean, 1990–1996

Years	Cubans	Dominicans	Puerto Ricans
1900–10	44,211	n/a	2,000
1911–20	25,158	n/a	11,000
1921–30	15,901	n/a	42,000
1931–40	9,571	1,150	18,000
1941–50	26,313	5,627	151,000
1951–60	78,948	9,897	470,000
1961–70	208,536	93,292	214,000
1971–80	264,863	148,135	165,817
1981–90	144,578	252,035	116,571
1991–96	94,936	254,832	168,475*
Total	913,014	806,390	1,258,863

Note: *1991–95.
Sources: Perez (1999/2000); Vega and Despradel (1999).

The newness of Dominican populations in the US expresses the special nature of the Dominican history of migration. It was, as was the case of Cuba before 1959, a country seeking settlers, not sending out people. As with the case of Cuba, Dominican intellectuals are seriously and constantly concerned with the issue of immigration. The importance of the movement to the US, the major immigrant destination by far, is reflected not only in the voluminous and substantive literature dedicated to it, but also in the strident nature of the theoretical debates over how best to study and understand it. This literature has unfortunately not emphasised geopolitics as a major causal factor in the changed US attitude towards migration from that country. A review of the major theories will reveal that gap.

Despite the existing challenges to its validity, the most widely used paradigm (implicitly and explicitly) to study migrant flows is some version of exchange theory, used alone or in combination with rational choice theory (Portes and Bach, 1984: 6–7). In both cases, it is assumed that individual migrants (or households) as well as national elites make a 'cost-benefit' analysis of migration. The decision-making of the individual appears straightforward enough: he looks at the difference between minimum wages here and there, the availability of jobs, and the differential rates of mobility. The last is judged in fairly straightforward ways: income, housing, purchase of a car, and very importantly, education of the children. Returning to the home town in the Dominican Republic to 'show and tell' is also an important incentive. It is assumed that Dominican elites, assessing the macro-sociological and macro-economic picture, make a similar calculation regarding the national benefits of the migration of their working class compatriots to the US. Among these considerations are a few imponderables and 'externalities', but generally they are quite specific as to benefits to the sending country. Migration to the US, they believe, has three beneficial results: (1) it relieves unemployment generally, and among the restless young specifically; (2) it engenders an infusion of hard currency through remittances and repatriated capital of successful immigrant capitalists, and; (3) and there is a repatriation of human capital in the form of new attitudes, skills and orientations.

The critical point, of course, is that the macro-sociological decisions of Dominican elites regarding the safety valve benefits of migration coincide with US geopolitical concerns. The granting of US immigrant visas to Dominicans during the tumultuous early years of the Cuban Revolution speaks to this fact.

Table 11.2 US Immigration visas to the Dominican Republic

Year	Visas issued
1960	464
1961	1,789
1962	3,680
1963	9,857
1964	5,671
1965	10,035
1966	16,321

Source: Ruiz, 1997: 3

The same critique can be made of the second paradigm used in the interpretation of the process: that based on 'world system', 'centre-periphery' or some variant of Marxian political economic theory. The fundamental argument here has to do with the distorting influences of imperialism (such as that of the US occupation of the Dominican Republic, 1914–28, and its intervention in the 1965 civil war) on the domestic economy and labour market. Migration is a result of this distortion, and migration, in turn, distorts the economy of the receiving country by 'segmenting' the labour force there into highly paid and poorly paid sectors. The problem with this approach is that it is too fixed in time and space, as a brief critique of the much-cited study by Andre Corten will illustrate (Corten, 1991).

Corten uses a variant of world systems theory to explain Haitian migration to the Dominican Republic which, in turn, had an impact on Dominican migration to the US. He argues that Haitians became an agricultural proletariat locked into the sugar industry from the early days of the foreign-owned plantation. The specific weakness in Corten's approach is the general weakness of this theoretical approach. Because it ignores the fact that national elites as well as individual migrants, or households, do make (rational) choices, they cannot explain the historical changes and variations in the characteristics of the migrants and the geographical areas from which they come and to which they go. Corten admits that although the Haitian presence in the Dominican Republic is an old one, the estimated 500,000 Haitians now settled there (90 per cent of whom are illegal according to Corten), are more than just the agricultural proletariat of old. They have new destinations and new occupations. For the past two decades, Haitians have been moving into the informal economy in urban centres of the Dominican Republic.

This movement of Haitians was occurring just as the US, concerned with the geopolitical threat from the Cuban Revolution, was opening up opportunities for Dominican migration in the mid-1960s. There was no Dominican crisis of man–land relations *à la* Haiti, nor did the migration result from a crisis in the Dominican state and political instability. Despite the political and social turmoil of the early 1960s, there was no major push for emigration. In 1966, the Cortens concluded that the lack of desire to migrate reflected a deep-seated 'patriotism' on the part of the Dominicans. Fully 70 per cent of their middle class sample expressed no interest in migrating; only 3.7 per cent wished that their children be born outside the Dominican Republic, although 70 per cent would have liked for their children to have studied abroad, preferably in the US. Reflecting the small number of actual migrants, only 20 per cent of their sample had resided abroad for over a year, and 51.6 per cent of these had done so as students (Corten and Corten, 1968: 128). When it did pick up, Dominican migration did not respond to a labour recruiting programme, but originated from US geopolitical considerations and, subsequently, to the family reunification provisions in US immigration legislation. As Christopher Mitchell put it, the '[o]pen use of immigration policy' by the US was done 'to further foreign policy aims' (Mitchell, 1992: 21, 89–123).

Evidence of the explicitly political use of immigration is central to the arguments of Grasmuck and Pessar (1991). After accounting for the various variables which have been emphasised by preceding studies (viz., the international division of labour and unequal terms of trade, social class relations in both sending and receiving countries, gender, generations, households and migrant social networks), they make a fine distinction between 'conditioning' and 'determining' factors, all of which have to be placed within carefully delineated historical periods. To them, social structural conditions and social class relations in the sending society are determining factors. In an approximation of exchange theory thinking they ask: To which domestic class or group is migration beneficial?

Their answer, as far as the Dominican Republic is concerned, is that the country's political elites and economic elites, to whom political elites are beholden, are the beneficiaries of the removal by emigration of potential sources of pressure and conflict. State policies in the Dominican Republic, they maintain, have consistently favoured certain socially and politically connected groups, 'who stand to benefit personally and politically by bolstering inefficient state enterprises and by favoring the interests of a politically powerful group of industrialists' (Grasmuck and Pessar, 1991: 200). Those studies, which have used rigorous canons of historiography, appear to bear out the Grasmuck and Pessar thesis.

While the movement of Cubans after 1959 has been studied extensively, the links between that revolution and movements elsewhere in the Caribbean have received less attention. The most comprehensive study of Haitian migration to the Dominican Republic describes three conjunctural causes of that migration. First, the crisis in agriculture and land tenure in the Central and Northern provinces of Haiti and the ready availability of this cheap labour to recruiters for Dominican sugar estates; second, the closing off of Cuba by the revolution of 1959; third, the closing off of work opportunities in the Bahamas after the crash of that country's building boom of the early 1960s (Lozano and Baez Evertsz 1992: 26). As a result, by the 1960s a Haitian agricultural proletariat already existed, moving year round from one crop to the other and increasingly becoming permanent residents of the Dominican Republic. By the late 1980s, 64.2 per cent of the Haitians working in coffee were already resident, and of the 35.8 per cent who came over from Haiti, 59 per cent indicated that they intended to stay. Although basically sympathetic to the plight of the Haitians, the authors continue the Dominican concern over the Haitian presence by concluding that the massive nature of that migration had dramatically changed the nature of agricultural labour in the Dominican Republic. They analyse three distorting changes wrought by this Haitian migration: (1) the Haitians displaced traditional Dominican seasonal agricultural workers who then moved to the cities; (2) they depressed salaries for agricultural work generally; and, (3) their presence dampened the spirit of progress by retarding any urgency among Dominican owners to modernise their agricultural establishments.

The logical consequence of this is that Haitian migration to the Dominican Republic helped enlarge the pool of potential migrants to the US, the other great destination for citizens of both nations. Indeed, by the early 1970s, the US had become the favourite destination for Dominican migrants. A major survey done in 1974 by the Dominican Ministry of Public Health and Social Assistance indicated that 71 per cent of the migration was to the US, 19 per cent to Puerto Rico, 6 per cent to the rest of Latin America and 3 per cent to Europe (Del Castillo and Mitchell, 1987: 41).

A fundamental aspect of Dominican migration was that the level of education and skills of Dominican migrants to the US has been below that of migrants from other Caribbean countries, including Haiti. As Max Castro noted, only Mexico and Italy among leading immigration countries has a proportionally higher working class immigrant population than the Dominican Republic. Castro calls it 'primarily a proletarian or proletarianizing migration' (Castro, 1985: 132).

As their numbers increased, they began organising and mobilising in the same way that others had done in New York. In that city, as in Miami, the role of voluntary organisations has been critical.

> Leadership positions in one of these organizations, no matter how ephemeral—provide a platform of visibility and can potentially serve as a means of political promotions within the Dominican community, or even in the wider New York political arena and/or in the Dominican Republic. (Georges, 1989: 198)

Georges describes the binational relationship in terms of the lyrics of a popular Dominican *merengue*, 'living with one foot here and the other there'.

The upshot of this Dominican migration to New York over thirty years has been the development of a solid community in New York and powerful economic impacts back home. Within this community, a bloc of some 20,000 small businessmen (*bodegeros*) form the backbone of the community and the major source of returning talent. These 'Tropical Capitalists' as two students called them, have contributed to a heavy stream of remittances which, since the early 1990s, has been twice as large a source of foreign exchange as the sugar crop. The World Bank calculates that between 1988 and 1995, funds remitted from the US to Dominican Republic increased from $188 million to $795 million (World Bank, 1997: 244). In addition, 'Tropical Capitalists' are a source of returning entrepreneurs who experience considerable social mobility upon their return to the Dominican Republic (Portes and Guarnizo, 1991). The contribution of the diaspora, however, is moving from cash remittances to a whole range of activities and investments. After studying the Size of remittances, the investments in various sectors, as well as their participation in the tourism and housing industries, Luis Guarnizo concludes that migrants are 'not only the primary source of hard currency—well above revenues from tourism and economic Free Trade Zones (FTZs), the flagships of the country's economic restructuring—but also the single most important social group contributing to the national economy' (Guarnizo 1994: 79). Not surprisingly, Guarnizo discovered the continued attachment of Dominicans to their country of origin, citing one immigrant: 'The ideal situation is to have a money-making business in the US but live in the Dominican Republic'. Despite the youth of Dominican settlements in the US, they have established deep roots that have had real consequences for the sending country generally and the sending towns specifically.

In 1968, Hendricks studied migration to the US from the little town of Mesa Real, 25 km south-east of the city of Santiago. Despite the fact that they began arriving only after 1965, the villagers adjusted speedily to life in New York and equally speedily began to remit monies to their village.

Remittances were the 'lifeblood' of this village. In a matter of a few years, the village of Mesa Real was in many ways 'an economic and social appendage of New York' (Hendricks 1978: 59). Of the 146 households in the village, 85 per cent had one or more relative living in New York and of the 200 letters which arrived in Mesa Real each day, 150 were from New York. Indeed, such are the attachments of Dominicans to their mother country and native towns, that they have one of the lowest naturalisation rates of any group of migrants in the US. Of the 204,000 admitted for permanent residency in 1960–80, and who qualified for naturalisation, only 7.8 per cent took that step. Their constant demand was that they be allowed to hold dual citizenship (Grasmuck and Pessar, 1991: 207).

Proving the widely-held hypothesis that the single most important determinant of naturalisation is time of residence in the US (Johnson et al. 1999: 24–26), Dominican naturalisation rates have increased from 7.8 per cent in 1960–1980 to 30.9 per cent from 1990 to 1997. In fact, Dominicans are now among the top ten countries of naturalisation in terms of absolute numbers (Table 11.3).

Table 11.3 Persons naturalised in US, FY 1996, by top ten countries of former allegiance

Top Ten Countries of Former Allegiance	
Mexico	217,418
Cuba	62,168
Vietnam	47,625
Philippines	45,210
Soviet Union	36,265
El Salvador	33,240
China	30,656
India	28,932
Dominican Republic	27,293
Columbia	26,115
All Countries	1,044,689

Source: US Department of Justice, I.N.S. *1996 Statistical Yearbook.*

However, the rates are still below that of all Asians, below the rate for Cubans (52 per cent), and below the median for all countries (45.9 per cent in 1995), but considerably higher than that for Europeans and most other Latin Americans. The critical issue is that the end of the Cold War, and thus the geopolitical imperatives which opened up migration from the Dominican Republic, has not slowed their rate of migration. Geopolitics opened the door; other factors contributed to the continued movement. During 1981–96, 509,902 Dominicans migrated legally to the US, placing Dominican Republic fifth among the top ten sending countries. To the extent that Dominicans, like most other Latin American immigrants, take a page from the Cuban experience of assimilation, naturalisation and political activism, Table 11.4 provides an interesting comparison.

Table 11.4 US Citizenship status, Cuban/Dominican-born

Status	Cubans	Dominicans
Total foreign-born	913,000	632,000
Naturalised US citizens	474,000	195,000
As percent of the foreign-born	51.9	30.9

Source: U.S. Bureau of the Census, 1998.

Table 11.5 Estimates of remittances by Cuban/Dominican US residents (US$ millions)

Year	Cubans	Dominicans
1989	48	300
1990	13	315
1991	18	329
1992	43	347
1993	255	722
1994	310	758
1995	532	796
1996	1,112	1,138

Source: CEPAL, Santiago, Chile.

An important additional comparison between Cubans and Dominicans is the amount of remittances to their native countries (Table 11.5).

The big difference between the Cuban and the Dominican relates to race. On the basis of the 'self-reported' definition, 84 per cent of Cubans reported themselves as white, but only 24.3 per cent of Dominicans (living in New York) so reported, and 44.2 per cent of the Puerto Ricans (US Census, 1993). This has an enormous bearing on the value of citizenship: non-white immigrants need it more than white immigrants.

By the late 1980s, the mood of the country began to shift against aliens: legal but especially illegal. That was when Mexican-American scholars began to lament the low rate of naturalisation of Mexican immigrants. It was, they said, a major obstacle to their political empowerment (Johnson et al., 1999: 37–43). The period of residence before naturalisation of the Mexican was invariably two to three times longer than for the European and Asian. By 1990, Mexicans represented the largest number of naturalisations (Table 11.6).

Table 11.6 Foreign-born aliens and naturalisations in US (1990)

Foreign-born 1990 Census: Top Ten Countries of Birth		Aliens 1990 Census: Top Ten Countries of Birth		Naturalised 1990 Census: Top Ten Countries of Birth	
Mexico	4,298,014	Mexico	3,328,310	Mexico	969,704
Philippines	912,674	Philippines	420,460	Germany	512,018
Canada	744,830	El Salvador	393,898	Philippines	492,214
Cuba	736,971	Cuba	361,019	Italy	440,143
Germany	711,929	Canada	341,876	Canada	402,954
United Kingdom	640,145	Korea	337,487	Cuba	375,952
Italy	580,592	United Kingdom	322,342	United Kingdom	317,803
Korea	568,397	Vietnam	311,463	Poland	242,294
Vietnam	543,262	China	296,438	China	233,399
China	529,837	India	293,196	Vietnam	231,799
All Countries	19,767,316		11,770,318		7,996,998

Source: INS Statistical Yearbook, 1996

Two factors, in addition to period in the US, have been adduced to explain this change (Johnson et al., 1999). First, the role of positive incentives, the most important of which was the 1986 Immigration Reform and Control Act (IRCA) which dramatically increased the numbers eligible for naturalisation by 1993. 'Those granted amnesty', notes one of the few studies on the topic, 'became eligible for naturalization starting in 1993, and by the end 1996 almost 2.5 million legalised immigrants became eligible to naturalize' (Johnson et. al., 1999: 55) The 1995 INS programme to clear up the large backlog of applications ('Citizenship USA' Programme) was less important but nonetheless indicated a changed US attitude. Second, and perhaps more important, were the potential negative consequences of non-citizenship. First, California's Proposition 187 of 1994 promised to cut off the delivery of social services to undocumented migrants, followed in 1996 by a welfare reform law denying federally-funded social services to non-citizens, i.e., to even *legal* immigrants.

It was not just anti-immigration spokespersons such as Roy Beck (1995) who filled the air with arguments about the need to return to 'traditional levels' of immigration, it was also those who argued that the whole process was 'devaluing' American citizenship (Schuck, 1989). Even the prestigious American Assembly meeting of experts on immigration noted in early 1996 that 'International migration is rising to the top of the foreign policy agenda' (Teitlebaum and Weiner, 1995: 299). In a book provocatively titled, *Threatened Peoples, Threatened Borders*, the experts concluded that aside from political and economic disasters, global economic integration, new communications and transportation networks, the availability of rights and benefits to migrants, and domestic debates about the costs and benefits of immigration have all forced re-evaluations of national immigration policies. Especially important was their assertion that the perceptions of threat posed by migration may or may not reflect reality, even though these were 'strongly felt and cannot simply be dismissed' (Teitlebaum and Weiner, 1995: 300). This issue of perceptions is especially important because of a fundamental fact regarding the natives' perception about immigration: that perception is hardly ever based on accurate knowledge and information.

All this goes a long way towards explaining why the overall naturalisation rate which had fallen from 63 per cent in 1965 to 38 per cent in 1993, had risen to 46 per cent in 1996. In fact, in just one year, 1995–96, naturalisation doubled from 500,000 to 1,045,000 (INS *Statistical Yearbook*, 1996: 11).

The irony of the process is evident: anti-immigrant feelings provide an incentive to naturalise which government encouragement alone could not. It is fair to say that the Hispanic population, soon to be the largest minority in the country, is moving rapidly to acquire the right to vote and with that potentially altering the dynamics of majority–minority group negotiations in the US. The fundamental question is: how solid a stake or an entitlement and resource is citizenship in the US?

CONCLUSIONS: CITIZENSHIP AS A RESOURCE

The concept of citizenship, writes Bickel, with approval, has played a very minor role in US Constitutional history. He notes:

> I find it gratifying that we live under a Constitution to which the concept of citizenship matters very little, that prescribes decencies and wise modalities of government quite without regard to the concept of citizenship (1975).

The emphasis, rather, has been on moral, political, and traditional sources, sources more complex than the simple contractual notion of citizenship which, he concludes, 'is at best a simple idea for a simple government' (Bickel, 1975: 53–4).

Rather than providing a consistent, hard and fast doctrine of guarantees and prerogatives to those that hold it, definitions and applications of the US concept of citizenship have depended on the temper of the times and on the outcome of the competition for power of those groups functioning in the system. Unfortunately, the results of stressing 'persons' rather than citizens, in legal and social action as well as in Constitutional and political theory and practices, have not always been that 'balance between order and liberty' that Bickel posits. It is clear that, driven in part by the force of historical guilt, attitudes toward black persons have changed. It is a fair question to ask how other immigrant groups fare in this respect.

Lacking an overriding moral dilemma about immigration (as contracted to race issues), US citizens, especially the white majority, did not believe that the opportunity given immigrants to enter the US had to be carried over into all areas of social relations. As early as 1928, Bogardus (1971) showed that while US citizens of all races were quite willing (but at different rates) to allow a large number of immigrants into the country and, indeed, to become citizens, this willingness to open up citizenship did not translate into acceptance as friends, club members, neighbours, employees, and, even less, spouses. The key question is just what rights did the legal status of citizenship entail, especially in the social and economic realms?

In a way, this distinction between the rights of legal citizenship, and the benefits to be expected therefrom, might help explain why some groups with high racial and ethnic acceptance by the dominant US majority and thus, mobility, such as many Europeans, do not acquire US citizenship, or do so for strictly strategic personal reasons. In 1995, of the ten nationalities with the lowest rate of US naturalisation, only one, Japan, was not a Caucasian country. As already noted, in the Caribbean, only Cuban refugees fit the 'white' racial category in substantial numbers.

Is the implication of all this that legal citizenship, as compared for instance with racial status, is a weak resource in the political fray of pluralist societies? Not completely. As with all forms of empowerment, citizenship does not involve principles of natural law. It is a developing principle that requires the active promotion of the rights and duties that are attached to it. Citizenship building is like community building in that both require full membership and participation in the enterprise.[6] T.H. Marshall is worth quoting at length here:

> There is no universal principle that determines what those rights and duties shall be, but societies in which citizenship is a developing institution create an image of an ideal citizenship against which achievement can be measured and towards which aspiration can be directed. The urge forward along the path thus plotted is an urge towards a fuller measure of equality, an enrichment of the stuff of which the status is made and an increase in the number of those on whom the status is bestowed. (Marshall 1964: 92)

If the functional idea of US citizenship has tended to create the idea of people being *mere* citizens, then the hope is that an emphasis on the developmental idea will change that to the idea of *fellow* citizens. To the extent that the pursuit of ethnic grievances inhibits the growth of community, it also obstructs the development of the fellowship of citizens. The process begun with the granting of citizenship to American ex-slaves through the Fourteenth Amendment has to be continued. As Kettner (1978) notes, 'it made a difference—both to him and to the wider community—whether Dred Scott was legally a citizen. It makes a difference still'. So it is with those immigrants from Mexico, the Dominican Republic and other parts of Latin America, in very large numbers working class. They received an opportunity to enter because of geopolitical considerations of the Cold War: they now have to acquire those attributes which will allow them to negotiate their rights.

Citizenship, writes Lenski (1966: 83), continues to figure prominently in the distributive process: those who lack other kinds of resources, together with those who, for ideological reasons, believe in social equality, 'have combined to fight for the enhancement of the value of citizenship at the expense of those resources which generate inequality'. What is involved is a process of political bargaining. Since citizenship is no longer perceived as a natural law or political absolute, its definition and its weight as a resource are matters to be bargained and fought for. Citizenship can be considered as a resource in the continual bargaining that characterises all social processes. It is one of many sources of power, but differs from other sources, such as social class or social status, in that, theoretically at least, it does not divide the society. Again, theoretically, it recognises all under a common definition of citizen. Paradoxically, citizenship allows the former immigrant alien to now refer to the American Creed and other US principles, in political theory and practice, of equal rights and equal treatment.

In the twentieth century struggle between those who favour human rights and those who emphasise property rights, it is the former that advocates the expansion of the concept of citizenship to make it more inclusive of social and economic rights. This fact has been ignored by those students of power who assume that citizenship, because it is shared by all, no longer has any relevance for the study of stratification. Those immigrant groups whose social class and ethnicity place them at the bottom of the social hierarchy can afford no such assumptions. They have to pursue every strategy of negotiation, not the least of which is naturalisation and using the status of citizen. It is, in the final analysis, the best way to force the national majority to continually reaffirm what Bhagwati calls a major 'defining principle' of the American identity: that the US is a nation of immigrants (Bhagwati, 1998). As they do this they should also keep in mind the less than absolutely firm status of citizenship in the American political culture. As Schuck notes in an important recent book:

> Americans view the relationship among citizens, strangers, and in-betweens in often nuanced ways that combine the symbolic power of myth; the emotional power of deeply held ideals, fears and antagonisms; the psychological power of family narratives; and the political power of clashing private and public interests. (Schuck 1998: 1)

In the American pluralist system, with its functional approach to citizenship, naturalisation is no substitute for political articulation and mobilisation. It provides, however, the opportunity to articulate and aggregate group demands more effectively. Doing those things successfully typically requires educated and skilled elites. The non-white and working class migrants from the Caribbean (except for the Cubans) need time to develop these elites, and time appears to be of the essence in the ups and downs in the American debate on immigration and naturalisation. The acceleration of naturalisations among Caribbean immigrants indicates that they are aware that they should strike while the iron is hot, that is, while there exists a relatively liberal climate towards naturalisations.

Transforming the often trite cliché 'fellow citizens' into an operational and inclusive principle remains a goal. Indeed, it is the challenge of this age of mass immigration to the US which still acknowledges what Myrdal's enduring phrase refers to as the 'American Creed' of equality.

NOTES

1. See the important essays in Mitchell (1992); Papademetriou and Miller (1983). See also the imaginative analysis in Mahler (1999).
2. A good illustration is the benefit derived by the nineteenth-century immigrant German population from the generally held, but erroneous, belief that their vote elected Abraham Lincoln in 1860. The significance of showing that they 'voted right' was an important sign that the immigrants 'owed' their new nation something for the privilege of entry (Schafer, 1968: 32-49).
3. This in part explains why the US has experienced none of the ethnic xenophobia or secessionism of other new nations. The incremental expansion of US territory, from the original thirteen colonies to the fifty states, did not involve the incorporation of large populations that were ethnically different. There were 200,000 inhabitants in the whole Mexican territory incorporated in the mid-nineteenth century.
4. This partly explains how Coleman (1941) could survey a very large body of literature on the American character and discover that, at one time or another, authoritative writers attributed virtually every known value, custom, and cultural trait to the Americans.
5. Charles Keely makes the important point that the original, largely NW European or Anglo-Saxon, majority continually absorbed new arrivals from Southern and Eastern Europe, ensuring thereby the continued dominance of a 'White European' group (Keely, personal communication, 3 March 2000).
6. The people of Massachusetts knew already in 1779 that citizenship had to be earned. Listen to their Constitution (Act VI): 'No man, nor corporation, or association of men, have any other title to obtain advantages, or particular and exclusive privileges, distinct from those of the community, *than what arises from the consideration of services rendered to the public*; and this title being in nature neither hereditary, nor transmissible to children, or descendants, or relation by blood.' (emphasis added).

REFERENCES

Appleyard, Reginald (1998, 1999), *Emigration Dynamics in Developing Countries*, four volumes on Sub-Saharan Africa; South Asia; Central America, Mexico and the Caribbean; and the Arab region, Cheltenham and Northampton, MA, Ashgate.

Beck, Roy (1995), *The Case Against Immigration: The Moral, Economic, Social and Environmental Reasons for Reducing Immigration Back to Traditional Levels*, New York: W.W. Norton.

Bhagwati, Jagdish (1998), *A Stream of Windows: Unsettling Reflections on Trade, Immigration, and Democracy*, Cambridge, MA: MIT Press.

Bickel, A.M. (1975), *The Morality of Consent*, New Haven, CT: Yale University Press.

Bogardus, E.S. (1971), *Immigration and Race Attitudes*, New York: Ozer (reprinted from 1928 edition, Boston: D. C. Health and Co.).

Borjas, George J. (1999), *Heaven's Door*, Princeton, NJ: Princeton University Press.

Castro, M. (1985), 'Dominican journey: patterns, context and consequences of migration from the Dominican Republic to the US', unpublished Ph.D. dissertation, Department of Sociology, University of North Carolina, Chapel Hill.

Coleman, L. 1941, 'What is American? A study of alleged American traits', *Social Forces*, **19**: 492–99.

Corten, A. (1991), 'Politique miratoire et societes de rente', *Canadian Journal of Latin American and Caribbean Studies*, **16** (32): 5–34.

Corten, A. (1968), *Cambio Social en Santo Domingo*, Instituto de Estudios del Caribe, Universidad de Puerto Rico; Rio Piedras, Puerto Rico.

De Conde, Alexander (1992), *Ethnicity, Race, and American Foreign Policy*, Boston, MA: Northeastern University Press.

Fix, Michael and Jeffrey S. Passel (1994), *Immigration and Immigrants: Setting the Record Straight*, Washington, DC: Urban Institute.

Fuchs, L.H. (ed.) (1968), *American Ethnic Politics*, New York: Harper & Row.

Furnivall, J.S. (1939), *Netherlands India: A Study of Plural Economy*, Cambridge: Macmillan.

Furnivall, J.S. (1945), 'Some problems of tropical economy', in Rita Hinden (ed.), *Fabian Colonial Essays*, London: George Allen & Unwin, pp 161–83.

Gordon, M.M. (1964), *Assimilation in American Life: The Role of Race, Religion and National Origin*, New York: Oxford University Press.

Grasmuck, S. and P. Pessar (1991), *Between Two Islands: Dominican International Migration*, Berkeley: University of California Press.

Guarnizo, L. (1994), ' "Los Dominicanyorks" ': The making of a binational society', *Annals of the American Academy of Political and Social Science*, vol. 553, May.

Hendricks, G. (1978), *Los dominicanos ausentes: un pueblo en transicion*, Santo Domingo, Dominican Republic: Editora Alfa and Omega.

Higham, J. (ed.) (1962), *The Reconstruction of American History*, New York: Humanities Press.

INS (Immigration and Naturalization Service), (various years) *Statistical Yearbooks*, INS Statistics Page: http://www.ins.usdoj.gov/graphics/aboutins/statistics/index.htm.

Jerome, H. (1926), *Migration and Business Cycles*, New York: National Bureau of Economic Research.

Johnson, H., B. Reyes, L. Mameesh and E. Barbour (1999), *Taking the Oath: An Analysis of Naturalization in California and the United States*, San Francisco: Public Policy Institute of California.

Kettner, J.H. (1978), *Development of American Citizenship, 1808–1870*, Chapel Hill: University of North Carolina.

Kilson, M. (1976), 'Blacks and neo-rthnicity in American political life,' in N. Glazer and D.P. Moynihan (eds), *Ethnicity: Theory and Experience*, Cambridge, MA: Harvard University Press, pp. 236–66.

Kuznets, S. and E. Rubin (1954), *Immigration and the Foreign Born*, National Bureau of Economic Research.

Lenski, G. (1966), *Power and Privilege: A Theory of Social Stratification*, New York: McGraw-Hill.

Lozano, W. and F. Baez Evertsz (1992), *Migracion internacional economia cafetalera*, 2nd edn, Santo Domingo, Dominican Republica: Centro de Planificacion and Accion Ecumenica, Inc.

Mahler, Sarah J. (1999), 'Transnational migration as grassroots diplomats', unpublished ms., Miami, Florida.

Maingot, Anthony P. (1994), *The United States and the Caribbean*, London: Macmillan.

Maingot, Anthony (1999), 'Emigration dynamics in the Caribbean: the cases of Haiti and the Dominican Republic', in Reginald Appleyard (ed.), *Emigration Dynamics in Developing Countries*, vol. III, Aldershot, and Brookfield, US, Ashgate.

Marshall, T.H. (1964), *Class, Citizenship and Social Development*, New York: Doubleday.

Mathias, C. (1981), 'Ethnic groups and foreign policy', *Foreign Affairs*, **59** (5): 975–8.

Mills, C. Wright (ed.) (1950), *The Puerto Rican Journey*, New York: Harper & Bros.

Mitchell, Christopher (ed.) (1992), *Western Hemisphere Immigration and Foreign Policy*, Penn: The Penn. State University Press.

Myrdal, G. (1944), *American Dilemma*, New York: Harper & Row.

Papademetriou, Demetrios G. and Mark J. Miller (eds) (1983), *The Unavoidable Issue: US Immigration Policy in the 1980s*, Philadelphia: Institute for the Study of Human Issues.

Perez, L. (1999/2000), 'De Nueva York a Miami', *Revista Encuentro*, invierno, 13–26.

Podhoretz, N. (1963), 'My negro problem, and ours', *Commentary*, **35**: 93–101.

Portes, Alejandro and Robert Bach (1984), *Latin Journey: Cuban and Mexican Immigrants in the US*, Berkeley: University of California Press.

Potter, D.M. (1962), 'The Quest for the National Character', in J. Higham (ed.), *The Reconstruction of American History*, New York: Humanities Press, pp. 197–220.

Roney, L.S. (1981), 'The present immigration system: its origins and operations', in US Select Commission on Immigration and Refugee Policy, *US Immigration Policy and the National Interest: Staff Report*, Washington, DC, pp. 295–351.

Ruiz, Larissa (1997), 'Migration as a political tool in the Dominican Republic', University of Florida, Gainesville, Florida.

Schafer, J. (1968), 'Who elected Lincoln?', in L.H. Fuchs (ed.), *American Ethnic Politics*, New York: Harper and Row.

Schuck, Peter H. (1989), 'Membership in the liberal polity: the devaluation of American citizenship', *Georgetown Immigration Law Journal*.

Schuck, Peter H. (1998), *Citizens, Strangers, and In-Betweens*, Boulder: Westview Press.

Senior, Clarence (1951), *The Puerto Ricans of New York City*, Washington, DC: Office of Puerto Rico.

Smith, Rogers M. (ed.) (1997), *Civic Ideals. Conflicting Visions of Citizenship in US History*, New Haven, CT: Yale University Press.

Teitlebaum, M. and M. Weiner (1995), *Threatened Peoples, Threatened Borders*, New York: W.W. Norton.

Turner, F.J. (1920), *The Frontier in American History*, New York: Holt and Co.

US Department of Commerce (1979), *Economic Study of Puerto Rico*, Washington, DC: Government Printing Office.

Vega, B. and R. Despradel (1999), *Migration Trends by Dominicans and other Caribbean Nationals to the United States*, Washington, DC: Embassy of the Dominican Republic.

World Bank (1997), *World Development Report, 1997*, New York, Oxford University Press.

12. Past Trends in International Migration and their Implications for Future Prospects

Hania Zlotnik[1]

INTRODUCTION

International migration has been a major feature of the twentieth century. The revolutionary advances made in transportation and communication systems are undoubtedly at the root of the sharp increase in population mobility that the century has witnessed. Yet only a very small proportion of the persons travelling from one country to another can be considered international migrants. Despite the unprecedented increase in number of persons living on earth, which is estimated to have risen from 1.6 to 5.3 billion between 1910 and 1990, international migration has continued to be comparatively rare. According to estimates made earlier in the century by the International Labour Office (ILO), in 1910 there were at least 33 million foreigners living in countries other than their own (International Labour Office, 1936). By 1990, the number of international migrants[2] in the world had risen to 120 million (United Nations, 1995). That is, over this century the number of international migrants has probably increased by a factor of 3.6 compared with the 3.25 times rise in world population so that, overall, international migrants still account for a small proportion of the world population (2.25 per cent in 1990).

In a world organised into mutually exclusive states whose borders are deemed to coincide with the social boundaries of the people under their jurisdiction, international migration can be seen as a deviant process whereby individuals are transferred from the jurisdiction of one state to that of another and thus cease being members of one society to become members of another (Zolberg, 1981). According to the premises of the social contract, the state's role is to maximise the collective welfare of society. To do that while maintaining the identity and exclusiveness of their respective societies, states have the right to restrict the entry of foreigners. It is this universally recognised attribute of sovereignty that both conditions and curtails international migration.

The crystallisation of the modern system of nation-states during the twentieth century has led both to a greater potential for international migration (the more units within the system, the greater the possible moves between them) and to the proliferation of barriers against such movement. In the developing world, the process of decolonisation and the emergence of newly independent states during the 1950s and 1960s transformed movements that used to occur within a single territory into international migration subject to control. Similarly, the recent subdivision of the Soviet Union into the Commonwealth of Independent States has internationalised population movements that used to be internal. The reconfiguration of nation-states, especially when it results from prolonged conflict as in Ethiopia or the former Yugoslavia, has the potential of generating significant flows of international migrants.

Although international migration often involves a certain tension between the interests of individual migrants and those of the receiving state, there are many instances in which both interests coincide or are compatible with each other. Thus, economic considerations often underlie the decision of states to allow international migration. When the land and capital within a state are not utilised to their full potential because of labour shortages, the admission of economically active foreigners is more likely. The market-economy countries of Europe opted for such a strategy during the 1950s and 1960s. A different strategy was adopted by Japan. When it found itself with under-utilised capital in the 1970s and 1980s, Japan decided to export capital to countries with excess labour rather than to admit foreign workers. Yet, neither Japan nor the market-economies of Europe have been able to avoid altogether the inflow of international migrants attracted by the demand for labour in specific sectors of their economies. In Europe such demand has persisted during the 1980s and 1990s even under high levels of overt unemployment.

Given that economic considerations are at the root of most international migration, the latter is significantly influenced by developments in the world economy. The process of globalisation that has strengthened the economic linkages between major economic actors in the world and given rise to regional trading blocs aimed at enhancing the competitive position of those actors in the global economy is deemed to have important consequences for international migration. The promotion of freer trade either within trading blocs or at a more general level—through GATT or the WTO, for instance—is expected to reduce the potential for international migration in the developing countries participating in such trade. Export-led growth is considered a key strategy to achieve development. However, since the process of development itself is recognised to set in motion forces that promote migration, it is not evident whether the successful participation of developing countries in the world economy and the trading system will enhance or reduce the potential for international migration. The prevailing view is that, as development based on export-led growth takes off, it is likely to increase the potential for international migration for some time. As development continues, however, that potential should subside (US Commission for the Study of International Migration and Co-operative Economic Development, 1990; United Nations, 1998). Given the deficiencies of international migration statistics and the complexity of the issues involved, the empirical bases for such assertions remain weak.

Although the genesis of international migration flows can often be traced to governmental or institutional actions—such as the recruitment of workers in a given country by agents working for employers or the government of another country—once established, international migration flows tend to develop their own momentum through the operation of migrant and institutional networks (Kritz and Zlotnik, 1992; Massey et al., 1993). Migrant networks link communities of origin and destination, serving as channels for information and resources. They contribute to insulate international migrants from the problems involved in adapting to the host society. Whereas economic and political processes operating at the macro level may explain why certain international migration flows emerge, the operation of networks is thought to be useful in explaining why certain persons migrate while the vast majority does not.

As the twentieth century drew to a close, a significant number of countries find themselves hosting sizeable migrant populations and having to deal with the long-term consequences of international migration and with the potential for increased inflows as new migrants are attracted through the operation of migrant networks. Furthermore, the rapidly changing dynamics of the world economy have serious repercussions on the configuration of international migration flows. For instance, the high levels of sustained economic growth experienced by the newly industrialising economies of East and South East Asia during the 1980s and early 1990s were responsible for labour shortages in certain sectors of the economy that were often met by the use of foreign labour. However, the economic downturn that affected those countries in 1997–98 resulted in measures fostering or even imposing the repatriation of migrant workers. Although the effects of such measures have not been reliably quantified, numerous workers undoubtedly were forced to return to their home countries, if only because of the serious economic difficulties they faced in the receiving countries. Fortunately, the economic situation has stabilised or improved in most of the countries of East and South East Asia that were affected and migration flows directed to them seem to have resumed. Economic difficulties have also contributed to erode the stability of some of the successor states of the former Soviet Union and migration flows are likely to be affected by such developments. Indeed, the end of the bi-polar era in world affairs has changed the nature of peace and security issues around the globe, opening better prospects for the solution of conflict in certain cases but at the same time leading to increased instability in others, instability that has often resulted in sizeable flows of people.

Most of the developments outlined above have had some impact on international migration flows, the most obvious being the role of conflict in generating refugees and asylum-seekers. At a time when the developed market-economies are pursuing strategies to ensure their continued advantage in the world economy, the increase in international migration brought about by instability and conflict in Europe's immediate vicinity or in certain developing countries has been greeted with alarm. Furthermore, given that the economies of advanced countries remain dependent on cheap, unskilled labour for the service, construction and agricultural sectors, the inflow of migrant workers has generally not ceased, despite the persistently high levels of unemployment experienced by a number of market-economy countries. These developments have been interpreted to mean that international migration is out of control and the governments of the countries concerned have been reacting by adopting more stringent measures to reduce migration. The rest of this chapter will be devoted to an assessment of international migration trends over the past two or three decades and of the prospects for the maintenance of those flows given the policy changes that are under way.

MIGRATION FOR PERMANENT SETTLEMENT

The United States is the major receiving country in the world. With a long tradition as a country of immigration, it has seen its number of immigrants rise steadily since 1960. Record numbers of immigrant admissions have been set in the 1990s, particularly because of the effects of the legalisation programme instituted by the Immigration Reform and Control Act of 1986. The Act has resulted in the legalisation of nearly three million persons, most of whom had entered illegally before 1986 and become established in the US. Even without such legalisation, the number of immigrants to the US had been increasing, to reach an annual average of 770,000 in 1990–94 and 814,000 in 1995–96.

Canada and Australia are also important countries of permanent settlement, though their immigrant intakes are considerably lower than that of the US. As Table 12.1 shows, the total number of immigrant admissions in Canada has risen since the mid-1980s, reaching 1,178,000 in 1990–94 or 236,000 annually. In Australia, a decline in the number of admissions occurred in 1990–94, so that the annual average fell from 123,000 in 1985–89 to 93,000 in 1990–93.

All countries of immigration have experienced diversification of immigrant flows in terms of origin. Such diversification is the direct result of changes in the immigration laws of those countries that occurred in 1965 in the US and in the 1970s in Australia and Canada. The laws adopted opened the door to the immigration of persons from non-European countries. As a result, the proportion of admissions from Asia increased markedly in all three countries and there were also important increases in the admissions from other developing countries in the sphere of influence of each receiving country. Thus, in Australia, the proportion of admissions from Oceania rose and so did, at least initially, the proportion of admissions from the Americas in Canada and the US. By 1975–79, the flows to all immigration countries showed clear signs of diversification. Since then, as Table 12.1 indicates, immigrants from countries in the less developed regions have constituted a clear majority in Canada and the US, and had risen to over 50 per cent in Australia as of 1985–89.

Table 12.1 Total number of admissions of permanent immigrants and percentage of immigrants by region of birth: Australia, Canada and the US, 1975–79 to 1995–96

Region of birth	1975–79	1980–84	1985–89	1990–94	1995–96
A. Australia[a]					
Africa	4.7	4.7	5.6	4.8	—
Americas	7.0	4.9	5.9	5.0	—
Asia	33.1	33.2	41.7	50.9	—
Europe	40.9	44.2	30.3	27.5	—
Oceania	14.2	12.9	16.4	11.8	—
Total number (thousands)	344.8	469.8	615.8	462.6	—
B. Canada[b]					
Africa	5.7	4.5	6.1	7.2	7.4
Americas	26.4	20.2	21.0	15.9	11.7
Asia	32.4	44.1	48.1	57.4	61.7
Europe	33.7	29.9	24.0	18.6	18.6
Oceania	1.7	1.2	0.8	0.9	0.6
Total number (thousands)	650.6	570.3	689.5	1,177.5	212.5[b]
C. United States[c]					
Africa	2.1	2.6	3.0	3.1	5.8
Americas	43.8	37.3	41.8	36.7	41.2
Asia	38.1	47.7	44.1	41.8	35.4
Europe	15.2	11.7	10.7	17.8	16.9
Oceania	0.9	0.7	0.6	0.6	0.6
Total number (thousands)	2,308.9	2,825.0	3,028.4	3,849.2	1,627.5

Notes: a Data refer to fiscal years which run from 1 July to 31 June.
b Data on immigrants by region of birth refer only to 1995.
c Data for the US exclude persons who legalised their status under the Immigration Reform and Control Act of 1986.

Sources:
Australia: Department of Immigration, Local Government and Ethnic Affairs, 1993; Bureau of Immigration, Multicultural and Population Research, 1996.
Canada: Employment and Immigration Canada, various years; Citizenship and Immigration Canada, various years; Statistics Canada, 1995.
US: Immigration and Naturalization Service, 1994 and various years.

Table 12.2 Diversification of immigration flows directed to the US

Country of birth	Immigrants in 1950–54	Cumulative percentage of total	Country of birth	Immigrants in 1990–94	Cumulative percentage of total
1 Germany	168,117	15.3	Mexico	416,769	10.8
2 Poland	133,604	27.5	Philippines	286,152	18.3
3 Canada	123,015	38.6	Vietnam	282,625	25.6
4 United Kingdom		46.1	Former USSR		
	82,098		(excl. the Baltic States)	243,315	31.9
5 Mexico	78,723	53.3	China	218,708	37.6
6 Italy	51,395	58.0	Dominican Rep.	199,014	42.8
7 Former USSR			India	169,367	47.2
(excl. the Baltic States)	39,642	61.6			
8 Yugoslavia			Poland	110,531	50.0
former	37,335	65.0			
9 Latvia	33,131	68.0	Korea, Rep. of	104,093	52.8
10 Ireland	23,923	70.2	El Salvador	89,414	55.1
11 Lithuania	19,657	71.9	Jamaica	84,937	57.3
12 Czechoslovakia	18,840	73.7	United Kingdom	81,312	59.4
13 Hungary	18,836	75.4	Iran	74,942	61.3
14 France	16,803	76.9	Canada	74,004	63.3
15 Greece	16,503	78.4	Taiwan	66,950	65.0
16 Netherlands	16,272	79.9	Cuba	60,797	66.6
17 Austria	15,869	81.3	Ireland	56,979	68.1
18 Cuba	15,644	82.7	Colombia	54,663	69.5
19 Norway	12,085	83.8	Haiti	49,405	70.8
20 Romania	11,999	84.9	Peru	46,121	72.0
21 Japan	10,961	85.9	Hong Kong	45,972	73.2
22 Estonia	9,129	86.8	Guyana	45,106	74.3
23 China	9,042	87.6	Pakistan	42,516	75.4
24 Sweden	8,358	88.3	Lao People's		
			Dem. Rep.	41,367	76.5
25 Switzerland	8,185	89.1	Nicaragua	40,317	77.6
26 Belgium	6,644	89.7	Guatemala	37,305	78.5
27 Denmark	6,396	90.3	Germany	37,262	79.5
28 Portugal	5,913	90.8	Japan	33,559	80.4
29 Philippines	5,214	91.3	Thailand	32,916	81.2
30 Colombia	5,006	91.7	Trinidad and		
			Tobago	30,785	82.0
31 Spain	3,464	92.1	Ecuador	30,655	82.8
32 Ecuador	3,338	92.4	Honduras	28,950	83.6
TOTAL	1,099,035	100.0	TOTAL	3,849,162	100.0

Another measure of the diversification of origins is that the smallest number of countries accounting for about seventy-five per cent of the immigrant intake in each receiving country increased markedly between 1965–69 and 1990–94, rising from 6 to 12 countries in the case of Australia,

14 to 24 in the case of Canada, and 18 to 26 in the case of the US (Zlotnik, 1998). Yet, when the highest numbers reached in recent years are compared with the fact that the world is now divided into 185 nation-states, it is clear that immigrant inflows are still dominated by relatively few countries. To provide a sense of the changes taking place, Table 12.2 presents the top 32 countries of origin of immigrants to the US in 1950–54, when Europe was still the main region of origin of immigrants to that country, and in 1990–94. Very few European countries remain in the list for the latter period, though it is noteworthy that the former Soviet Union and Poland are high on the list and that Germany, Ireland and the UK, countries that have dominated immigration to the US over its history, are still important sources of immigrants today. But the key message of the lists is that developing countries in the Americas and Asia are today the main sources of immigrants to the US, a trend that is expected to continue well into the next century. Mexico, in particular, has been the main source of legal immigrants to the US since 1980 at least, and is also the origin of the largest proportion of unauthorised migrants. Partly as a result of the IRCA legalisation, where Mexicans accounted for 75 per cent of those legalised (United Nations, 1998), the number of Mexicans among the foreign born has soared, passing from 760,000 in 1970 to nearly seven million in 1997, and the increase during 1990–97 has been of the order of 2.7 million (US Census Bureau, 1999). Though much of that increase can be attributable to legal immigration, it is also true that the number of unauthorised Mexican migrants in the US has been rising, despite the measures taken to prevent illegal entry. Indeed, perhaps partly because of the success of those measures, the circulatory pattern that has characterised Mexican migration to the US is less prevalent and has been substituted by longer stays in the northern neighbour. It is not expected that the first decades of the twenty-first century will witness a sharp reduction in migration from Mexico, though economic development and the less rapid increase of the Mexican labour force may have a dampening effect over the medium term.

To conclude, it is worth noting that by favouring the selection of immigrants on the basis of family ties with residents, immigration flows have tended to show high proportions of women. In the US, for instance, 55 per cent of the 2.1 million immigrants admitted on the basis of family ties during 1972–79 were women or girls (United Nations Secretariat, 1995) and women have tended to outnumber men among all immigrants during most of the 1950–90 period. In Canada, the proportion of females among immigrants has fluctuated between 49 and 52 per cent since 1960, and it has been as high as 58 per cent among persons admitted under family reunification criteria. In Australia, the proportion of females among immigrants has been lower than in Canada but has generally been above 48 per cent.

THE MARKET-ECONOMIES OF EUROPE

Within continental Europe, the reconstruction undertaken after World War II and the economic boom that ensued led to labour shortages, especially in the countries whose populations had been most affected by the War. Consequently, during the 1950s and 1960s, Belgium, France, Germany (Western), the Netherlands, Sweden and Switzerland all resorted to the import of foreign workers on a temporary basis. Smaller countries, such as Andorra, Liechtenstein, Luxembourg, Monaco and San Marino have always been highly dependent on foreign workers but have largely satisfied their needs by importing people from their immediate vicinity. Larger countries adopted the same strategy at first. Thus, Sweden imported workers from Finland; Switzerland from Italy and Germany; and France from Algeria (a French department at the time), Belgium, Italy and Spain. But as labour demands continued to rise and supplies from neighbouring countries became tight, the labour-importing countries opted for new sources of labour. Former or current colonial ties, traditional geo-political alliances and other historical links determined which countries were selected as possible suppliers of workers. By the end of the 1960s, the main labour importing countries in continental Europe were hosting significant expatriate populations, with large contingents of persons originating in Algeria, Greece, Italy, Morocco, Portugal, Spain, Turkey and the former Yugoslavia.

All the major labour-importing countries in continental Europe adopted similar policies to manage labour migration during the 1950s and 1960s: their aim was to make the stay of foreign workers strictly temporary and to ensure the 'rotation' of labour, meaning the replacement of one worker by another once the permit for the first expired. Elaborate systems of work and residence permits were introduced to regulate and control labour migration. Recruitment was often organised by the prospective employer or by representatives of the governments of receiving countries. Private recruiters were rare. Statistics on inflows and outflows of migrants during the 1960s indicate that rotation was fairly effective. Out of a gross inflow of 17.2 million persons to Belgium, Germany (Western), the Netherlands and Sweden during 1960–69, a net gain of only 2.3 million migrants was recorded (Zlotnik, 1994). That number, however, was viewed as too high in countries that wanted a net gain of zero. Thus, although the economic recession that affected Europe during the late 1960s led to the departure of substantially higher numbers of migrant workers than in previous years, it also proved that not all would leave when no longer wanted. By 1973–74, when the sharp rise in oil prices caused an even deeper recession, the receiving countries had changed their minds about the utility of labour migration. Consequently, by 1974 all major labour importing countries in continental Europe had scrapped their labour migration programmes or introduced sharp restrictions on the admission of migrant workers. The period that followed was one of 'stabilisation', where migrants already present in the labour-importing countries were granted longer residence permits and, provided certain conditions were met, were allowed to bring in their immediate family members (spouse and minor children). Incentives were provided to foster the return of migrants to their home countries, including cash bonuses and the payment of pensions abroad. Despite the inflows for family reunification, return flows were sizeable and net migration remained low during 1975–84, amounting to only 218,000 persons over the whole decade in Belgium, the Netherlands, Germany (Western), Sweden and the UK taken together (Zlotnik, 1994).

By the early 1980s the economic configuration of the market-economies of Europe was changing. The European Community, which had expanded to include Denmark, Ireland and the UK in 1973, approved the membership of Greece as of 1981. Although Greek workers were granted the right of free movement only as of 1988, the admission of Greece into the Community was a sign that that country was no longer a supplier of labour. In 1986, Portugal and Spain joined the Community, but their workers were granted free movement rights only in 1992. In all three cases, as with Italy earlier in the 1960s, free movement rights within the European Community were granted when they were no longer likely to lead to major worker outflows. On the contrary, by the mid-1980s it was clear that Italy and Spain were themselves attracting migrant workers from other countries as were, but to a lesser extent, Greece and Portugal.

The mid-1980s also marked a turning point with respect to migration from Eastern bloc countries. As liberalising currents took hold in that region, the strong restriction on travel that had characterised those countries during the Cold War era began to be relaxed and a growing number of persons opted for migration to the West. With labour migration restricted, there were mainly two avenues for admission to market-economy countries: by belonging to an ethnic group with special ties to particular countries (i.e. being ethnic German, Jewish, Pontian Greek, Armenian, etc.) or by seeking asylum. Both types of flows increased markedly but that of asylum-seekers soon became controversial because, although under Cold War tenets almost anyone fleeing a Communist regime had been considered a refugee, as the Cold War waned and Communist regimes weakened, the rationale for admitting large numbers of migrants from Eastern bloc countries lost validity. Furthermore, not only was there a rise in the number of asylum-seekers originating in Eastern bloc countries, but those originating in developing countries where conflict raged also increased markedly (Zlotnik, 1991). The asylum systems of the market-economy countries were not prepared to cope with the numbers involved. Although refugee status was granted to only a small proportion of applicants, many others were allowed to stay legally for humanitarian reasons. Even those whose applications for asylum was ultimately denied could often spend two or three years working in the receiving country while their applications were being processed. Given the characteristics of asylum systems in developed countries, the potential for abuse was high. To reduce that potential, countries have undertaken a series of concerted actions to tighten the asylum system and make it more efficient. Co-ordination among European Union member states has been common, although it has not always been carried out through European Union mechanisms. The reforms introduced to the asylum system in recent years seem to have been effective in reducing the number of asylum applications, which peaked in 1992 at about 690,000 applications but have declined since (UNHCR, 1999). As Table 12.3 shows, the total number of applications for asylum lodged in European countries fell by 37 per cent between 1989–93 and 1994–98. The change in the German Basic Law, that used to guarantee the right to seek asylum, had a significant impact on such reduction. Coming into effect on 1 July 1993, the new legislation permitted the rejection of asylum claims by persons entering Germany through neighbouring countries considered to be safe under German asylum provisions (United Nations, 1998).

As Table 12.3 indicates, the asylum route has been important for the diversification of countries of origin of migrants to the market economies of Europe. Both Eastern bloc countries and developing countries have been major sources of asylum applicants to Europe and although most of those applicants have not been granted refugee status, their presence in receiving countries can act as anchor for further migration. It is important to note, however, that some of the main sources of asylum applicants were already important sources of migrants to the market-economies of Europe. Turkey, for instance, occupies third place and the former Yugoslavia, together with Bosnia and Herzegovina, account for about twenty-three per cent of all applications filed during 1989–98. Furthermore, nearly 43 per cent of all asylum applications filed during the period were lodged by citizens of other European countries, whereas Asian countries other than Turkey and African countries accounted for about the same proportion.

In terms of receiving countries, half of all the asylum applications filed in Europe were lodged in Germany and among them, half were lodged by citizens of other European countries (Table 12.4). Over the period 1989–1998, the number of applications filed in France, the Netherlands, Sweden, Switzerland and the UK ranged between 250,000 and 320,000 in each, and implied a special burden for countries with smaller populations, such as Sweden or Switzerland. In terms of region of origin, asylum applicants evinced a selectivity associated with economic and colonial ties to the receiving State. Thus, in the UK the highest proportion of applicants was from Africa; in France and the Netherlands, applicants from Asia accounted for 44 per cent of the total; whereas in Sweden and Switzerland, those from Europe were more numerous. In all receiving countries, however, the proportions of asylum-seekers from Africa, Asia and Europe were substantial.

Table 12.3 Main countries of origin of the persons filing asylum applications in European countries during 1989–98

Country or area of origin	Number of asylum applications			Percentage		
	1989–93	1994–98	1989–98	1989–93	1994–98	1989–98
Yugoslavia, Fed. Rep. of	491,840	276,830	768,670	19.8	17.7	19.0
Romania	340,610	60,240	400,850	13.7	3.9	9.9
Turkey	212,880	159,560	372,440	8.6	10.2	9.2
Iraq	41,140	116,730	157,870	1.7	7.5	3.9
Bosnia and Herzegovina	89,740	65,630	155,370	3.6	4.2	3.8
Sri Lanka	91,890	62,140	154,030	3.7	4.0	3.8
Bulgaria	96,050	16,270	112,320	3.9	1.0	2.8
Iran	63,200	48,350	111,550	2.5	3.1	2.8
Somalia	58,980	52,110	111,090	2.4	3.3	2.7
Dem. Rep. of the Congo	69,620	38,510	108,130	2.8	2.5	2.7
Afghanistan	37,170	62,170	99,340	1.5	4.0	2.5
Pakistan	47,270	37,140	84,410	1.9	2.4	2.1
India	49,150	31,910	81,060	2.0	2.0	2.0
Lebanon	63,850	11,240	75,090	2.6	0.7	1.9
Poland	67,530	7,420	74,950	2.7	0.5	1.9
Vietnam	54,910	17,570	72,480	2.2	1.1	1.8
Nigeria	40,180	29,580	69,760	1.6	1.9	1.7
Albania	44,590	18,800	63,390	1.8	1.2	1.6
Algeria	27,050	34,980	62,030	1.1	2.2	1.5
Russian Federation	34,310	24,670	58,980	1.4	1.6	1.5
Ghana	44,530	10,070	54,600	1.8	0.6	1.3
China	23,120	25,550	48,670	0.9	1.6	1.2
Angola	32,390	14,340	46,730	1.3	0.9	1.2
Ethiopia	28,050	11,020	39,070	1.1	0.7	1.0
Armenia	8,230	25,650	33,880	0.3	1.6	0.8
Bangladesh	16,050	13,590	29,640	0.6	0.9	0.7
Syrian Arab Rep.	16,630	12,950	29,580	0.7	0.8	0.7
Liberia	17,600	9,660	27,260	0.7	0.6	0.7
Togo	12,960	12,120	25,080	0.5	0.8	0.6
Palestinians	20,200	3,430	23,630	0.8	0.2	0.6
Africa	455,240	312,890	768,130	18.3	20.0	19.0
Asia	753,190	671,390	1,424,580	30.3	43.0	35.2
Europe	1,209,460	527,380	1,736,840	48.6	33.8	42.9
Latin America and the Caribbean	30,870	2,850	53,720	1.2	1.5	1.3
Other/Unknown	40,450	27,330	67,780	1.6	1.7	1.7
Total	2,489,200	1,561,810	4,051,010	100.0	100.0	100.0

Source: UNHCR, (1999), Table VI.7.

Table 12.4 *Percentage distribution of asylum applications in European countries by region of origin of the applicant, 1989–98*

Country of asylum	Africa	Asia	Europe	Latin America and the Caribbean	Other or unknown origin	Number of asylum applications (000)
Austria	6.3	34.1	58.1	0.1	1.4	131.5
Belgium	35.3	25.7	37.8	1.1	0.2	153.1
Denmark	18.7	29.4	40.5	0.2	11.2	71.2
Finland	28.5	19.3	50.1	0.8	1.2	15.4
France	34.9	44.2	17.6	3.0	0.3	324.2
Germany	13.2	35.2	50.0	0.2	1.4	2,025.0
Greece	5.9	83.0	10.5	0.0	0.5	26.1
Italy	14.9	13.8	70.5	0.3	0.6	44.5
Netherlands	25.2	44.5	28.0	0.6	1.7	296.8
Norway	15.7	23.8	57.4	1.2	1.9	48.3
Spain	25.5	13.3	30.1	23.7	7.3	77.6
Sweden	9.3	23.5	60.8	3.3	3.0	263.8
Switzerland	14.1	38.0	45.1	0.6	2.2	261.0
United Kingdom	43.6	37.4	15.7	2.4	0.9	312.8
Total	19.0	35.2	42.9	1.3	1.7	
Number of asylum applications (000)	768.1	1,424.6	1,736.9	53.7	67.8	4,051.0

Sources: UNHCR, 1999, Table VI.6.

Table 12.5 *Persons admitted as spouses under the family reunification provisions of France and the UK, selected years*

Year	Female spouses	Male spouses	Total	Percentage of women
United Kingdom, persons admitted under family reunification				
1985	17,990	6,680	55,360	72.9
1988	15,120	7,950	49,280	65.5
1991	19,010	11,160	53,900	63.0
1993	19,100	12,000	55,640	61.4
1995	19,940	12,680	55,480	61.1
1996	21,520	12,450	61,730	63.4
France, persons admitted under family reunification				
1991	12,765	3,745	16,510	77.3
1992	11,417	3,741	15,158	75.3
1993	11,341	3,540	14,881	76.2
1994	7,538	2,245	9,783	77.1
1995			14,360	
France, persons admitted as spouses of French citizens				
1991	9,314	9,449	18,763	49.6
1992	9,413	9,632	19,045	49.4
1993	10,524	9,556	20,080	52.4
1994	7,426	5,719	13,145	56.5
1995	—	—	13,387	—

Source: Kofman (1999), Tables 1 and 2.

Aside from asylum, the other two avenues open for admission to Western bloc countries in Europe are the repatriation of ethnic groups and family reunification. The largest flow of the first type is undoubtedly that experienced by Germany where 3.1 million ethnic Germans (*Aussiedler*) repatriated during 1968–96, 2.3 million arriving between 1988 and 1996. Among them nearly 50 per cent originated in the former Soviet Union (especially in Kazakhstan), 34 per cent in Poland and 13 per cent in Romania. Flows generated by family reunification have not been easy to quantify because most receiving countries do not tabulate statistics on inflows by type of admission. Data relative to France and the UK reveal that even in terms of admissions of spouses (without counting minor children), the numbers have been substantial and that, as in the flows directed to immigration countries, women predominate among migrants admitted because of family reunification (Table 12.5).

What has been the effect of recent migration trends on the migrant stock in the market-economy countries of Europe? Data necessary to answer this question are not available for the major receiving countries. The most comprehensive set of data available refers to the foreign stock in each country. Changes in the foreign stock, however, are not only indicative of the effects of the net migration of foreigners but also of the processes of naturalisation and natural increase (in countries where *jus sanguinis* is the basis for obtaining citizenship). Nevertheless, the number of foreigners in a country has been commonly used to gauge the impact of international migration. Table 12.6 presents changes in the foreign stock of the main receiving countries in Europe for 1985, 1990 and 1996. Trends vary considerably among them. Among those hosting the largest numbers of foreigners, Germany has experienced a marked net increase in the foreign stock (nearly 3 million during 1985–96), the UK has recorded a modest rise, concentrated mostly in the 1990s, and France may have seen its foreign population remain largely stable (the number for 1996 is an estimate, since France lacks data on the foreign population after 1990). Among the next tier of receiving countries, Belgium, the Netherlands and Switzerland have experienced low to moderate increases of their foreign populations, whereas Italy, Spain and Denmark have seen their foreign populations rise by more than a factor of 2. Increases in the foreign stock of Portugal, though large, have been moderate in comparison. But the country experiencing the most marked rise of the foreign population has been Finland, whose foreign stock in 1996 was still the smallest among those of all countries considered.

The rapid rise of the foreign stock in Italy and Spain deserves some comment. In the 1980s, it became clear that those countries, which had been major sources of migrants to the labour-importing countries of the region, were themselves attracting foreign workers. As a response to such developments, between 1985 and 1991, Italy and Spain introduced legislation to regulate worker migration and conducted several regularisation drives aimed at providing permits to foreigners working in their territories. Despite the high numbers of undocumented migrants said to exist, the numbers regularising their status during 1985–91 were modest: a total of less than 200,000 in the regularisations carried out in 1985–86 and 1991 in Spain and about 320,000 in those carried out in 1987–88 and 1990 in Italy (Zlotnik, 1998). Consequently, whether through regularisations, the admission of refugees (especially in the case of Italy), or the legal migration of foreigners, particularly those from other EU member states, both countries have seen their foreign stocks rise markedly and become fairly diversified in terms of origins.

Table 12.6 Foreign population in selected European countries with market economies

Receiving country	1985	1990	1996	Percentage increase 1985–96
Germany	4,378.9	5,342.5	7,314.0	67.0
France	3,669.7	3,596.6	3,510.9	–4.3
United Kingdom	1,731.0	1,723.0	2,066.0	19.4
Switzerland	939.7	1,100.3	1,337.6	42.3
Italy	423.0	781.1	1,095.6	159.0
Belgium	846.5	904.5	911.9	7.7
Netherlands	552.5	692.4	679.9	23.1
Spain	242.0	278.8	539.0	122.7
Sweden	388.6	483.7	526.6	35.5
Denmark	117.0	160.6	237.7	103.2
Portugal	94.7	107.8	172.9	82.6
Norway	101.5	143.3	157.5	55.2
Luxembourg	97.9	113.1	142.8	45.9
Finland	17.0	26.6	73.8	334.1

Sources: United Nations, 1998, Table 15 and OECD, 1998.

At the level of the Western bloc countries of Europe, however, a few countries of origin still account for most of the migrant stock in the region. Table 12.7 presents estimates of the stock of migrants in Europe from selected countries of origin as it has evolved over time. As of 1996, citizens of Turkey, the former Yugoslavia, Italy and Morocco living in countries other than their own within Europe amounted to 7.3 million, but their numbers showed varied trends of change over the previous 10 or 15 years. Migrants from the former Yugoslavia had declined in numbers between 1980 and 1985 but were already rising by 1990 and their numbers have nearly doubled between 1990 and 1996. The number of Italians has declined steadily but in 1996 there were still nearly 1.5 million living in other European countries, a figure surpassing the foreign stock in Italy. In contrast, the numbers of Moroccans and Turks have been rising steadily, especially as they expand their array of destinations (Moroccans, for instance, have been migrating in moderate numbers to Southern European countries). However, as the proportions of migrants living in the main receiving countries listed in Table 12.7 attest, concentration in a few destinations is still typical. Table 12.7 shows estimates for two other groups of migrants whose numbers in 1996 were moderate but that exemplify two different trends. The number of Polish migrants in Europe rose rapidly after 1980 as a result of the rise of the Solidarity movement in Poland and of the eventual liberalisation of exit regulations in that country. Though Poles remain largely concentrated in Germany and France, their traditional destinations, they can also be found in a number of other countries. United States citizens in contrast can be found in small to moderate numbers in almost every country of Western Europe. The number of Americans living in Europe has been rising steadily and, although they move for a variety of reasons (training, marriage, work), their increase is likely to be tied to the process of globalisation and the increasing American presence in international business and finance.

Table 12.7 Number of migrants in the market economies of Europe originating in selected countries and percentage distribution by main country of residence

Region, country of citizenship and country of residence	1980	1985	1990	1996
Africa				
Morocco (000)	—	785.0	1,030.3	1,268.5
France	—	62.0	55.6	54.9
Belgium	—	15.7	13.8	10.9
Netherlands	—	14.8	15.2	10.9
Asia				
Turkey (000)	1,844.7	1,875.1	2,312.1	2,729.1
Germany	79.3	74.8	73.3	75.1
Netherlands	7.5	8.3	8.8	4.7
France	5.9	7.8	8.6	10.4
Europe				
Italy (000)	1,832.5	1,612.9	1,547.3	1,495.7
Germany	33.7	32.9	35.7	40.1
Switzerland	23.0	24.3	24.5	23.4
France	20.0	18.9	16.3	13.5
Belgium	15.4	15.7	15.6	13.9
Poland (000)	—	189.7	326.8	367.8
Germany	—	55.3	74.1	77.1
France	—	30.3	14.4	10.1
Yugoslavia, former (000)	809.6	798.5	960.4	1,832.4
Germany	78.0	74.0	69.0	70.8
Switzerland	5.4	8.7	14.7	16.6
Northern America				
United States (000)	—	268.4	313.0	351.9
Germany	—	27.0	29.6	35.4
United Kingdom	—	32.0	32.6	29.6
Italy	—	19.0	18.6	15.5

In the medium-term future, the Western bloc countries of Europe are likely
to continue recording positive net migration, though their desire to
discourage further inflows, especially those triggered by the involuntary
movements of persons fleeing conflict, is likely to dampen inflows in the
near future. Nevertheless, the need for unskilled labour continues and the
affluent European Economic Area is a powerful magnet for both the large
numbers of underemployed workers in developing countries and those trying
to cope with the effects of economic transformation in the economies in
transition of Eastern and Central Europe. Furthermore, because of their
liberal tradition, the Western bloc countries will continue to be called upon to
aid and provide security to persons fleeing, if not individualised persecution
in their home countries, at least the very real threats posed by internal conflict
or outright war. The destabilising effects of the disintegration of the former
Yugoslavia have already had a large impact on migration flows to the West.
The potential for more flows of that type has not entirely abated.

THE ECONOMIES IN TRANSITION OF EUROPE

After having successfully sealed their borders for nearly half a century,
Eastern bloc countries were largely unprepared to cope legally or in practical
terms with the migration flows unleashed by both the relaxation of exit
controls and the disintegration of nation-states. With the dissolution of a
State, movements that used to be internal have become international. In the
Russian Federation alone, at least 10 million persons who were born in other
republics of the former Soviet Union qualify as international migrants
(Russian Federation, 1992). Furthermore, at the time of the 1989 census,
there were 25 million Russians living in non-Russian republics, many of
whom have since opted to return to the Russian Federation instead of staying
'abroad'.

Until the early 1990s, the international migration experienced by Eastern bloc
countries had been directed mostly to the market-economies of the developed
world and to Israel, but with the disintegration of the Soviet Union in 1991 a
number of migration flows have converged on the Russian Federation. Data on
inflows and outflows experienced by the Russian Federation show that average
annual net migration rose from 147,000 during the 1980s to 341,000 in 1990–94
and to nearly 400,000 in 1995–97. The rise of net migration after 1990 was
mostly the result of sharp declines in the outflow of migrants from the Russian
Federation to other member States of the Commonwealth of Independent States
(CIS). That is, whereas when the Soviet Union was united inflows to and
outflows from the Russian Federation to other republics were similar in
magnitude, after the dissolution of the union, inflows changed less than
outflows. The latter dropped from an annual average of 730,000 in 1985–89, to
477,000 in 1990–94 and still further to 190,000 in 1995–97. In contrast, the
average number of annual inflows from other republics rose at first from

891,000 in 1985–89 to 920,000 and then declined somewhat, but was still at a high 685,000 per year during 1995–97 (Zlotnik, 1998).

In the late 1980s and 1990s the former Soviet Union has been the origin of very sizeable flows of migrants directed to Western bloc countries, mainly to Germany, Israel and the US. In the US, the number of immigrants from the former Soviet Union increased eleven-fold between 1985–89 and 1990–94, rising from 22,000 to 243,000. In Israel, the number of Soviet Jews admitted between 1989 and 1996 ascended to 669,000, 597,000 of whom arrived during 1990–95 (Della Pergola, 1997).

Table 12.8 Number of refugees and other persons of concern to UNHCR in the members of the Commonwealth of Independent States (CIS), 1995 and 1997

	Number of refugees			Others of concern		
	End of 1995	End of 1997	End of 1998	End of 1995	End of 1997	End of 1998
Transcaucasian republics						
Armenia	218,000	219,000	310,000	72,000	72,000	—
Azerbaijan	233,700	233,700	221,600	622,000	551,100	576,300
Georgia	100	200	20	288,600	273,400	277,000
Central Asian republics						
Kazakhstan	—	15,600	8,300	8,000	—	—
Kyrgyzstan	13,200	15,300	14,600	800	—	—
Tajikistan	400	2,200	3,600	18,700	—	—
Turkmenistan	3,000	15,800	14,600	—	—	—
Uzbekistan	900	3,200	1,100	40,600	—	—
Other European republics						
Belarus	—	100	80	30,800	160,000	160,000
Republic of Moldova	—	—	—	—	1,300	1,300
Russian Federation	42,300	237,700	128,600	1,335,000	1,294,000	1,025,500
Ukraine	5,200	4,600	6,100	—	35,000	105,700
Total	516,800	747,400	708,600	2,416,500	2,386,800	2,145,800

Sources: UNHCR, 1996, 1998 and 1999.

The conflicts that have erupted after the disintegration of the Soviet Union have led to important flows of persons in need of protection among the successor states. Reports provided by governments to UNHCR permit an overview of the situation in the various countries affected by such movements. As Table 12.8 shows, by the end of 1998 there were 709,000 refugees and 2.1 million internally displaced persons in the 12 member states of the CIS. The largest groups of displaced persons were concentrated in the Russian Federation and Azerbaijan. The number of refugees was also largest in those countries plus Armenia. The continued conflict in Chechnya is likely to further increase the number of persons in need of assistance within the

Russian Federation. Given the lack of stability that still characterises most of the CIS countries, both in economic and political terms, it is likely that the next decade or two will witness further conflicts leading to forced migration. In addition, emigration to Western bloc countries will continue though its magnitude will largely depend on the willingness of receiving countries to allow the admission of citizens from the former Soviet Union or from other countries with economies in transition.

The contentious disintegration of the former Yugoslavia has been at the root of the rising number of refugees and other persons in need of protection in Europe. War in Croatia exploded in 1991 and was followed by a protracted confrontation in Bosnia and Herzegovina that began in 1992. At the peak of the upheavals in 1993, there were two million persons in need of protection within the territory of the former Yugoslavia, including 810,000 internally displaced persons in Bosnia and Herzegovina. During 1995 the refugee population in Yugoslavia more than tripled, increasing from 200,000 to 650,000 because of the influx of persons from Bosnia and Herzegovina and from Croatia (United Nations, 1998). In December 1995, the Peace Agreement (signed at Dayton) between Bosnia and Herzegovina, the Republic of Croatia and the Federal Republic of Yugoslavia (Serbia and Montenegro) brought the four years of war to an end, but tensions persist between different ethnic groups and the repatriation of uprooted persons has been slow. By mid-1997, there were still 900,000 people displaced in Bosnia and Herzegovina and another 900,000 living as refugees in other states (UNHCR, 1997). Furthermore, in 1998–99 the conflict in Kosovo produced again major displacements of population. By early 1999, the Federal Republic of Yugoslavia was hosting 502,000 refugees (UNHCR, 1999).

THE DEVELOPING COUNTRIES

Forced Migration

In much of the developing world, the dominant flows of migrants are those of refugees or persons in search of asylum. As Table 12.9 shows, since 1981, at least three-quarters of all refugees in the world have found asylum in developing countries. Until the early 1990s, the number of refugees had been growing steadily but over the course of the 1990s declines have been common, partly as a result of successful repatriation drives made possible by the resolution of long-standing conflicts, and partly because of the growing reluctance of governments to grant refugee status to persons in need of protection who are not victims of individual persecution. As of early 1999 there were 11.5 million refugees in the world, about a quarter less than at the peak of nearly 15 million in early 1990.

Table 12.9 Percentage distribution of the number of refugees by region of asylum, 1981–96

Region of asylum	Early 1981	Early 1985	Early 1990	Early 1995	Early 1999
Africa	44.6	28.0	30.9	46.6	28.5
Asia	27.7	47.7	45.6	34.6	41.3
Europe	7.2	6.5	5.4	13.0	23.2
Latin America and the Caribbean	2.4	3.7	8.1	0.7	0.6
North America	14.5	13.1	9.4	4.7	5.7
Oceania	3.6	0.9	0.7	0.4	0.6
Total number (millions)	8.2	10.5	14.9	14.5	11.5

Sources: UNHCR

Over the past two decades, Africa and Asia have hosted the largest numbers of refugees in the world. In Africa there has been a diversification of both the sources and the countries of asylum of refugees. The end of the colonial period left a number of multi-ethnic states whose political and economic stability was tenuous. In some states, inter-ethnic conflict had predated decolonisation and intensified after it. During the Cold War, internal conflicts were couched in terms of the larger confrontation between the super-powers and, in order to gain influence, the latter provided overt or covert support to one group over another, thus exacerbating existing antagonisms. The countries of the Horn of Africa were especially affected by such problems and became the major sources and hosts of refugees in the region during the 1970s and early 1980s. Thus, in 1980, Ethiopia alone was the major source of refugees in Africa: 1.6 million, hosted mostly by Somalia and Sudan. Since the 1970s and all through the 1980s, Burundi and Rwanda were also important sources or receivers of refugees, as Hutus and Tutsis fought each other for political ascendancy. Uganda under Idi Amin produced sizeable outflows of refugees until the mid-1980s when a change in government allowed the eventual repatriation of most Ugandan refugees. In Southern Africa, the protracted conflict in Angola produced a steady outflow of refugees during the 1980s, so that by 1990 there were 400,000 Angolan refugees in other African countries; and in Mozambique, intensification of the civil war during the late 1980s led to the outflow of 1.1 million persons, the majority of whom found asylum in neighbouring Malawi.

With the end of the bi-polar era, several long-standing conflicts found resolution. After years of war and famine, a change of government in Ethiopia prompted the repatriation of nearly a million refugees, primarily from Djibouti, Somalia and Sudan. In 1993, Eritrea achieved independence and the repatriation of its citizens became possible. Nevertheless, by 1997 there were still 328,000 Eritreans in Sudan. Between 1992 and 1996, some

1.7 Mozambican refugees returned to their country from Malawi, South Africa, Swaziland, Tanzania, Zambia and Zimbabwe. Despite these positive developments, Africa witnessed a series of new or renewed conflicts during the 1990s. In Somalia the disintegration of the Siad Barre regime in the early 1990s led to conflict among clans and their warlords, producing large refugee outflows directed to several neighbouring countries but particularly to Ethiopia and Kenya. In early 1999 there were 475,000 Somalian refugees in Africa.

In Sudan, the government continued to battle rebel forces in the south and about 430,000 Sudanese remained in Uganda, the Democratic Republic of the Congo, Ethiopia and Kenya in 1997 (UNHCR, 1997). By early 1999 372,000 Sudanese were still refugees in the region. In Rwanda, a long and complex history of inter-ethnic conflict produced a crisis in 1994 when nearly half a million Tutsis and moderate Hutus were killed over a period of six weeks. The genocide was stopped when the Government was ousted by the Rwandese Patriotic Front led by Tutsis. Those who organised the genocide, fearing for their lives, organised the mass evacuation of the Hutu population: around 1.75 million persons moved to the Democratic Republic of Congo, Tanzania and Burundi. As Hutus left, about 700,000 Tutsi refugees returned, many after years of exile. In 1994 itself, 160,000 Hutu refugees returned voluntarily to Rwanda. In Burundi, the Hutu refugees from Rwanda were not welcome by the Tutsi-dominated Government and by 1996, 90,000 had been forced back to Rwanda and 30,000 had moved to Tanzania. In the Democratic Republic of Congo, the forces of the Alliance of Democratic Forces for the Liberation of Congo-Zaire (ADFL), led by Laurent Kabila, advanced over the camps of Rwandese refugees, obliging them to repatriate. Thousands returned between 15 and 19 November 1996. By the end of the year, 600,000 Rwandese refugees had returned from the Democratic Republic of Congo, but another 450,000 had fled into the country's interior and fell prey to attacks by the ADFL. By June 1997, 215,000 refugees remained unaccounted for, whereas 234,000 had been able to return to Rwanda with UNHCR assistance. By the end of 1996, an estimated 483,000 Rwandese refugees had returned from Tanzania (UNHCR, 1997). As a result of such repatriations, by early 1999 only 70,000 Rwandese were still living as refugees outside Rwanda.

Western Africa, a region that had experienced few refugee flows during the 1970s and 1980s, began having to face the problem of forced population displacements when war erupted in Liberia in 1989. By early 1991, neighbouring countries were hosting 740,000 Liberian refugees and as late as 1999, 257,000 Liberian refugees remained in the countries of asylum, hosted in their majority by Côte d'Ivoire and Guinea. Also in 1991, internal conflict began to rage in Sierra Leone (UNHCR, 1999). By 1997, when the country's civilian government was overthrown by armed rebels, there were 800,000 internally displaced persons in the country. Although the civilian government was reinstated in 1998, conflict continued and by early 1999 there were 407,000 refugees from Sierra Leone, about 300,000 in Guinea and 100,000 in Liberia (UNHCR, 1999).

Table 12.10 shows countries hosting the largest numbers of refugees in Africa at different points in time. In the early 1980s, most refugees in the continent were concentrated in the Eastern part, including Sudan and Somalia in the north and Tanzania and Mozambique further south. By 1995, the conflicts raging in Western Africa had given rise to sizeable refugee populations hosted by Guinea, Côte d'Ivoire, Liberia and Ghana. Senegal had replaced Ghana by 1999. The Democratic Republic of Congo was hosting 137,000 refugees from Angola, 35,000 from Rwanda and 31,000 from Sudan, whereas in the United Republic of Tanzania the main group enjoying asylum was refugees from Burundi which numbered 474,000 in early 1999.

In Asia, involuntary migrations on a massive scale have occurred several times during the twentieth century. One of the largest was the movement of 8.5 million Hindus and Sikhs who fled from Pakistan and 6.5 million Muslims who left India when the country was partitioned in 1947. In 1971, an additional 10 million Bengalis and Hindus left Bangladesh after it seceded from Pakistan (Dowty, 1987). Better known is the plight of Palestinian refugees, 600,000 to 700,000 of whom were displaced in 1947–48 as a result of the events that led to the creation of the State of Israel and whose numbers have since increased to 3 million (United Nations, 1994b).

More recently, the end of the Vietnam War in 1975 marked the beginning of major refugee outflows from the countries of Indo-China. At least 1.2 million refugees from the region were resettled in overseas countries; nearly 300,000 ethnic Chinese from Vietnam were granted asylum in China; and a further 370,000 Cambodians who were not recognised as refugees remained under the mandate of the United Nations Border Relief Organization (UNBRO) in camps located on the border between Cambodia and Thailand. The repatriation of Cambodians became possible following a negotiated settlement reached in 1991 between the warring factions. Most of the displaced Cambodians had returned to their areas of origin by the time elections were held in Cambodia in April 1993. For Vietnamese asylum-seekers as well, repatriation has become a more likely prospect than resettlement in third countries, especially since 1989 when countries of asylum in East and South East Asia introduced individual screening procedures to establish who qualified for refugee status. Prior to that date, Vietnamese arriving in countries of the region had been granted refugee status on a group basis. Individual screening resulted in low refugee-recognition rates and a growing number of persons held in camps. Between 1989 and 1996, over 90,000 Vietnamese asylum-seekers whose claims to refugee status had been rejected repatriated voluntarily from camps throughout South-East Asia and many others returned involuntarily (UNHCR, 1997).

International Migration into the 21st Century

Table 12.10 Major countries of asylum in Africa, 1985 to 1999

Country of Asylum	Early 1980	Country of Asylum	Early 1985	Country of Asylum	Early 1990
Africa	2,727,847	**Africa**	2,929,450	**Africa**	4,608,590
Sub-total	2,437,400	Sub-total	2,460,100	Sub-total	4,118,200
Percentage	89	Percentage	84	Percentage	89
Somalia	1,275,000	Somalia	700,000	Malawi	822,500
Sudan	441,000	Sudan	690,000	Sudan	767,700
Dem. Rep. of		Dem. Rep. of		Ethiopia	710,200
the Congo	299,000	the Congo	317,000	Somalia	600,000
Tanzania	160,000	Burundi	256,600	Dem. Rep. of	
Mozambique	150,000	Tanzania	178,500	the Congo	340,700
Uganda	112,400	Algeria	167,000	Burundi	267,500
		Uganda	151,000	Tanzania	265,100
				Zimbabwe	175,400
				Algeria	169,100

Country of Asylum	Early 1995	Country of Asylum	Early 1999
Africa	6,752,190	**Africa**	3,270,860
Sub-total	6,029,600	Sub-total	2,911,700
Percentage	89	Percentage	89
Dem. Rep. of		Tanzania	543,900
the Congo	1,724,400	Guinea	413,700
Tanzania	883,300	Sudan	391,500
Sudan	727,200	Ethiopia	262,000
Guinea	553,200	Dem. Rep. of	
Côte d'Ivoire	360,100	the Congo	240,300
Ethiopia	348,100	Kenya	238,200
Burundi	300,300	Uganda	204,500
Uganda	286,500	Zambia	168,600
Kenya	252,400	Algeria	165,200
Algeria	219,100	Côte d'Ivoire	119,900
Zambia	141,100	Liberia	103,100
Liberia	120,200	Senegal	60,800
Ghana	113,700		

Sources: United Nations, 1994a, Table 2; UNHCR, 1999, Table 1.4.

Table 12.11 Main countries of asylum in the world in 1990, 1995 and 1999

Country of Asylum	Early 1990	Country of Asylum	Early 1995	Country of Asylum	Early 1999
Total	14,914,160	Total	14,488,740	Total	11,491,710
Sub-total	13,405,800	Sub-total	13,061,900	Sub-total	10,331,300
Percentage	90	Percentage	90	Percentage	90
Pakistan	3,275,700	Iran	2,236,400	Iran	1,931,300
Iran	2,850,000	Dem. Rep. of the Congo	1,724,400	Pakistan	1,202,500
United States	1,000,000	Pakistan	1,055,400	Germany	949,200
Malawi	822,500	Germany	1,004,600	Tanzania	543,900
Sudan	767,700	Tanzania	883,300	United States	524,100
Ethiopia	710,200	Sudan	727,200	Yugoslavia, Fed. Rep. of	502,000
Somalia	600,000	United States	591,700	Guinea	413,700
Canada	447,200	Guinea	553,200	Sudan	391,500
Mexico	356,400	Côte d'Ivoire	360,100	Armenia	310,000
Dem. Rep. of the Congo	340,700	Ethiopia	348,100	China	292,300
China	280,500	Armenia	304,000	Ethiopia	262,000
Costa Rica	278,600	Burundi	300,300	Dem. Rep. of the Congo	240,300
Burundi	267,500	China	287,100	Kenya	238,200
Tanzania	265,100	Uganda	286,500	Azerbaijan	221,600
Honduras	237,100	India	258,300	Uganda	204,500
Guatemala	223,100	Kenya	252,400	India	185,500
France	188,300	Azerbaijan	231,600	Sweden	178,800
Zimbabwe	175,400	Algeria	219,100	Zambia	168,600
Algeria	169,100	Yugoslavia, Fed. Rep. of	195,500	Algeria	165,200
Germany	150,700	Croatia	183,600	France	140,200
		France	152,300	Thailand	138,300
		Zambia	141,100	Canada	135,700
		Liberia	120,200	Netherlands	131,800
		Iraq	119,600	Russian Federation	128,600
		Bangladesh	116,200	Nepal	126,100
		Ghana	113,700	Côte d'Ivoire	119,900
		Nepal	103,300	United Kingdom	116,100
		Thailand	100,800	Iraq	104,100
		South Africa	91,900	Liberia	103,100
				Switzerland	81,900
				Austria	80,300

Sources: UNHCR, 1998, Table 1.4.

During the 1980s, the largest recognised refugee population in the world was that of the Afghans, who started fleeing their country after the Soviet intervention of 1979. Between 1980 and 1989, the Afghan refugee population increased from 400,000 to 5.6 million, 60 per cent of whom found asylum in Pakistan and the rest in the Islamic Republic of Iran (United Nations, 1998). Following the withdrawal of Soviet troops from Afghanistan during 1988–89, a slow process of repatriation began. Despite the continued fighting in their homeland and the absence of a central government, more than 2.7 million Afghans repatriated from Pakistan and Iran between 1992 and 1996 (UNHCR, 1997). Yet, by early 1999 there were still 1.2 million Afghans in Pakistan and 1.4 million in Iran (UNHCR, 1999). Other sizeable refugee populations in Asia during the 1990s include those who fled civil war in Iraq during the aftermath of the Gulf War, 1.3 million of whom were present in Iran in early 1993 and 531,000 of whom remained by 1999 (UNHCR, 1999); the 184,000 refugees from Afghanistan, Sri Lanka and Tibet reported by India; and the 106,000 Bhutanese in Nepal (UNHCR, 1999).

Table 12.11 shows the countries of asylum accounting for 90 per cent of the world's refugee population in 1990, 1995 and 1999. Their number has been rising steadily, from 20 in 1990, to 29 in 1995 and 31 in 1999. Among countries hosting most of the world's refugees in 1990, four were developed countries (the US, Canada, France and Germany, in order of importance). By 1995, the Federal Republic of Yugoslavia and Croatia had been added to that list and Canada had dropped from it, but by 1999, 11 developed countries were among those providing asylum to most refugees. The number of Asian countries in the list also rose markedly, from 4 in 1990 to 11 in 1999. There was less change in the number of countries in Africa: from 9 in 1990 to 11 in 1999, though the latter group includes more countries from Western Africa and fewer from Southern Africa than the former. There was a marked change in the number of countries hosting large refugee populations in Latin America and the Caribbean: from four in 1990 to none in 1999. The International Conference on Central American Refugees (CIREFCA) held in May 1989, the creation on 6 September 1989 of the International Support and Verification Commission and the negotiations to end civil wars in various Central American countries, led to the repatriation of most refugees and displaced persons in the region by 1995 (United Nations, 1998).

Despite successes in achieving the resolution of a number of long-standing conflicts and in maintaining stability in the countries affected, the international community is not able to find speedy solutions to all the eruptions of violence in the developing world. Although regional institutions, particularly in Africa, have become more proactive in containing conflict and working toward the peaceful resolution of internal disputes, success has been limited and population displacement or outright refugee outflows continue to be common. Over the medium-term future, therefore, involuntary migration will likely continue, especially in contexts where the process of nation building is still at its early stages. That is particularly the case of Africa and some countries of Asia, especially those that have gained independence recently.

Voluntary Migration

The most common type of voluntary migration in the developing world is the movement of workers. In Western Africa, labour migration dates from colonial times when the development of plantation agriculture in the forested rainy areas along the Gulf of Guinea required the movement of workers from drier grasslands along the southern border of the Sahara Desert. After independence, some of the countries occupying coastal areas kept on importing labour from their inland neighbours. Thus, Côte d'Ivoire has been persistently the destination of agricultural migrant workers from Burkina Faso, Mali and Guinea; Senegal has hosted sizeable numbers of migrants from Guinea and Mauritania; and Ghana was a major pole of attraction in the region until the late 1960s, when it expelled international migrants and economic difficulties began to transform it into a source rather than an importer of labour. A decade or so later, Nigeria expelled large numbers of Ghanaians, Togolese and others who were working illegally in the country (United Nations, 1985). They had been attracted by Nigeria's oil boom during the late 1970s, but their expulsion in 1983 and again in 1985 was brought about by a return of economic difficulties in Nigeria. At present, that country is not believed to be hosting large numbers of irregular migrants. Instead, another oil-rich country, Gabon, whose foreign population surpassed 100,000, according to preliminary data from the 1993 census (Gabon, n.d.), introduced, early in 1995, stringent work permit requirements that resulted in the repatriation of considerable numbers of migrants from neighbouring countries. In Côte d'Ivoire, the foreign population, which was about 1.5 million in 1975, had nearly doubled by 1998, but the result of surveys carried out in 1993 indicated that Côte d'Ivoire may have experienced net migration losses in the early 1990s (United Nations, 1998).

In Southern Africa, the Republic of South Africa has been a major importer of unskilled workers for its coal and gold mines. Foreign workers originated mostly in neighbouring countries—Botswana, Lesotho, Malawi and Mozambique—and were subject to strict controls related to length of stay, type of work and place of residence. Labour rotation was strictly enforced and transportation to and from South Africa was provided through organised groups so that the return of workers whose contracts had expired could be assured. During the early 1970s, the average annual number of foreign workers employed by the Chamber of Mines of South Africa exceeded 300,000, but by the early 1980s it had declined to less than 200,000 and by 1990–93 stood at 179,000. The reduction was brought about by an explicit policy favouring the substitution of foreign workers by black South Africans, a policy that continued through the 1980s. During the 1990s, as apartheid was being dismantled, prosperous South Africa has become increasingly attractive to workers from other countries, particularly those with the skills needed to fill the gaps existing among the black population of the Republic. Irregular migration from as far away as Ghana or Nigeria has reportedly been increasing, together with that of unskilled workers from neighbouring countries. According to statistics on authorised migration, South Africa has maintained a positive net migration balance with other African countries since 1976, but a negative balance with developed countries except during 1980–84 (Zlotnik, 1998).

In Latin America during the 1970s, Argentina and Venezuela attracted migrants from neighbouring countries to work in low-paying jobs. However, economic difficulties during the 1980s may have dampened migration to those countries. In Venezuela, for instance, the foreign-born population remained almost unchanged at about one million between 1981 and 1991, and Argentina recorded a decline of the foreign-born population between 1980 and 1991 (from 1.9 to 1.6 million). In Venezuela, the vast majority of Latin American migrants originate in Colombia, with the Dominican Republic being a distant second. In Argentina, Latin American migrants originate mainly in Bolivia, Chile, Paraguay and Uruguay. In both cases, migrants from neighbouring countries largely begin by working illegally in low-status occupations (agriculture, construction, domestic service, etc.). Argentina conducted a number of regularisations during the 1970s and 1980s, and Venezuela conducted a regularisation drive in 1980 where 267,000 applications were received, 92 per cent from Colombians. Though less important in numerical terms, the movement of Haitian agricultural workers to the Dominican Republic, of Guatemalan agricultural workers to the South-eastern states of Mexico, and the migration of skilled personnel from Caribbean states with more advanced educational systems to the less advanced but prospering tourist economies of other Caribbean states, are worth noting. Because some of these migration movements are only temporary (Haitian or Guatemalan agricultural workers move only during the harvest season, for instance), and because most Latin American countries lack statistical systems to account for those flows, they remain ill documented. Census data, which provide only a snapshot of a very dynamic situation, confirm that most international migration originating in Latin American and the Caribbean is directed to the US (United Nations, 1992). Intra-regional migration has been small in comparison.

In Asia, immigration has been a major factor in the population growth of Israel. In 1992, 80 per cent of the 5.1 million persons living in the country were either immigrants or children of immigrants. Immigrants to Israel have been almost exclusively Jews and their immediate relatives. Since the late 1970s, the major source of new settlers to Israel has been the Soviet Union, with the outflow of Jews from Soviet territory increasing sharply during the late 1980s and early 1990s. In 1990 alone, nearly 200,000 Soviet Jews arrived in Israel (Table 12.12). An estimated one million Jews remain in the Russian Federation and other successor states of the former Soviet Union, all of whom are potential future emigrants to Israel (United Nations, 1994a). In addition to admitting Jewish immigrants, Israel began to admit migrant workers in 1987, partly to reduce its dependence on Palestinian workers from Gaza and the Occupied Territories. As Table 12.12 shows, the number of foreign workers admitted by Israel has grown markedly since 1993. Migrant workers are granted temporary permits of stay and work, and are concentrated mostly in construction and agriculture. The main countries of origin of migrant workers are the Philippines, Romania and Thailand.

Table 12.12 Different types of migrant inflows to Israel, 1985–96

Year	Jewish Immigrants (000)	Non-Palestinian foreign workers (000)	Number of foreign workers in			Percentage of foreign workers in			Number			Percentage	
			Construction	Agriculture	Other	Constsruction	Agriculture	Other	Palestinian workers	Construction	Agriculture	Construction	Agriculture
1985	106	—	—	—	—	—	—	—	892	425	141	47.6	15.8
1986	98	—	—	—	—	—	—	—	947	456	148	48.2	15.6
1987	130	25	—	—	—	—	—	—	1,089	497	158	45.6	14.5
1988	130	33	—	—	—	—	—	—	1,094	542	167	49.5	15.3
1989	240	34	—	—	—	—	—	—	1,049	561	142	53.5	13.5
1990	1,992	42	—	—	—	—	—	—	1,077	641	126	59.5	11.7
1991	1,761	81	—	—	—	—	—	—	978	670	117	68.5	12.0
1992	771	77	—	—	—	—	—	—	1,156	859	104	74.3	9.0
1993	768	96	33	17	46	34.4	17.7	47.9	838	608	86	72.6	10.3
1994	800	302	195	50	57	64.6	16.6	18.9	467	298	50	63.8	10.7
1998	76	689	485	122	82	70.4	17.7	11.9	406	268	37	66.0	9.1
1996	688	1,030	753	169	108	73.1	16.4	10.5	191	—	—	—	—

Source: Bartram (1998), Tables 1, 2 and 3.

Labour migration has been essential for the development of the oil-exporting countries of the Gulf Cooperation Council (GCC), namely, Bahrain, Kuwait, Oman, Qatar, Saudi Arabia and the United Arab Emirates. With small and largely unskilled populations, these countries lacked the human resources needed to exploit the vast oil reserves found in their territories. Consequently, they depended on foreign workers to expand oil production, especially after the 1973 rise in oil prices, and to build the infrastructure and improve the services needed by their native populations. It is estimated that between 1975 and 1990, the foreign population of the GCC countries increased from 1.9 million to 8 million. Although initially most foreign workers originated in other Arab countries, during the late 1970s a calculated diversification of labour suppliers took place and more workers from India and Pakistan began to be hired. Later, the Republic of Korea, the Philippines, Thailand, Indonesia and Sri Lanka joined the list of major labour suppliers. During the early 1980s, as oil prices declined and major construction projects were completed, the demand for foreign male workers dropped, but that for female domestic workers rose as the standard of living of nationals in the GCC countries improved. Another important change in the system took place during 1990–91, when the invasion of Kuwait by Iraq led to the repatriation of some 700,000 migrant workers. After liberation, the work of reconstruction in Kuwait again boosted the demand for foreign labour. Furthermore, political realignments associated with positions taken by various governments during the war resulted in the repatriation of important groups of foreigners, including Jordanians, Palestinians and Yemenis from Kuwait and Saudi Arabia. Egyptians were admitted to fill the public service jobs left vacant by the departure of those workers. In addition, demand for workers from Eastern and South East Asia increased (Table 12.13). During 1990–94, the number of permits issued to workers going to Western Asia reached all-time highs in Bangladesh, India, Pakistan, Sri Lanka and the Philippines. As a result of these trends, it is estimated that by 1997 there were about 10.5 million foreigners in the GCC countries (Hugo, 1999).

Table 12.13 Average annual number of migrant workers originating in the major labour-exporting countries of Asia and percentage distribution by region of destination: 1975–94

Sending country/receiving region	1975–79	1980–84	1985–89	1990–94
Eastern Asia				
China[a]				
Western Asia	—	80.1[b]	48.2	3.7[c]
Other Asia	—	6.0[b]	18.6	37.6[c]
Outside Asia	—	14.0[b]	33.3	58.6[c]
Number of clearances	—	37,600[b]	61,100	135,000[c]
Republic of Korea				
Western Asia[d]	97.3[e]	90.0	81.7[f]	50.4[c]
Other Asia	1.7[e]	8.5	12.2[f]	37.7[c]
Outside Asia	1.0[e]	1.5	6.0[f]	11.9[c]
Number of clearances (land based)	79,900[e]	142,600	52,100[f]	20,218[c]
South-central Asia				
Bangladesh				
Western Asia	88.3[g]	92.0	95.9	83.5
Other Asia	0.2[g]	1.0	0.5	15.6
Outside Asia	11.5[g]	7.0	3.6	0.9
Number of clearances (land based)	17,300[g]	53,000	78,000	174,100
India				
Western Asia	—	92.4[b]	95.8	96.0[h]
Other Countries	—	7.6[b]	4.2	4.0[h]
Number of clearances (land based)	67,000[g]	223,500[b]	139,800	297,225[h]
Pakistan				
Western Asia	87.3	97.2	99.9	99.6
Other Asia	2.7	0.0	0.0	0.2
Outside Asia	10.0	2.7	0.1	0.2
Number of clearances	90,600	124,500	76,800	143,000

Sending country/receiving region	1975–79	1980–84	1985–89	1990–94
Sri Lanka				
Western Asia	—	—	94.5[i]	95.4
Other Asia	—	—	4.3[i]	3.3
Outside Asia	—	—	1.2[i]	1.3
Number of clearances	—	31,300	18,900[i]	52,300
South-eastern Asia				
Indonesia				
Western Asia	73.7[j]	64.9	78.0	40.6[c]
Other Asia	8.5[j]	20.5	13.1	55.5[c]
Outside Asia	17.8[j]	14.6	8.9	3.9[c]
Number of clearances	10,400[j]	24,400	63,500	118,100[c]
Myanmar				
Number of clearances	—	—	8,100[k]	9,100[l]
Philippines[m]				
Western Asia[n]	67.4	84.8	71.8	61.6
Other Asia	17.7	11.2	22.5	30.6
Outside Asia	14.9	4.0	5.7	7.9
Number of clearances (land based)	42,400	274,000	353,900	471,000
Western Asia[d]	7.5	81.7	72.4	24.4
Other Asia	7.7	5.3	14.6	71.9
Outside Asia	16.9	13.1	13.0	3.7
Number of clearances	6,300	60,100	89,600	86,800

Notes: (Table 12.13)

a. Excluding Taiwan.
b. Average for 1982–84.
c. Average for 1990–91.
d. Including Libya.
e. Average for 1977–79.
f. Average for 1985–88.
g. Average for 1976–79
h. Average for 1990–93.

I. Average for 1986–89.
j. Figure for 1979.
k. Figure for 1989.
l. Figure for 1990–92.
m. Figures for 1975–79 and 1980–84 refer to those processed but not yet deployed.
n. Including Libya and Algeria.

Sources:

China: State Statistical Bureau, *China Statistical Yearbook 1996,* China Statistical Publishing House; China's Foreign Economic Relations and Trade, *Almanac of China's Foreign Economic Relations and Trade,* 1993, 1994, and 1995.

India: Ministry of Labor, *Annual Report 1994–95* (New Delhi, n.d.).

Pakistan: data supplied by Bureau of Emigration and Overseas Employment through personal communication (1995).

Philippines: Philippines Overseas Employment Administration, *Statistical Compendium 1975–87* (Manila, n.d.); Philippines Overseas Employment Administration, Comparative Overseas Employment Statistics 1992 vs. 1993, in *Overseas Employment Info Series,* Vol.7, no.1 (Manila, 1994); Battistella, Graziano, 'Data on migration from the Philippines,' *Asia and Pacific Migration Journal,* Vol.4, no.4 (Manila, 1995).

Sri Lanka: data supplied by Bureau of Foreign Employment through personal communication.

Thailand: National Statistical Office, *Quarterly Bulletin of Statistics,* various years (Bangkok).

Various countries: International Labour Organization, Regional Office for Asia and the Pacific, *Statistical Report 1990,* mimeograph; Asian Regional Programme on International Labour Migration, United Nations Development Programme—International Labour Organisation project RAS/88/029 (Bangkok, 1990), various tables; Scalabrini Migration Center, 'Trends in labour migration 1992,' *Asian Migrant* (Manila, 1993), Vol.4, no.1, various tables.

In East and South East Asia, the rising affluence of Japan and the newly industrialising economies during the 1980s converted them into attractive destinations for migrant workers from other countries in the region. Not only Hong Kong and Singapore, which had long been importers of labour, but Japan, Malaysia, the Republic of Korea and Taiwan began to absorb foreign workers destined to take the low-paying jobs that natives shunned. As Table 12.13 shows, until 1985–89 nearly three-quarters of all Thai workers had gone to Western Asia but in 1990–94, 72 per cent found employment in other Asian countries. Large increases in the proportion of migrant workers going to Asian countries other than those in Western Asia were also noticeable in the cases of Indonesia, the Philippines, the Republic of Korea and China.

Japan deserves special attention because, until the early 1980s, the country had achieved high economic growth without resorting to foreign workers. In 1975 there were 752,000 foreigners residing in Japan, 86 per cent of whom were Koreans who had been brought as forced labour during World War II and their descendants who do not have the right to Japanese citizenship. In the 1980s and especially after 1985, Japan began receiving migrant workers, many of whom remained in an irregular situation because Japanese law does not allow the admission of unskilled workers. Between 1985 and 1995, the number of legally resident foreigners rose by 60 per cent, from 851,000 to 1,362,000. Most of the growth (44 per cent) stemmed from the increase in persons originating in Asian countries, especially China, the Philippines, Thailand, Vietnam and Iran. Increases in the number of foreigners of Japanese descent originating in Brazil and Peru accounted for a further 41 per cent of the growth in the foreign stock (Zlotnik, 1998). In addition, in 1995 Japanese authorities reckoned that there were about 280,000 foreigners residing illegally in the country (they were visa overstayers).

Echoing developments in Japan, Malaysia, the Republic of Korea, Taiwan and Thailand began to experience labour shortages in the late 1980s and to attract undocumented foreign workers. In Malaysia, official statistics showed that the number of registered foreigners stood at 88,000 in the late 1980s (Abella, 1991) and a regularisation drive undertaken in 1990 led to the legalisation of 130,000 Indonesian workers (Hugo, 1992). However, the number of migrants remaining in an irregular situation is thought to remain high. Hugo (1999) reports 2.3 million for 1996, a figure that seems to be on the high side. In the Republic of Korea, the number of employment-related visas issued by the Government in 1986 surpassed for the first time the number of Korean workers departing to work abroad, when the former stood at 116,000. By 1989, the number of employment-related visas issued by the Republic of Korea reached 162,000 and the number of apprehensions of international migrants in an irregular situation was still rising (United Nations, 1994a). By 1996, the number of migrant workers in the Republic of Korea was estimated at 210,000 (Hugo, 1999). In Taiwan, the number of visa overstayers was estimated at 40,000 in 1990 (Tsai, 1991) and by 1995 the stock of foreign workers was estimated at about 300,000 (Hugo, 1999). In Thailand, rough estimates of the number of foreign workers put them at 1.3 million in 1997. In both Malaysia and Thailand, the number of migrant workers is likely to have declined as a result of the economic crisis in those countries in late 1997 and 1998, especially because of repatriation drives. However, studies of the labour situation suggest that those countries have a structural need for unskilled labour and that the financial crisis of the late 1990s would not reduce that need in the long run.

If economic dynamism has contributed to transforming the newly industrialising economies of Asia from sources to receivers of foreign labour, the same is unlikely to happen in the largest industrialising country of all, China. The economic liberalisation that the country has experienced since the late 1970s has brought about important changes in spatial mobility, though they have tended to be played out mostly within the country itself. Thus, China now recognises that rural–urban migration has been rising, and it is likely that the continued economic transformation of the country will increase such flows. China has also attempted to become a labour-exporting country, but the few statistics released indicate that only small numbers of workers have been placed temporarily abroad (Shengjin, 1995). Of greater concern is the potential for emigration from China. Already its economic success has permitted a number of persons to obtain the funds necessary to pay the costly passage to a developed country. Reports on the existence of organised criminal groups that engage in the international trafficking of migrants have become more frequent, and Chinese migrants have been smuggled into various European countries, the US and certain developing countries. The numbers detected are generally low but reliable indicators of the magnitude of trafficking are elusive. However, even in the absence of trafficking, the potential for large migration flows to originate in China and find legal means of being admitted in countries that already have important nuclei of Chinese migrants is growing, and it is a factor likely to become more salient in the future.

CONCLUSION

Over the past one hundred years, international migration has often been at the centre stage of major events that reshaped the world. The twentieth century began with a decade where transatlantic migration reached unprecedented levels and it has closed with one in which migration from developing to developed countries and from Eastern bloc countries to the West has been at a high. Since the late 1980s, as the dynamics of globalisation in the economic sphere have gained momentum and the geo-political organisation of the world has undergone a major transformation, international migration has been seen as a pervasive force that affects and is affected by those processes of change. Both the increasing economic disparities between countries that have managed to advance in the development path and those that have made little progress in that direction, and the lack of stability of states that are still in the early stages of the nation-building process, have fostered flows of international migrants attracted by better economic opportunities abroad or repelled by danger and persecution at home. With the end of the bi-polar era, the asylum regime that was constructed after the end of World War II and withstood 40 years of Cold War tensions, is being eroded. Although the revolution that ended Communist rule in Eastern and Central Europe was mostly peaceful, the bloodiness of Yugoslavia's break-up has brought again the spectre of mass displacement and large refugee flows to Europe. And the international community is still struggling to find lasting solutions to multi-ethnic conflict. The creation of Western protectorates, such as Kosovo, is unlikely to be viable in other cases and whether through civil strife or outright conflict, the root causes of refugee flows and forced population displacement are not likely to abate soon. The first decades of the twenty-first century will witness the recurrence of such events, whether as a continuation of past antagonisms or as the eruption of new ones. Increasingly, containment of the resulting flows within the region of origin will be the main strategy pursued, a strategy that may put in jeopardy the well-being of affected populations if effective means to ensure their protection are not deployed.

Economically motivated migration will almost surely continue, though not necessarily rising steadily in all contexts. As in the past, fluctuations are likely to occur, as some countries advance more than others in both the transition to lower population growth and higher development levels or suffer reverses in economic terms. Maintaining the ideal balance between labour demand and supply is not easy, and migration trends will be affected by both deficits and surpluses of labour. In the more developed countries, deficits are restricted to a few sectors of the economy even when overall unemployment levels are high. Such structural deficits are at the root of the attraction exerted by the more developed countries on unskilled workers from developing countries. Both the expected reduction of the labour force in relative terms and the continued need for workers in selected sectors of the economy are likely to fuel migration well into the twenty-first century, though receiving countries in the developed world will continue to exert pressure to keep that migration at a minimum or at least under tight control.

For, despite the increasing economic disparities among countries, the lower transportation costs, the easier access to relevant information, the expansion of trans-national networks of individuals and institutions capable of fostering migration, and the multiplication of nation-states, international migration remains a relatively rare phenomenon. From this perspective, the demise of the state as controller and decider in the migration process has been prematurely announced. Control and selectivity, both exercised by the state, are very much in operation today and, although traffickers or adventurous migrants may on occasion break the barriers in existence, those barriers still keep the majority of potential migrants out. The issue is whether the leakage that accompanies any control system can be tolerated and under what circumstances leakage may increase. In many of the more developed countries, tolerance levels have been diminishing and barriers are on the rise. The extent to which they will be effective will play a key role in determining a large part of future migration flows.

NOTES

1. The views and opinions expressed in this chapter are those of the author and do not represent those of the United Nations.
2. International migrants are defined as persons born in a country other than that in which they live.

SELECT BIBLIOGRAPHY

Abella, Manolo I. (1991), 'Manpower movements in the Asian regions', paper presented at the Second Japan–ASEAN Forum on International Labour Migration in East-Asia, organized by the United Nations University and the International Labour Organization. Tokyo, 26–27 September.

Bartram, David (1998), 'Foreign workers in Israel: history and theory', *International Migration Review*, **32** (2): 303–25.

Bureau of Immigration and Population Research, *Australian Immigration: Consolidated Statistics, 1991–1992*, No. 17 (Canberra, 1993).

Bureau of Immigration and Population Research, *Immigration Update*, September Quarter 1995 (Canberra, 1996).

Bureau of Immigration, Multicultural and Population Research, *Australian Immigration: Consolidated Statistics, 1993–1994*, No.18 (Canberra, 1995).

Citizenship and Immigration, Canada. *Immigration Statistic 1992* to *1995* (Ottawa, various years).

Della Pergola, Sergio (1997), 'The Global Context of Migration to Israel', in E. Leshem and J. Shuval (eds), *Studies in Israeli Society*, vol. VIII, New Brunswick, NJ: Transaction.

Department of Immigration, Local Government and Ethnic Affairs, *Australian Immigration: Consolidated* Statistics, various years (Canberra).

Dowty, Alan (1987), *Closed Borders*, New Haven, CT: Yale University Press.

Employment and Immigration Canada. *Immigration Statistics*, various years (Ottawa).

Gabon, Bureau Central du Recensement (nd). Recensement Général de la Population et de l'Habitat, preliminary results.

Hugo, Graeme (1992), 'Indonesian labour migration to Malaysia: trends and policy implications', paper presented to the International Colloquium on Migration, Development and Gender in Southeast Asia, Kuantan, Malaysia, 28–31 October.

Hugo, Graeme (1999), 'Key issues in international migration today: trends', in *Migration at the Threshold of the Third Millennium*, Proceedings of the IV World Congress on the Pastoral Care of Migrants and Refugees held at the Vatican, 5–10 October 1998.

Immigration and Naturalization Service, *Annual Report of the Immigration and Naturalization Service 1992* (Washington, DC, 1994).

Immigration and Naturalization Service, *Statistical Yearbook*, various years (Washington, D.C).

International Labour Office (ILO) (1936), *World Statistics of Aliens: A Comparative Study of Census Returns 1910–1920–1930*, Studies and Reports, Series O (Migration), No. 6, Geneva: International Labour Office.

Kofman, Eleonore (1999), 'Female "birds of passage" a decade later: gender and immigration in the European Union', *International Migration Review*, 23 (2): 269–99.

Kritz, Mary M. and Hania Zlotnik (1992), 'Global interactions: migration systems, processes, and policies', in Mary M. Kritz, Lin Lean Lim and Hania Zlotnik (eds), *International Migration Systems: A Global Approach*, Oxford: Clarendon Press, pp. 1–16.

Lim, Lin Lean (1994), 'International labour migration in Asia: patterns, implications, and policies', in *International Migration: Regional Processes and Responses*, United Nations Economic Commission for Europe and United Nations Population Fund, Economic Studies No. 7, (United Nations Sales No. GV.E.94.0.25).

Massey, Douglas S., Joaquin Arango, Graeme Hugo, Ali Kouaouci, Adela Pellegrino, J. Edward Taylor (1993), 'Theories of international migration: a review and appraisal', *Population and Development Review*, 19 (3): 431–66.

OECD (1998), Trends in international migration, Annual Report, Statistical Appendix, Paris: OECD.

Russian Federation (1992), 'Narodnoe Xoziaistvo 1992', Moscow: Goskomstat Russia.

Shengjin, Wang (1995), 'China's export of labor and its management', *Asian and Pacific Migration Journal*, (Manila, Philippines), 4 (2–3): 429–47.

Statistics Canada, *Annual Demographic Statistics, 1994* (Ottawa, 1995).

Trends in International Migration, Annual Report (1998), Statistical Annex (Paris, 1998).

Tsai, Hong-Chin (1991), 'Foreign workers in Taiwan: demographic characteristics, related problems, and policy implications', *Industry of Free China* (Taipei), September, 53–70.

UNHCR (United Nations High Commissioner for Refugees) (1995), *The State of the World's Refugees, 1995*, New York: Oxford University Press.

UNHCR (United Nations High Commissioner for Refugees) (1996), 'Populations of concern to UNHCR: a statistical overview', 31 December 1995, mimeograph, UNHCR: Geneva.

UNHCR (United Nations High Commissioner for Refugees) (1997), *The State of the World's Refugees: A Humanitarian Agenda*, Oxford: Oxford University Press.

UNHCR (United Nations High Commissioner for Refugees) (1998), 'Refugees and others of concern to UNHCR: 1997 statistical overview', mimeograph, Geneva: UNHCR.

UNHCR (United Nations High Commissioner for Refugees) (1999), 'Refugees and others of concern to UNHCR: 1998 statistical overview', Mimeograph, Geneva: UNHCR.

United Nations (1985), *World Population Trends, Population and Development Interrelations and Population Policies*, 1983 Monitoring Report, vol.1, Population Trends, (United Nations Publication, Sales No. E.84.XIII.10).

United Nations (1992), *World Population Monitoring 1991*, United Nations Publication, Sales No. E.92.XIII.2.

United Nations (1994a), *World Population Monitoring 1993*, (ESA/P/WP.121).

United Nations (1994b), Report of the Commissioner-General of the United Nations Relief and Works Agency for Palestine Refugees in the Near East, General Assembly. Official Records A/49/13.

United Nations (1995), 'Trends in the International Migrant Stock', Database maintained by the Population Division, United Nations.

United Nations (1998), *World Population Monitoring 1997: International Migration and Development*, United Nations Publication, Sales No. E.98.XIII.4.

United Nations Secretariat (1995), *International Migration Policies and the Status of Female Migrants*, United Nations Publication, Sales No. E.95.XIII.10.

US Census Bureau (1999), *Profile of the Foreign-Born Population in the United States: 1997*, Census Population Reports, Special Studies pp. 23–195, Washington, DC: Government Printing Office.

US Commission for the Study of International Migration and Cooperative Economic Development (1990), 'Unauthorized Migration: An Economic Development Response', Washington, D.C.: Government Printing Office.

US Immigration and Naturalization Sevice (1994), Annual Report of the Immigration and Naturalization Service 1992, Washington, DC.

US Immigration and Naturalization Service (various years), *Statistical Yearbook*, Washington, DC.

Zlotnik, Hania (1991), 'South-to-North migration since 1960: the view from the North', *Population Bulletin of the United Nations* (New York), No. 31/32: 17–37.

Zlotnik, Hania (1994), 'International Migration: Causes and Effects', in Laurie Ann Mazur (ed.), *Beyond the Numbers*, Washington, DC: Island Press, 359–77.

Zlotnik, Hania (1998), 'International migration: 1965–96: an overview', *Population and Development Review*, **24** (3): 429–68.

Zolberg, Aristide R. (1981), 'International migrations in political perspective', in Mary M. Kritz, Charles B. Keely and Silvano M. Tomasi (eds), *Global Trends in Migration: Theory and Research on International Population Movements*, Staten Island, NY: Center for Migration Studies, pp. 3–27.

13. International Personnel Movement and the Emergence of an International Migration Regime

Charles B. Keely

INTRODUCTION

The recent increase in the temporary migration of highly skilled labour has been widely noted by migration scholars.[1] The phenomenon of interest is the movement for more than brief visits by managers, engineers, and scientists. Three time-related categories of interest are persons hired in temporary statuses, typically after university graduation, but with a high probability of more or less permanent settlement; persons relocated for periods of a year or longer, typically with their families, and also typically intracompany transferees; and persons who spend shorter periods, one to six months on assignment, often providing a service that was outsourced, including highly specialised financial and business-related services (legal, consulting, insurance, and accounting services, for example).

Unlike seasonal workers or those involved in 'guestworker' programmes in post-war Europe, current workers involved in temporary migration typically have high education or advanced experience or specialised knowledge, often related to their being employees of a particular firm. Their job classifications include researcher, scientist, engineer, manager, and executive. They may also have an unusual set of skills, for example, a fluent Japanese-speaking accountant able to service Japanese companies located outside Japan.

One of the difficulties of studying the increased movement of highly-skilled personnel and trying to analyse its implications involves definition. Most analysts focus on skill level and the idea that it usually involves relocation for appreciable periods, but not necessarily permanent residence. For each of these attributes—skill and duration—there are important exceptions to the typical cases. Service workers who fulfil contracts that firms outsource to foreign companies, such as computer programmers designing, creating, and installing customised programs, may work for two or three months on a project. A lawyer, accountant, or management consultant may also spend similar periods on a project, perhaps from time to time over a long period while providing on-going services to a client. On the other hand, some global firms have programmes to train middle-level staff in such areas as financial control, facilities management, and human resources which may involve classroom training followed by a period of practical experience. The objective is to increase predictability and control of staff functions in global firms. The workers are not particularly highly skilled when relocated. The intent of the relocation, in these and other career development schemes operated by firms, is to train employees with potential for leadership in world-wide operations to move into positions of greater responsibility as a result of the overseas training experience, often at headquarters locations.

The reference to intra-company transfers highlights the important role of private sector firms in the development of this phenomenon and their continuing role in trying to influence government regulation of its development. One characteristic of the movement is that to a large extent private actors are *de facto* establishing the criteria and choosing the candidates for highly skilled international personnel movement.

While multinational firms have a long tradition of sending some personnel overseas, especially managers, more recent migration of the highly skilled seems to go well beyond management relocation to overseas facilities and subsidiaries of a key manager or two. Current initiatives in the movement of international personnel are dominated by firms that think of themselves as global, rather than multinational. Global firms make decisions about markets, manufacturing, distribution and, more recently, personnel with an eye on company goals. Attempts are made consciously not to let nationalist considerations or 'home' country or domestic operational health interfere with business decisions affecting the firm. This does not mean that there are no remnants of the originating country's corporate culture or even dominance of nationals of the originating country in top management. Ford Motor Company, which has had a British national as CEO, is still an American company in many ways, just as Siemans is German, and so on.

Global perspectives have antecedents in sectors such as oil and automobile manufacturing. The development of more globally oriented firms, however, which is related to the increases in trade as a proportion of world output, has led to sea changes in the way many large firms in a broad array of sectors see their businesses. Restructuring of economies toward services and away from manufacturing, the emergence of the so-called light economy with a heavy reliance on intellectual property for value and productivity, also has contributed to internationalising staffs and creating global outlooks. Service sectors such as finance, equities, insurance, accounting, consulting (and more recently law firms), have 'gone global', which has affected how services are delivered in both developed and developing countries. However, the phenomenon is not confined to the light economy or to industries heavily reliant on knowledge creation. Some traditional heavy industry firms are definitely competing in a global market place, including employment of international staff.

While the private sector has led in these developments, there are areas in which organisations that are part of government, or parastatal in nature, have also participated. The major sector is in research where scientists move internationally to 'world class' facilities. Examples include the European Center for Nuclear Research (CERN) in Switzerland and the National Institutes for Health in the US. In addition, university research centres continue the long tradition of internationalism in the recruitment of scientists and research faculty.

This chapter does not attempt to solve issues of scope and definition concerning the international movement of highly skilled personnel. While important, these problems should not deter attempts to determine the broad outlines of what is occurring and to begin to sketch the implications of such movements for migration policy. While lack of precision about details carries the possibility of making important mistakes, there is room to begin to analyse the contours of what is taking place in a tentative way, conscious of the preliminary nature of such attempts.

The thesis here is that the temporary movement of international personnel with high skills is altering political decision-making about international migration. There is a movement from state organs making decisions almost exclusively, toward greater involvement of regional groupings of states regulating migration of this sort. Further, we are in the initial stages of a shift of immigration policy-making toward the trade arena, in which both some states and firms seek to fold temporary migration of workers into the international trade regime, especially as part of the emerging regime of trade in services. This may signal the initial concrete elements of an international migration regime that extends beyond the refugee regime that addresses migration forced by political factors.

Experience tells us that such shifts are typically never absolute or complete. What we are witnessing will probably result in mixed decision-making, conflict about competence, and a continuous contesting between competing views and interests to locate decision-making in a context likely to result in outcomes favourable to the interests of contesting parties. The parties will include the whole panoply of states from the rich to poor, the powerful and dominant to the weaker and developing. Various regional intergovernmental structures, such as the European Union, can also be players. Additionally, non-governmental interests, often spanning international boundaries will be involved, including business firms, organised labour, and advocates about the environment and human rights.

A shift of migration into the context of trade in services may not only change decision-making about migration but also influence the mode and outcome of international trade negotiations. The Millennial round of negotiating the General Agreement on Trade and Services (GATS), and the eventual operation of the World Trade Organization (WTO), may be quite different because non-governmental parties attempt to influence outcomes in a more public set of negotiations, more open to influence by broad constituencies. The days of trade agreements fashioned in private by diplomats, trade negotiators, and a limited group of influential insiders may be history. Parallel meetings by non-governmental groups, more typically found at United Nations international conferences, may become an ordinary aspect of international trade negotiations, both at the preparatory stages and at the more formal negotiating sessions.

THE LOGIC OF EXCLUSIVE STATE REGULATION OF ECONOMIC MIGRATION

Attempts begun in the early nineteenth century by European states to control the entry of immigrants, which flowered into broad state controls in the early twentieth century, signalled the initiation of a fundamental shift in global political economy. Throughout the nineteenth century, the model of the nation state gained as the modal form of geopolitical structure. The exaltation of the nation as the legitimate basis for a claim to a state coincided with the replacement of mercantilism by liberalism as the dominant economic model for international trade. The result was a heightened concern about homogeneity within states. The mercantilist maxim, 'To rule is to populate', was seen as an insufficient guarantor of social integrity and stability within the nation state context. States gradually switched from a preoccupation with prohibiting expatriation to concern about control of entry. In the late nineteenth century, even the 'traditional immigrant' states, which leaned in the direction of being civic nations that did not heavily emphasise ethnic purity in their self-conceptions, adopted laws to exclude racially defined groups, notably Asians. Progressively, tighter restrictions on the overall number of immigrants and their ethnic origins came to characterise even those countries historically most open to immigration. The tension between the nation-state political model and the emerging dominance of liberal economic and trade models was somewhat addressed by the stronger hegemonic states of Europe and North America through colonialism, whether a formal political system or a form of economic colonialism such as the dominance relationships of the US with some countries of Latin American and the Caribbean.

The period after World War I saw the consolidation of restrictive immigration policies. It was (not merely coincidentally) the period in which the elements of an international refugee regime began to take shape with an emphasis on repatriation rather than simple absorption of migrants/refugees as was the policy norm in mercantilist theory. The political economy changes, allied with the growing acceptance of concepts like 'excess population' and 'reserve armies' to describe rural to urban migration, urban unemployment, and large-scale emigration from nineteenth century Europe, led to acceptance of the idea that international migration was normatively deviant and should lessen more and more over time. Everybody belonged somewhere (to some state) and people should reside where they belong. A corollary was that persons should be citizens of only one country. Statelessness and dual nationality were both to be minimised. One of the first European covenants after World War II had as its objective the reduction of dual nationality.

Decline in authorised international settlement migration through immigration restriction during the twentieth century led to important norms about labour and society. Immigration was to be tightly controlled. It might be allowed for family purposes of citizens, but even there the scope of familial needs of citizens was often narrowly construed. As for economic migration or immigration for labour force purposes, most countries took a minimalist view. Workers might be needed in special circumstances, like seasonal labour, and would then go home. Perhaps a temporary bottleneck in labour supply might justify temporary entry. Truly world class persons, in the arts, sciences and other learned professions, could be admitted with little detriment. In the late 1930s while the world-wide economic depression was the dominant economic reality, few states could be convinced to admit even a nominal number of politically persecuted people from Nazi racialist policies. States and their constituencies basically assumed that they were, and of right ought to be, sufficient unto themselves in labour. The role of the state in regard to immigration was to a large extent defined as protecting the jobs that rightly belonged to natives.

Towering over both familial and economic migration were policies emanating from 'scientific racism', or theories about the inherent superiority and inferiority of people classified into racial groups. The use of racial and nationality quotas and administrative methods to restrict entry by 'inferior races' who might 'pollute the gene pool' are well known. But while such theories dominated selection of immigrants and led to the wholesale restriction of various peoples, the labour policy of autarky also became deeply embedded in immigration policy thinking. A correlative was that nationals had rights to jobs within their territories and that governments were supposed to protect those jobs for their own citizens.

The implication of such thinking was a subtle, or at least largely unnoticed, parallel between restrictive trade practices and immigration law as applied to labour migration. Immigration laws that prohibit or tightly restrict entry of migrants act like non-tariff barriers in trade. They provide a subsidy to domestic labour as tariff and non-tariff barriers to trade subsidise protected industries. Recent discussions (leading up to the 1996 immigration legislation) about labour immigration in the US even included proposals to charge employers fees for temporary worker visas, even if no domestic workers could be found after government supervised market searches. The similarity of this to a tariff on the importation of goods did not seem to occur to the protagonists.

Similarly, governments were supposed to protect native jobs by not entering into trade agreements that encouraged the transfer of operations to overseas locations. In the US, the Reform Party presidential candidate in 1992, Ross Perot, joined by others in mainstream parties and organised labour, criticised the North American Free Trade Agreement (NAFTA) by referring to 'a giant sucking sound' of jobs being pulled south into Mexico. Similar criticisms about loss of jobs to the US were heard in Canada in reference to the NAFTA predecessor agreement between Canada and the US. Protectionist stances continue to be voiced during national elections and legislative debates about international trade policy. Little of this sort of criticism seems to have emerged within the European Union's history, toward Italy in the 1950s and 1960s or more recently toward Spain and Portugal. Perhaps the focus on creating a more inclusive single market, along with the political implications of deepening the EU, meant that the goal of strengthening all the economies deflected criticism away from nationalist approaches about loss of jobs and focused it more on transfers to the weaker member states.

There is a fundamental notion in many countries that there is no need demographically or normatively for immigrants to fill jobs. Labour 'need' is presented by proponents of labour autarky as an economic variable. They argue that one need only to get the price right and there will be sufficient domestic workers. Against the backdrop of presumed labour self-sufficiency, the power of the market to get the price of labour right would work better without the interference of admitting foreign labour. This scenario seemed normal rather than a view that immigration regulation was government interference in the free market. Normatively, liberal immigration was seen as government intervention in the labour market which would serve to undercut domestic wages and working conditions, disciplining the domestic workforce to the advantage of capital. A contrasting view is that any government regulation of immigration, no matter how generous and open, is interference in the market. The conclusion of such a view, parallel to liberal trade theory, is minimal government regulation of immigration. Even for supporters of liberal trade regimes, minimally regulated immigration is not taken as a serious policy option. Even a dual policy goal of facilitation of access by firms to needed labour and protection of domestic labour was seen as a radical and a slippery slope to creating unemployment by allowing cheap labour to displace citizens from their jobs.

Any analogy between tariff and non-tariff trade barrier and immigration regulation must take notice of a crucial difference between free trade and free migration. Migrants are moral actors who enter society, play important roles, and begin to make social demands based on their humanity, their presence, and their economic contributions. Video recorders, automobiles, and food staples do not do this. Thus, there may be important social reasons for government regulation of migration that go beyond economic criteria. The ideology underlying immigration control and restriction of labour-related migration, however, was not typically articulated as a social policy. The reason, of course, was that the articulation of social considerations could easily skirt very close to racist ideas or other invidious comparisons. The experience of World War II, and the general repudiation of racist ideas as manifest justifications for government policy, meant that policy debate by proponents of control tended to focus on economic reasoning, rather than arguments about social cohesion and the effects of immigration on society and political life. This did not mean that such calculations and considerations were absent. Their articulation, however, was avoided. When they emerged, their appearance, in guises such as referenda against 'over-foreignisation', were politically embarrassing and a source of political divisiveness.

Firms engaged in global operations challenge the fundamental assumption of the labour autarky view. Global firms maintain that in order to operate and compete, they need to have international labour forces for many of their operations and as a strategy for socialising executives to assume ever greater responsibilities. Global firms use examples like economies of scale in locating research and development facilities in a single place, or in a few locations, and attracting the scientific and engineering skills to those places. Such a strategy may require periodic relocations of R&D team members when innovation is translated in manufacturing. For example, research on motor technology for an appliance firm may be in a European country, and carried on by an international R&D team. A breakthrough in motor noise reduction may mean that various team members disburse to manufacturing plants in many countries to integrate the innovation into manufacturing.

Similarly, design of a product for multiple country introduction or a marketing plan for simultaneous introduction of a new product in many markets, would both require international teams. Global firms contend that the nature of such work requires international groups, and reject the view that assembling such a group in a country robs natives of jobs, as an outdated view of business. So too, do service providers who are advising on projects that cross international boundaries and involve different state laws, regulatory bodies, and review procedures need international specialist teams. Finally, global firms want executives that have international experience and understanding of the global aspects of the sector and firm's specific place in international business.

Employers pursuing global human resource policies have used domestic law to allow them to achieve their ends to a great extent. There has been an increase in temporary international movement of personnel. The transition has not necessarily been smooth and firms feel that they encounter delays, roadblocks, and arbitrary decisions by various layers of government bureaucracies whose officials continue to operate within a labour autarky framework for immigration decision-making.

Employers have moved on three fronts: domestic law changes; regional economic integration agreements; and international trade negotiations. International legal firms that specialise in international personnel movement are quite proud of their databases about laws in various countries about visas, work permits, residence permits, licences, registrations, and other requirements for personnel relocation. Law firms no longer confine themselves to assisting in getting a work visa in their own country for their clients. They have expanded in two directions as providers of expert advice and assistance in human resource relocation. They help, through various partnering arrangements with law firms in other countries, to provide for visas to a wide range of countries. Second, they realise that the work visa is often only the first step in a series of administrative requirements to allow a worker and his or her family to relocate.

When major obstacles inhibit the achievement of global human resource objectives, global firms and their legal allies seek to change national regulations that impede movement and have little rationale other than tradition. The business justification typically notes changed business conditions in a global economy. Migration policies based on protecting citizen jobs exclusively (autarky) are labelled as outmoded and actually harmful in the long run to the domestic labour market. Labour autarky policies, it is argued, stifle innovation, impede reaction to market opportunities, and reduce competitiveness of national firms in a global market.

REGIONAL ECONOMIC INTEGRATION

The second focus of global firms wishing to facilitate international personnel movement is regional trade agreements. The most notable arrangement in this regard is the European Union (EU) and its predecessors, the European communities arrangements (Christian, 1999). The European Economic Area (EEA) arrangements allowed quite similar access to labour markets by citizens of European Free Trade Area (EFTA) states that chose to do so to EU member states. The original vision of the EU included free movement of goods, capital, services, and people. The people component has had a checkered history (Russell, et al., 1999). Currently, citizens of an EU member can freely relocate residence and take a job in another member state. Third country nationals legally resident in an EU state, however, may not freely relocate or enter the job market of another member state.

Similar arrangements have been included in other regional economic integration and trade agreements. A notable success in terms of free movement has been the common Nordic labour area, agreed to in 1954 and with amendments in 1982. Less successful have been agreements among developing countries, such as those in the Caribbean, among the Mercosur in South America, and the Central American trade agreements. While the goal of free labour mobility has been embraced in these agreements, actual implementation has fallen far short of interstate mobility. Successful interstate movement of labour within regional trade or economic integration agreements seems to require state participants with fairly robust economies and similar levels of development.

The NAFTA provides an example that falls between the EU and agreements in developing countries. The US trade negotiators had little desire to include wholesale provisions about free movement of labour in the NAFTA agreement because of internal immigration politics. There were provisions that allowed for movement of very limited classes of skilled labour with a special visa designation of TN (for temporary entrant). Even in this case, the agreement was more generous toward Canada in the number of entries, which were limited in the case of Mexico over a period to end in 2004.

Regional agreements about trade or economic integration have generally not been restricted to merely the highly-skilled sectors of the labour force. NAFTA is the exception to this general characteristic, a situation related to the economic disparity of Mexico and the US and its implications for domestic immigration politics in the US and in Mexico–US relations. Regional integration agreements, however, do move migration decision-making about access of foreigners out of the domestic sphere exclusively. The goal is to integrate economies for efficiency of markets and greater productivity and growth for all members. The focus is not so much on micromanaging labour markets as to opening up markets to allow for factor mobility with its presumed beneficial effects for all economies involved. The lack of operational success in developing countries, and the NAFTA example, can be interpreted as labour protectionism rearing its head because of domestic fears of losing jobs, which gets translated into limiting, by regulation or otherwise, free access of labour.

TRADE IN SERVICES AND MOVEMENT OF THE HIGHLY SKILLED

The most recent development in global labour mobility policy has been the focus by firms and some labour supplying countries on access of 'natural persons' in international trade agreements affecting services, and the attendant spillover of arrangements for labour mobility in the provision of services.[2]

Trade in services as of 1997 represented $1.3 billion in export value. This was about twenty per cent of the total value of all exports and was an increase of over twenty-five per cent between 1994 and 1997. The Uruguay Round of negotiations on the General Agreement on Trade in Services led to signing of the agreements in Marrakesh in April 1994. Four service topics remained uncompleted at the end of the Uruguay Round: market access in financial services, basic telecommunications, maritime transportation, and the movement of persons in the provision of services. Negotiations on movement of natural persons resumed in May 1994 and ended July 1995 with commitments attached to the Third Protocol of the GATS.

Trade in services is divided in the GATS into four modes. The first is cross-border supply of services from one country to another. The second is consumption abroad in which the service is supplied in the territory of the service supplier to the consumer from another country. The third is commercial presence whereby a supplier locates in another country and supplies the service locally (e.g., a branch office of a merchant bank or consulting firm). The fourth is the presence of natural persons in which the service supplier's employee travels from the country of the supplier to another country for a temporary period to supply the service.

Some developing countries were interested in access of lesser-skilled persons, in construction for example. But developing countries also had appreciable numbers of well-qualified professionals who could provide services in the international market. Some of these states also noted that their firms lacked the capital to establish a commercial presence through branch offices and subsidiaries (the third mode). Developed countries, and especially the Quad (US, EC [the EU is called the European Communities in WTO business], Japan, and Canada) were requested to expand their positions on the fourth mode. The US responded that the 65,000 visas for temporary professional level workers under the H-1B program would be 'bound' (that is, committed as a minimum that would be difficult to change).[3]

The negotiations had modest success. With innumerable qualifications, one can generally say that three categories of temporary business migrants are listed (in their schedules reported to the WTO that a state is willing to bind itself about). Business visitors entering for short stays (typically for up to 90 days) to do business that does not include sales to the general public or supplying a service for pay is the first group. This is the continuation of general practice for business to business sales, negotiations about sales, mergers, partnering, joint ventures, and so on. The second group is intracompany transfers of executives, senior managers, and specialists with uncommon knowledge of the firm and its business. Again, many countries have provisions for such transfers. There is, however, no common definition of executive, senior, manager, uncommon, and so on. Country by country practice differs and is influenced by firms' impact on legislators and regulators that affect decisions. Countries also differ about whether accompanying spouses may enter the labour force and ages of children permitted to reside with parents. The area is clearly of interest to corporations as a topic for further work to achieve comparability and predictability for human resource decisions. The third group is qualified professionals and practitioners. Of concern here is whether prohibitions about service provision are imposed not by immigration regulation but by licensing or other forms of qualifications, recognition. Doctors, architects, accountants, lawyers, engineers, and many other professions are affected. A WTO working party is looking at ways to avoid use of licensing, technical standards, and other methods as an indirect way to erect barriers to trade.

The new round of negotiations on GATS in Seattle in November 1999, and its preparation, was to be the site for activity on the part of states and global firms to focus on greater specificity and common agreement about details in definition, scope of coverage, and avoidance of backdoor methods of using red tape to frustrate the terms of the trade agreement. The new public activism regarding trade issues all but crippled the process and little headway was made. Political activism related to global trade has continued at meetings of the World Bank and International Monetary Fund in April 2000 in Washington and at the meetings of the Organization of American States in June 2000 in Canada.

A second gambit by global firms is to develop model legislation to be accepted by states either individually or within the trade framework concerning the international migration of labour. The focus of global firms is clearly on executive, managerial, and R&D personnel with high-level qualifications. This includes the by-now familiar intra-company transferees. It also includes new hires, especially of recent graduates with advanced degrees. The strategy comes to a large extent from US corporations and their legal advisors who adopt an accustomed model developed because of the separate jurisdictions on many legal matters in the 50 states of the United States. Model laws are developed and presented to state legislatures for adoption. Thus, separate jurisdictions operate, in effect, with the same or very similar law about an issue. Translated into the international arena, the hope is that a common legal model, with standard definitions and provisions, will be adopted as metropolitan law by states. Common practice and uniform procedures will be typical, rather than a welter of different laws, rules, definitions, appeals processes, and so on. This would reduce legal barriers to transfers within companies, and other forms of temporary movement of the highly skilled. A strategy of a model laws is clearly compatible with an objective of lowering barriers to the trade in services.

A hurdle for any private sector initiative to affect interstate agreements on trade or the movement of international personnel is the simple difference in interests among firms, among states, and between firms and states. It has been already noted that some developing states had interests in the temporary movement of lesser skilled workers, for example, in construction. To press such demands, they have proposed linking movement of natural persons with greater access for financial services.

Further, US companies want access to new graduates from US universities who are not citizens. Often temporary visas are either convenient or preferred for these hires. This is different from interests about intra-company transfers which are more broadly shared with firms in many countries where foreign students in domestic universities are not targeted by firms for entry-level recruitment of the highly educated.

The drive for greater openness to temporary migration and to facilitation of such movement by common laws, trade agreements, and so on is not being pursued by either countries or firms whose interests and objectives are identical. It is not merely nationalist trade restrictionists who may prevent the attainment of agreements to allow greater and more predictable movement of personnel internationally among state-bounded labour markets.

CONCLUSION

The outcome of the increased incorporation of temporary movement of personnel within the global trade regime or wide adoption by states of model legislation or significant parts of model laws will be the initial stages of an international migration regime. There seems to be no reason to presume that such a regime, if developed in the area of labour migration, will be extended to family migration. More likely are separate migration regimes that cover refugees and temporary labour migration, while family migration remains firmly embedded within traditional state control. Because we are only in what may become the initial stages of a regime, it is too early to say whether the regime will be confined only to temporary movement and to persons of more or less high qualifications.

What seems to be true, however, is that decision-making about some forms of labour migration (especially temporary movement by the highly skilled) is being contested and the direction seems to be that legal competence in this policy area will move beyond exclusive nation state control. Not all together surprisingly to students of international migration in the twentieth century, the topic continues to evolve and there are challenges ahead for another generation of migration scholars to document and analyse.

NOTES

1. For some of the US literature see Lindsay (1999), and Keely (1998), and the bibliographics and references cited there. For Europe, Salt has been writing for years about the movement and the recent growth taking place. See also Straubhaar (1998). The literature grows constantly.
2. The reference to 'natural persons' refers to mode four in the GATS agreement concerning provision of services. The reference is to humans, as opposed to corporate legal persons, and to the fact that some services require the presence of a person to deliver the service.
3. Press Brief, Movement of Natural Persons. This is an unpaginated press release from the WTO web site (http://www.wto.org/wto/archieves/natpers.htm). The quotation and much of the summary here is taken from the brief. A legal footnote

yet to play itself out is that the US Congress has jealously guarded its prerogatives in the field of immigration legislation. It may not react kindly to the realization that trade negotiators have inhibited, at least, their capacity to reduce the H-1 programme if they should ever desire to do so.

REFERENCES

Christian, Bryan Paul (1999), 'Comparative study: policies and programs for the admission of highly skilled foreign workers in Europe', working paper, Institute for the Study of International Migration, Georgetown University.

Keely, Charles B. (1998), *Globalization and Human Resource Managemene*, New York: Center for Migration Studies.

Lindsay, Lowell B. (ed.) (1999), *Foreign Temporary Workers in America*, Westport, CT: Quorum Books.

Russell Sharon Stanton, Charles B. Keely, and Bryan Paul Christian (1999), 'Multilateral diplomacy to harmonize asylum policy in Europe: 1984–1993', unpublished paper, Institute for the Study of International Migration, Georgetown University.

Straubhaar, Thomas (1998), 'Experience with temporary workers: some evidence from selected European countries', Third International Metropolis Conference, Zichron Yakov, Israel.

14. Compelled to Move: the Rise of Forced Migration in Sub-Saharan Africa

Sally E. Findley

INTRODUCTION

Although Sub-Saharan Africa has a long history of migrations, recent decades have seen huge increases in the numbers and types of migrations. Post-colonial economic forces and the economic recession of the 1980s were associated with a dramatic increase in labour migrations, especially circular and seasonal migrations. Between 1970 and 1990, millions of Africans were migrating between communities within the borders of their country, with an estimated 130 million lifetime migrants in 1990 accounting for about twenty per cent of the total population (Findley, 1997). International migrations also have been on the rise in Sub-Saharan Africa. By the end of the 1980s, there were an estimated 30 million voluntary international migrants in Sub-Saharan Africa, accounting for about 3.5 per cent of the total population (Russell, 1993). At any given time, this stream of economically-motivated, voluntary migrants has included persons forced by drought or political battles. During some years, the numbers forced to move due to drought and other environmental disasters reached hundreds of thousands, as in the Sahel and Southern Africa after the droughts of 1983–85 (Findley, et al., 1995; Milazi, 1995). Until the recent decade, these forced migrants had been substantially outnumbered by voluntary migrants, but the 1990s has seen an unparalleled increase in numbers of forced migrants fleeing conflict and the destruction of their communities. By the mid-1990s, refugees and internally displaced persons in some countries outnumbered voluntary emigrants by more than two to one.

This rise in forced migration has had great repercussions for the structure of communities receiving the forced migrants. The circumstances of departure and settlement of the forced migrant differ so vastly from those of the labour migrant that there can be little expectation that they will quickly adapt and find economic niches in the same way. When the forced migrant fails to find an economic niche, there is no home that he/she can return to, and choices for onward movement are limited. Nor can the forced migrant expect to receive food and shelter indefinitely.

Just as governments and communities learned throughout the 1970s and 1980s how to cope with rural-urban migrants and facilitate their accommodation (Findley, 1979; Simmons, 1979; Fuchs and Demko, 1979; Laquian, 1979), it is possible for governments, communities, and organisations to take steps that will enable forced migrants to become accepted, productive members of communities. Some may be able to return home; others may not. Some may stay in the country of asylum against the wishes of the country or the refugees. As with voluntary migrants, some solutions may not be immediately obvious or be the ones preferred by all groups. But we expect that forced migrants will be equally pragmatic, and seek compromises which help them get some of what they need without incurring great cost to their families and their old and new communities.

TRENDS IN FORCED AND VOLUNTARY MIGRATIONS

Throughout the last two decades, increasing numbers of African countries have been engulfed by violent political conflicts or outright civil wars as ethnic groups competed for hegemony and control of vital resources in the post-colonial period. In the 1960s, refugees came from only eight countries, those governed by white minority governments or which had been Portuguese colonies (Kibreab, 1985). By 1996, refugees were fleeing conflict in 21 Sub-Saharan African countries (UNHCR, 1997).

The rising tide of violence in post-Cold War, Sub-Saharan Africa removed the element of choice for millions of internal migrants. By the mid-1990s, millions of Africans had sought refuge in communities outside the areas of conflict. In 1995, 14 countries had significant internally displaced populations (Cohen and Deng, 1998). Many of the internally displaced are farmers and pastoralists who seek refuge in other rural areas outside the conflict zone, hoping to return when the conflict simmers down. However, when massive numbers are involved, many are forced to move to the cities. During periods of intense civil war, many capital cities have been inundated with 'urban refugees' fleeing the rural conflicts (UNHCR, 1997).

Droughts and other extreme forms of environmental degradation exacerbate the plight of farmers in conflict zones. Away from the conflict, many families have found ways of coping with drought which allowed them to maintain their home, at least as a base, while some members migrate to work in less affected zones (Findley, 1994; McCann, 1987; Bratton, 1987). Thus, the migration response to drought is usually a differentiation of internal and voluntary international migrations, except in the case of major droughts in 1983–85 and 1992, when adjustments inside the country were not sufficient. During the 1992 drought, thousands were forced to leave Zimbabwe and other parts of Southern Africa to avoid starvation (Richmond,

1993). When drought occurs in an area already experiencing political instability and conflict, food relief systems do not function and people have no choice but to leave the country, as in Sudan and Somalia during the 1990s droughts (Otunno, 1992). These drought refugees are also likely to go to the cities because opportunities for farming are necessarily limited by the drought. Another category of environmental refugee is persons forced out of their homes by development projects, such as the construction of dams and governmental irrigation projects (Cernea, 1995).

Economic forces have simultaneously been affecting options for international migrants, both voluntary and forced. Throughout the last two decades, African governments have confronted the economic shambles left in the wake of structural adjustment programmes and global recession. During the 1980s, most African countries experienced negative economic growth (United Nations, 1998b) and could no longer afford to offer jobs to immigrants who were perceived as competing with their own citizens. By 1995, over one-third of the African countries had abandoned their 1980s non-interventionist policies towards immigration. Djibouti, Malawi, Zambia, Gabon, South Africa, Côte d'Ivoire, and Gambia took steps to restrict immigration and encourage international migrants to go home (United Nations, 1998b). Others, responding to political pressures, asked immigrants to leave (for example, Senegal sending Mauritanians home). This climate of xenophobia, together with visible constriction of economic opportunities, led to a decline in economically motivated international migrations within the continent.

In addition, recent decades have witnessed an increase in internal conflicts in countries and regions previously relatively unaffected by civil war (Adekanye, 1998). Hopes for peaceful transitions of leadership and resolution of disagreement over resource allocations were dashed in one country after another when disagreements turned violent. Further, unlike historical border skirmishes that have long troubled several Sub-Saharan African nations (for example, Chad), these conflicts were of such intensity and duration that they seriously disrupted settlements and livelihoods. Political unrest and civil war in Togo, Liberia, Senegal, and Sierra Leone forced hundreds of thousands of persons out of their homes and into neighbouring countries. Ethnic conflicts over control of the best agricultural land, oil, diamonds, and other precious resources, sparked battles and created refugee flows in Rwanda, Burundi, Kenya, Sudan, Ethiopia, and Somalia (Oucho, 1996).

As a result of these transformations in the migration landscape, the 1990s had become a decade of massive displacement for many African countries. Tables 14.1 and 14.2 contain the latest estimates of numbers of forced and voluntary migrants. While at times the distinction between forced and voluntary may seem artificial, it is nonetheless an important distinction that has been used in traditional assessments of international migrants, and is

Table 14.1 Total migrations by type of migration and origin

Region	Country of Origin	Refugees 1996	Internally Displaced 1994–97	All Forced Migrants	Total Emigrants Circa 1986	Forced/ Voluntary
East Africa &	Burundi	425,289	882,900	1,308,189	65,633	19.9
Horn of Africa	D.R. Congo	122,743	504,000	626,743	79,774	7.9
	Congo	—	—	—	71,786	—
	Djibouti	18,000	—	18,000	—	—
	Eritrea	328,307	6,000	334,307	—	—
	Ethiopia	51,467	65,000	116,467	—	—
	Kenya	8,678	120,000	128,678	127,071	1.0
	Madagascar	—	—	—	13,701	—
	Malawi	—	—	—	57,940	—
	Rwanda	460,304	1,200,000	1,660,304	209,703	7.9
	Somalia	482,118	1,170,000	1,652,118	—	—
	Sudan	460,140	4,000,000	4,460,140	65,959	67.6
	Tanzania	—	—	—	68,416	—
	Uganda	22,714	400,000	422,714	4,900	86.3
Middle Africa	Cameroon	—	—	—	9,970	—
	C. African Rep.	—	—	—	19,532	—
	Chad	50,057	—	50,057	46,610	1.1
	Gabon	—	—	—	1,409	—
Western Africa	Benin	—	—	—	75,957	—
	Burkina Faso	—	—	—	956,657	—
	Côte d'Ivoire	—	—	—	73,129	—
	Ghana	12,285	192,000	204,285	76,917	2.7
	Guinea-Bissau	—	—	—	31,016	—
	Guinea	—	—	—	246,325	—
	Liberia	776,268	1,190,000	1,966,268	11,612	169.3
	Mali	54,928	100,000	154,928	413,975	0.4
	Mauritania	80,794	200,000	280,794	22,967	12.2
	Niger	10,181	—	10,181	59,316	0.2
	Nigeria	—	—	—	245,620	—
	Senegal	66,000	5,000	71,000	81,265	0.9
	Sierra Leone	120,001	800,000	920,001	7,022	131.0
	Togo	20,258	—	20,258	262,082	0.1
Southern Africa	Angola	238,108	1,300,000	1,538,108	38,458	40.0
	Botswana	—	—	—	57,745	—
	Lesotho	—	—	—	137,375	—
	Mozambique	33,202	30,000	63,202	76,449	0.8
	Namibia	—	—	—	52,709	—
	South Africa	—	500,000	500,000	22,829	21.9
	Swaziland	—	—	—	36,649	—
	Zambia	—	—	—	21,168	—
	Zimbabwe	—	—	20,001	147,370	0.1
Total		3,841,842	12,964,900	16,806,742	3,997,016	4.2

Sources:

For Refugees: UNHCR (1997).

For IDP's: UNHCR (1997) for Burundi, Liberia, Sierra Leone, and Somalia. Remaining countries from J. Hampton (1998).

For Emigrants: Russell (1993).

continued here with recognition that the realities are not as clearly differentiated as the terms imply.

Forced migrants are those *compelled* to move by political or environmental crises, and include refugees whose flight takes them across the border, thus making them a special category of international migrant, and internally displaced, whose flight takes them to another district or region in their home country. Most are fleeing generalised violence and human rights abuses in which whole groups of persons are targeted and forced to flee in order to find safety. Economic and environmental crises often coexist with the conflict and abuse and exacerbate the insecurity and impossibility of staying (UNHCR, 1997; Cuny and Hill, 1999). Refugees conform to the 1951 Convention relating to the Status of Refugees, namely that they have a well-founded fear of being persecuted in the country of origin for reasons of race, religion, nationality, membership of a particular social group or political opinion (United Nations, 1998a). In Africa, the Organization of African Unity (OAU) has modified the definition of refugee to include persons who are compelled to leave their habitual residence due to external aggression, occupation, foreign domination or other events seriously disturbing public order (Oucho, 1996; United Nations, 1998a). If this definition is interpreted to allow for generalised violence at the community of origin, many of the internally displaced would also conform to the refugee definition.

In contrast, voluntary migrants are persons who exercise *some freedom of choice* in moving to another location, usually motivated by economic realities. They include foreigners admitted for education, training, or employment; migrants for family reunification or for family formation; and migrants for settlement or retirement. International labour migrants are a well-known example of the voluntary migrant, leaving their home to work either seasonally or for extended periods in a foreign labour market (United Nations, 1998a).

In reality, the distinction between a forced and voluntary migrant is often blurred. The root causes of armed conflicts are often economic, involving a struggle to gain control over limited, precious economic resources. Countries with dismal and deteriorating economic situations, rising unemployment, rampant inflation, and declining living standards are particularly at risk for political chaos, complex emergencies, and forced migrations (UNHCR, 1997). Many forced migrants, including those who are internally displaced, have faced economic stress for long periods prior to their departure, so that actual flight can be seen as the culmination of an extended period of economic duress in the face of insurmountable conflicts. Many Sierra Leonians fleeing during their country's prolonged civil war fell into this category of economic and political duress. The professional Ugandans who fled Uganda during the Amin years are another example of mixed voluntary and forced migrants, whose departure was hastened by impending economic demise and threatened murder if they stayed (Oucho, 1996). In contrast, some voluntary migrants move precipitously in the face of a crop failure or localised crisis, their move having some of the compulsion elements of forced migration. Drought-related migrations from the Sahel are another example of these voluntary-forced migrants (Adepoju, 1996).

Recognising that there are elements of compulsion and choice for both forced and voluntary migrants is essential to the message of this chapter, namely that these migrants may share more commonalities than might be apparent on the surface. Nonetheless, their situations are different, particularly in terms of the forced migrant's access to the society and resources of the host country or region. Forced migrants lack the resources and networks that are so vital to the success of voluntary migrants. In addition, there are different national and international protocols for responding to forced migrants, particularly refugees, and statistical systems report on forced and voluntary migrants separately. Studies conducted throughout the 1990s highlight the marked rise in refugees in Sub-Saharan Africa, a continent known for its large number of environmental refugees (Adepoju, 1998). Therefore, the tables in this chapter differentiate forced and voluntary migrants, any murkiness of their differential definitions not withstanding.

To properly understand international migration, we need to consider numbers from a dual perspective: country of origin and host or destination country. Large numbers coming from each country signal areas where expulsive forces are greatest, where steps need to be taken to reduce the exodus. Countries with disproportionately large numbers of immigrants, on the other hand, are areas where steps need to be taken to facilitate the reception and settlement of migrants.

Unfortunately, there is no standard data source of migration estimates by origin and destination. International migration statistics come from a variety of sources, each with its weaknesses in terms of coverage and accuracy. The systems for assessing international and internal migrations are incomplete at best. While countries may register arrivals, they do not systematically register departures. Further, countries do not have continuously observed borders, whole segments of which can involve undocumented crossings. Even among those officially counted, there are many who arrive as businessmen, tourists, or family visitors, and not for purposes of establishing a permanent residence in the host country. Not all who cross are migrants, forced or voluntary. For this reason, statisticians have relied on an alternative method for assessing migration status, namely questions asked about place of birth and/or place of residence five years ago. The difficulty with this method is that it captures the migrant after settlement in the destination, and to obtain a complete count of migration from a specific country, all potential destinations need to be completely surveyed. Inevitably, for one reason or another, the documentation based on questions asked at the destination miss some emigrants. An alternative to the survey at the destination is a survey conducted at the place of origin. While this does not capture the entire families who have emigrated, it does allow family members at the origin to report on previous migrations by individual family members. In addition, a survey at the place of origin will include returned migrants and circular migrants, who can report on the migrations they have undertaken prior to their latest return to the place of origin.

While the tables presented contain the most current and comprehensive estimates available at time of writing, it must be emphasised that these *are* only estimates. Most estimates of numbers of forced migrants are flow statistics, which do not accurately indicate total in flight over an extended period. The estimates of forced migrants, both refugees and internally displaced, are probably the most incomplete being based on observation of refugee flows at particular locations by non-government organisations and government agencies concerned with their reception and welfare. Forced migrants who do not go to areas covered by such programmes would not be captured in the assessment, nor would persons crossing the border at unmanned observation points. Finally, only rarely do estimates of refugees include information on repatriation and return. For areas with little repatriation or movement, refugee statistics begin to resemble stock data, as persons still in the designated area could be counted again during their second year of residence. In contrast, voluntary migration statistics may be either flow or stock statistics. Estimates of emigrants by country of origin are flow estimates, based on the countries' estimates from border crossings and internal surveys. Estimates of voluntary immigrants are stock estimates, obtained from the question in censuses on foreign birth. The estimates resulting from surveys conducted at the place of origin will miss persons who were members of entire families who departed, persons from regions not included in the survey, and persons who moved and returned before the survey was conducted. Estimates based on censuses or surveys conducted at the place of destination will yield an accurate estimate of all migrants, namely all foreign born, but will not accurately estimate migrant flows in any given year unless the estimate includes only persons arriving in the past year or five years. Because undocumented and internally displaced migrants are not eager to be observed and counted, they are less likely to be captured by the survey, and the numbers are likely to be underestimates. Use of border statistics will generate large numbers, because of the inclusion of traders, students and others making visits but not migrating, as in the case of some Francophone African countries requiring exit visas.

Table 14.1 contains estimates of forced and voluntary migrations by country of origin. The estimates of refugees are from the UNHCR (1997), as reported in the 1997 report on the state of the world's refugees. These estimates derive from annual reports from government and non-government sources active in areas receiving refugees. The refugee group includes persons who met the 1951 Convention standards for definition as a refugee, as well as others may not meet that definition but are granted temporary protection or admission for humanitarian reasons. Estimates of internally displaced persons are taken from the UNHCR or from Earthscan's Global Survey of Internally Displaced Persons, 1998. Both sets of estimates vary from year to year as conflicts wax and wane, and migrations go up and down. Finally, the emigration statistics for the preceding decade were reported by Russell (1993), and use a variety of census, survey, and government statistics which varied by country.

Table 14.2 contains the estimates of immigrants by type of migration and host or destination country. The voluntary migration estimates are based on the 1998 electronic database 'Trends in Total Migrant Stock by Sex', prepared by the United Nations Population Division and based on census or survey sources. The voluntary migration total reported in Table 14.2 excludes refugee stocks included in this database for each country. The refugee estimates are drawn from the 1997 UNHCR report, supplemented where the United Nations refugee stock estimate was available in the absence of a UNHCR estimate.

Table 14.1 also contains the numbers of forced and voluntary emigrants by country of origin. In 1996, there were 16.8 million forced migrants, including 3.8 million refugees and 13.0 million internally displaced persons. Countries which reported having a high level of refugees leaving were also likely to have a high level of internally displaced persons. More than 100,000 persons had fled each of the following countries as refugees: Burundi, Democratic Republic of Congo, Eritrea, Rwanda, Somalia, Sudan, Liberia, Sierra Leone, and Angola. Together, these nine countries accounted for 89 per cent of all refugees. These countries also had at least 100,000 internally displaced persons, with the exception of Eritrea. The number of forced migrants exceeded a million in Burundi, Rwanda, Somalia, Sudan, Liberia, and Angola, with Sierra Leone almost in this category. Several additional countries had high levels (>100,000) of internal displacement, without a correspondingly high level of refugee flight: Kenya, Uganda, Ghana, Mali, Mauritania, and South Africa. No longer were refugees concentrated in Southern Africa and the Horn of Africa, with their history of civil war and battles for political hegemony. In the 1990s, refugees could be found throughout the continent.

High levels of 1986 emigration were not associated with high levels of 1996 forced migration. If anything, there is an inverse relation. In 1996, Burkina Faso, Guinea, Nigeria, and Lesotho had very high levels of economic/voluntary emigration but no refugees or internally displaced. In the mid-1980s, Angola, Liberia and Sierra Leone had very low levels of economic/voluntary emigration, but then experienced sharp reversals in the numbers of persons leaving, as refugees flooded over the borders fleeing conflict. Burundi, the Democratic Republic of Congo, Sudan, Mauritania, and South Africa also went from fairly low levels of economic/labour emigration to high levels of forced migration, including refugees. Mali had high levels of economic emigration in the 1980s, but then experienced major displacement and refugee flight in the 1990s as conflicts escalated in the northern zone of the country.

The forces driving refugees and other forced migrants may have underlying economic components similar to those driving labour migrants, but in itself labour migration in no way predicts whether the country will subsequently experience the violent paroxysms of conflict and refugee flight. In only a handful of countries did 1986 voluntary migrations come close to or exceed forced migrations observed in 1996 (Kenya, Chad, Mali, Niger, Senegal, Togo, Mozambique, and Zimbabwe). In most countries with groups fleeing conflict, there were on average four times more forced migrants than economic/voluntary emigrants (assuming the economic/voluntary emigration rate continued at least at the same level into the 1990s, refer to the last column, Table 14.1). In several countries, the ratio of forced to voluntary migrants exceeded ten: Burundi, Sudan, Uganda, Liberia, Mauritania, Sierra Leone, Angola, and South Africa. While it is likely that the estimates of the 1986 emigrants are low due to missed categories of family and undocumented emigrants in most countries with both types of migrations, forced migration volumes in these countries vastly outnumber voluntary emigrations.

There does appear to be a relation between a history of receiving economic/labour immigrants and receiving large numbers of refugees (Table 14.2). Most of the countries hosting the largest numbers of refugees had a long history of receiving economic migrants, including Democratic Republic of Congo, Kenya, Sudan, Tanzania, Uganda, Côte d'Ivoire, Liberia, and Zambia. Only Ethiopia and Guinea received hundreds of thousands of refugees with no prior experience of receiving voluntary immigrants.

Table 14.2 shows that there were 4.1 million refugees residing in Sub-Saharan Africa.[1] The number of host countries for refugees is fewer than the number of countries from where refugees are fleeing. Ten countries (listed in the previous paragraph) each receive more than 100,000 refugees, together hosting 90 per cent of the total 1996 refugee population in Sub-Saharan Africa. Three of these countries, Democratic Republic of Congo, Liberia, and Sudan, have thousands fleeing in both directions.

Perhaps the most striking finding from this comparison of patterns of forced and voluntary migration is that the number of refugees hosted by Sub-Saharan African countries is still only 38 per cent of the number of economic/voluntary migrants hosted. The 10.9 million voluntary migrants in Sub-Saharan African countries outnumber refugees by more than 2 to 1. Twenty-five countries each had at least an estimated 100,000 immigrants as of 1990. In a few countries there is a balance of refugees and immigrants, as depicted by the ratios of about 1.0 for refugees to immigrants (Democratic Republic of Congo, Sudan, Guinea-Bissau, Liberia, Zambia). For most,

Table 14.2 Immigrants by type of immigration and host country
(countries with at least 10,000 immigrants or refugees)

Region	Host country	Refugees (1996)	Immigrants (excluding Refugees) (1990)	Ratio of refugees to immigrants
East Africa and	Burundi	0	65,954	—
Horn of Africa	Comoros	—	38,520	—
	D.R. Congo	675,973	700,000	0.97
	Djibouti	25,076	4,402	5.70
	Ethiopia	390,528	57,104	6.84
	Kenya	223,640	156,014	1.43
	Madagascar	0	127,101	0.00
	Malawi	—	282,515	—
	Reunion	—	58,770	—
	Rwanda	25,257	48,810	0.52
	Somalia	—	21,897	—
	Sudan	393,874	417,628	0.94
	Tanzania	498,732	313,169	1.59
	Uganda	264,294	200,000	1.32
Middle Africa	Cameroon	46,407	220,000	0.21
	C. African Rep.	36,564	55,000	0.66
	Chad	—	17,007	—
	Congo	20,451	126,238	0.16
	Gabon	—	100,000	—
	Zaire	—	700,000	—
Western Africa	Benin	5,960	47000	0.13
	Burkina Faso	23,381	417,602	0.06
	Cote d'Ivoire	327,696	3,370,419	0.10
	Gambia	6,924	101,183	0.07
	Ghana	35,617	137,160	0.26
	Guinea	663,854	17,318	38.33
	Guinea-Bissau	15,401	17,000	0.91
	Liberia	120,061	127,101	0.94
	Mali	18,234	110,000	0.17
	Mauritania	15,880	54,894	0.29
	Niger	25,845	115,000	0.22
	Nigeria	8,486	250,000	0.03
	Senegal	65,044	125,000	0.52
	Sierra Leone	13,532	197,791	0.07
	Togo	12,589	140,000	0.09
Southern Africa	Angola	9,381	15,000	0.63
	Botswana	—	21,182	—
	Lesotho	—	20,000	—
	South Africa	22,645	1,118,369	0.02
	Swaziland	—	33,742	—
	Zambia	131,139	187,707	0.70
	Zimbabwe	—	600,000	—
Total		4,124,461	10,888,587	0.38

Sources:

For refugees: UNHCR (1997).
For immigrants: United Nations (1998a).

however, there is a preponderance of one type of immigrant over another. Middle Africa and Southern Africa stand out as regions with significantly greater voluntary immigrants, while only three Western African countries receive more than 100,000 refugees. East Africa and the Horn of Africa harbour the largest shares of refugees.

That so many countries receiving refugees have had experience with the reception of voluntary labour migrants is actually a positive situation. While refugees may receive assistance from international agencies for some time after their initial flight, this assistance may not continue for the duration of their residence in the country of asylum. At some point, the host country and the refugee must adopt an alternate course, one which leads him/her towards self-sufficiency and survival, whether through return home or settlement in the host country or another asylum country. The countries which already have received immigrants have labour markets, housing, and social networks that assist the refugees to shift to immigrant mode.

Both the forced migrants and the host community want to see their residence in the country as temporary, and that refugees will return home after the conflict has been resolved (Koser and Black, 1999). Throughout Africa, as conflicts have simmered down and regions become 'pacified', tens of thousands have returned home. In 1996, 1,690,800 persons had been repatriated in 10 countries: Angola, Burundi, Eritrea, Ethiopia, Liberia, Mali, Mauritania, Rwanda, Somalia, and Togo (UNHCR, 1997). Most of these returnees were Rwandans. Without this massive repatriation, the number returning would have been only about 300,000, less than one-tenth the number of refugees. These figures suggest that many fewer return than are forced out. Although negotiations towards a return may continue for years, forced migrants cannot wait indefinitely to restart their lives and become self-supporting. They will start to explore non-return options as soon as it becomes possible. For many, this will imply an onward move to the place that will become their home.

THE CHALLENGES OF LOSS OF CHOICE

This section examines the situations of forced and voluntary migrants, highlighting the salient features of forced migration which make it particularly difficult for the forced migrant to regain a sense of choice and transform the compulsory flight to chosen resettlement. From the often hasty flight through the possible protracted period of residence in the initial host community, the forced migrant has fewer options and resources to support return or resettlement. Challenges are related to lack of choice in the timing or direction of movement and the urgency of the flight and correspondingly minimal preparation time. Circumstances prior to and accompanying the flight also leave the forced migrant endangered, precarious, and subject to legal and political barriers to movement or integration into the host community, as well as suffering the psychological trauma of the loss of home, family and community. Many of the coping mechanisms available to voluntary migrants have been disrupted, and replacement or repair of these mechanisms slows the integration or return experiences.

The quintessential aspect of migration has been that it is a decision, a choice to improve one's life. This does not mean that there is not any element of compulsion, as there are always 'push' and 'pull' factors behind any migration decision. Many migrants report that they 'had no choice' but to leave if they were ever going to find work. Nonetheless, economically motivated migrants have a fairly large range of choices over their moves: who would go, where to go, when to go, who would help them get settled, how long to stay before returning, whether to settle permanently.

In contrast, forced migrants have fewer choices (Van Hear, 1998). Their moves are dominated by fear, the need to get away from the threat on their lives. Indeed, the refugee definition includes the criterion of fear of persecution due to race, religion, nationality or political opinion (United Nations, 1998b). Within the forced migration group are both refugees (international forced migrants) and internally displaced persons. The latter are subject to no less fear, but seek refuge within their own country. If barred from entering the neighbouring country, they may be more disadvantaged than refugees, since they do not benefit from international assistance (Hampton, 1998). Others prefer to stay as close as possible to home, staying near or with friends or persons with whom they feel safe, until they have the opportunity to return (Cohen and Deng, 1998).

The urgency of the forced flight from violence does not mean that the migration does not have underlying economic factors. The zones most involved in political struggles are also those with economic or environmental factors that increase the chance that the refugees might have adopted some form of voluntary migration at some future date (Van Hear, 1998). Richmond (1993) proposed a typology of 'reactive' migrants, whose migration is in response to various combinations of political, economic, environmental, social, and bio-psychological factors. For example, refugees from war zones and political exiles would be reacting to purely political forces, while those fleeing drought exacerbated by institutional inability to deliver food relief would be environmental/political refugees.

An alternative way of viewing the degrees of choice involves consideration of how much advance planning precedes the move. As proposed by Cuny and Hill (1999), the process of displacement begins with a generalised pressure on economic resources, deterioration of the food supply, and inability to purchase food. Persons leaving at such a time are economic refugees who have choices regarding when and where they go: preparing for their departure by selling off assets, selecting a destination, and proceeding to that destination through ordinary means of transport. Many South Asians left Uganda just prior to the mass expulsions of the Amin days (Van Hear, 1998).

As the situation enters an emergency stage, families prepare hastily to evacuate, selling assets if they can, and moving quickly. At this stage, the actual move often occurs in large groups; whole clans or villages under one leader. The group may still have some liberty in choosing where to go. Where they go will be influenced by locations of sanctuaries (churches, schools, and other 'neutral' zones), proximity to a border, locations of jobs and income sources, routes to safety and the locations of conflict zones to be avoided (Maynard, 1999). Forced migrants may continue to move, as the situation changes, and their safety is again imperilled. At some point, the refugee or forced migrant hopes to enter the phase where resettlement or repatriation can occur (Koser and Black, 1999) and he/she becomes a voluntary migrant, if possible, moving on in search of employment, land, better living conditions, and, in general, a place to settle. At this stage, the move becomes more considered, containing elements of the decision-making of economic/ voluntary migrants. The forced migrant will seek out friends and family for refuge. In the absence of such ties, he/she may move to cities or other areas perceived to have job opportunities. Depending on success at that location, he/she may or may not make a final move: return home.

The refugee resettlement process may also be viewed from the angle of enrichment. As the forced migrant flees, she/he becomes impoverished, losing land, home, assets. In taking steps to become settled, whether in a new host community or by return, resettlement is not only a process of increasing choices, it is also one of enrichment, building options, resources, and ultimately assets (Cernea, 1995). Assistance given during the post-flight stage should therefore be offered in a developmental context, helping the displaced to find or create opportunities to generate income and build communities (Cuny and Hill, 1999). In the ideal world, each move brings the forced migrant closer to the situation of labour migrant, with rebuilt economic and social networks enabling him/her to settle successfully in a host community.

Although the process looks similar to that experienced by migrants, who also move onward until they either develop their niche or return home, the forced migrant has much fewer choices at each point. These are limited by legal status, the often unwelcoming attitude of the host community, distance and sense of 'otherness' between the refugee and the host community, lack of friends or family, government regulations and barriers to free movement, and absence of money for financing new ventures or travel. Case studies of repatriation and resettlement suggest that the educated and those with marketable skills are least constrained by their refugee status and are therefore better able to overcome barriers to successful integration with the host community (Koser and Black, 1999; Preston, 1999).

The limited resources and advance planning necessitated by their flight make it much harder for forced migrants to resettle successfully. In their haste, most are able to take little to help them through the journeys (Cohen and Deng, 1998; Ager, 1999). Further, the flight and journey are extremely taxing, and many forced migrants arrive malnourished and ill. Refugees in Ethiopia, Kenya, Malawi, and Zimbabwe experienced crude death rates three to ten times higher than the baseline rate for their country of origin. Internally displaced persons tend to face even higher risks of death (Toole and Waldman, 1993) In contrast, voluntary migrants generally take a long time to prepare for their move so that they can maximise their chance of success (Findley, 1977). They move to a place where they know they can work, with savings to tide them over until new earnings are acquired.

Another major difference between the voluntary and forced migrant relates to group composition. Voluntary migrants usually move alone, or in very small groups of friends or family. In contrast, forced migrants are likely to move en masse. In Liberia and Sierra Leone, whole villages followed leaders to a safer location (Van Damme, 1999). While group flight enables more persons to be evacuated, it leads to clustering which tends to make absorption more difficult (Maynard, 1999). Even though forced migrants seek out communities where they know friends or family, limited resources in the host community make it difficult for the entire group to be received. In Guinea, for example, early arrivals from the conflict in Liberia were warmly received by the host groups, but for later arrivals, kin relations between the host and the arriving group were weak and hosts felt they were 'saturated'. The result was that refugees were less able to 'self-settle' among hosts, and forced to establish camps, dependent on aid and food distributions (Van Damme, 1999).

Although the voluntary migrant leaves home, home is still there, and is a psychological if not actual available retreat, as well as a source of support during difficult times. The forced migrant has no such comfort zone. While he/she may travel with people from 'home', the forced migrant no longer has a home. If not already destroyed by conflict engendering the flight, the home is likely to be completely destroyed after the family has left. With the loss of home, the migrant loses not only assets and belongings, but also family, social networks based in the home community, and a sense of community; namely the normative identity which ties a people and a place (Zetter, 1999). Without this normative identity, the group has no communality (Summerfield, 1999). The loss of a sense of place, a home place, has profound psychological consequences for the forced migrant (Fullilove, 1996). The community gives people a sense of acceptance and mutual respect. They trust each other and interact to solve common problems. People in a community can use knowledge of the community to survive. Without this trust and respect, community members are easily disoriented and find difficulty in interacting freely with persons (Fullilove, 1996). Social interactions are no longer easily mapped out in space, and become much more difficult to locate and activate. Many options open to migrants are closed to the forced migrant who has lost his/her home and community:

circulation between the city and home village, reliance on the home community's social networks for information on opportunities, availability of social and monetary support from the home community.

For most forced migrants, the loss of home includes loss of many loved ones. Men are more likely to be voluntary or involuntary participants in the conflict, and are usually the first to be killed when a situation deteriorates into chaos. Even if they had not witnessed the murder of their own family members, refugees are haunted by the fear that those they cannot locate have been killed. They live with the uncertainty of not knowing if they still have a family. Some Vietnamese refugees did not know if their family members had survived ten years after fleeing. Their circumstances make it practically impossible to stay in touch with the community or any family left behind (Allden et al., 1996). Just when they most need family to help them grieve over the deaths, they are unable to find or be with surviving members. Without mourning, it is much more difficult for the forced migrant to take the first steps in establishing a new family and community (Fullilove, 1996; Allden, et al., 1996; Harrell-Bond, 1999).

In contrast to voluntary migration groups which have tended to be dominated by men, refugee and forced migrant groups are dominated by women and children who have either seen their husbands and fathers killed or have left them fighting (UNHCR, 1997). While women made up 44 per cent of international voluntary migrants in Sub-Saharan African in 1990, they comprised 52 per cent of refugees (United Nations, 1998b). When the internally displaced are included, some estimate that the female proportion may be as high as 60–80 per cent (Dirasse, 1995).

This preponderance of women among forced migrants has significant implications for the women and their attempts to re-establish lives. In their flight, many women became heads of households, and despite their traumatic experiences they still have to find food and shelter for family members they were able to save. Unlike voluntary migrant women who at least have some choices about how to provide support for children (Findley, 1997; Makinwa-Adebusoye, 1997), the forced migrant is ill-equipped to suddenly take on this role. She has lost her land, possibly her tools, and may herself be injured or in very poor health. At the camp or other initial asylum location, she may have no access to land or other income-generating opportunities, yet she continues to be responsible for feeding her family (Dirasse, 1995; Callamard, 1999). In a camp situation, authorities may not recognise women as heads of household, instead distributing food rations to men. Experience shows that men often sell their rations, leaving the family without food (Dirasse, 1995). There are also serious social problems associated with this sudden shift in the gender balance. The absence of men is an indication that the social ties and norms that governed gender relations are no longer operational. Surveys show alarmingly high rates of rape and abuse in refugee camps (Dirasse, 1995). In the Kakuma refugee camp for Sudanese refugees, 12 per cent of the surveyed women had been beaten by their spouse or partner in the past month (International Rescue Committee, 1999). Instead of feeling safe and protected, women may continue to live in fear, and be further delayed in the work of starting new lives. In both Kenya and Democratic Republic of Congo, women have been unable to prosecute their attackers, and police have continued to ignore their plight (Callamard, 1999). To compound matters, women may be excluded from all decision-making regarding camp operations, including distribution of assistance and resources. Although they are the de facto household heads, they may not receive any training or resources to support their efforts (Dirasse, 1995).

Family groups also will have been broken up in the process of flight. There are exceptionally high rates of orphanage among the displaced. Of the twelve million children made homeless by conflicts as of 1996, one million were orphaned or separated from their parents. Approximately 5 per cent of all refugees are unaccompanied children, (Summerfield, 1999). Surveys conducted in Democratic Republic of Congo and Mozambique show that 20–33 per cent of households contained foster children. Children separated from their parents have great difficulty in finding them (Ahearn, et al., 1999). In Guinea, for example, many families had been split up before arriving from Liberia or Sierra Leone (Van Damme, 1999).

Refugees and others fleeing violence have experienced the very worst humanity has to offer: psychological traumas of war and conflict, death of family members, witness to unbearable cruelty and inhumanity, suffering and injury, rape and sexual abuse, loss of hope and all sense of dignity (Cohen and Deng, 1998; UNHCR, 1997). The stress and psychological pain appears to be most severe for women who, in today's conflicts, not only see their fathers, brothers, husbands and sons murdered, but are themselves raped as a means to further terrorise and control the women and their (surviving) partners (Carballo, et al., 1996). Rape has been widely used by militia in Liberia, Rwanda, Somalia, and Sudan (Dirasse, 1995).

The experience of systematic public torture much used in current conflicts destroys the social fabric, leaving people helpless and at a loss about what to do (Summerfield, 1999). As a result, severe depression and lasting post-traumatic stress syndrome are widespread among refugees and the internally displaced (Summerfield, 1999; Hauff and Vaglum 1995; Locke et al., 1996). Unlike the voluntary migrant who is able to connect with existing solidarity groups, the forced migrant must start with the daunting task of building trust and community solidarity. The challenge for many refugee groups is the reconstruction of familiar family and community structures in unfamiliar surroundings and often with non-family members (Maynard, 1999; Kibreab, 1995).

Having come through a long period of violence and fear of violence, a communal sense of safety is essential to begin the process of rebuilding community (Maynard, 1999). Refugees are necessarily preoccupied with establishing conditions of safety. With safety assured, they can turn to mending the torn social fabric of their lives. Not surprisingly, the normal 'coping' units and strategies of the society are disrupted by the conflict, and those fleeing cannot turn to the traditional supports or sanctuaries of churches, schools, or hospitals. Indeed, health care workers and teachers are often the explicit targets for terror (Cuny, 1983). In the absence of traditional social networks, many refugees have turned to each other to build networks of support (Maynard, 1999). Refugees who have fled together and stayed together may be more likely to have a distinct aggregational and relational community (Dona and Berry, 1999). In Rwanda, women's survivor groups became a national network of support for thousands of widows in and out of exile, providing the possibility of group support which was their preferred way to cope emotionally through self-counselling (Bennett, 1998).

Although voluntary migrants often face depression as they find that life is much more difficult than they had expected, they are able to find satisfaction out of effecting changes in their lives. Forced migrants are severely demoralised by their situations, yet they may be deprived of the ability to take charge of their situation. Despite recommendations that refugees be given more autonomy and authority to govern themselves and control the development of their community, such participation is often denied by the aid agencies controlling food and shelter (Harrell-Bond, 1999). Ironically, the dependence on aid only compounds the stress experienced by the refugees (Harrell-Bond, 1999).

Another major difference between forced and voluntary migrants is their degree of choice for onward moves. While the voluntary migrant has a full range of options from staying to returning, the forced migrant has very limited choices, generally confined to: (1) staying put (long-term residence in country/zone of initial refuge); (2) third country resettlement; (3) permanent resettlement in the initial refuge or host country; and (4) voluntary return or repatriation. The challenge for the forced migrant is to find a way to reinstate choice (Van Hear, 1998).

Though most refugees and internally displaced persons (80–90 per cent) want to return home, repatriation and return are an elusive goal rarely achieved by the forced migrant. For those whose homes were completely destroyed, repatriation may be more a goal of the host country than of the individual refugee (Koser and Black, 1999). Returning home is highly politicised, a complicated negotiation between the origin and host countries, with the refugees themselves having little control over their return, as in the case of repatriation of Eritrean refugees (McSpadden, 1999). In contrast, the voluntary migrant has fairly wide latitude over the timing and nature of a return home. The 'return' of forced migrants can be anything but empowering. Very often the refugees won't go 'home' but to a new location which lacks not only their own community of family and friends, but also the infrastructure the community had supported: schools, clinics, roads and wells.

Thus, when ultimately given a choice to return, many refugees may exercise this new freedom in a seemingly contrary manner, to resettle in the host country and not return, which may be seen as a greater threat to the family's health and the education of its children. In Mozambique, for example, these concerns kept many women in Maputo who would have considered returning (Agadjanian, 1998).

SHARED CIRCUMSTANCES BETWEEN FORCED AND VOLUNTARY MIGRANTS

While forced migrants have had much less choice in their original flight, like migrants everywhere they want to make their own choices about how long to stay at the initial asylum, and where next to move. While they may have been victims of violence, in the post-emergency situation they actively seek ways to support themselves and take charge of their lives. As with all other migrants, they want to find an economic niche, and get 'beyond' the past, if not ahead. The forced migrants' survival strategies encompass food supplementation activities such as cultivating vegetables for sale in the camp to the pursuit of full-time farming or trade (Dirasse, 1995; Cuny and Hill, 1999). This pursuit of economic opportunity is a fundamental element of the process of re-gaining confidence and control over one's life and of recuperating a sense of community and a place in the world (Bennett, 1998). As we learned with rural development and settlement programmes that failed because they did not foster individual initiative and responsibility (Findley, 1979; Oberai, 1988), it is important that assistance to forced migrants be structured to enable this search, rather than to foreclose it by excessive control and dependency (Harrell-Bond, 1999). In contrast to the stereotype of refugees as helpless and dependent, refugees and internally displaced persons can and must be seen as agents of their own development (Cuny, 1983; Harrell-Bond, 1999; Maynard, 1999; Koser and Black, 1999).

Voluntary migrants exercise their choice of destination prior to their move, but the forced migrant begins to consider and choose among options after the initial flight. While most would like to go home, this may not be feasible immediately or even ever. The entire community fabric is likely to have been destroyed by the conflict, and returnees may find only chaos when they return. Their homes may have been destroyed or appropriated for others' use. Their lands will have become uncultivated or, worse, distributed to supporters of the controlling group. The land itself may be mined (Koser and Black, 1999). Questions of land tenure become unresolvable with no intact community structure. Those who return may in fact find no access to land, and no home for their families (Cohen and Deng, 1998; Eastmond and Ojendahl, 1999).

Refugees and internally displaced persons face different choices, at least in terms of the timing and relocation possibilities. Refugees in a camp situation obviously have a different range of choices than those who have spontaneously settled, and there may be less pressure to move on immediately for those receiving food and shelter from international relief agencies. Refugees outside a settled refugee camp and the internally displaced begin to confront settlement and onward migration choices almost immediately after arrival. While forced migrants seek economic opportunities, just like voluntary migrants, their pursuit of opportunity is priority only after establishing a safe and secure residence. Thus, the forced migrants tend to prefer adaptive and flexible solutions that enable the family to maintain security while allowing individual pursuit of jobs and income (Cuny, 1983).

Despite the generally horrendous circumstances which forced them out of their homes, eighty to ninety per cent of the internally displaced and refugees want to go home (Agadjanian, 1998; Cohen and Deng, 1998; Dona and Berry, 1999). Those forced out have a strong desire to reclaim their lands and homes, to assert their citizenship and membership in the community, and to be 'home' even if the physical home is destroyed. Also important is the desire to avoid being a social outcast. Strong as the pull is, however, return home, particularly as a voluntary returner, is achieved by fewer than one in five (Dolan, 1999). A wide range of factors directly prevent or indirectly forestall a return: demilitarisation and safety in the origin community; only moderate levels of destruction or moderate efforts to replace destroyed infrastructure and homes; access to land and housing; willingness to accept the returnees and integrate them into the society.

A successful return is more likely if the person regains control of land and other assets. Those who are displaced only to the edges of conflict may more easily return (Maynard, 1999). A host of circumstances can prevent or long forestall any return. Continuing conflict and absence of security will prevent returns. Even if the area is calm, returnees may fear being recruited by the army to fight in the war. As they learn more about the destroyed communities they fled, refugees begin to realise that home is not what it was. With this recognition, they see that the life they had led no longer exists, and slowly recognise that they cannot go home (Maynard, 1999). The return itself can be unsuccessful. Many of the Rwandans returning from the Democratic Republic of Congo found others in control of their home and lands, and they were forced to move to other locations in Rwanda (Cohen and Deng, 1998). Regaining possession may or may not be feasible. Return also can fail if the returnee has no support to cover transportation costs. Finally, the longer the person remains in exile, the more likely he/she is to stay in exile (Maynard, 1999).

When large numbers of refugees or demobilising soldiers are involved, they may be able to participate in a programme of mass repatriation, with agencies negotiating for land where groups of refugees can be resettled and integrated into the local economy, as in the case of repatriated demobilised soldiers in Angola, Chad, Mozambique, Namibia, Uganda, and Zimbabwe (Preston, 1999). This mass repatriation enables the refugee to plan the return, and to use the power of their numbers to push for a higher level of support than might be possible if individual refugees were mobilising for return. Those returning from South Africa to Mozambique, for example, agitated for schools, clinics and infrastructure (Dolan, 1999).

Although refugees and persons of concern to UNHCR may qualify for resettlement assistance, the constraints on these programmes often lead individuals to pursue return on their own. For the many forced migrants who do not qualify for UNHCR assistance, the return is an ongoing process of attempting to secure an adequate location and situation. Unless they are forced to return (as was the case for many Rwandan refugees in the Democratic Republic of Congo), returnees have some choice about when to return and whether they will return to their original community or to another one in a less destabilised zone. Obviously, those returning home to their farmlands would prefer to delay return until the situation stabilises, and even then the group may return only temporarily to reclaim farming rights. This compromise situation characterised the temporary return of Liberian and Sierra Leonian men returning from Guinea to their homelands to farm during the planting season, leaving women and children in safety in Guinea (Van Damme, 1999). Temporary returns also allow migrants to assess the situation and determine realistically whether it is possible or desirable to return permanently to the original community or a nearby region. For example, returnees coming back from Mozambique with reports of drought and a destroyed cattle economy led many to delay their return from South Africa (Dolan, 1999).

Settlement in the host community or another 'neutral' zone actually may be the safest and least risky option for many forced migrants. For many internally displaced persons who are unable to return home, local integration is the preferred option, as they have the opportunity to stay within the culture and economic system they know and can use to their advantage (Cohen and Deng, 1998; UNHCR, 1997). Integration into the host community can work if the host community is receptive, offering land and opportunities to build homes and become members of the community. At its best, local integration is like spontaneous settlement of migrants in previously uncultivated areas, where there is less potential for conflict over access to land and resources. Where there are existing communities, integration can occur through self-settlement processes, where the displaced ask for land and acceptance by a host community (Cuny and Hill, 1999).

While the self-settlement process appears to work best for the displaced and the host community, it may not be feasible if the community is already saturated with displaced. Areas receiving hundreds of thousands of forced migrants experience stress to the existing social, economic, and physical structures, which in turn lead them to reject further migrations. Among the stresses that can cause a host community to force or 'encourage' migrants to go elsewhere are: a sense that the forced migrant group upsets a delicate ethnic balance and threatens their own political stability; heightened militarisation of their own region; ecological degradation associated with the intense demands posed by the forced migrants for firewood, water, food; and a recognition that the economic opportunities can't stretch to cover the immigrant groups (Nnoli, 1998). Thus, many displaced find themselves shunted to distant second destinations.

Whether in the original or second host community, local integration implies becoming part of a community where the forced migrant feels safe, helping overcome fears of betrayal, and renewed violence. Local integration offers the possibility of inclusion in an existing social structure, thus reducing isolation and sparing the forced migrants the difficulty of establishing these social reference points. The key to local integration is host country acceptance and support of the displaced persons. In addition, the host community must be supportive, not viewing the refugees as competitors or usurpers of their benefits. Needless to say, local integration should be economically viable. The new arrivals need to gain access to land in rural areas, or to jobs in the cities. If necessary, assistance should be provided to train the displaced in skills they need to rebuild their economic survival strategies. Just as governments have provided training and loans for farmers settling new lands or migrants starting new businesses, the displaced should receive aid that will enable them to get established. Ultimately, refugees settling on new lands need to have the opportunity to acquire citizenship in the host country. Without citizenship, their full social and economic integration with the country of asylum may be difficult or impossible.

Like voluntary migrants, forced migrants pursuing economic and settlement opportunities tend to follow the emigration routes of those who have gone before. Successive waves of forced migrants contribute to the development of the diaspora, namely the dispersal into recognised and expected destinations (Van Hear, 1998; Adepoju, 1998). Not only are there concentrations of persons in the initial asylum locations, but also in the onward migration locations. This tendency to adopt the same migration destinations is shared with voluntary migrants, who also have clustered in a few preferred African countries. In 1986, the primary migration destinations for Africans dispersed in Africa were: Côte d'Ivoire, Cameroon, Ghana, Malawi, Uganda, Zambia, and South Africa (Russell, 1993). These continue to be prominent, but new destinations for onward migrations have been added with the increase in refugee flows in the continent: Burundi, Democratic Republic of Congo, Kenya, Rwanda, Tanzania (related to the Tutsi–Hutu conflicts) Liberia and Sierra Leone, Mali, Niger, Senegal (the last three related to the conflicts in the North of the Sahel), Somalia, Ethiopia, and Sudan, and Togo (United Nations, 1998a).

Like voluntary economic migrants, some forced migrants have prior migration experience, having been compelled by economics to search for work elsewhere before being forced to flee (Van Hear, 1998). Many more are members of families which had already participated in some form of migration. For example, one member migrated to the city to look for work, leaving others behind (Agadjanian, 1998). Many women fleeing the rural zones of conflict in Mozambique fled to the capital city of Maputo, the only option remaining after the nightly refuges from RENAMO raids no longer provided sufficient protection. Maputo was perceived as the only safe destination where the women could find work (Agadjanian, 1998).

Again, in a pattern similar to the voluntary migrants, forced migrants may move onward several times before finally reaching a location where they can stay and establish themselves permanently (Cuny, 1983; Maynard, 1999). These onward moves may be trial attempts and failures at establishing a community, or they may be stages at which the migrant is accumulating skills and resources to prepare for the move to the final preferred destination. One study shows how Eritrean refugees worked in their initial asylum communities while earning money to go to the Gulf States or to US/Canada (Kibreab, 1995).

The stages of settlement for forced migrants parallel those for voluntary migrants: arrival, initial settlement, adaptation, acculturation. As for voluntary migrants, the speed of transition between settlement stages and also the extent to which they ultimately move to integration versus separation varies widely. The pace at which the forced migrant becomes acculturated and fully settled in a new location depends on many factors, including the degree of choice of the migration, and degree of permanence in the contact between the refugees and the settlement/host community (Kibreab, 1995). Potential conflicts between newcomers and the host community over limited resources for housing, water or food will slow or stall the transition to acculturation (Van Hear, 1998). This may propel the migrants to make repeat 'initial settlements' until they arrive at a location where adaptation is possible. Acculturation and stable resettlement are facilitated, as they are for voluntary migrants, by a sense of openness and inclusion with the host society. Just as voluntary migrants seek support and assistance from co-ethnics or persons from the same origin, the same is true for the forced migrants. Successful settlement will be difficult for groups facing constant prejudice and discrimination. Also important are the levels of resources available to the refugee group (Dona and Berry, 1999).

Like immigrants who establish migrant associations focusing on maintaining their home culture and supporting developments back home, forced immigrants also develop social organisations and customs that help reinforce connections with the communities they have fled (Hammond, 1999). This is most striking among enclaves of refugees, working and waiting to return home, as has been found among forced migrants in South Africa and Sudan (Donal, 1999; Hammond, 1999; McSpadden, 1999).

Where possible, forced migrants will seek opportunities to continue in the same work or professions they had before fleeing. Like migrants everywhere, the easiest course for the forced migrant is to use skills and experience from the pre-flight life. Two years after returning to Yemen from Saudi Arabia, returnees who were working were in their pre-exile occupations (Van Hear, 1998). Those who had lived and worked in urban areas will seek work in cities; forced migrants going from rural to urban areas will be disadvantaged in seeking jobs, just like rural-urban migrants everywhere (Kibreab, 1995). Gender-specific roles are likely to be maintained, with women seeking work that uses their traditional skills of mother and housewife (Findley, 1997). Like their rural-urban migrant sisters, Eritrean women refugees in urban Sudan found work in domestic service or cooking/catering in 'community restaurants'. Maintenance of gendered roles does not always happen, however. Ironically, self-settled women in urban areas fare better than their sisters in the settlement camps/areas (Kibreab, 1995). Subordination of women is greater in transit and resettlement centres than in rural areas, where all the food, land, tools, and seeds go to men, leaving women dependent (Dirasse, 1995; Callamard, 1999).

In the absence of targeted assistance to help the forced migrants get back into farming, the many hundreds of thousands who were farmers before fleeing may not be able to continue farming. Farmers may have no access to land; women may have no access to markets with which to start their trading activities. Limited land and resources in the host community will propel migrants to search elsewhere for work. This search for work can be facilitated by assistance from international agencies. Specifically, if refugees receive training and loans to start new economic undertakings, this can be a vehicle for their economic mobility, a cherished dream of all migrants, particularly female migrants (Findley, 1997).

Lessons from rural development and resettlement programmes for migrants are also relevant here. Skills training programmes should be guided by a well-thought-out, locally researched and development based assistance programme (Chambers, 1986; Harrel-Bond, 1999). If the forced migrant is trained in new farming techniques, he/she needs to have access to the necessary inputs, loans for equipment purchase, and assistance with marketing (Findley, 1979). Given the preponderance of women among the displaced, it is vital that these programmes be targeted to women (Dirasse, 1995; Callamard, 1999). Attention to skills development must be in occupations where there is a demand for the work or products, and for which the refugees (especially women) are supported in developing their own businesses after completing training. A refugee training programme in Malawi encountered difficulties in launching the women on the occupations for which they were trained, including beekeeping, because insufficient attention was paid to building a market for their products (Knudsen and Halvorsen, 1997). If carefully chosen, however, a major advantage of job training programmes is that the investment can go with the person, who may apply them wherever he/she goes. Refugees and host communities can develop mutually beneficial commercial interactions, as in the case of Mozambican refugees in Malawi. The refugee camp in Luwani, Malawi became the site of an active market, where local women were able to sell their produce, and refugee men sold excess and inappropriate food aid. Refugees arriving with any assets sold them to start a business in Luwani (Callamard, 1994).

Displacement often prompts changes to economic roles, including specialisation by gender. Eritrean men who brought donkeys or camels with them to Sudan began earning money by hauling water and fuel, previously the job of women and to the detriment of the Eritrean refugee women (Johnson, 1981). In other cases, men and women evolve a division of labour which is more complementary, as in Zambia where married Angolan couples developed effective survival strategies (Spring, 1979). As a group, the refugees may find a new economic role which minimises competition with the local host population. Instead, they can develop a non-competitive mutually supportive pattern (e.g. trade with each other, with refugees selling excess and unwanted donated food in order to buy the food they want, as in Malawi) (Callamard, 1994). With positive linkages, antagonism can be averted, as in Somalia and Thailand (Christensen, 1983; Harrell-Bond, 1999.

Like migrants everywhere, forced migrants seek to settle where there are other family members or co-ethnics Dirasse, 1995; Bennett, 1998). Within this group, they will develop support through mutual aid (Cuny, 1983). Among refugees to Guinea in 1990–91, virtually all settled themselves among kinfolk, even when they established a de facto camp (Van Damme, 1999). There is evidence that emotional and social support is critical for migrants trying to establish a new life. A study of political exiles returning to South Africa showed that after controlling for the level of re-entry difficulties (specific functions including getting work, children in school), emotional social support had the strongest effect on psychological well-being, while instrumental social support from the family was most important for perceived quality of life. Problem-focused coping was also important for quality of life, although emotion-focused coping did not relate to well-being (Majodina, 1995).

Like voluntary migrants who want others to see them as successful and refuse to return until they can do so with a sense of pride and accomplishment (Findley, 1997), forced migrants need to see themselves as successful at coping, and avoiding an appearance of failure. Burmese exiles in Thailand want to portray themselves as helping the struggle and self-confident about their futures (Allden et al., 1996). Groups working with forced migrants can facilitate cooperation and cooperative programmes which would help the refugees regain self-confidence (Oucho, 1996; Cuny and Hill, 1999). This solidarity also is equally important for those returning, who face reverse cultural shock (Majodina, 1995).

As among voluntary migrants who use a variety of strategies to create fictive kinship (Findley and Diallo, 1988; Bledsoe and Isiugo-Abanihe, 1989), forced migrants also develop quasi-familial social relations. Late arrivals to Guinea arrived in heterogeneous kin groups that had not lived together prior to fleeing (Van Damme, 1999). In Rwanda, 21 per cent of the refugee households fostered unaccompanied children (Maynard, 1999). One-third of internally displaced women in Maputo had foster children living with them (Agadjanian, 1998). Women who had fled from rural Mozambique to Maputo found that their only opportunity to build a social world was the church, especially the healing churches. Through these new communities, the forced migrants re-establish standards for 'right' with the family and newly formed migrant solidarity group (Maynard, 1999).

REGAINING DEGREES OF FREEDOM

At least for the foreseeable future, we are going to continue to see hundreds of thousands of forced migrants, both refugees and internally displaced. While the circumstances of their departure may have been vastly different from those accompanying economic migrants, the forced migrants share many of the motives of voluntary migrants: establishing a new home, building community, staying healthy, becoming economically self-sufficient. Unlike voluntary migrants, however, the forced migrants face an uphill battle in claiming their new lives. Many arrive at their initial destinations malnourished and in poor health, some with serious injuries that need treatment. The trauma they experienced before fleeing continues to live in their sense of loss, depression, and isolation. They have lost family and community and must build a new support network. To make matters worse, they may be unwelcome where they arrived and be forced to move on, further delaying when they can finally begin establishing a new community. Despite these very significant differences between forced and voluntary migrants, there are certain lessons we can apply from what we have learned in managing and facilitating the integration and success of voluntary migrants.

Stabilise through Development

While the conflicts driving forced migrants are complex in origin, economic disparities and conflict over rights to resources play a role in sharpening hostilities. Thus, promotion of economic development is a long-term strategy to prevent both forced and voluntary migrations. This is comparable with earlier recommendations to stimulate socio-economic development to create opportunities for families and enable them to survive or even prosper without having to migrate (Findley, 1979). Several regions subject to conflict are at risk for drought, which exacerbates the risk of famine and flight. Steps need to be taken in these regions to increase protection from drought, and to develop mechanisms to maintain agricultural production (Cuny and Hill, 1999). Unfortunately, promoting development is a very long-term strategy for areas already experiencing conflict. In the short term, it is extremely difficult to plan or invest when investors don't even know who will be in control or what rules and regulations they may have to honour, even if the security of their workers and physical structures could be maintained. As their economic and political resources are pulled into conflict, governments lose their ability to plan or invest in social welfare or infrastructure (Adekanye, 1998). It may be possible, however, to undertake stabilisation and development activities in marginal areas, which would help them better cope with the arrival of persons fleeing the conflict zones (Cohen and Deng, 1998).

Protect the Right to Stay

Additional steps can be taken in potential hot spots, as for example in Eastern Africa and the Horn of Africa, to promote good governance, implement systems to mediate conflicts and protect human rights. An important right that needs to be protected is the right to stay, namely not to be displaced (Cohen and Deng, 1998). Ironically, while migrants seek to open opportunities for moving, those at risk for internal displacement and flight need protection from being arbitrarily forced out of their homes.

Expect Forced Migrations

Over the last two decades there has been an increase in voluntary internal and international migrations in Sub-Saharan Africa, despite governmental concern that these were too high and 'undesirable' (Findley et al., 1995; Findley, 1997; United Nations, 1998b). The same lesson holds for forced migrations. Much as we would like to be able to prevent the situations which lead to displacement, extremely explosive forces propel these migrations, and as with the voluntary economic migrants, governments seeking to suppress the movements will find little success. When refugees cannot enter at a particular location, they will seek entry elsewhere. And if they cannot cross the border, they will join the ranks of the internally displaced at the margins of conflict. But they will definitely move (Schmeidl, 1998; Cohen and Deng, 1998). Anticipation of displacement can help communities and organisations who will end up having to cope with the displacements.

Act on Early Warning of Conflicts

For years before conflicts reach the stage where people are forced to flee, there are many indications of trouble (Kibreab, 1985). There are many signs: human rights violations, curtailment of political rights, terrorist events, mounting ethnic diatribes and attacks, arbitrary control of food distribution systems, destruction of crops by conflicting forces. Establishment of a conflict early warning system based on these danger signals could help those involved prevent escalation of the conflict (Cohen and Deng, 1998). Such early alerts also could assist organisations prepare for massive displacement when conflicts cannot be prevented from escalating. Theoretically, such a system could be used to help governments develop programmes to mediate conflict and address the sources of these conflicts and stabilise the communities, much as Sub-Saharan African governments have established famine early warning systems which use a variety of indicators to signal incipient drought and food shortages (Cuny and Hill, 1999; Autier et al., 1990). In this case, signals could be used to determine the need for increased human rights surveillance, teams trained in negotiations and conflict resolution, as well as to protect and stabilise food supply and other vital resources. The United Nations has developed a Humanitarian Early Warning System (HEWS) which is used to compile a list of 'hot spots', but the system is not linked to a programme of early action (Cohen and Deng, 1998). This linkage between alert and action needs to be in place for the system to work as it has for FEWS. It needs to include all groups monitoring and responding to human rights abuses, including non-governmental organisations. Agencies could support the development of a network of communication points to assist communities in relaying information about their situation to the aid groups. Religious leaders in Burundi, for example, long warned of impending crisis and sought assistance in mediation. Mediation efforts can be successful even after the conflict has started to escalate, as in the example of the successful efforts to bring about a treaty between the Tuareg and the government in Mali (UNHCR, 1997). Although we would like all mediation efforts to succeed, experience shows that it often takes years to broker a settlement, and then additional time to enforce and maintain the settlement. As recommended by Cohen and Deng (1998), regional and international agencies need to be involved in preventing escalation of conflicts. In Sub-Saharan Africa, the OAU could play a much larger role in mediating and resolving conflicts within its member states. Both regional and international peacekeeping forces could be deployed before war breaks out. Perhaps by beginning a presence early in the conflict stage, the peacekeeping force can actually be more successful than has been the recent experience in Sierra Leone. In so doing, the horrendous experiences of the refugees threatened and terrorised by militia might be avoided.

Manage or Channel Displacement Flows

For countries where there are signs of impending and seemingly unavoidable displacement, emergency escape plans could be drafted to identify locations where the displaced can go, much like disaster preparedness plans for areas frequently struck by hurricanes and tornadoes. Agencies could prepare possible asylum sites as emergency shelter locations, with provisions for shelter, sanitation, water and food supplies. While this may sound needlessly hopeless about the chances of resolution, this advance planning, if even by a short time, could help reduce the suffering of displacement. With less suffering, migrants could be ready sooner for the tasks of resettlement or return. Both the forced migrants and the countries affected by their flows will benefit from migration management, as recommended by the United Nations in their 1997 report on international migration (United Nations, 1998b). Many countries with large forced migration flows are the ones which traditionally have had large numbers of voluntary migrants.

Management can start with integration of the monitoring, review, and strategy development process regarding both voluntary and forced migrant flows. As we learned with internal migration flows, governments have a large array of programmatic and policy tools that can help channel migration to areas and migrants to economic niches which are more likely to be mutually beneficial to the migrant and the host community (Findley, 1977, 1979; Findley et al., 1995). Government agencies and non-government organisations have development and relief programmes that could be reviewed for their 'migration friendly' characteristics, and changed if need be to make the programmes more migration-friendly and prepared. Countries which have traditionally hosted hundreds of thousands of immigrants need to work with their 'partner' sending countries to elaborate alternative plans for hosting migrants that will be better tailored to their own economic situations. For example, rather than restricting entrants and sending others home, countries could channel immigrants toward zones needing seasonal or temporary labour, facilitating circular migrants rather than permanent workers. The existence of pre-established options will also facilitate the management of crisis-related displacement flows as these emerge.

Nurture Migrant Communities

Just as migrant associations have provided many invaluable services for the settlement and acculturation of successive waves of immigrants, forced migrants need their own organisations (Harrell-Bond, 1999; Maynard, 1999). Among the displaced who have lost their family and communities, these organisations are an essential step towards rebuilding social networks, helping families mourn their losses, and re-establishing norms of trust, mutual aid, and self-help. These associations also play a major role in facilitating provision of services in a way that empowers the community to resume responsibility for the vital functions of health and education. All services and training should be given in a participatory mode, with involvement of the refugees in planning the receipt and distribution of the services or goods (Oucho, 1996; (Harrell-Bond, 1999). In addition to the establishment of routine and preventive health care services, migrant communities need to take steps to help each other address the psycho-social stresses of the forced migration experience. The migrant community can assist families in tracking lost family members, including helping them through the trauma of verifying the deaths of lost family. The migrant social network also will play a key role in assisting families through the individual and collective bereavement process. Where possible, those providing assistance and counselling should be members of the migrant group (Carballo et al., 1996).

Preference for Gradual and Complementary Changes

After their difficult flight, there is a tendency to think that the refugee or internally displaced person has lost material possessions and is too traumatised to want to take an active role in building the community. Although they may suffer emotionally, refugees have no less interest than voluntary immigrants in actively participating in building their new lives. The work with refugee communities to establish self-help mechanisms to manage daily life, establish business and trade activities, construct schools, houses, and so on, all show the empowering effect of active participation in problem solving (Harrell-Bond, 1999). Progressive strategies are needed that will help the forced migrants expand the domain over which they have choice, first over their daily lives and then over their own futures.

Support Women in Rebuilding Community

Women migrants have been on the increase throughout Sub-Saharan Africa. They are increasingly involved in migrations to cities where they work as domestics or traders, supporting children with them in the city or sending money home to sisters, parents, or aunts caring for family remaining in the rural areas (Findley, 1997). Given the predominance of women among the displaced, it is not surprising that in the 1990s, thousands of forced migrant women have joined their migrant sisters in the pursuit of work in major cities. These migrations need to be expected, facilitated, and supported. Job training programmes should equip women with skills they can use to develop their own economic niches in the city or town. Small-scale loan programmes that benefit women need to be open to the refugees, not just to citizens of the country. Establishment of women's refugee associations can facilitate the re-establishment of the social networks that are so vital to women's productive and reproductive activities. Particular attention needs to be paid to the health and emotional needs of women refugees. As indicated above, many refugee women must not only cope with grieving but also with the aftermath of sexual abuse, including unwanted and stigmatised pregnancies. The reproductive health needs of displaced women need to be included in assistance programmes, whether for women in camps or self-settled (Dirasse, 1995). Women's associations also can play a major role in developing trauma counselling programmes, family planning services, and health education, as in Côte d'Ivoire (Dirasse, 1995).

These same recommendations apply to working with women who stay in the rural zones, either in camps or self-settlement areas. Their economic and social roles in building community need to be recognised and supported. Women in particular need to be trained to adapt their traditional roles to the new setting. In Ghana, for example, a pilot programme helped women build their own centre at the Buduburam camp. In the process of building the centre, they learned how to make and lay bricks, construct window and door frames, and put up roofs. The Liberian women participating in the construction not only developed a centre for themselves but also learned new income-generating skills. At the same time, the involvement of local non-government organisations helped build linkages between the refugees and the local women's community (Dirasse, 1995).

Support Resettlement

Although resettlement in separate zones may not be ideal for the forced migrants, this may be one of few viable solutions for those who cannot return and who do not want to move on to a city. Governments and international agencies resettling families to rural sites can learn much from the resettlement experiences of the last two decades (Cernea, 1995). These lessons range widely over the minutiae of making a settlement work: site selection, preparation for agriculture, clarification of land title, water or irrigation systems, construction of housing, physical and social infrastructure, training of settlers for their new economic roles, including training for women and for men, arrangements for marketing. Perhaps the most important lesson is to facilitate self-help and participatory development, as has been recommended for rural development and resettlement programmes (Findley, 1979; Harrell-Bond, 1999). Another important lesson transferred from the experience of creating settlements is to attend equally to the needs of the host community and to avoid creating a protected, privileged group of displaced at the expense of the host community (Cernea, 1995). The other lesson is to explore ways to support spontaneous settlers, in both large and small groups. For internal migrants, the spontaneous settlement experiences often proved to be much more economical than the large government-sponsored settlement programmes (Oberai, 1988). This self-settlement also works better for the forced migrants (Cuny and Hill, 1999). A wide array of supportive services (loans, marketing assistance, housing construction assistance, health services) are needed to give settlers the choices they need. The most effective help is provided through a dispersed set of local organisations and communities, leaving choices to the migrants, both forced and voluntary, to find the niches which best suit their capacities and situations.

Integrate Assistance for Onward Migrations

Both voluntary and forced migrants prefer to move to places where they can be with family and friends, preferably locations with economic opportunities.

For the forced migrants, this means assisting them in going to destinations popular with voluntary migrants, especially the cities which have traditionally received thousands of circular and permanent migrants. Forced migrants need additional assistance to be able to migrate. Important facilitators for onward migration among the forced migrants are assistance with transportation and support for the initial period after the move. Information and assistance with networking are also vital. Just as governments and organisations have helped voluntary migrants through improved information about jobs and opportunities, similar information could be provided to forced migrants. More important for the forced migrant is information about family. The network itself can be used to facilitate the dissemination of information and resources. As we learned from internal migrants, there are many ways that the migration process can be assisted, but one of the most effective means is through the informal networks of dispersed migrants. Rather than targeting all relocation assistance through major planned settlements, these alternative channels can be used as a structure for making loans and assistance available to onward migrants, to both rural and urban areas. This will foster both self-help and integration of forced and voluntary migrants, reducing the sense of isolation experienced by the forced migrants.

Last Words

Many governments wished to turn back the seething hordes of migrants coming to cities to search for work in the 1970s and 1980s, but they were unable to do so (Findley, 1977). By the end of the 1990s we had begun to appreciate the positive contributions made by the many immigrant groups, and most governments and organisations no longer emphasise programmes that blindly return family members to their home regions (Findley, 1997). In 1997, only six Sub-Saharan countries wanted to reduce immigration. The same kind of recognition that forced migrants are 'with us' has not yet permeated war-torn regions. This recognition is long overdue. The estimates of forced migrants presented in this chapter underscore the large number of persons involved in forced migrations. Similarly, just as economic migrants can and are channelled through indirect mechanisms changing the contours of opportunity, the concrete strategies outlined above could be implemented to assist in preparing communities for their role as host communities. It promises to be a very complicated and exceedingly difficult and politically challenging task. However, just as we learned from migrants themselves how they solved problems and were able to establish themselves in unlikely locations, it is likely that we will learn much from the forced migrants as they rebuild community and recapture lives for themselves.

NOTE

1. The total refugees in Tables 14.1 and 14.2 are not equal because some refugees from Sub-Saharan Africa are not in Sub-Saharan African countries, and vice versa.

REFERENCES

Adekanye, 'Bayo J. (1998), 'Conflicts, loss of state capacities and migration in contemporary Africa', in Reginald Appleyard (ed.), *Emigration Dynamics in Developing Countries*, vol. 1, Aldershot, Ashgate, pp. 165–206.

Adepoju, Aderanti (1996), 'The links between intra-continental and inter-continental migration in and from Africa', in Aderanti Adepoju and Tomas Hammar (eds), *International Migration in and from Africa: Dimensions, Challenges and Prospects*, Dakar: PHRDA, pp. 13–38.

Adepoju, Aderanti (1998), 'Emigration dynamics in Sub-Saharan Africa', in Reginald Appleyard (ed.), *Emigration Dynamics in Developing Countries*, vol. 1, Aldershot: Ashgate, pp. 17–34.

Agadjanian, Victor (1998), 'Trapped on the margins: social characteristics, economic conditions, and reproductive behaviour of internally displaced women in urban Mozambique', *Journal of Refugee Studies*, **11**: 284–303.

Ager, Alastair (ed.) (1999), *Refugees: Perspectives of the Experience of Forced Migration*, London and New York: Pinter.

Ahearn, Fred, Maryanne Loughry, and Alastair Ager (1999), 'The experience of refugee children', in Alastair Ager (ed.), *Refugees: Perspectives on the Experience of Forced Migration*, London: Cassell, pp. 215–36.

Allden, K., C. Poole, S. Chantanavich et al., (1996), 'Burmese political dissidents in Thailand: trauma and survival among young adults in exile', *American Journal of Public Health*, **86,** 1561–9.

Autier, P., J.P. D'Atilia, J.P. Delamalle, and Vincent Vercruysse (1990), 'The food and nutrition surveillance systems of Chad and Mali: The SAP after two years', *Disasters*, **13** (1): 9–32.

Bennett, Jon (1998), 'Problems and opportunities of displacement', in Janie Hampton (ed.), *Internally Displaced People: A Global Survey*, London: Earthscan Publications, pp. 10–16.

Bledsoe, Caroline and U.C. Isiugo-Abanihe (1989), 'Strategies of Child Fosterage among Mende Grannies in Sierra Leone', in Ron Lesthaeghe (ed.), *African Reproduction and Social Organization*, Berkeley: University of California Press.

Bratton, Michael (1987), 'Drought, Food and the Social Organization of Small Farmers in Zimbabwe', in Michael H. Glantz (ed.), *Drought and Hunger in Africa*, Cambridge: Cambridge University Press, pp. 213–44.

Callamard, Agnes (1994), 'Refugees and local hosts: a study of the trading interactions between Mozambican refugees and Malawian villagers in the district of Mwanza', *Journal of Refugee Studies*, **7**: 39–62.

Callamard, Agnes (1999), 'Refugee Women: A Gendered and Political Analysis of the Refugee Experience', in Alastair Ager (ed.), *Refugees: Perspectives on the Experience of Forced Migration*, London: Cassell, pp. 196–215.

Carballo, Manuel, Mandy Grocutt, and Asja Hadzihasanovic (1996), 'Women and migration: a public health issue', *World Health Statistics Quarterly*, **49**: 158–64.

Cernea, Michael M. (1995), 'Understanding and preventing impoverishment from displacement: reflections on the state of knowledge', *Journal of Refugee Studies*, **8**: 245–64.

Chambers, Robert (1986), *Rural Development – Putting the Last First*, London: Longman

Christensen, H. (1983), 'Survival strategies for and by camp refugees in Somalia', *Horn of Africa*, **5**: 3–20.

Cohen, Roberta and Francis M. Deng (1998), *Masses in Flight: The Global Crisis of Internal Displacement*, Washington, DC: Brookings Institution Press.

Cuny, Frederick C. (ed.) (1983), *Disasters and Development*, Oxford: Oxford University Press.

Cuny, Frederick, Richard B. Hill (1999), *Famine, Conflict and Response: A Basic Guide*, West Hartford, CT: Kumarian Press.

Dirasse, L. (1995), 'Gender Issues and Displaced Populations,' in Noeleen Heyzer, Sushma Kapoor and Joanne Sandler (eds), *A Committment to the World's Women: Perspectives on Development for Beijing and Beyond*, New York: United Nations Development Fund for Women (UNIFEM), pp. 214–25.

Dolan, Chris (1999), 'Repatriation from South Africa to Mozambique – Undermining Durable Solutions?' in Richard Black and Khalid Koser (eds), *The End of the Refugee Cycle? Refugee Repatriation and Reconstruction*, New York: Berghahn Books.

Dona, Giorgia and John W. Berry (1999), 'Refugee Acculturation and Re-acculturation', in Alastair Ager (ed.), *Refugees: Perspectives on the Experience of Forced Migration*, London and New York: Pinter, pp. 169–95.

Eastmond, Marita and Joakim Ojendal (1999), 'Revisiting a "Repatriation Success" The Case of Cambodia' in Richard Black and Khalid Koser (eds), *The End of Refugee Cycle? Refugee Repatriation and Reconstruction*, New York: Berghahn Books.

Findley, Sally E. (1977), 'Planning for internal migration: a review of the issues and policies in developing dountries', *International Research Document No. 4, International Statistical Programs Center, U.S. Bureau of the Census*, Washington, DC: Government Printing Office.

Findley, Sally E. (1979), 'Rural development programmes: planned versus actual migration outcomes', in Population Distribution Policies in Development Planning, papers of the United Nations/UNFPA Workshop on Population Distribution Policies in Development Planning, Bangkok, 4–13 September 1979, United Nations, (1981), pp. 144–63.

Findley, Sally E. (1994), 'Does drought increase migration? A study of migration from rural Mali during the 1983–85 Drought', *International Migration Review*, Fall **28** (107): 539–53.

Findley, Sally E. (1997), 'Migration and Family Interactions in Africa', in Aderanti Adepoju (ed.), *Family, Population and Development in Africa*, London: Zed Press, pp. 109–38.

Findley, Sally E. and Assitan Diallo (1988), 'Foster children: Links between rural and urban populations', in *Proceedings of the African Congress on Population*, Liege, Belgium: IUSSP.

Findley, Sally E. and Salif Sow (1998), 'From Season to Season: Agriculture, Poverty and Migration in the Senegal River Valley, Mali', in Reginald Appleyard (ed.),

Emigration Dynamics in Developing Countries, Vol. 1, Aldershot, Ashgate, pp. 69–144.

Findley, Sally E., Sadio Traore, Dieudonne Ouedraogo, and Sekouba Diarra (1995), 'Emigration from the Sahel', *International Migration,* December, **33** (3/4): 469–520:

Fuchs, Roland J. and George J. Demko (1979), 'Population distribution measures and the redistribution mechanism', in Population Distribution Policies in Development Planning, Papers of the United Nations/UNFPA Workshop on Population Distribution Policies in Development Planning, Bangkok, 4–13 September 1979: United Nations, pp. 70–85.

Fullilove, Mindy T. (1996), 'Psychiatric implications of displacement: contributions from the psychology of place', *American Journal of Psychiatry,* **153**: 1516–23.

Hammond, Laura (1999), 'Examining the Discourse of Repatriation: Towards a More Proactive Theory of Return Migration', in Richard Black and Khalid Koser (eds), *The End of Refugee Cycle? Refugree Repatriation and Reconstruction,* New York: Berghahn Books.

Hampton, Janie (ed.) (1998), *Internally Displace People: A Global Survey,* London: Earthscan.

Harrell–Bond, Barbara (1999), 'The Experience of Refugees as Recipients of Aid', in Alastair Ager (ed.), *Refugees: Perspectives on the Experience of Forced Migration,* London and New York: Pinter, pp. 136–68.

Hauff, Edvard and Per Vaglum (1995), 'Organised violence and the stress of exile: predictors of mental health in a community cohort of Vietnamese refugees three years after resettlement', *British Journal of Psychiatry,* **166**: 360–67.

International Rescue Committee (1999), *Kakuma Refugee Camp: Reproductive Health Survey Results,* New York: International Rescue Committee.

Johnson, T. (1981), 'Eritrean Refugees in Sudan', *Disasters,* **3**: 418–24.

Kibreab, Gaim (1985), *African Refugees: Reflections on the African Refugee Problem,* Trenton, NJ: Africa World Press.

Kibreab, Gaim (1995), 'Eritrean women refugees in Khartoum, Sudan, 1970–1990', *Journal of Refugee Studies,* **8** (1): 1–25.

Knudsen, Are J. and Kate Halvorsen (1997), 'Income-generating programmes in Pakistan and Malawi: a comparative review', *Journal of Refugee Studies,* **10**: 462–75.

Koser, Khalid and Richard Black (1999), 'The End of the Refugee Cycle?' in Richard Black and Khalid Koser (eds), *The End of Refugee Cycle? Refugee Repatriation and Reconstruction,* New York, Berghahn Books, pp. 2–17.

Laquian, Aprodicio B. (1979), 'Review and evaluation of urban accommodationist policies in population redistribution', in Population Distribution Policies in Development Planning, Papers of the United Nations/UNFPA Workshop on Population Distribution Policies in Development Planning, Bangkok, 4–13 September 1979: United Nations, 1981, pp. 101–12.

Locke, Catherine J., et. al. (1996), 'The psycological and medical sequelae of war in Central American refugee mothers and children', *Archives of Pediatric Adolescent Medicine,* **150**: 822–28.

Majodina, Zonke (1995), 'Dealing with difficulties of return to South Africa: the role of social support and coping', *Journal of Refugee Studies,* **8** (2): 210–28.

Makinwa-Adebusoye, Paulina K. (1997), 'The African Family in Rural and Agricultural Activities', in Aderanti Adepoju (ed.), *Family, Population and Development in Africa*, London: Zed Press, pp. 97–108.

Maynard, Kimberly A. (1999), *Healing Communities in Conflict: International Assistance in Complex Emergencies*, New York: Columbia University Press.

McCann, James (1987), 'The Social Impact of Drought in Ethiopia: Oxen, Households, and Some Implications for Rehabilitation', in Michael H. Glantz (ed.), *Drought and Hunger in Africa*, Cambridge: Cambridge University Press, pp. 245–68.

McSpadden, Lucia Ann (1999), 'Contradictions and Control in Repatriation: Negotiations for the Return of 500,000 Eritrean Refugees', in Richard Black and Khalid Koser (eds), *The End of Refugee Cycle?*, New York: Berghahn Books, pp. 69–84.

Milazi, Dominic (1995), 'Emigration dymanics in southern Africa', *International Migration*, **33**, 3/4: 521–49.

Nnoli, Okwudiba (1998), 'Ethnicity, Ethnic Conflict and Emigration Dynamics in Sub-Saharan Africa', in Reginald Appleyard (ed.), *Emigration Dynamics in Developing Countries,* vol.1, Aldershot: Ashgate, pp. 207–63.

Oberai, A.S. (ed.) (1988), *Land Settlement Policies and Population Redistribution in Developing Countries: Achievements, Problems, and Prospects*, New York: Praeger.

Otunnu, O. (1992), 'Environmental refugees in Sub-Saharan Africa: causes and effects', *Refugee*, **12**: 11–14.

Oucho, J. O. (1996), 'Refugees and Displacement in Sub-Saharan Africa: Instability due to Ethnic and Political Conflicts and Ecological Causes', in Tomas Hammar and Aderanti Adepoju (eds), *International Migration in and from Africa: Dimensions, Challenges and Prospects*, Dakar: PHRDA, pp 161–88.

Preston, R. (1999), 'Researching Repatriation and Reconstruction: Who is Researching What and Why?' in Richard Black and Khalid Koser (eds), *The End of the Refugee Cycle? Refugee Repatriation and Reconstruction*, New York: Berghahn Books, pp. 18–37.

Richmond, Anthony H. (1993), 'Reactive migration: sociological perspectives on refugee movements', *Journal of Refugee Studies*, **6**: 7–24.

Russell, Sharon Stanton (1993), 'International Migration', in Karen A. Foote, Kenneth H. Hill and Linda G. Martin (eds), *Demographic Change in Sub-Saharan Africa*, Washington DC: National Academy Press, pp. 297–349.

Schmeidl, Susanne (1998), 'Comparative Trends in Forced Displacement: IDPs and Refugees, 1964–96' in Jamie Hampton (ed.), *Internally Displaced People: A Global Survey*, London: Earthscan Publications, pp. 24–33.

Simmons, Alan B. (1979), 'A Review and Evaluation of Attempts to Constrain Migration to Selected Urban Centers and Regions', in *Population Distribution Policies in Development Planning, Papers of the United Nations/UNFPA Workshop on Population Distribution Policies in Development Planning*, Bangkok, 4–13 September 1979: United Nations, 1981, pp. 87–100.

Spring, Anita (1979), 'Women and men as refugees: differential assimilation of Angolan refugees in Zambia', *Disasters*, **3**: 423–28.

Summerfield, Derek (1999), 'Sociocultural Dimensions of War, Conflict, and Displacement', in Alastair Ager (ed.), *Refugees: Perspectives on the Experience of Forced Migration*, London and New York: Pinter, pp. 111–35.

Toole, Michael J. and Ronald Waldman (1993), 'Refugees and Displaced Persons: War, Hunger, and Public Health', *Journal of the American Medical Association*, **270**.

UNHCR (1997), *The State of the World's Refugees*, Oxford: Oxford University Press.

United Nations (1998a), *Trends in Total Migrant Stock by Sex*, New York: United Nations.

United Nations (1998b), *World Population Monitoring Report: International Migration*, New York: United Nations.

Van Damme, Wim (1999), 'How Liberian and Sierra Leonean refugees settled in the forest region of Guinea (1990–96)', *Journal of Refugee Studies*, **12** (1): 36–53.

Van Hear, Nicholas (1998), *New Diasporas: The Mass Exodus, Dispersal and Regrouping of Migrant Communities*, London: UCL Press.

Zetter, Roger (1999), 'Reconceptualizing the myth of return: continuity and transition amongst the Greek-Cypriot refugees of 1974', *Journal of Refugee Studies*, **12** (1): 1–22.

Index

Abella, Manolo I., 256, 259
Adekanye, J., 52, 71, 277, 300, 306
Adepoju, Aderanti, v, xi, 5, 10, 50, 52, 53, 56, 57, 59, 62, 63, 66, 67, 71, 72, 280, 295, 306, 307, 309
Afghan, 250
Afolayan, A.A., 53, 56, 72
Africa
regional institutions, 250
Agadjanian, Victor, 292, 293, 296, 299, 306
Ageing, 154, 156, 157, 160, 162, 163, 164, 166, 167, 168, 169, 170, 174, 176
Ager, Alastair, 288, 306, 307, 308, 309
Algeria, 65, 234, 237, 249, 255
Aliens, 16, 18, 33, 44, 47, 56, 61, 62, 63, 64, 76, 77, 79, 81, 83, 84, 99, 101, 105, 218, 219
Compliance Order of 1969, 61
Allden, K., 289, 298, 306
Alliance of Democratic Forces for the Liberation of Congo-Zaire (ADFL), 246
Altonji, Joseph, 79, 84
Alvarado, J., 157, 158, 160, 161, 162, 163, 168, 169, 170, 176
American Creed, 204, 206, 207, 209, 222, 223
ANC, 8, 63
Andorra, 234
Angola, 11, 52, 54, 58, 69, 237, 245, 247, 278, 282, 283, 284,

285, 294
Appadurai, Arjun, 110, 122
Appleyard, R.T., v, xi, xv, xvi, xvii, xviii, xix, xx, 1, 43, 45, 48, 71, 72, 73, 198, 202, 223, 225, 306, 307, 309
Argentina, 10, 252
Asante, S.K.B., 53, 70
Asian dragon economies, 126, 130, 131, 149, 150
Asian economic crisis, 133, 148
Asylum, 15, 16, 22, 86, 236, 237, 238, 249
conflict, 230
seekers, 6, 22, 23, 25, 27, 43, 88, 98, 99, 100, 107, 130
Australia, v, xi, xii, xv, xvi, xvii, xviii, xix, 1, 2, 3, 8, 9, 13, 48, 65, 74, 82, 87, 92, 93, 102, 112, 113, 114, 115, 119, 123, 124, 136, 137, 153, 154, 155, 156, 159, 160, 162, 163, 164, 166, 167, 170, 172, 173, 174, 175, 176, 177, 183, 184, 196, 198, 200, 230, 231, 232, 233
birth and death rates, 154
immigration, xvii, 161
Azerbaijan, 243, 249

Bach, Robert, 72, 73, 212, 225
Bahrain, 94, 253
Bak, M., 97, 106
Baker, M., 92, 106, 116, 122
Bangladesh, 191, 237, 247, 249, 254